Writing
Clear
Essays

Writing Clear Essays

SECOND EDITION

ROBERT B. DONALD
BETTY RICHMOND MORROW
LILLIAN GRIFFITH WARGETZ
KATHLEEN WERNER

Community College of Beaver County

Illustrations by Raymond E. Dunlevy

Prentice-Hall, Inc., Englewood Cliffs, New Jersey   07632

Library of Congress Cataloging-in-Publication Data

Writing clear essays/Robert B. Donald . . . [et al.]; illustrations
  by Raymond E. Dunlevy.—2nd ed.
       p.   cm.
     Includes index.
     ISBN 0-13-970971-1
     1. English language—Rhetoric.   I. Donald, Robert B.
PE1408.W772   1992
808'.042—dc20   91-26360
                                                     CIP

Editorial and production supervision: **Michael R. Steinberg**
Cover and interior design: **Butler Udell Design, Inc.**
Prepress Buyer: **Herb Klein**
Manufacturing Buyer: **Patrice Fraccio**
Acquisitions Editor: **Tracy Augustine**
Editor-In-Chief: **Phil Miller**

Credits and copyright acknowledgments appear on page 407,
which constitutes an extension of the copyright page.

 © 1992, 1983 by Prentice-Hall, Inc.
A Simon & Schuster Company
Englewood Cliffs, New Jersey 07632

Printed in the United States of America

10 9 8 7 6 5 4 3 2 1

ISBN 0-13-970971-1

PRENTICE-HALL INTERNATIONAL (UK) LIMITED, *London*
PRENTICE-HALL OF AUSTRALIA PTY. LIMITED, *Sydney*
PRENTICE-HALL CANADA INC., *Toronto*
PRENTICE-HALL HISPANOAMERICANA, S.A., *Mexico*
PRENTICE-HALL OF INDIA PRIVATE LIMITED, *New Delhi*
PRENTICE-HALL OF JAPAN, INC., *Tokyo*
SIMON & SCHUSTER ASIA PTE. LTD., *Singapore*
EDITORA PRENTICE-HALL DO BRASIL, LTDA., *Rio de Janeiro*

C O N T E N T S

P R E F A C E

A few years ago when we were writing the preface to the first edition of this book we told an anecdote from World War II about a group of rookies waiting for their first military assignment. To the question, what did you do when you were a civilian, the new soldiers answered "machinist" or "cook" or "accountant" or whatever they had been in peacetime. The officer in charge had need for all of them. One man, however, remained unassigned until the officer learned that he could write.

When the men were mustered out at the end of the war, they returned to the original base. All had been working hard at their jobs, but the writer, in his challenging and stimulating job, had traveled over all of Europe for writing is necessary every place.

We told the story, of course, to make the point that the ability to write can improve one's chances *for* a job or *on* a job. We are still convinced of this. What's more important, industrial engineers agree; their studies show that all jobs, even the most technical, are 60 percent communication. The bulletins of the National Association of Accountants, also agreeing, maintain that written communication is the most highly required skill in management.

Today, however, there is an issue far more imperative than the success and personal satisfaction of an individual. All indicators show that other industrialized nations are outstripping us in education. *Nationally* we are falling behind other nations in scientific knowledge and the ability to communicate it. To retain a leading position in the world, the United States must maintain an educated citizenry. All the able people of the nation *must* understand the science that underlies the modern world and *must* know how to communicate that knowledge.

It is the responsibility of all, not only of a few, to do their educated best to support the nation's position of leadership.

ACKNOWLEDGMENTS

We are pleased to thank our colleagues in the Community College of Beaver County who have generously given us help and enthusiasm in putting together this textbook. We want particularly to thank our librarian, Linda Ciani, who always made the time and had the talent to capture the elusive reference. Thanks, too, to Marsha Spano, our secretary, who was consistently cheerful, careful, and conscientious.

To colleagues outside our own college, we owe appreciation for their helpful and perceptive critical opinions on the job we are all trying to do. Our thanks to Carolyn Crowley of Tarrant County Junior College, South Campus; Janet H. Hobbs of Wake Technical Community College; Mary Neil Kivikko of Tarrant County Junior College, South Campus; Betty Koch of York Technical College; Jencie Rucker of Florida Community College; Hope Toler of York Community College.

We send our thanks also to the staff of Prentice-Hall for their invaluable assistance and support.

Our students, of course, we appreciate above everyone else, because we learned together. They and we have worked together to understand and utilize the principles that result in clear, simple, and effective writing. They have lent us their essays to give examples of those principles at work. We are grateful to Jay Bauer, Maggie Henson, Bob Pfeiffer, Dorothy Gaydos, Mark Custer, Jackie Kunzmann, Ron Alberti, Bonnie Shamrock, Erin Duffy, Pat Tonkovich, Jim Krauza, and David McNutt.

Writing
Clear
Essays

P R O L O G U E

In an old play, a character called Jourdain is surprised and pleased to find that he has been speaking prose all his life. He had supposed that it was very difficult to do. Like Jourdain, you may be pleased and surprised to find that you know more than you thought you did about writing an essay. An essay is simply a piece of writing built from the paragraph.

The paragraph has a three-part form. First, it has a *topic sentence*, which includes a subject and an attitude toward that subject. The attitude is what you think or feel about the subject: For example, in the sentence "Despite the appeal of mistletoe and Santa Claus, Thanksgiving has some definite advantages over the more popular end-of-the year holidays." *Thanksgiving* is the subject, and *some definite advantages* is the attitude.

The second part of the paragraph is the *development* (also called the *body*). In the development, you pull together enough supporting detail to convince your reader that you are right to have that attitude toward that subject. For example, to support your idea about Thanksgiving, you might include such points as:

1. Thanksgiving is the first of several big holidays all happily huddled together at the end of the year, so you not only have Thanksgiving itself to enjoy but others to look forward to.
2. Because there are other holidays soon to come, you are not too upset if some little thing goes wrong. You can be relaxed about Thanksgiving.
3. This relaxation extends to getting ready for Thanksgiving. You don't feel as if you have to have the whole house scrubbed and polished. So what if you don't get the upstairs windows washed. There's plenty of time to do them before the other holidays.
4. The Thanksgiving cooking is as much work as the other holiday cooking, but you don't have to worry about trimming the tree, wrapping the presents, decorating the whole house. You can just plunk Aunt Miranda's beautiful china turkey in the middle of the table and enjoy making those pumpkin pies and your own special stuffing.
5. On Thanksgiving you have all the joy of gathering with your family, but you don't have to worry about whether to give Uncle John a good sweater or just a case of beer.
6. On Thanksgiving you have a feast day and you love seeing all your family, but you're not broke for the next two months.

These six points make an adequate development. They show why you like Thanksgiving better than the other holidays. (They don't have to persuade your reader to like it better. They just have to show why *you* do.)

The third part of the paragraph form is the *concluding sentence.* This sums up your development and states again your topic idea. It must not, of course, bring in new ideas because it is an ending, not a beginning.

A possible concluding sentence for the paragraph about Thanksgiving might be:

Thanksgiving is the best holiday of all—feast and family without pressures and with more fun to come.

WHAT IS AN ESSAY?

An essay is a written interpretation of experience. What an essay communicates is not facts or information but an *interpretation* of such facts or information. There are many ways it can interpret, but the important thing is that *it does* interpret, not simply report.

The subject of your essay can be almost anything; it can be primarily factual or primarily opinion. It can be of serious concern, or it can be humorous. The vital point is that its attitude, its interpretation, reflects your personal feelings about the subject matter.

As you study this book you will learn that a good essay requires a good thesis statement, which is a statement of the controlling idea as a whole. That controlling idea is made up of the subject and the attitude: the subject, what you are going to write about, and the attitude, how you are going to write about it. Having written your thesis statement, you then explain it, analyze it, define it, dramatize it in a story, argue for or against it, or try to persuade someone else to see it as you do in the *body* of your essay.

Since it is *your* interpretation, an essay is highly personal. As the writer, you are extremely important. The information on which you base your interpretation may be important or trivial, but the personal expression of your reaction to it is always important.

This emphasis on the personal point of view and the personality of the writer goes back to the so-called father of the essay, the French philosopher Montaigne, who in 1580 published a volume called *Essais.* This means "attempts," efforts to communicate his thoughts and ideas in the light of his own personality. Montaigne said, "It is myself that I portray," and writers since his time have attempted to convey their responses to the world and ideas surrounding them through essays that also portray themselves.

Essays and You

If your experience is like that of many other Freshman Composition students, sometime during the first week of class your instructor will ask you to write a short essay, probably on a subject of your own choosing, perhaps a personal experience. Your instructor may refer to it as a "writing sample." This may leave you confused. What does the instructor want? What does the instructor expect you to say? You pick up a pencil or roll a sheet of paper into your typewriter, but the paper remains stubbornly blank.

This confusion comes about because writing for a class is an artificial situation. In a class, you write because you must to pass the course; your instructor reads because it's a large part of the job. But the natural arrangement between writer and reader is different. Writers write because they have something they want to say; readers read because they want to be entertained or they want to learn something.

If you adopt this natural association between writer and reader, some of your problems will vanish. Change your first question from "What does the instructor want?" to "What do I want to say?" Change your second question from "What does the instructor expect me to say?" to "How can I best say it?"

Every time you think about your writing assignments, you will have to consider two key terms—*narrow* and *choose.* To begin with, among the various forms of writing, your concern will be narrowed to expository writing. *Expository writing* is nonfiction prose that aims at communicating facts, ideas, or opinions. *Exposition,* which means "explanation," does most of the everyday work of communication. It is the writing in textbooks, in business and industry, in politics, in religion, in journalism. Exposition is also the writing of much self-expression. In personal letters, in diaries, in autobiographies, writers say who they are, what they think, what they feel. All of these types of writing are specialized essays.

Within the wide reaches of expository writing, you will narrow your choice again by the type of expository writing you are doing. Eight chapters in this book are discussions narrowed to one type. Depending on what you want to say, you choose definition, narration, comparison/contrast, persuasion, or whatever type best suits your purpose.

It is true, of course, that usually writers do not stick to just one type of writing. Their essays generally combine several types; each one is chosen to make its point effectively and to complement the other types. After the individual modes, or types, have been discussed and practiced, you will go on in Chapters 8 through 12 to practice the essay that uses more than one mode.

GETTING STARTED

In starting your paper, there are three separate ideas to consider:

1. Finding a topic
2. Establishing a purpose
3. Deciding on your audience

There is no hard and fixed order for these things, but this given order is the most frequently used.

Finding a Topic

Although you may fear you have nothing to write about, you do. You have all your personal experiences to draw on—school, jobs, friendships, hobbies, games, family life, disappointments and pain, successes and joys. You also have all you have learned. What have you experienced or learned that interests you? That is a key term, interest—if it interests you, you can almost always make it interesting to others.

What follows are some techniques that will help you find interesting topics.

Brainstorming

Derived from advertising copywriters seeking topics for ads, *brainstorming* consists of throwing out an idea and having others respond to it with their first thought. Each response generates another response until group members decide they have enough possible topics.

You can even do this alone by letting your mind wander from subject to subject in the thinking mode that psychologists call "free association."

Free Writing

Similar to brainstorming is *free writing*, where for a short period (usually ten minutes), you put on paper the ideas that flow through your mind. You don't pause for correctness or even for complete statements—just suggested ideas.

Keeping a Journal

This takes a little time, and it is truly rewarding. In a small notebook, preferably small enough to go into a pocket, write down ideas, observations, or comments that strike you as amusing, touching, or interesting in any way. Don't wait for an earth-shaking event, for it seldom occurs. Remember that there is fascination in everyday occurrences.

Reading

Although all of these devices will stimulate your thinking so that you find better topics, nothing is so rewarding for all intellectual life, and especially for *writing*, as reading and more reading. Sometimes just the title of a book, magazine article, or even a newspaper headline will suggest a subject that will make an interesting paper for you.

Books

The Strong Brown God

The Closing of the American Mind

Single Parents Are People Too

Golf Begins at 50

Bury My Heart at Wounded Knee

Magazine Articles

"Can This Marriage Be Saved?"

"Positively the Last Word on Baseball"

"Born Beautiful: Confessions of a Naturally Georgeous Girl"

"What We Know about the Homeless"

"The Pursuit of Politeness"

Newspaper Headlines

"Math Skills Linked to Job Earnings"

"Scholarship Is Not a Frill"

"Greek Letter Fraternities Endangered"

"Memoirs of a Football Maverick"

"Little Wishes Form the Big Dream"

"Consumer Trust: An Elusive Quarry"

ESTABLISHING A PURPOSE

Establishing a purpose is something you probably have been accustomed to doing almost subconsciously. You are only asking yourself a series of questions: What do I want to achieve in this paper? What method of development will be most effective for it? What tone or style do I choose to use for it? What audience am I addressing? Do they have any special needs?

In some respects, all of these questions depend on the first. You want to tell somebody something; that is, you want to teach them something, or you want to entertain them. Usually, you want to do both. To do this, you must determine the development of your paper: Will you tell a story, describe a scene, arrange facts and examples, or perhaps use several methods?

The tone also depends on what you expect your paper to achieve. You could not be frivolous and lighthearted about hunger, nor could you be somber and concerned about someone's punk hair-do. Unless you are treating it ironically, your subject and your tone must agree.

NARROWING TO A SPECIFIC SUBJECT AND ATTITUDE

Suppose the subject you have found and decided to write about is your family. Your family is, after all, what you know best and feel most strongly about. What's more, all of your readers have family feelings, too, so they are willing to be interested. Therefore, family is a good subject, what is known as a "universal" subject because it has universal appeal. Since you are writing only a short essay, however, you quickly realize that your family is too broad a subject. You must decide on a narrower, more specific subject.

For example, at the family reunion picnic last summer, twenty-seven relatives showed up. Obviously, you must narrow "family" to a smaller unit—perhaps just one person. Which person? This is a rather hard decision, since you like almost all of them—even some that you didn't like when you were a child.

Cousin Chris is a good example. When you were both youngsters she was a real pain. Your mother used to say she was the type who "got into things." You didn't mind so much that **she** got into things. The real problem was that she got **you** into things, all of them trouble. She always wanted to have adventures; she always wanted to know **why** anything happened. She once persuaded you to "explore" an empty house, where **your** foot went through a rotten board so you had a sprained ankle. She persuaded you to climb into an empty freight car to see how hobos traveled. When the train pulled out, you were both afraid to jump and you ended up thirty-one miles from home. **Your** father had to come for you, and he had tickets for that day's ball game. She was a pain then, but now she's fun.

She's a magazine reporter who has traveled all over Europe. She's met a lot of famous people and quite a few oddballs. She's really enthusiastic about what she's doing, and she can persuade other people that things are as exciting as she sees them.

When you come to think of it, Cousin Chris as a child had most of these characteristics. She just controls them better now. Maybe, you think, that's what's meant by growing up—channeling your interests and energy to get something good, not just trouble. So, you have found yourself a specific topic, the growing up of Cousin Chris.

Thinking of Cousin Chris reminds you, through the process your psychology instructors call "free association," of Cousin Lucy. She was another pain when you were both youngsters. First of all, her looks annoyed you. Her hair, cut very short, curled all over her head. You would have loved a haircut like that, but your ears stuck out.

What was worse, she always managed to stay clean. Even her knees were clean, but yours were always grimy and scabby. Somehow, her hems never came out, looping down in untidy scallops like yours. Worst of all, she always wanted to play with dolls when you wanted to play some good game like kick-the-can. Even in the tree house your grandfather had made, she wanted to have tea parties instead of playing pirates. She certainly was a pain.

But last summer at the reunion you realized that she was a pretty, pleasant, hard-working woman. Although she had a large, rollicking, loving family, she also was a teacher in elementary school. Her childhood characteristics, too, determined the kind of woman she turned out to be, as Chris's had.

As you think about this, you became aware of a third possibility for a subject. You know now that neither of them was a pain; they were just individuals. Perhaps your changed attitude toward your cousins was not so much their growing up as your growing up. As you recognize that, you know you have thought your way to a good subject: Growing up means liking people for their own merits, not just for their effect on you.

You could have chosen either Cousin Chris or Cousin Lucy as your narrowed subject; however, by thinking further about these people and your reactions to them, you have come up with a far better subject.

DEVELOPING A THESIS STATEMENT

Once you have decided on a subject, the next step is to decide what you want to say about that subject; you have to develop an attitude. This process takes some time and some hard, logical thinking, but it is well worth the effort. It is impossible to write a coherent, focused essay on a broad, vague topic. A narrowed topic does not make your task simple, but it does make it possible.

Suppose you have decided to write about sports:

TOPIC:
Sports

You now must decide what you want to say about these sports— your attitude:

TOPIC:
Sports

ATTITUDE:
taught me a lot

Now you begin the process of narrowing. After deciding on your attitude, you realize your subject is not just sports but:

Sports that I have participated in taught me a lot.

This is narrower, but if you participated in a lot of sports, you still have a broad topic; perhaps it should be narrowed further:

Two sports that I participated in. . . .

And perhaps you want to narrow it by time:

> Two sports that I participated in during high school. . . .

And perhaps you can narrow it further by being more specific:

> Playing football and tennis in high school. . . .

Once you have a narrowed subject, you should go through the same process with your attitude:

> taught me a lot
> Playing football and tennis in high school taught me a lot.

This attitude is still broad. Do you want to discuss "a lot" of things that you learned? You would have a better essay if you concentrated on one or two important things these sports taught you rather than merely listing "a lot" of items:

> taught me several important things

This is acceptable as an attitude, but perhaps you want to narrow it further, to be more specific:

> taught me several important things about myself as a person and as a competitor

Now you put your narrowed subject and narrowed attitude together in a thesis sentence:

Playing football and tennis in high school taught me several things about myself as a competitor and as a person.

EXERCISE

Narrow the following topics to one suitable for a 500-word essay. Add an attitude and write a clearly worded thesis sentence for each.

1. Topic: Cartoon Characters

Narrowed subject: _____

Narrowed attitude: _____

Thesis sentence: _____

2. Topic: A Best Friend

Narrowed subject: _____

Narrowed attitude: _____

Thesis sentence: _____

3. Topic: Vacations—Delightful or Disastrous

Narrowed subject: _____

Narrowed attitude: _____

Thesis sentence: _____

4. Topic: Favorite Film or TV Program

Narrowed subject: _____

Narrowed attitude: _____

Thesis sentence: _____

5. Topic: The Class That Taught Me the Most

Narrowed subject: _____

Narrowed attitude: _____

Thesis sentence: _____

OUTLINING

One way to avoid a rambling essay is to make an outline before you begin to write your first draft. Through the process of making an outline, you can eliminate serious problems that might otherwise appear in the first draft of your essay. For example, you might discover that some of your material is irrelevant or that your essay is not logically organized or that you don't have enough details to prove your point. In other words, a good outline can help to ensure that your essay will be unified, coherent, and adequately developed.

Having decided that you want to write an essay about your mother, you try brainstorming. You begin by jotting down all the details that stand out in your memory. You might end up with a list like this:

doing housework all day long and then working again at night
living with an alcoholic
having a baby at age 44

trying to keep peace in the family
the steelworkers' strike of 1959—losing the house
cooking extra meals just for my father
moving to West Virginia and raising seven children alone
making the decision to leave my father
how I thought about my mother when I had my first child
   comparing her to other women in the labor room
   thinking about her after I got home from the hospital
lying to my father in order to protect us
working in an apple orchard
living in a house without running water
learning to drive when she was 59
starting life all over again in her late forties
finally getting a better job in Winchester, Virginia
dealing with the problems of older children
   her sons going to Vietnam
   two of her children getting divorced

Now that you have your thoughts down on paper, you can begin to narrow your topics; you see that the details reflect primarily your mother's courageous spirit, her determination to face any problem that confronted her. This idea is your thesis. Now you must decide how to arrange the details about your mother's strength in some sort of rough chronological order. Your list might look like this:

living with an alcoholic
cooking extra meals just for him
trying to keep peace in the family
lying to him in order to protect us
doing housework all day long and then working again at night
the way she faced pregnancy at age 44
how I thought about her when I had my first child
   comparing the other women in the labor room to her
   thinking about her when I got home from the hospital
the steelworkers' strike in 1959—losing the house
finally making the decision to leave my father
moving to West Virginia and raising seven children alone
starting life all over again in her late forties
working in an apple orchard
living in a house without running water
finally getting a better job in Winchester, Virginia
dealing with the problems of older children
   her sons going to Vietnam
   two of her children getting divorced
learning to drive when she was 59

After you examine this list, you see that most of your details are examples of your mother's courage in facing two situations: living with an alcoholic, and making a new life for herself. You could then arrange all of your details under these two headings:

living with an alcoholic
    cooking extra meals just for him
    trying to keep peace in the family
    lying to him in order to protect us
    doing housework all day long and then taking over my father's
        chores in the evening
    the way she faced pregnancy at age 44
    how I thought about her when I had my first child
        comparing the other women in the labor room to her
        thinking about her after I got home from the hospital
starting life all over again in her late forties
    finally making the decision to leave my father
    moving to West Virginia and raising seven children alone
    the steelworkers' strike in 1959—losing the house
    working in an apple orchard in West Virginia
    living in a house without running water
    finally getting a better job in Winchester, Virginia
    dealing with the problems of older children
        her sons going to Vietnam
        two of her children getting divorced
    learning to drive when she was 59 years old

These two ideas should then become the major headings in the body of your outline, and the sum of the two ideas, the two halves of your essay's total idea, will be its thesis, the key ingredient in your essay's introduction.

THESIS STATEMENT:

One phase of my mother's personality is consistent: her determination to do whatever needs to be done.

OUTLINE

Introduction

One phase of my mother's personality is consistent: her determination to do whatever needs to be done.

Body

A. Coping with my father's alcoholism
B. Facing life alone

Conclusion

Concluding paragraph

You now have a basic outline. Next you decide how you are going to develop each of the paragraphs in the body of your essay. You examine the details you have listed to see how they can be divided further and put under more specific headings. Concentrating first on *A*, "Coping with my father's alcoholism," you find that your mother's actions were basically to protect the children and to set an example of perserverance.

    I. Coping with my father's alcoholism
        A. Protecting her children
        B. Setting an example of perserverance

Now you ask yourself, "How did she protect her children?" You look back at your list and see that you have already pointed out several ways in which your mother protected her children. These points would then become supporting details for subtopic A.

    I. Coping with my father's alcoholism
        A. Protecting her children
            1. Shielding them from emotional pain
            2. Shielding them from physical pain

Continuing that way, you might end with a final outline that looks like this:

Introduction   One phase of my mother's personality is consistent: her determination to do whatever needs to be done.

Body
    I. Coping with my father's alcoholism
        A. Protecting her children
            1. Shielding them from emotional pain
            2. Shielding them from physical pain
        B. Setting an example of strength and perserverance
            1. Overworking herself
            2. Enduring pregnancy at the age of 44
   II. Facing life alone
        A. Adjusting to financial and emotional traumas
            1. Losing her home
            2. Leaving her husband
        B. Moving to West Virginia
            1. Working in an apple orchard
            2. Living in a house without running water
        C. Moving again, to Winchester, Virginia
            1. Improving the family's living conditions
            2. Dealing with the problems of her older children
            3. Learning and changing at the age of 59

Conclusion   Final paragraph

After reading the outline above, you can see some basic patterns emerging:

    1. An outline has a specific structure. Major ideas are indicated by Roman numerals, subtopics of major ideas are indicated with capital letters, and so forth. In general, as you move from left to right in an outline, your ideas become more and more specific. The basic pattern looks like this:

I
  A
  B
     1
     2
        a
        b

2. All the major headings—those indicated by Roman numerals— must be expressed in parallel form, and all headings of **equal** rank under the same major heading must be in parallel form. Notice that each detail in the outline above begins with an *-ing* verb (*coping, shielding,* etc.). An outline such as the one above, which uses phrase or incomplete sentence headings, is called a *topic outline.* If each idea in the outline were stated in complete thoughts, it would be called a *sentence outline.* For example:

I. She coped with my father's alcoholism
  A. She protected her children
  B. She set an example of strength and preserverance

Note that even if you are not using a sentence outline, each outline item is capitalized.

3. Each heading that has subheadings should have at least two subheadings. In other words, you can't have an A without a B or a 1 without a 2, and so on. The logic behind this concept is clear: you can't divide anything into fewer than two parts.

4. Usually, your final outline will not include everything that you thought of when you were writing your first list of details. For example, you would eliminate the details about the birth of your first child because they have nothing to do with your thesis—your mother's strength of character.

Once you have a good outline, you can begin to write your paper. Your final draft might look like this:

....
A TRIBUTE TO MOM
....

Today the words "I can't" seem to be a part of everyone's vocabulary. But when my seven brothers and sisters and I were growing up, these were words that we never heard. We were taught, by our mother, that we could do whatever we needed or wanted to do. Anything was possible if the need or desire was strong enough. Mom was and is a perfect example of the truth in these words. There are so many facets in her personality that

**Thesis
Statement**

she reminds me of a chameleon. In the space of a moment, she can change from a gentle, tender mother to a tough, demanding drill sergeant to a lighthearted, laughing gypsy; but **one phase of her personality is consistent—her determination to do whatever needs to be done.**

The first example of her courage and determination that I saw as a child was her reaction to my father's alcoholism. Somehow, she shielded us from most of the hurt and ugliness that surrounds an alcoholic. She was our strength; she taught us perserverance, not anger. When Dad came home drunk and obnoxious, she did whatever was necessary to soothe him. Many times, hours after we had eaten our dinner, she would go back into the kitchen to cook another meal for him because he had stayed out and missed his supper. Although she hated lying, sometimes she lied to him to protect us from his anger.

**I. Coping with
my father's
alcoholism**

Still, when he wasn't drunk, she worked by his side to provide for us. After a full day of washing, ironing, and constant cooking, she would go out and help him plow the garden, and after it was planted, she took complete care of it, protesting offers of help from the older children. At another time, I can remember seeing her on the roof of our house, helping my father put new shingles on it, even though she was always afraid of high places.

She stood beside him, whether he was drunk or sober, for many years. Her life had to be a living hell, yet she never became the bitter, angry woman she had a right to become. At age forty-four, when other women worry about where to have their hair done, my mother had her last child. I was with her when this child was born, and even during the pain of childbirth, she was a perfect example of strength and courage.

It was in 1959 that the combination of my father's drinking and a four-month strike by the steelworkers caused them to lose the house that she loved and had worked so hard to care for. Still her courage did not falter. I was married by this time, and so I escaped much of the sadness surrounding this event, but my brothers and sisters were not as fortunate. As time passed, my father's drinking became worse, and it was no longer possible for her to shield the children from his violence. Leaving him, she took her family to West Virginia to live. She still had seven children with her, the oldest being sixteen, the youngest one-and-a-half. Now the courageous example she set sustained all of us. With determination, bred of necessity, she set about raising her children alone. She took a job working in an apple orchard and raised my brothers and sisters in a house without running water. As a result, she soon became thin and haggard-

**II. Facing
life alone**

looking. When I visited her, I saw a frightened look in her eyes, which tore at my heart. I could not help her financially, but part of the time I was able to bring the baby home with me in the wintertime, and in the summertime, when the other children were not in school, they were able to visit me too. I hoped that this would ease her plight at least a little. My father contributed nothing, nor did his family, except to offer to split up the children among themselves, which, of course, my mother would not even listen to. She supported the children financially, took care of their physical needs, kept their spirits up, and planted seeds of their dreams. In her early fifties, with five children still in her care, she moved again—this time to Winchester, Virginia. There she took a job in a sewing factory. She rented an apartment, and at last their living conditions improved. She began to regain her health, and the frightened look in her eyes faded. During these next years she watched two of her sons leave for Vietnam, saw two of her daughters married, and another daughter and a son divorced. By this time, Mom should have been too tired to keep on learning and changing, but she continued to do whatever was necessary for the family and herself. For instance, when she was fifty-nine years old, she bought a car and learned to drive it. She's retired now, and the family is scattered over several states, but we never know when we will look up and see her coming down the road in her little car.

Conclusion   To some people it might seem that we were disadvantaged or deprived children, but her desire to raise us well knit the ties of love among us tighter and stronger than most people ever know. **It is the memory of her strength and determination which gives each of her children the will to win against adversity.**

Dorothy Gaydos
(Student)

DECIDING ON YOUR AUDIENCE

Closely related to finding your topic and establishing your purpose is identifying your audience. It will almost always determine the way you say what you have to say. You certainly would consider your audience when writing a love letter or an application for a job. You don't speak to your boss as you do to your grandmother. Likewise, when you write a theme, you think about your audience even though it is not an individual.

Each group is a separate audience with different requirements.

You would not write in the same way for your son's kindergarten class as for your graduation address, your bowling league's April Fool's Day party, or your term project for sociology class.

Each audience may have subgroups which each have a wide variety of specific needs for information. A group of enthusiastic skiers, for example, may differ widely in their skills and so require widely different instructions in techniques or in advice about choosing a satisifying ski resort.

Much writing is presented to a general audience: adult, intelligent, reasonably well-educated people. Yet even if you are writing to a general audience, there are different subclassifications who have special interests. The audience for *Field and Stream*, for example, is a general audience with a special interest in outdoor sports, particularly hunting and fishing. The audience for *Psychology Today* is also a general audience (that is, the magazine is not directed exclusively to practicing psychologists), but one that is especially interested in learning more about psychology. The audience for *Seventeen* is somewhat restricted, as its name suggests; writers writing for *Seventeen* limit their subjects to concerns of high schoolers, particularly girls. You probably would not write a technical article on nuclear fission for *Sports Illustrated* or describe the ten most swinging discotheques in New York for *The Farm Journal*.

Granted, any subject can be made appealing to various audiences. The subject, however, must be tailored to fit the interests of each audience. Your own audience, your instructor and classmates, is essentially a general audience. Your concern as a writer is to handle your writing so you appeal to an interest of theirs.

The following essay, by a psychoanalyst, discusses a *topic* the writer is an authority on, so he has chosen his subject from his professional learning and his *attitude* comes from his considered *opinion* about this aspect of "inner people." His *purpose* he establishes with the statement that . . . "I, in fact, do not acknowledge the existence of inner people." His *audience* is a general, college-educated one, identified as such by the topic itself, the vocabulary, the references, the figures of speech. He chooses several *methods of development*, although overall his development is persuasive.

Title—Seeks to interest the reader through his or her self-interest

....

WHAT YOU SEE IS THE REAL YOU

....

Introduction—Sets up contrast with popular figure

It was, I believe, the distinguished Nebraska financier Father Edward J. Flanagan[1] who professed to having "never met a bad boy." Having, myself, met a remarkable number of bad boys, it might seem that either our experiences were drastically differ-

---

1. Founder (1917) of Boys Town, a self-governing community for homeless and abandoned boys, for which he was also an energetic fund raiser.

ent or we were using the word "bad" differently. I suspect neither is true, but rather that the Father was appraising the "inner man," while I, in fact, do not acknowledge the existence of inner people.

Purpose of the essay

Definition of the "inner man"

Since we psychoanalysts have unwittingly contributed to this confusion, let one, at least, attempt a small rectifying effort. Psychoanalytic data—which should be viewed as supplementary information—is, unfortunately, often viewed as alternative (and superior) explanation. This has led to the prevalent tendency to think of the "inner" man as the real man and the outer man as an illusion or pretender.

While psychoanalysis supplies us with an incredibly useful tool for explaining the motives and purposes underlying human behavior, most of this has little bearing on the moral nature of that behavior.

Use of psychoanalysis

Comparison of x-ray with portrait

Definition of author's belief

Like roentgenology, psychoanalysis is a fascinating, but relatively new, means of illuminating the person. But few of us are prepared to substitute an X-ray of Grandfather's head for the portrait that hangs in the parlor. The inside of the man represents another view, not a truer one. A man may not always be what he appears to be, but what he appears to be is always a significant part of what he is. A man is the sum total of *all* his behavior. To probe for unconscious determinants of behavior and then define *him* in their terms exclusively, ignoring his overt behavior altogether, is a greater distortion than ignoring the unconscious completely.

Appeal to authority

Kurt Vonnegut has said, "You are what you pretend to be," which is simply another way of saying, you are what we (all of us) perceive you to be, not what you think you are.

Consider for a moment the case of the ninety-year-old man on his deathbed (surely the Talmud must deal with this?) joyous and relieved over the success of his deception. For ninety years he has shielded his evil nature from public observation. For ninety years he has affected courtesy, kindness, and generosity—suppressing all the malice he knew was within him while he calculatedly and artificially substituted grace and charity. All his life he had been fooling the world into believing he was a good man. This "evil" man will, I predict, be welcomed into the Kingdom of Heaven.

Comparison of "good" and "bad" old man

Continued comparisons of "good" and "bad"

Similarly, I will not be told that the young man who earns his pocket money by mugging old ladies is "really" a good boy. Even my generous and expansive definition of goodness will not accommodate that particular form of self-advancement.

It does not count that beneath the rough exterior he has a heart—or, for that matter, an entire innards—of purest gold, locked away from human perception. You are for the most part what you seem to be, not what you would wish to be, nor, indeed, what you believe yourself to be.

Spare me, therefore, your good intentions, your inner sensitivities, your unarticulated and unexpressed love. And spare me also those tedious psychohistories which—by exposing the goodness inside the bad man, and the evil in the good—invariably establish a vulgar and perverse egalitarianism, as if the arrangement of what is outside and what inside makes no moral difference.

Comparison, contrast

Saint Francis[2] may, in his unconscious, indeed have been compensating for, and denying, destructive, unconscious Oedipal impulses identical to those which Attila projected and acted on. But the similarity of the unconscious constellations in the two men matters precious little, if it does not distinguish between them.

I do not care to learn that Hitler's heart was in the right place. A knowledge of the unconscious life of the man may be an adjunct to understanding his behavior. It is *not* a substitute for his behavior in describing him.

Definition of "inner man"

The inner man is a fantasy. If it helps you to identify with one, by all means, do so; preserve it, cherish it, embrace it, but do not present it to others for evaluation or consideration, for excuse or exculpation, or, for that matter, for punishment or disapproval.

Conclusion: Definition of "real you"

Like any fantasy, it serves your purposes alone. It has no standing in the real world which we share with each other. Those character traits, those attitudes, that behavior—that strange and alien stuff sticking out all over you—*that's the real you!*

Willard Gaylin
1981 (Anateus)

2. Saint Francis of Assisi, who early in the thirteenth century renounced parental wealth, entered on a life of poverty, and founded the Franciscan order of begging friars.

C H A P T E R   1

Into the Essay

Moving from the paragraph to the essay is not a difficult procedure. It requires expanding the basic elements of the paragraph, either saying more about a small subject or choosing a bigger subject. The basic structure remains the same, as you can see in the diagram on page 21.

EXPANDING THE TOPIC SENTENCE TO THE INTRODUCTION

A good topic sentence, you remember, is vital for any paragraph, whether it stands alone or is part of a longer essay. A good topic sentence must be complete, clear, and specific, and it must have a narrowed subject and a specific attitude.

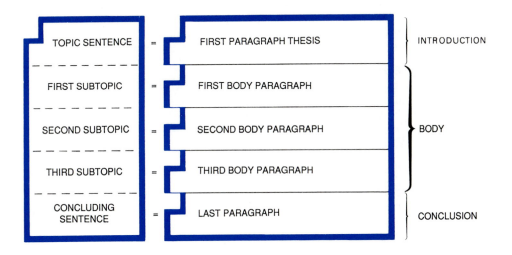

TOPIC SENTENCE	=	FIRST PARAGRAPH THESIS	INTRODUCTION
FIRST SUBTOPIC	=	FIRST BODY PARAGRAPH	
SECOND SUBTOPIC	=	SECOND BODY PARAGRAPH	BODY
THIRD SUBTOPIC	=	THIRD BODY PARAGRAPH	
CONCLUDING SENTENCE	=	LAST PARAGRAPH	CONCLUSION

FAULTY:

That the poor in American are largely invisible and ignored and the homeless as well. [This is a poor topic sentence because it is not a sentence at all; it is a fragment.]

IMPROVED:

Perhaps one reason that the poor and the homeless are ignored in America is because they are hidden from the sight of most citizens; they're the invisible Americans.

FAULTY:

Fishing is fun but dangerous. [This is a poor topic sentence because "fishing" is not clear and specific. What type of fishing is meant: trolling from a row boat, fly casting from the shore, deep sea fishing from a commercial boat, spear fishing, ice fishing, or net fishing? And how is it "dangerous"? Is the danger from falling out of the boats, or stabbing oneself with the hook, or being bitten by fish or snakes or insects, or being bored to death?]

IMPROVED:

Ice fishing is fun, but the dangers from the elements are deadly serious.

FAULTY:

Athletes and actors are overpaid in the American society. [This is a poor topic sentence because the subject, "athletes and actors," is too broad. Many athletes, 95 percent of all professional boxers and golfers, for example, don't even make expenses while many actors depend on unemployment compensation and welfare between roles.]

IMPROVED:

Top hockey players such as Wayne Gretsky and Mario Lemieux receive higher salaries than our government leaders and most of our heads of industry and business.

FAULTY:

The old and deteriorating house sat on the top of the knoll. [This is a poor topic sentence because it expresses no attitude that can be developed.]

IMPROVED:

The old and deteriorating house on the top of the knoll both frightened and fascinated the children in the neighborhood.

EXERCISE 1A: TOPIC SENTENCES

Which of the following would be acceptable topic sentences? Be prepared to tell why they would or would not be.

1. That a man like Danny DeVito could be a leading star in Hollywood is amazing.
2. Writing a research paper is difficult.
3. Golf is hard on the nerves.
4. Women are treated unfairly in the job market.
5. College students should be able to take only the courses they choose on their way to a degree.
6. The library was open until 2:00 A.M. last night.
7. The favorite activities of couch potatoes are watching television and eating pizza.
8. Making the Dean's List while working part-time and raising a family is terribly difficult but incredibly satisfying.
9. Mark Twain often uses humor to disguise his bitterest comments.
10. There are more Hindus in the world than Protestants.

Just as the main idea of a paragraph is expressed in the topic sentence, the main idea in an essay is expressed in a *thesis sentence*, usually the last sentence in a short introductory paragraph. The additional length of the essay allows the writer to use a few sentences to attract the reader's attention by including a relevant incident or anecdote or by presenting factual background for the topic. The introduction can also provide space for a clarification of terms and lead smoothly into the body of the essay. The function of the thesis sentence is the same as that of the topic sentence in that it is also a clearly worded statement presenting the topic to be discussed and a specific attitude toward that subject.

EXPANDING SUBTOPIC SENTENCES TO TOPIC SENTENCES

The body of the essay is made up of paragraphs, so if you can write a paragraph, you can write an essay. Each paragraph in the body has a topic sentence that presents a subject and a controlling idea, which is developed by adequate, relevant, and specific detail. Each topic sentence in the essay supports the thesis statement just as each subtopic sentence in the paragraph supports the topic sentence. In fact, if your paragraph was developed by subtopics, you need only use the subtopics as topic sentences and add relevant detail to each to expand your paragraph to an essay. (However, make sure that the paragraph needs more development. Sometimes a single paragraph is all the development a subject needs.)

Outlining

Before beginning a paragraph or an essay, you may find it useful to write an outline. An outline can do two things: First, it can save a lot of rewriting, and second, it can allow you to check quickly to see whether or not your paragraph or essay is unified.

AN EXAMPLE OF EXPANDING

Let's say that you want to expand the following paragraph that you have written on your problems with certain classes in high school.

> Although generally I liked high school, there were three classes that I really hated because the teachers, all for different reasons, ignored me. My physics teacher ignored me because I couldn't do the math problems associated with the science. He thought I was too stupid to know anything, so he ignored me even when I volunteered some answer not associated with the math. My gym teacher ignored me because she was terrified that I would get hurt. I was overweight (fat is the word, I believe) and somewhat awkward, and the poor woman trembled when I tried any activity more strenuous than walking. My English teacher ignored me for still a third reason: She thought that I already knew the material she was covering. I was never allowed to recite because she always wanted to see "if any of the others know the reason." I hated these three classes while I was in high school, and I still hate, for whatever reason, to be ignored.

If you examine the above paragraph, you will see that it contains a topic sentence, three subtopic sentences, and a conclusion. It could be outlined thus:

I. Topic sentence: Although generally I liked high school, there were three classes that I really hated because the teachers, all for different reasons, ignored me.

II. Body
  A. Subtopic: My physics teacher ignored me because I couldn't do the math problems associated with the science.

    B. Subtopic: My gym teacher ignored me because she was terrified that I would get hurt.

    C. Subtopic: My English teacher ignored me because she thought I already knew the material she was covering.

III. Conclusion: I hated these three classes when I was in high school, and I still hate, for whatever reason, to be ignored.

If you wanted to expand this paragraph into an essay, the outline would be much the same.

    I. Introduction, including thesis sentence
  II. Body
      A. Topic sentence: My physics teacher. . . .
      B. Topic sentence: My gym teacher. . . .
      C. Topic sentence: My English teacher. . . .
 III. Conclusion

DEVELOPING THE INTRODUCTION

Before you start to write, you want to decide what general statement you want to illustrate by your essay. Why do you want to tell the story of the three teachers who ignored you? Is your purpose to show your individuality? To point out weaknesses in the public schools? To show incompetency of teachers? To show differences in students or teachers? To emphasize the different methods of solving problems? The introduction to your essay enables you to focus the reader's attention on the reason for telling your experience: the purpose of your writing, the general truth beyond the actual experience.

In other words, what is the significance of the essay? Why did you choose this subject? What do you want the reader to get from your experience?

The introduction could be developed by any one of the following, each of which could lead into the thesis statement.

If your purpose is to emphasize your individuality, to show that you are not like many other people, you might use this introduction:

Significance

Thesis statement

    Some people try to slip through life unnoticed, feeling that if no one notices them, they won't get blamed for anything. I am not one of those people. If I do poorly at something, I want people to notice and to help. If I do well at something, I want people to notice and to appreciate. I do not want to be ignored. *Although generally I liked high school, there were three classes that I really hated because the teachers, all for different reasons, ignored me.*

If your purpose is to emphasize the different methods teachers use, you might use this introduction:

Significance

Thesis statement

Some teachers scream at their students, ridicule them, and chastise them. Some teachers always have encouragement for their charges. And some teach only selected students while ignoring the ones who are different. *Although generally I liked high school . . . .*

If you want to emphasize what teachers teach besides subject matter, you might use this introduction:

Significance

Thesis statement

I've had a lot of teachers, and all of them have taught me something. Some taught me math, some taught me science, and some taught me to spell and punctuate. But some taught me other things: how long fifty minutes can be, how unfair a test can be, how much fun learning can be. And three taught me to hate being ignored. *Although generally I liked high school . . . .*

If you want to emphasize how different people handle problems, you might use this introduction:

Significance

Thesis statement

People have different ways of dealing with problems. Clint Eastwood uses a Magnum, Sylvester Stallone uses his fists, and Jimmy Carter uses prayer. And some people ignore their problems, probably hoping they'll go away. I met three of the people who use the latter way, but their problems wouldn't go away. The problem ignorers were teachers and the problem was me—a captive student in public school. *Although generally I liked high school . . . .*

If you want to emphasize what you could not stand in the attitudes of teachers, you might use this introduction:

Significance

Thesis statement

Teaching is an art, and some teachers are more artful than others. I've been spanked, yelled at, smiled at, fawned upon, berated, encouraged, told off, and put in my place by teachers. I could stand all of these tactics but I hated being ignored. *Although generally I liked high school . . . .*

DEVELOPING THE BODY

If you are expanding the essay from a paragraph, you need only use your subtopic sentences as topic sentences.

In an essay you want to give more specific details to support your topic sentences. You think about your three classes and expand upon the ideas in the paragraph. On the first class, physics, you might think about why Mr. Boggs acted as he did. Was he a frustrated math teacher? Did he think you were stupid? You might also think about why his ignoring you bothered you so much. Was it because you really enjoyed the theory and you wanted to talk about it, but he wouldn't call on you?

You think about your gym class. Again, you know Mrs. Songerlym acted as she did because she was afraid you would get hurt. Here you think of specific incidents that happened in class and include them in that paragraph.

In this way you develop your body paragraphs by thinking of specific details to support your topic sentences. Include quotations, anecdotes, examples, or comparisons to support or prove the statement made in your topic sentence.

Then you can develop each topic sentence into a paragraph:

My physics teacher ignored me because I couldn't do the math problems associated with the science. Mr. Boggs must have been a frustrated math teacher; he spent all his class time explaining mathematical problems to the four or five boys who understood them. I couldn't do the math, but I loved the theory. I wanted to discuss the things I learned from the book. I raised my hand continually, but Old Bogger never called on me. He always looked pained when he saw my hand up, and he always looked away quickly. He was sure I was severely retarded at best and idiotic at worst. He beamed when one of his boys asked a question about the precious problems and ignored the rest of us. After about four weeks, I stopped raising my hand and started hating Boggs and physics.

My gym teacher, Mrs. Songerlym, was a much nicer person than Mr. Boggs, but she ignored me too, because she was terrified that I would get hurt. Because I was a bit overweight when I was in high school (fat is the word, I believe) and a bit awkward, the poor woman trembled when I tried any activity more strenuous than walking. When it was my turn to vault the horse, Mrs. Songerlym would leap in front of it and move it away. "Now that we've all tried the horse, let's move to the parallel bars, class." If I got to the front of the line for the parallel bars, she would ask me to stand on the base "to steady it." I got three credits for gym but not one hour of exercise.

But neither Bogger nor Mrs. Songerlym was my biggest dislike in high school. I was really good at one subject: English. My English teacher ignored me for still a third reason; she thought I already knew the material she was covering. When I volunteered to diagram a sentence, she would smile and say, "Let's see if someone else knows," and I was ignored. When I rushed into class bursting with indignation over the exploits of Macbeth, I was shushed and nodded to but not called on to discuss his motivation.

DEVELOPING THE CONCLUSION

Like the introduction, the conclusion is a necessary part of your essay. You don't just stop—you conclude. Because the conclusion is the last thing you put in your readers' minds, you want it to be a high point. You want it to be strong, interesting, and convincing. You want it to satisfy your readers that you have done what your introduction promised.

If the essay above stressed individuality, you might use the following conclusion:

> I hated these classes and I hated these teachers who ignored me. I wanted to be taught or helped or applauded, but instead I was labeled too dumb or too fat or too smart. Maybe ignorance and ignore have more in common than their opening letters.

If your purpose was one of the other ones suggested above, the conclusion would be different. If you used the introduction on teachers' methods of handling students, for example, you might use the following conclusion:

> Teachers use different methods to control their classes and teach their students, and students have their own preferences on the teachers' methods. Most perform better if the teachers encourage them; some do better if they fear ridicule and chastisement; some undoubtedly do better if the teacher is a pal. But no one does better if he or she is ignored.

In addition to this type of conclusion (the summary), you might conclude with a paragraph of quotation, a little story that dramatizes your thesis, a warning or remedy, or a reminder of the significance of your essay.

TITLES

Another difference between paragraphs and essays is that essays have titles whereas paragraphs do not. Choose your title carefully. It should do three things:

1. It should gain readers' interest.
2. It should give some idea of what the essay is about, its subject or content.
3. It should provide some indication of the author's tone, the author's attitude toward the subject, and some clue to the author's style.

Sometimes a title is just a literal label, especially if the author's intent is to be straightforward and factual—for example, "Ten Sources of Student Complaint." Frequently, however, it is imaginative or allusive as it indicates the author's tone and style. For instance, E. M. Forster titled one of his essays "Two Cheers for Democracy." In this title Forster indicates his subject—democracy—and because he says two cheers instead of the more customary three cheers, he indicates that his attitude is not wholly favorable toward democracy.

The title should also be short and snappy. It should be precise rather than vague. It should indicate whether it is sober, serious, satiric, or humorous. Alliteration, the use of two or more words having the same initial sounds, is sometimes a convenient device to make a title catchy: "Adolescent Agony," for example.

What is the difference of attitude in the titles *Soldiers Three* and *Three Soldiers?*

EXERCISE 1B: CHOOSING A TITLE

Read the following essay and think of a good title.

Young people enjoy playing the cowboy in wacky outdoor games. The end of a game of "Cowboys and Indians" occurs when the cowboys win, only the cowboys. That's the way it goes—with cowpokes, of course, always coming out on top or going out in grand style. Cowboys, good and bad, always make a good showing.

A cowboy is not only a field hand employed on a large cattle ranch, but is also a person who gets what he wants. The cowboy is a famous/infamous character whom people regard with either love or hatred. They have strong personalities and powerful charisma. Cowboys are outstanding people and cannot be ignored.

Examples of cowboys are easy to find. Steve McGarrett, super police chief of the television show "Hawaii Five-O," is such a person. If he wants a person arrested, he gets them arrested by fair means. He is a good cowboy. Jimmy Swaggart, television evangelist, saw that Jim Bakker was gaining a religious empire rivaling his own. Swaggart learned a dark secret and revealed it to everyone, eliminating Bakker. He is a bad cowboy. Godzilla fought to save the world, even if it meant destroying some buildings in the process. He is a good cowboy. Al Capone killed people to further his own ends. He was also a bad cowboy. A cowboy is easily recognizable.

A cowboy is not someone who loses or goes down without a fight. Gary Hart is not a cowboy, because he quit fighting after he was damaged. Mick Jagger, singer for the Rolling Stones, is not a cowboy because he changed his music in order to make money. Ghadaffi is not a cowboy, because after one attack, he was apparently quieted. Non-cowboys are quitters.

Cowboys go down in history as movers and shakers. They further their cause with extreme conviction. They blaze new frontiers so that others may follow. A cowboy is a great thing to be. In fact, cowboys are the powers that be.

Jay Bauer
(Student)

EXERCISE 1C: TITLES

What can you intelligently guess about the subject and attitude of the following essays from their titles?

1. "Friends, Good Friends—and Such Good Friends"
2. "The Ant as a Fraud"
3. "Co-existence or No Existence: The Choice Is Ours"
4. "I'd Rather Be Black than Female"
5. "Custer Died for Your Sins"
6. (And another comparable title) "Socrates Died for Your Sins"
7. "Why Americans Hate Politics"
8. "To a Small Boy Who Is Standing on My Shoes While I'm in Them"
9. "The Sand Cranes"
10. "Helping Children Reach Their Potential"
11. "Manchild in the Promised Land"
12. "Lying in a Hammock at William Duffy's Farm in Pine Island, Minnesota"

PITFALLS TO AVOID

1. Don't fail to include enough introductory material to make your thesis statement clear and indicate the significance of your essay.
2. Don't begin your essay with a vague introductory phrase such as "It all began when. . . ." Unable to identify the "It," your reader is apt to abandon your writing and turn on the television.
3. Do not permit sentences in the body of your essay to go in numerous or contradictory ways. Don't say "Competition is good and bad for many. The world today lives on competition. Competition is life." The baffled reader will have no notion of which idea he or she is to follow. You as the author must choose a line of development and follow it throughout the essay.

4. Don't end your essay without reaching some conclusion.
5. Don't use as a title the subject of your essay. "Cats" may be a good title for a Broadway play, but it won't entice a reader to snatch up your essay.

TECHNIQUES OF CLEAR WRITING

TRANSITIONS

In the beginning of this chapter you learned that since an essay is made up of paragraphs, all you have to do to write an essay is to expand upon your paragraph-writing skills. Recalling what you know about writing the paragraph, you remember how important it is to have *coherence*, continuity between your sentences, so your ideas come across smoothly to your reader. Coherence is achieved through *transition*.

The first part of the word, *trans*, meaning "across," suggests movement from one place to the other. Thus, to *transport* means "to carry across," to *transmit* means to "send from one place to another," and even the *transmission* of your car is so named because it is the part of your car that sends power from the engine to the wheels. Transition in a paragraph or essay means to move the reader from clause to clause or from sentence to sentence or from paragraph to paragraph smoothly and easily.

Notice the differences between these two sentences:

I don't like musicals; I loved Gregory Hines' *Tap.*
Although I don't usually like musicals, I loved Gregory Hines' *Tap.*

By adding two words, you make the relationship between the thoughts much clearer. Note too how the choice of the transitional word affects the meaning.

I started to study; I liked school.
After I started to study, I liked school.
Before I started to study, I liked school.
Because I started to study, I liked school.
Although I started to study, I liked school.

OR

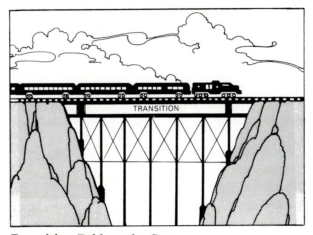

Transition Bridges the Gap.

> I started to study; consequently, I liked school.
> I started to study; nevertheless, I liked school.

What are the differences? Notice how careful you must be in choosing transitional words to make sure that you are showing the correct relationship. Among the more common transitions are the following:

TO SHOW ADDITION:
and, too, furthermore, moreover, in addition

TO SHOW COMPARISON OR SIMILARITY:
likewise, similarly, in comparison, comparable to, in similar fashion

TO SHOW CONTRAST:
in contrast; on the contrary; on the other hand; however; but; not only . . . but also. . . .

TO SHOW CONCESSION:
however, yet, still, nevertheless, but, despite, although

TO SHOW SEQUENCE OR TIME:
first . . . second . . . third; to begin with . . . later . . . finally; then; next; as soon as; just before; immediately after

TO SHOW CONCLUSION OR RESULT:
consequently; as a result; thus; therefore; obviously; in short; surely

TO SHOW ALTERNATIVE:
if . . . then; either . . . or; neither . . . nor

In writing both the paragraph and the essay, you can use several other devices for showing the connecting relationships among the sentences. Basically, these are divided into two types: the transitional devices and a logical sequence of organization. The most common transitional devices are these:

1. Enumeration
2. Pronoun reference
3. Repetition of key words and phrases or close synonyms
4. Parallel structure

Enumeration

Enumeration—the use of *first, second, third,* and similar connective words—offers a convenient way of indicating a chronological sequence:

> First, the trees must be felled . . .
> Second, the brush must be burned . . .
> Third, the stumps and rocks . . .

Pronoun Reference

A simple and natural way of providing transition is through the use of pronoun reference. As long as the antecedent (what the pronoun refers to) is clear, pronouns can be used quite effectively to link ideas smoothly:

> The librarian sent a message to the dean of students, **who** suggested. . . .
> The children must have immunization shots before entering school. **They** must be protected. . . .

A variation of this is the use of *demonstrative adjectives,* which point toward something previously discussed and tie the new sentence or paragraph to the previous discussion:

> **These** people . . .
> **Those** incidents . . .
> **This** notion . . .
> **That** principle . . .
> As a result of **this** action . . .
> The main point of **that** argument is . . .

Repetition of Key Words and Phrases

Note how repeating key words or phrases keeps the central idea before the reader and keeps the relationship between the parts clear.

> Although Thoreau was not a great **naturalist,** what he did supremely well was to extract meaning from **nature.** He tasted **nature** and extracted from **nature's** essence a higher meaning.

Sometimes groups of words can be repeated to give coherence to your writing. See, for example, how the repetition of *things* and the use of *depression* and *depressing* makes the second set of sentences more informative than the first set below:

UNCLEAR:
Many things contributed to my depression last semester. Biology was very difficult for me.

IMPROVED:
Many things contributed to my depression last semester. One of the depressing things was the difficulty I had with biology.

Repetition of the same word or phrase at the beginning of each of a series of sentences can increase both clarity and emphasis:

> It is not a task for the cowardly. . . . It is not the place for the timid. . . . It is not a haven for reckless fools. . . . It is one place where you get just one shot a being a hero or a bum.

Parallel Structure

Parallel structure is a writing technique that increases clarity by putting similar ideas into similar grammatical form. Parallelism makes ideas clear; it also makes reading pleasant and words and ideas easy to remember. Everyone uses it. Remember when you were a kid?

> One for the money
> Two for the show
> Three to get ready
> And four to go.

and Lincoln's

. . . of the people,
. . . by the people,
. . . and for the people . . .

with malice toward none;
with charity for all; . . .

And an oldie:

One for all
and all for one.

Much parallel structure comes automatically, especially single-word parallelism:

Bob,
Tom, and
Jim   went to the party. [Parallel subjects]

Sue   hopped,
       skipped, and
       jumped   through the park. [Parallel verbs]

Every day he went out for
                    breakfast,
                    lunch, and
                    dinner. [Parallel objects]

Some forms of parallelism, however, are more complex. For instance, the following sentence:

He lied   to his mother,
           to his wife,
           and
           to his boss.

The words do not have to be the same; just the structure is the same:

She thought   that roses were nice,
               that perfume was romantic, but
               that diamonds were overpowering   for a birthday
                                                  present.

Whole paragraphs can be held together by making most or all of the sentences parallel.

> Keito tried to be competitive as the U.S. culture demanded, but when he played basketball, he forgot to keep score. When he took timed tests, he forgot to raise his hand when he was through. When he did something brave, he forgot to tell anyone. But when he was praised for his work, he never forgot to give credit to the others who helped. Keito's god was cooperation, not competition.

> Pete wanted to be a scholar without studying; he wanted to be an athlete without practicing; he wanted to be thin without dieting; he wanted to be strong without exercising. He couldn't understand why he failed consistently.

APPLICATION OF OLD SKILLS

Remember, all these devices will make essays coherent just as they make paragraphs coherent. In the essay, however, the transitional word or phrase may be expanded into a transitional sentence to move the reader from paragraph to paragraph. For example, suppose you are writing an essay about the power wielded by various groups in the United States. In the first paragraph of the body you have discussed the power of the industrial leaders. In the second, you have discussed the power of the political leaders. In starting the third paragraph, you might write a transitional sentence like the following to prepare the reader for your last and most important thought:

> But the power held by the chiefs of industry and by the politicians combined cannot equal the power of still a third group in the United States. . . .

ORGANIZATION AS TRANSITION

Apart from transitional devices, transition also depends on good organization (again an expansion of the 1−2−3 form, introduction−body−conclusion). For the moment, we will ignore the introduction and the conclusion. **Focus on the development or body section,** which in the essay is usually made up of several paragraphs.

Like all other paragraphs, these body paragraphs have a topic sentence, with a subject and an attitude. But something else must be added: transition. Almost every topic sentence in the body of the essay supplies links to what has gone before, as well as announcing its subject and attitude. Often this kind of sentence begins with a subordinate clause that looks back to the preceding paragraph and continues with an independent clause that announces the topic of the current paragraph. For instance:

> **While** the Germans fought the disastrous Battle of Stalingrad, the British. . . .
>
> **Once** he has gotten himself elected, he. . . .
>
> **Until** drastic changes bring the revolution, we. . . .
>
> **As soon as** we free the hostages, the United States. . . .
>
> **As** I see it, no simple answer. . . .
>
> **If** there is no simple answer, the administration. . . .
>
> **Although** Roger was handsomer than most of his friends, he was too vain to be popular.

In the last sentence the subordinate clause "Although Roger was handsomer . . ." refers to a preceding paragraph in which his good looks were discussed. The independent clause, "he was too vain to be popular," gives the topic of the paragraph now to be written.

Sometimes these transitional links are not so obvious as the subordinate clause, but they are nevertheless precise. In the sentence *All these causes have led to the happiest result*, it is clear that the "causes" have already been discussed and the demonstrative adjective *these* points to those particular causes. Even the occasional use of *but, and, yet, for,* or *so* at the beginning of a topic sentence provides clear and simple transition. However, as these words are connecting words and not introductory words, they should be used very sparingly to begin a sentence.

Note how the writer of the following essay uses topic sentences as transitions:

ORIGINAL SIN

My mother, the daughter of an Old World clergyman, was a strict Calvinist. To my mother's way of thinking, the devil lay in wait at every corner, ready to ensnare me before I could even reach maturity and the safety of marriage. Thus while I was growing up, my life was hedged about with all sorts of restrictions and taboos. **Indeed, there was scarcely an activity that was not somehow tinged with sinfulness.**

Among the lesser sins of my early years, for example,

was the impulse to whistle. Now boys, of course, could whistle all they wanted to, but for me it was definitely condemned as unladylike. To compound my offense, I developed an uncontrollable urge to whistle during the dullness of Sunday afternoon. Now, in my mother's house on Sunday afternoons, nothing—and I mean nothing—stirred. Dullness clung to the motes of dust in what my mother insisted on calling the "parlor," except when the silence was shattered by my off-key whistling. Promptly banished to my room, I continued to whistle softly to myself while I was suppposedly contemplating my sins.

The cardinal sin of those years was playing spin-the-bottle in an empty garage two doors down the street. Although at going-on-fourteen I had only the furriest of notions about relations between the sexes, there was something enticingly wanton about kissing one particular neighbor boy. Wilbur was—if such a thing is possible—even more ardently fumbling than I. But whenever chance spun us together, we kissed until my lips were bruised. To this day my mother, of course, remains blissfully unaware of those pubescent interludes. Had she caught me, I'm sure that I would have been condemned, on the spot, to the eternal fire reserved for sinners beyond redemption.

When I look back on those years, what I feel now is not lust or sinfulness but whimsy tinged with pain. Today, my mother grudgingly accepts me as a grown woman, now that I have a daughter of my own; but there is still a certain reserve, a doubt, perhaps, of my having grown up in snow-white purity.

EXERCISE 1D: SENTENCE COMBINING

The following groups of sentences are choppy. Improve their coherence by supplying transitions to join short sentences.

1. It was cold. The wind was blowing. I said no to a date for the movies. I curled up in the big easy chair. I read a book.
2. James had beautiful furniture. Expensive pictures hung on the wall. His apartment was in the best section of town. He had good food and fine wine. He had no one to share these things with. He cried.
3. Jerry had failed every test. He did not turn in his research paper. He asked the teacher why he got an F.
4. Mark Twain was a critic. He wrote novels and short stories. He also wrote essays. He was a major American writer.

5. Movie heroes have changed. Big macho men like John Wayne seem to be a thing of the past. Sensitive men like Dustin Hoffman and weak ones like Dudley Moore and Woody Allen are in. They don't even have to be handsome anymore. Look at Danny DeVito.

6. On the beach in Miami are beautiful, expensive resort hotels. Not too far away are black ghettoes. Cubans control the city's businesses and outnumber the blacks by half a million. Over 100,000 Haitians live there. Seventy thousand more are expected.

7. He looked and sounded sincere. His behavior was reprehensible. His lack of consideration for others was intolerable. He was constantly late for appointments. His excuses were hollow.

8. David is a distraction in class. He questions everything the professor says. He laughs at questions other students ask. He reads a magazine when the subject doesn't interest him.

9. The scientist became absorbed with her work. She hurt people; she disdained the advice of her associates. She forgot about ethics. She even falsified her results.

10. Aerobic exercise strengthens the heart. It is good for the lungs. Weightlifting builds muscles.

EXERCISE 1E: UNITY AND COHERENCE

Although the sentences in the following paragraphs relate to the controlling idea, the paragraphs, as a whole appear choppy and disjointed. Using whatever transitional words and phrases may be necessary, rewrite the paragraphs to improve unity and coherence without changing the basic ideas.

I have a friend to whom ridiculous things happen. She is not silly or careless; things just happen to her. She was driving home from bowling once, humming to herself because she'd had good scores. She stopped, still humming, at a red light, and a car crashed into the rear of her car. She roared out of her car to complain. She observed that the other car was driven by her teen-age son. She breathed in deeply, popped the button on her skirt band, and her skirt fell to the street—to the cheers of the spectators.

One time she and her daughter took a short trip. They stopped in New York City for a couple of days. She bought her daughter some clothes to wear back to school. While she was gone, her husband made out the salary checks for the employees in his little business. He accidentally made them out on their personal account. The bank phoned to say that their account was overdrawn by several thousand dollars. She was appalled. "Oh, heavens," she moaned. "I knew I was spending too much money. I never dreamed it was that much." She fainted dead away.

These are trivial things. They are never her fault, really. They make her feel that she can't control anything in her life. She feels that she is a victim of circumstances.

<hr>

WORD POWER

ACTION VERBS

Your essential job as a writer is to make your material interesting to the reader. There are several ways to do this; one way is to **show** the readers what you are thinking or seeing, not just **tell** them. Readers have to be able to see someone or something doing something. Action verbs enable them to do this. They also add clarity. Note the difference here:

The ketchup **was spilled** all over.
The ketchup bottle **slid** through his fingers, **hit** the floor, and **exploded,** the ketchup shooting in all directions.

The car **went** down the expressway.
The car **hurtled** down the expressway.

The collector **knocked** on the door.
The collector **pounded** on the door.

The cow *jumped* over the moon.

Verbs such as those in the second sentence of each example give a sense of life, action, forward movement. Readers are carried along with you, when they can "see" the action.

ACTIVE VERSUS PASSIVE VOICE

In the active voice, the doer of an action, the **actor,** is the subject of the sentence:

Jonas   read   the assignment   carefully.
Actor   *Action*   *Object*

Betty   spoke   to the militant   students.
Actor   *Action*   *Object*

What would be the object or receiver of the action in a sentence in the active voice is the subject of the sentence in passive voice.

The assignment was read carefully by   Jonas.
        Object   *Actor*

The militant students were spoken to by   Betty.
        Object   *Actor*

Notice that using the passive voice adds words to a sentence without adding meaning. Passive slows the pace of the writing and is generally not so clear and direct as active voice. As a general rule, use the active voice.

Note that there are times, however, when the passive voice is more natural and effective than the active. It is the **overuse** of the passive that is to be avoided. The passive voice works effectively in the following cases:

1. When the subject (the doer of the action) is unknown or unimportant:

    The bridge was built in 1927. The process was first developed in Egypt. [Who built the bridge or developed the process is unimportant.]

2. When the writer wants to place the emphasis on the receiver of the action:

Old Mrs. Phillips was badly beaten by the mugger.
Detectives were totally baffled by the crime.

Choose the form that best suits your purpose.

REPLACING WEAK AND COLORLESS VERBS

Weak and colorless verbs, such as *to have, to make, to get, to do*, can often be replaced by more vivid and lively verbs:

WEAK:
After he **had a quarrel** with his boss, Jerry quit.

IMPROVED:
After he **quarreled** with his boss, Jerry quit.

WEAK:
A distinction **must be made** between *imply* and *infer*.

IMPROVED:
You **must distinguish** between *imply* and *infer*.

WEAK:
The lucky one **gets** a prize.

IMPROVED:
The lucky one **wins** a prize.

WEAK:
The combine **does** the harvesting of the grain.

IMPROVED:
The combine **harvests** the grain.

Note how another word in the sentence can frequently be converted into an action verb.

REPLACING UNNECESSARY *TO BE* VERBS

The weakest of all verbs is the one we use most often: *to be*. The *to be* verbs—*is, was, were, could have been, should have been*, and so on—provide no sense of action. For example, compare the following sentences:

There **was** a tropical storm off the east coast of Florida.
A tropical storm **lashed** the east coast of Florida.

It **was** the finding of the committee that there **had been** bribes paid by company executives to foreign officials.

The committee **found** that company executives **had bribed** foreign officials.

Most sentences can be strengthened by getting rid of weak verbs. Just change the subject from a nonactor to the doer of the action. For example:

The high scoring record for Alviani High School was broken last night by Ricky "Action" Jackson, who was high man with forty-four points.

Last night, Ricky "Action" Jackson scored forty-four points to break the high scoring record at Alviani High.

Notice that you also become more concise and precise as you eliminate weak verbs.

THE ACTIVE VOICE IN ACTION

As its name implies, the active voice is particularly expressive in displaying action, which is why sports writers use it to describe the fast-moving activities of the sports world.

In a collection of sports stories titled *Upset: The Unexpected in the World of Sports*, the writing, like that of all good sports writing, is especially vigorous and lively because the writers use so many active verbs. Notice the verbs in the following short quotations. (From the story of the shocking defeat of the Brooklyn Dodgers by the New York Giants in the 1951 playoff game.)

. . . As shortstop Alvin Dark strode towards the batter's box, Durocher clapped his hands. Newcombe, the Dodger starter, buzzed two quick strikes past Dark. On the next pitch, Dark rapped a grounder between the first and second basemen.

As Newcombe raced to cover the bag, Hodges lunged, backhanded, for the ball. The tip of his huge mitt deflected the ball away from Robinson. The next batter bounced a single into right field.

Bobby Thompson stepped into the batter's box. He swung, his arms following through perfectly and the big, black 23 on his back twisting with his six-foot, 195-pound frame. The ball sailed out toward left field. It bored through the cool autumn air, over the high green wall and deep into the crowd of jumping, waving fans.

Bobby Thompson knew he had won the pennant for the Giants. He skipped and danced around the bases. At the plate he leaped into the arms of his teammates who half-carried, half-pulled him across the outfield to the clubhouse.

The use of the active voice makes sentences briefer, and also makes them more specific, and so more colorful and vivid. Somehow bland verbs—passive, weak, or colorless—lead to colorless and weak nouns, adjectives, and adverbs.

Notice how the use of the passive voice and general and weak verbs flatten the following example.

As shortstop Alvin Dark went towards the batter's box, Durocher applauded. Newcombe, the Dodger starter, threw two quick strikes past Dark. On the next pitch, Dark hit a grounder between the first and second basemen.

As Newcombe went to cover the bag, Hodges reached, backhanded, for the ball. The tip of his huge mitt sent it away from Robinson. A single was hit into the right field by the next batter.

Bobby Thompson went into the batter's box. He hit, his arms following through and the big, black 23 on his back turned with his movement. The ball went out into left field. It went through the cool autumn air and over the high green wall into the crowd of active fans.

Bobby Thompson knew he had won the pennant for the Giants. He hurried around the bases. At the plate he joined his teammates who hustled him to the clubhouse.

Here are some other examples of the use of active verbs in sports writing (From the story of the triumph of Cassius Clay over the heavyweight boxing champion Sonny Liston in 1964):

Cassius Clay burst into the aisle. The crowd, seeing him, jeered as the challenger jogged toward the ring. He hopped up the small wooden steps and leaped through the maroon ropes. As he turned in quick circles, everyone was able to read the two words in red on the back of his white robe: The Lip.

He was "on stage" almost every minute. Whenever he saw a sportswriter with a pencil or a TV-radio newsman with a microphone, he started his spiel. "I am the greatest."

The following is from a short story by Jack London in which he describes a single blow in a prize fight.

The third round began as usual, one-sided, with Sandel doing all the leading and delivering all the punishment. A half-minute had passed when Sandel, overconfident, left an opening. King's eyes and right arm flashed in the same instant. It was his first real blow—a hook, with the twisted arch of the arm to make it rigid, and with all the weight of the half-pivoted body behind it. It was like a sleepy-seeming lion suddenly thrusting out a lightning paw. Sandel, caught on the side of the jaw, was felled like a bullock. The audience gasped and murmured awestricken approval. The man was not muscle-bound after all, and he could drive a blow like a triphammer.

EXERCISE 1F: ACTIVE—PASSIVE

Of the following sentences, some clearly must be passive, some would obviously be improved by making them active, and some, depending on what you wish to emphasize, might be either. If they are correct as passives, mark them C. If they ought to be active, rewrite them. If they might be either, say **how** *the use of the active or passive changes the emphasis.*

1. It was proposed by the Council that three streets in the borough be paved by Turner Asphalt.

   _____

2. The bridge was built in 1953.

   _____

3. Heavy damage to crops and homes was caused by the tornado.

   _____

4. His performance was regarded as substandard by the critics.

   _____

5. Little Eva was terrorized by the pit bull.

   _____

6. Her application was accepted, and the job offered to her by Advanced Pyrotechnics before it was discovered that arson had been committed by her a year before.

   _____

7. The ride through Space Mountain was enjoyed by everyone.

   _____

8. There was no way Chernobyl could have been prevented.

   _____

9. The whole sky was filled with locusts; by daybreak everything in their path was eaten.

   _____

10. Francesca was honored on Thursday.

_____

11. The explanation was given by Professor Richmond in such a way that it was never forgotten by the class.

_____

_____

12. The conversation was interrupted by the ringing of the telephone.

_____

13. The stop sign was hidden by the heavy growth of azalea bushes.

_____

14. The serial murderer was caught and eventually executed by the Florida authorities.

_____

15. The building was professionally demolished, and none of the buildings around it were harmed.

_____

_____

C H A P T E R 2

Narrating

ORGANIZATION

Often the best source of material to write about is personal experience, for this is one vital resource everyone has. What's more, personal experience has the two great qualities that make stories convincing and interesting. First, personal experience has "universality"—that is, your experience resembles the experiences of other people's enough so that others can recognize it and identify with it. Second, personal experience has "individuality"—that is, even though your experience is similar to the universal human experience, you are unique and so your response and the significance of your response make your narrative special.

Walt Whitman expressed this once by saying, "I am the man; I suffered; I was there." Whitman was saying that suffering is general, but his suffering is his own. Good writing permits us to share in the common human experience and express our version of that experience.

To use your experience effectively, you must first sift through your memory of people and events and then select the details that suit your purpose.

THE THREEFOLD STRUCTURE FOR NARRATION

In the narrative essay you are not just telling a story; you are using a narrative to illustrate, support, or prove a clearly stated thesis. The narrative itself is not an essay but rather a relevant story than can be used as the body of your essay. Thus you have the same three-part organization as in other essays: (1) the introduction leading up to your thesis sentence, (2) the narrative body of the essay using an incident from personal experience to illustrate your thesis, (3) the conclusion, which serves to reemphasize or reinforce the controlling idea of your thesis sentence. When properly shaped to the purpose, your experience may provide powerful testimony. The narrative essay provides a form for using your story to bring home to your reader something that you have learned from experience.

In confronting our own experience, we are often forced to reexamine our feelings and beliefs. You, too, might well begin by examining your own experience and asking yourself some questions:

What is it that I feel that others don't seem to understand?

How did I come to feel this way?

What seems to have been decisive in shaping my attitude?

You might then go on to reexamine a specific event which in some way shaped your life:

A childhood illness or accident

A move to new surroundings

A chance meeting that led to new experiences

An event that revealed something about yourself

In writing an essay based on personal experience, your best chance for success is to focus upon a single event (or possibly a chain of closely related events) of particular significance to you. Thousands of incidents in your life could be used for this essay: Many were funny, some were sad, others were embarrassing, or enlightening, or surprising, or terrifying, or rewarding. Any of these incidents that changed you in any way is worth writing about. Choose an incident that taught you something or made you braver or more cowardly, or made you trust people more or less, or changed you from a loner to a joiner, or helped you decide on a career, or changed your plans. In other words, choose an incident that has had significance in your life. In sifting through your memory of events, the central question you need to ask is, "What did this mean to me?"

Once you have chosen your subject, you must write a clear, concise thesis sentence presenting your subject and its significance. You might start with just the controlling idea: the subject and the attitude.

Subject	Attitude
Going away to college	Drawbacks of independence
Being arrested	Frightening
My trip to Italy	Appreciation of my heritage
Playing basketball in high school	Confidence
My ride down the Grand Canyon	Stifled my adventurousness

Once you have this much, you only have to get this controlling idea into a sentence, making it as interesting to the reader as possible.

I was as eager as any seventeen-year-old to get away from home and parents, but going away to college taught me that there are horrors involved in independence.

Calling a cop a "pig" is one thing, but being arrested is a different matter; it is frightening.

My "overly" emotional and sentimental parents were an embarrassment to me before I learned to appreciate my heritage on an enlightening trip to Italy.

I played ball because I liked it, but playing basketball in high school did more for me than build by muscles; it built my confidence in myself.

Whenever I get the desire to do something daring, I remember my ride down the Grand Canyon—and my adventurousness is stifled.

Having determined your thesis, you need to shape the narrative to suit your purpose. If your essay is to be successful, your reader must see that your story does illustrate the controlling idea. In determining what to include and what to leave out, you must keep your reader in mind. Telling everything "just the way it happened" may provide a poor illustration of your thesis. You must be highly selective. Don't burden your narrative with irrelevant or insignificant details. For example, don't bother telling what you ate for lunch or how much the bus ticket cost unless those details are essential to the story. Don't fuss about whether the event occurred on a Friday or a Tuesday unless that is somehow important to your story. Your purpose is not to bore the reader but to illustrate your point effectively through the story that you tell.

To write an effective narrative essay, you have to remember only one principle of organization: the one–two–three form that governs all standard expository paragraphs and essays. When you apply this three-part form to your essay, remember that one and two and three form a unit. You cannot drop off the introduction or the conclusion. A writer of fiction, on the other hand, need not include all three parts. Indeed, fiction writers usually use only the second, the body, wishing to leave the interpretation up to their readers. Fiction writers often do not explicitly state a controlling idea because they are interested in telling a story for the story's sake. When they do state their theme explicitly, they frequently bury that statement in the text.

But you, as a writer of exposition, must state your controlling idea clearly in your introduction and again in your conclusion. You are interested in telling a story **for the sake of the idea you want to support.**

INTRODUCTIONS

If you look again at the diagram at the beginning of Chapter 1, you will see that the introductory paragraph is comparable to the topic sentence, except that it is longer. The introduction should attract the reader, should tell the reader what the topic is, should narrow it enough that it can be handled, and should indicate what the author's attitude toward the topic is. Also like the topic sentence, the introductory paragraph commits the essay to that topic and attitude. The essay can do no more or less than the introductory paragraph says it will do.

But how does the writer write interesting introductions? How do you "attract the reader"? There's an old piece of advice to writers that says nothing is interesting—except sex— unless the writer *makes* it interesting. But how is this to be done? Here are some standard approaches:

Technique 1

One of the most effective methods of introduction is to relate the topic to a contemporary event, especially a controversy. If at the end of the 1980s you had been writing about public health, you would have attracted readers by beginning with details of diet as a contribution to good health. Look around you. What is in the news today?

Technique 2

Another good introductory approach is justification. Sometimes you have to show your reader that you are qualified to write on a particular subject, that your thoughts have merit. It may be that you have studied the matter for years, or that you have had personal experience, or that you have met or are a personal friend of the one you are writing of. For example:

> I have been a lifelong fan of Mark Twain's. I started reading his books at the age of twelve and have continued reading his works for thirty years. I wrote my doctoral dissertation on Twain's later years. Yet, I cannot say I understand all the man believed in, although he did believe in Satan.

Technique 3

In a method closely related to the preceding one, the introduction gives the background or reason for the topic you are proposing to support. That is, the paragraph is explaining why you are writing. The final sentence, of course, is the statement of the topic.

In an essay titled "The Egalitarian Error," Margaret Mead uses this type of introduction:

> Almost all Americans want to be democratic but many Americans are confused about what, exactly, democracy means. How do you know when someone is acting in a democratic—or an undemocratic—way? People who do want to be democratic are frequently muddled.

She then goes on to explain what democracy is and why people are muddled about it.

Technique 4

Another good introductory device is to state your opinion very firmly, especially if it is less popular than opposing opinions. This is sometimes referred to as "the argumentative edge." Its purpose is to provoke the reader into some response. For example, you might wish to start a discussion of the Forty-Niners with the controlling idea that teams that constantly win are boring.

Technique 5

A relevant incident or little anecdote that introduces your topic usually gets immediate reader attention (as was mentioned earlier, everyone loves a story). If you were writing on the basketball story mentioned earlier, you might start this way:

> I dribbled down the floor, palms sweating, heart pounding. I felt as though there was a film over my eyes. I looked for Sanchez in the keyhole, Wilson in the corner. I was too nervous to see. Suddenly my opponent reached in and snatched the ball. He threw to his forward

breaking down the floor. He was nervous, too, but he could still function.

Then go on with your thesis sentence.

Technique 6

Another method of introducing is to present factual background. You may find that before your reader can understand your essay, he or she must know some details that you do not want to present in the body. Often it is best to give the background at once—in the introduction:

> Thoreau believed that we individuals are the prisoners of our own wants. We want so many things that we must work hard and give up the pleasures of leisure in order to satisfy these wants. He went to Walden, not to study nature, but to "live deliberately, to front only the essential facts of life."

Technique 7

A quotation is often a good way to start an introduction for two reasons: (1) it attracts the reader's attention (and it often makes the reader feel good if he or she recognizes it), and (2) it often states a universal truth. Try to use a less well-known quotation rather than a cliché. A book of quotations or poetry is often a good source.

CAUTION: Make sure the quotation illustrates the significance of your essay. (Don't put it in just because you like it.)

If writing on prejudice, for example, you might use one of these:

> After all, there is but one race—humanity.
>
> *George Moore*

> I am a citizen, not of Athens or Greece, but of the world.
>
> *Socrates*

> How seldom we weigh our neighbor in the same balance with ourselves.
>
> *Thomas à Kempis*

Technique 8

The use of startling statistics is also a good way to get a reader's attention if they lead up to the subject you will write on. Suppose you were going to write an essay on the odd value system in the United States. You might start out:

> A beginning schoolteacher in the United States makes about $20,000 annually. An engineer with a good academic background can

start at about $28,000. A legislative assistant to a U.S. Senator earns $65,000 to $70,000 a year. The salaries of many professional athletes top one million per year. And talk-show host Oprah Winfrey reportedly earns over thirty million dollars a year.

Technique 9

A slightly more complicated version of the above is a striking contrast between an idea commonly held and the one you are introducing. If you were writing an essay to support the idea that even famous men had difficulties to overcome on their way to success, you might start with an introduction like this:

> Babe Ruth struck out more times than any other major league player (1,330 times). Humphrey Bogart was thirty-seven years old before he made his first successful film. George Washington lost more battles than he won. Nevertheless, these men became heroes.

Technique 10

Perhaps the most obvious introductory paragraph is one that makes a direct statement of the idea to be supported. Bruce Catton does this in an essay titled "Grant and Lee: A Study in Contrasts."

> When Ulysses S. Grant and Robert E. Lee met in the parlor of a modest house at Appomattox Court House, Virginia, on April 9, 1865, to work out the terms for the surrender of Lee's Army of Northern Virginia, a great chapter in American life came to a close, and a great new chapter began.

He then goes on to tell what ended and what began.

These are only a few of the possible introductions you might use. They can be used in many varieties, combinations, and lengths, although generally the introductory paragraph is shorter than the body paragraphs. All you need is an opening that attracts the reader's interest and introduces your thesis and tone. The thesis statement is generally the last sentence of your introduction.

Introductions to Avoid

In almost all areas of writing, there are many ways to be correct. Unfortunately, there are many ways to be incorrect, too. Here is a list of openings almost sure to turn off your reader:

1. The **complaint** or the **apology** is a boring way to begin an essay. Avoid such openings as "Racism is too large a subject to be discussed in a short essay." You're right. It is. So narrow your

topic before you begin to write. Or, "I don't really know too much about racism." If you don't, learn something about it before you begin to write.

2. The **panoramic opening** is poor because it offers so broad a background that it fails to introduce what you are going to talk about. Suppose you are going to write a personal narrative about how your VA benefits have helped your education. A "panoramic opening" might begin by saying, "Warfare has bedeviled man all through history. From the days of Homer men have suffered from war. Any history book records the suffering from warfare. I, however, . . ."

3. Another poor opening is the so-called **mystery introduction** because no one knows what the topic is. Avoid openings like "This book interested me because the leading character reminded me of my Uncle Henry." Or, "It all began when my sister ran into the house screaming." Or, "That experience left me suspicious of dark-haired men with mustaches."

4. **Loading your introduction with definitions** is another poor way to begin your essay. Even though you will find it necessary to clarify the meaning of important terms, squeezing them all into an introduction is a serious mistake. Your readers will become either bored or so confused that they will lose all interest in reading the rest of your paper.

THE BODY

The body of the narrative consists of several paragraphs, each controlled by a topic sentence. The easiest and most logical order for a narrative is **chronological:** just tell it as it happened—first this, then this, then this, finally this. If you are to demonstrate your thesis by sharing your experience with your reader, you must present the events of your story in the proper time sequence so that you take your reader with you.

Make an Outline

If you were writing the essay mentioned earlier about the ride down the Grand Canyon, you could arrange the details in chronological order. You might jot down the major events as they happened, and then divide them into logical divisions such as those shown in the left column. These notes become your outline.

1. The night before: making the decision to go down into the canyon

2. The next morning
   before we started: bad weather
                           guide's warnings about what could happen
3. The ride down: who went: members of the train
                           not too bad at the top
                           narrow, scary path
                           what mules did "at rest"
4. The trip up: same dangers
                           Sheila's idiosyncrasy
                           the hikers' appearance
                           Sheila climbs the wall
                           other mules' actions
                           my terror

Once you have this list, having removed all the irrelevant detail, you are ready to write topic sentences for each body paragraph.

TOPIC SENTENCE, PARAGRAPH 1

The decision was a tough one to make, but three of us decided the trip was worth the trouble.

TOPIC SENTENCE, PARAGRAPH 2

We realized that the trip down would be rough.

TOPIC SENTENCE, PARAGRAPH 3

The trail was not too bad at the very top, but it got worse quickly.

TOPIC SENTENCE, PARAGRAPH 4

The trip back up the path was a nightmare, punctuated by sheer terror.

Provide Transitions

As you write the paragraphs, remember that the reader does not have the outline before him or her and can't see the divisions you have set up (*the night before, the next morning,* etc.). Therefore, you must inform him or her of the changes: use phrases such as *the night before, the next morning, we started down the trail, later, after three hours, when we reached the bottom,* and the like. Tell your reader of every change in time, place, or direction.

Be Specific in Detail

In developing your paragraphs, be specific and concrete. If quotations are relevant, use them. Describe the setting so that the reader can see, hear, feel, smell, or taste the situation. Don't say, "It was a frightening situation"; **show** the reader how frightening it was. Don't say, "The man acted crazy"; **show** the man acting insanely: "He threw his arms around wildly, windmilling them; the veins stood out in his neck like ropes; his eyes bulged, and he lunged at me, but unsteadily, slewing to the left and right."

Be Consistent in Tense

Usually, the simple past tense is best for a narrative essay. You must be careful not to switch into present tense as you begin to relive your experience.

Be Unified and Concise

You must make your narrative unified (having no irrelevant details) and concise. You will probably do this best as you revise. As you read over your first draft, check to see that all of your details develop your thesis. Throwing out irrelevant details will serve two purposes: it will unify your essay and it will make it more concise.

The following essay is a good chronological narrative.

....

It's Easy to Be Brave from a Safe Distance.

....

Every time I think about my trip to the Grand Canyon, I am reminded of how easy it is to be brave from a distance. Our adventure began when three of my friends and I decided to head west one summer to see the country. When we got to Arizona, I decided that I wanted to see the Grand Canyon—from the bottom. The trip cured me of my adventurousness. Now, whenever I get the urge to do something daring, I remember my ride down the Grand Canyon—and my desire for adventure is promptly stifled.

The decision to go down was not an easy one to make, but three of us decided it was worth the trouble. When we went to the "Mule Trips" office, we found that the trip took eight hours. The cost, we thought, was exorbitant—after all, we didn't want to buy the mules, just rent them for a day. By this time, one friend, Irene, decided that eight hours on a mule was not for her, but I convinced the others to go.

The next morning, when we actually got on the mules, we realized that the trip down would be rough. It had rained the previous night and the day dawned cold and damp and very foggy. Our train leader (the line of mules was called a train) gave us explicit orders and strong warnings:

"Don't lean to either side, or the mule will step out from under you." (Did you ever sit perfectly erect for eight hours?)

"The mules like to walk right on the chasm edge so that they can see it. Don't try to move them in for they might think you are signaling them to turn around and start back. If they do go back, they'll knock every other mule and rider off the trail into the canyon." (I could be a murderer!)

"Don't let your mules eat." (How can you stop them?)

And most frightening: "The trail is only wide enough for one mule. There is no way that I or my assistants can get to you if you get in trouble." (Good grief!)

At this point, I thought Irene was the wisest of us all, but I couldn't quit; it was my idea. We started down the trail, twelve customers, one train leader, two assistant leaders, and one extra mule carrying the lunches. The trail was not too bad at the very top, but it got worse quickly. It became so narrow that my left foot scraped the sheer canyon wall while my right foot hung over the 3,000-foot drop to the canyon floor. The path, knocked out of the canyon wall, was clay, and it was slippery because of the rain. The mules slipped and slid while the neophyte riders gasped and moaned, and it was so foggy I couldn't see across the canyon. The mules had to be rested frequently, so our leader would stop us at some slightly wider area of the trail, and the mules would face the edge of the canyon. My mule, Sheila, would always see some delectable vegetation, seemingly just out of reach, and lean forward to get it while I, horrified, gazed over her shoulders into the sheer drop to the canyon floor. It didn't seem to bother Sheila, though; nothing could have kept her from her repast. After three hours of slipping and sliding, we finally reached the floor of the canyon. Once at the bottom, I heaved a sigh of relief, but my troubles were not over. In fact, the worst part of the journey was yet to come.

The trip back up was a nightmare, punctuated by sheer terror. All of the discomfort and fears of the trip down were still there, but I had an added worry. The train leader had explained to me that Sheila was "head-shy" and that this might be a problem if we met any hikers. I was to keep her head as close as possible to the tail of the donkey just ahead of her. Two thirds of the way up, we met some hikers: a mother and three small children. Since the mules would not pass anyone on the wall

"Whoa, Sheila, whoooa!"

side of the canyon, the woman and her children had to stand on the canyon edge, holding on to trees or bushes for support. Our train leader shouted back to me to keep Sheila close to the mule ahead, and the train started moving again. I urged Sheila forward, but as soon as she saw the hikers, she bolted. One leap took her ten or twelve feet up the sheer rocky wall. Her feet raced frantically to take her still higher, but the wall was steep and there were no footholds. She started sliding back down. Mules are smart. The ones ahead galloped ahead, away from where Sheila was performing her anti-gravity stunt, and the mules behind us stopped dead; they wanted no part in this escapade. "Whoa, whoa," I pleaded, but to no avail: Sheila could not stop her slide down the cliff. I figured I was dead and wondered fleetingly if they would bring my body up from the canyon floor. Probably they would—on a mule. Then, as Sheila's hooves hit the path, she miraculously caught herself, her legs straightened, and, now twenty feet past the hikers, she calmed down. Nothing could ever erase those terrifying moments from my memory; I can still see myself sitting in glassy-eyed fear atop a crazed, leaping, scrambling mule as she tried to climb straight up a Grand Canyon wall.

Today, although I am tempted when someone offers me the chance to learn to ski, and I am still fascinated by the birdlike freedom of the skydiver, I always say "no." Every time I am approached by skiers or skydivers or hang gliders or skin divers, I remember my experience with Sheila the Mule and the Grand Canyon, and I decline. I have become a devout coward.

CHRONOLOGICAL ORDER IN WRITING OTHER THAN NARRATIVE

The chronological sequence is important in many types of writing other than the narrative essay. If you are telling someone how to make brownies or color Easter eggs, you need to describe the process in the exact sequence that is to be followed. In various forms of on-the-job writing, too, a precise chronological sequence is crucial; it clarifies descriptions of a process, progress reports, and accident or other reports. After all, your own career or someone else's might depend on the clarity of your report.

The example that follows is from a police report of an accident resulting from a high-speed chase:

> On November 6, 1977, at approximately 2:25 A.M., Officer Louis Velasquez was traveling west on Fulmer Street, approaching the intersection of Fulmer and South Barrington Avenue. As he came up to the intersection, he saw a car traveling north on Barrington at a high rate of speed. According to his testimony, Velasquez estimated this car's speed at 85 to 95 mph.
>
> Officer Velasquez testified that he immediatelly turned on the flasher and siren, swung right into South Barrington Avenue, and began to pursue the violator. Traveling north in pursuit of the offender, Officer Velasquez reached speeds in excess of 115 mph, according to his own testimony.
>
> In the 2100 block of North Barrington Avenue, Velasquez began to overtake the offender. According to his testimony, he was approximately three car lengths behind the offender when he braked suddenly and swung east into Marston Street Extension. Officer Velasquez attempted to follow the car, but he failed to negotiate the turn. The patrol car struck a fire hydrant 20 feet from the intersection of North Barrington and Marston Street Extension. It rolled over and skidded 156 feet, coming to rest on its top on the front lawn of the Carmine residence, 108 Marston Street Extension.

Note the accuracy with which the sequence of events is recorded. Whether you are reporting an auto accident, the results of an experiment, or the behavior of a mental patient, you record your observations in narrative form. Although such reports are expected to be objective and impersonal, they follow the narrative form and adhere to a strict chronological sequence.

THE CONCLUSION

There are several successful techniques for concluding an essay.

The Summary

This method of concluding, though the most common, can be boring and repetitious. Make sure that you summarize only the highlights and that they all emphasize your thesis.

Final Quotation

To conclude with a strong quotation is good because it is brief, has the authority of its author, and pleases the reader's sense of style. Suppose you had written an essay on the age-old question of women's equality with men. An effective close to your thesis might be the quotation from Samuel Johnson when he was asked, "Which is more intelligent, man or woman?" Dr. Johnson answered, "Which man and which woman?"

The Anecdote

A little story that dramatizes your thesis is an effective conclusion. Suppose, in writing an essay on the popular arts for your sociology class, you want to make a final point that the popular story always ends happily even though such a happy ending is not credible in real life. You might write something like the following:

Ignoring reality, the popular story substitutes sentimentality to provide a happy but unlikely ending. The heroine, Mary Lou, is rescued from her drab life clerking in the fish store to support her worthless brother by Prince Charming, Homer Hoskins. Homer just happens by, happens to see her, and sweeps her off to romance in his ice-cream truck.

The Warning or Remedy

If you have been writing about something that ought to be changed, you might want to give a warning about what might happen if things don't change or suggest a remedy for making them change. Suppose you had been writing about the student body's failure to elect the best candidates to student government. You might conclude with the following warning:

If the students continue to elect student government officers who are interested only in social events and who ignore academic responsibilities, we will soon have a social committee, not a government. If we have only a social committee, we will have resigned our rights to any control of our academic careers.

If you wanted to conclude on an affirmative note, you might conclude the same essay with this remedy:

> If we wish our student government really to be a governing body, we must assign social affairs to a social committee and elect to office persons who are concerned with the academic responsibilities and privileges of students. We must have officers who understand that the responsibilities of self-government are at least as important as the privileges. We must elect officers who take themselves and self-government seriously.

The Emphasis on Significance

Especially in a narrative essay, in which readers may become so interested in the story you are telling that they almost forget your thesis, you may conclude by reminding them of it. In the essay about the mule trip, you will notice that the writer concluded by restating the significance of his narrative. After all, you've learned something from this experience or you wouldn't be writing about it. Tell what you learned. The rider on the mule learned to be "a devout coward."

Conclusions to Avoid

1. A **verbatim repetition** of the thesis sentence, usually preceded by "So you can easily see. . . ."
2. **The colorless summary** which says something like "Students have many problems. They have to worry about their grades. They are frightened about going into a vocation. They are unsure of themselves."
3. **The unsupported claim to interest.** "I have always liked to read about bird watching. This book was an interesting book about bird watching. I couldn't put it down. My mother couldn't put it down. My grandmother couldn't put it down. The dog couldn't put it down." This may show a happy community of interest in your family but tells nothing about the book.
4. **The vague moral.** Moralizing is never very popular and the vague moral is boring as well. "We all should be kind to each other" will not advance your thought or the cause of kindness.
5. **The new idea.** Above all else, make sure your conclusion does conclude and does **not** introduce a new thought: "This reminds me of another thing I should have mentioned. . . ."

PITFALLS TO AVOID

1. Don't shrink from using the first-person pronoun *I*. Efforts to avoid *I* often lead to a wordy, impersonal style that deprives your story of its vitality.
2. Don't make the mistake of thinking that you must have an earth-shaking story of events in some exotic place. Stick to what you know best. An everyday experience can be transformed into an effective essay by careful observation and thoughtful evaluation. Rather than searching for some bizarre subject, try to present a fresh and vivid personal view that will make even a common experience unique.
3. Avoid any apologetic phrasing throughout the essay as well as in your introduction:

> This may sound dumb, but . . .
> Although I didn't have much time to think about it, . . .
> After all, I was only a third grader, so . . .

Try to present a candid account of your experience, without bragging or apologizing. Even if you acted with less than perfect honesty or wisdom, your reader will more readily accept an honest account than lame apologies or efforts to impress someone.

4. Don't move back and forth from one tense to another needlessly. Stick to the simple past tense in telling your story: *We* **went**. . . . *We* **saw**. . . . *We* **heard**. . . . If you need to relate details that took place before the time of your story, use the past perfect:

> We **had seen** bear tracks on the day we **arrived** at camp.
> We **had heard** about the abandoned mine shaft, so we **went**. . . .

5. Don't use *it, this,* or *that* as a vague reference to your title or thesis. For example, in a paper titled "The Day the World Was to End," about your youthful conviction that the world was coming to an end, the following opening sentences start with vague references:

FAULTY:
That was twelve years ago when I was staying at my grandparents' farm for the summer.

FAULTY:
It was not because of anything my grandfather had said.

6. Don't leave a gap between the introduction and the body of your essay. Provide a transition to tie the body of the essay to the introduction and the thesis statement. Look at the following example:

Introduction

    My aunt, with whom I lived for several years, was a lady whose dignity few people cared to question. That my mother had married a common millwright who had the indecency to get himself killed seemed, to her, a personal insult. Throughout my stay at my aunt's home, I was constantly reminded of how low in the world my mother had fallen. Since my uncle—poor, harmless fellow—was usually absent on some sort of business, my aunt had an abundance of free time in which to pour into my small ears all the details of my mother's disastrous marriage choice. But the day came when I grew tired of hearing my aunt refer to my father as having been a failure. **In something less than a straightforward way, I determined to take my small revenge.**

First body paragraph

    Throughout the hot, motionless days of August, I spent much of my time on the banks of the Souris River. I walked along its banks for miles, exploring tiny creeks and ravines. . . .

Note the gap between the introduction and the first body paragraph. A slight revision could supply the transition needed to tie the body of the essay to the introduction.

IMPROVED:

During the hot, motionless days of August, a plan of revenge slowly began to take shape in my mind. Wandering the river bank not far from my aunt's home, I developed, bit by bit, a devious scheme to strike a blow at her dignity. . . .

This revised version provides smooth transition and keeps the story's central idea uppermost in the reader's mind.

SUGGESTED TOPICS

Write a narrative essay on one of the following topics.

1. A blind date
2. A traffic accident
3. A childhood prank
4. A courtroom battle
5. A wedding reception
6. A vacation
7. A barroom brawl
8. A hunting trip
9. A surprise party
10. A fraternity party
11. An accident at work
12. An embarrassing incident

13. Your first date
14. Your wedding day
15. Your first child
16. Your first plane ride
17. Your first birthday away from home
18. Your first day on a new job
19. Your first encounter with death
20. Your first attempt at public speaking
21. Your first attempt at skiing (or hang gliding or other activity)
22. Your high school prom
23. Your first job interview
24. Your first trip to another country
25. Your first experience in unemployment
26. Being arrested
27. Witnessing a crime
28. Getting lost
29. A military experience
30. Winning a championship game
31. Losing your job
32. Learning an important lesson
33. Meeting your future in-laws
34. Getting caught in a lie
35. Making a crucial decision
36. Dealing with an irate customer
37. Being thrown from a horse
38. Running in a marathon
39. Losing a friend
40. Playing a practical joke on someone
41. An experience that taught you:
    a. to think before you act
    b. to respect age
    c. to spend more time with your kids
    d. to change your priorities
    e. to be less critical of others
    f. to appreciate your parents
    g. to appreciate your roots
    h. to have more confidence
    i. to look at both sides of an issue
    j. to appreciate your education

TECHNIQUES OF CLEAR WRITING

THE CORE SENTENCE

Often a sentence fails to communicate the writer's idea clearly because the core sentence is faulty. The core sentence consists of the subject, *S*; the verb, *V*; and the completer, *C*. (The completer is anything that completes the sentence; it can be a direct object of an active verb, a complement of a linking verb, or other kinds of words that complete the thought of the sentence.)

Subject	Verb	Completer
Donnie	passed	French.
S	*V*	*C* [object]

| Mother | felt | sick. |
| *S* | *V* | *C [adjective]* |

| Stella | is | a good cook. |
| *S* | *V* | *C [predicate nominative, complement of linking verb]* |

| Ricky | went | to the game. |
| *S* | *V* | *C [prepositional phrase]* |

| The storm | moved | east. |
| *S* | *V* | *C [adverb]* |

| David and Lisa | eloped. | |
| *S* | *V* | *C [needs none]* |

Whatever the completer might be, it is one of the trio, *SVC*, that must make sense if the sentence is to be clear.

Clarity is sometimes lost because the sentences start off in one direction but stray away in another. Either the subject and verb don't make sense together or the verb and the completer don't go together logically. For instance, in the sentence "Evidence of theft was committed last night," the **subject** is *evidence* and evidence cannot be *committed.* The writer presumably means that theft was committed and evidence was found to prove it. In the sentence *The committee's report replaced John's job*, it is unlikely that a report could take the place of a job. The writer probably meant "The committee reported that John's job was unnecessary."

If words come between the elements of the core sentence, seeing the error is difficult; in order to correct the sentence, you must pick out the **Subject, Verb,** and **Completer** to see if they make sense. For example:

Any one of the members of the Homecoming Queen's Court who didn't show up would mean an unbalanced float.

You may be able to figure out what is meant in such a sentence, but it isn't easy. The *reason* for its obscurity *is* that the SVC is faulty.

| Anyone | would mean | unbalanced float |
| *S* | *V* | *C* |

Once you see the error, it is not difficult to create a correct sentence:

If anyone in the Homecoming Queen's Court is absent, the float will be unbalanced.
The absence of any of the Homecoming Queen's Court would unbalance the float [*or* destroy the balance of the float].

Here is another faulty core sentence:

As you know, the situation in the cafeteria must be resolved.

Situation   must be resolved
   S   V

Situations are not resolved; problems and differences are. Situations can improve or worsen, but there is nothing in a situation to resolve.

As you check your sentences to make sure the Subject-Verb-Completer in each makes sense, don't limit your attention only to the independent clause or clauses. The core within a dependent clause must also be a logical *S-V-C*. For example:

Although the decline in prosperity was turned around, unemployment remained a problem.

Here the main clause, *unemployment remained a problem,* has a correct *S-V-C*. But in the dependent clause the subject, *decline,* and the verb, *was turned around,* are illogical. A *decline* may level off or bottom out, but it cannot turn around.

EXERCISE 2A: CORE SENTENCE

*Pick out the core sentences in the following. If a core sentence is faulty, correct it. Remember that the core sentence must be correct in **all** clauses, not just in the main clause.*

1. The possibility of a flood may happen since three inches of rain has fallen in two days.

   _____

2. The mistakes the teacher has explained will make our writing better.

   _____

3. A college is where you go to get advanced training.

   _____

4. The blueprint for our new library will take eight months to build.

   _____

5. The newspapers that we sell this year should triple in the next two years.

_____

6. The tendency, on your part, to procrastinate is hurting your grades.

_____

7. The contrast between Sylvester Stallone and Dudley Moore determines the audience of the movies of each actor.

_____

8. These solutions will help the lack of participation of the students.

_____

9. One example of Franscesca's shyness is when she meets boys.

_____

10. The glorious mixture of sun and sand in Miami houses racial discrimination.

_____

EXERCISE 2B: CORE SENTENCE

In the following, find the core sentences. Correct any faulty cores so that all sentences are logical.

1. Unless the problem improves, the solution will get worse.

_____

2. The question of the authorship of Shakespeare means the ignoring of dramatic history.

_____

3. The contrast between Eliot's ideas and his dedicated readers is a discussion of morals.

_____

4. The tendency to 'put off 'til tomorrow' causes inefficiency.

_____

5. The love of money is the root of all evil.

_____

6. When the situation is resolved, the worries will improve.

_____

7. The improvements grow worse as the members decline.

_____

8. Every time Ben complains, his complaints come back to him as more obstacles he must submit to.

_____

9. John recommended council adding its failures to its agenda.

_____

10. As soon as the mistakes were committed, the new president asked that council be called upon to improve them.

_____

POINT OF VIEW

One of the ways writers sometimes confuse their readers is by changing point of view. Point of view refers to **when, where, how,** and **by whom** the situation is viewed. Errors in point of view can occur in five areas: **person, tense, number, voice, and tone.**

Person

Errors in person are the most common errors in point of view. The writer may start off correctly using the third person:

> **The students** were starting to feel uneasy as the smell of smoke grew stronger.

Then he or she lapses into first person:

> Someone screamed, and **we** panicked.

Or when starting a narrative, the writer may start with a first-person generalization for the thesis sentence:

> Moving to **my** own apartment required some major adjustments.

Then he or she shifts to the second person:

> **Your parents** were very much against **your** moving out.

Shifts in person occur frequently in everyday conversation. In fact, you have probably become so used to **hearing** these errors that you automatically shift from one person to another without even realizing that you have changed your point of view. For example:

INCORRECT:
Those students thought that **you** could breeze right through Mrs. Griffith's sociology class, but **they** got a rude awakening after the first test. [This sentence shifts from third person (*students*) to second person (**you**), then back to third (*they*).]

CORRECTED:
Those students thought that **they** could breeze right through Mrs. Griffith's sociology class, but **they** got a rude awakening after the first test.

INCORRECT:
I thought that **I** could breeze right through Mrs. Griffith's sociology class, but **you** get a rude awakening after the first test.

CORRECTED:
I thought that **I** could breeze right through Mrs. Griffith's sociology class, but **I** got a rude awakening after the first test.

NOTE: Avoid inappropriate use of second person. Keep your reader in mind. For example, it would sound ridiculous to write for a male English instructor, "While washing your nighties in Lux. . . ." It is preferable to use the second person only when you are addressing someone directly. Do not use *you* when you mean *everybody*.

Tense

Shift in tense is also a common error, especially for inexperienced writers. It is sometimes caused by the writer's getting caught up in the story, especially in a narrative. A student is writing, let's say, about a wreck that changed his choice of careers. He begins correctly using the past tense, but then, excited by his memories, switches to the present tense.

I started down the narrow twisting road that led to the picnic area. I had the car in second gear because the last thing I wanted from the car was speed. Suddenly, up pops the gear shift. I'm in neutral! The car gathers speed as I brake frantically.

Number

Errors in number, making illogical switches between singular and plural, are usually errors in referring to antecedents: errors in agreement between subject and verb and between subject and pronoun. Essentially errors in grammar, they also confuse the point of view.

They are discussed in the Techniques of Clear Writing section in Chapter 4. They include errors such as these:

Each child was told to bring **their** own marbles.
Everybody knows **their** own mind.

Voice

Changes in voice are changes from active to passive or passive to active. These changes interfere with the flow of thought and force the reader to reread the sentence to understand.

I ordered a ham sandwich, and a hamburger was served to me.
Harry Truman loved bourbon and poker, and an occasional session at the piano was enjoyed by him.

Tone

Basically tone is word choice. Tone can be formal or informal, conversational or pedantic, sardonic or serious. Whatever tone you choose, stick, with it; be consistent. When you change tone, you jar the reader.

The ambulance arrived immediately. The white-coated attendants moved quickly and effectively to stem the flow of blood. Cripes, what a mess! The poor sucker looked like he'd been blown away.

Boy, were we having fun. Kids were all over the place, some climbing trees, a few wading in the creek, and a gang playing touch football. A cool breeze permeated the entire area although the sun was a brilliant orb.

The concert was a real bummer. The whole performance was pedestrian.

My brother is a real jerk at school. He mouths off to the teachers, clowns around in class, and neglects his academic preparation. In short, he is a maladjusted, regressive deviant.

You really confuse your reader if you change your point of view.

EXERCISE 2C: POINT OF VIEW

Revise the following sentences to eliminate needless shifts in point of view.

1. If students keep their work up-to-date, you will find studying for exams relatively easy.

2. I go to all my high-school basketball games, for each one is exciting.

_____

3. The instructor rapped on his lectern for attention and then begins his class.

_____

4. Everybody is going to their own classrooms.

_____

5. As we joined the group, the tension was clearly felt by us.

_____

6. The valley stretched to the horizon, on which the setting sun cast up its rays of red and gold. Wow, what glitz!

_____

7. The students were given a three-day study time before exams; you are better prepared this way.

_____

8. As we come down the path, the cabin sprang into view.

_____

9. Each voter ought to know the issues, so that they can cast their votes intelligently.

_____

10. Guests should check your coats in the front hall where the management had set up coat racks.

_____

EXERCISE 2D: POINT OF VIEW

Identify the types of errors in point of view in the following sentences and correct them.

1. San Francisco is a great city; they have wonderful restaurants, beautiful sights, and fabulous stores.

_____

_____

2. I think capital punishment should be abolished; you'd think an advanced country like the U.S. would have eliminated this barbarian custom years ago.

_____

_____

3. Everyone cried when they watched E.T. even if you won't admit it.

_____

_____

4. Bill started down the hill, and suddenly he's going seventy miles per hour.

_____

_____

5. Anyone who wants to be physically fit is going to find they have to work to attain it.

_____

_____

6. Julio took first place in the mile; second and third were taken by Domingo and Alex.

_____

_____

7. The night club had crazy, flashing strobe lights, wild frescos on the walls, and gracious appointments.

_____

_____

8. If you want to make an *A*, everyone will have to hit the books.

_____

_____

9. As Carla leaves, she bowed to the audience.

_____

10. Before he went for dinner, George eats a few sandwiches.

_____

EXERCISE 2E: POINT OF VIEW

Familiar though you may be with the Declaration of Independence, you will have difficulty at times understanding the version below. It has been rewritten with an inconsistent point of view. Underline the inconsistencies in person, tense, number, voice, and tone. Then revise the inconsistencies so that the excerpt is logically acceptable.

We hold these truths to be self-evident: That all men will be created equal; that his Creator endowed you with certain unalienable rights;

that among these will have been life, liberty, and the pursuit of happiness; that, to secure these rights, governments will be instituted among men, deriving its just powers from the consent of the governed: that whenever any form of government becomes destructive of these ends, it was his right to alter or abolish them, and to have a new government instituted by them, laying their foundations on such principles, and organizing its powers in such form, as to you shall seem most likely to effect their safety and to give them whatever they damn well want whenever they damn well want it. Prudence, indeed, will dictate that governments long established should not be changed for itsy-bitsy causes; and accordingly all experience will show that mankind was more disposed to suffer, while evils are sufferable, than to have yourself righted by abolishing the forms to which we are accustomed. But when a long train of unintentional mistakes, pursuing invariably the same object, evinces a design to reduce you under absolute despotism, it is his right, it is duty, to throw the bloody twits out.

WORD POWER

THE CHOICE IS YOURS

Much of what is involved in writing is a matter of making the right choice for what you want to achieve. There are, of course, some matters that are completely correct or incorrect. However, the great majority of the decisions you make in your writing will be your choice of what you think will be preferable in any given circumstance.

You decide what you want to say and then determine the best way to say it.

The Choice of Verbs: Active or Passive Voice

As you learned in the Word Power section of Chapter 1, you must choose between the active and the passive voice. As you recall, the passive voice is preferred when you wish to emphasize what happens rather than who does it. ("The passive voice is preferred" is an example of the use of the passive voice.)

Usually, however, the writer chooses the active voice. ("The writer chooses . . ." is an example of the active voice.)

The Choice of Verbs: General or Specific Verbs

A **general** verb indicates a broad action or an action taken by a great number of people.

The wind **blew** through the trees.
A mob **ran** through the streets.

A **specific** verb indicates a more precise action or an action done by a more limited number of people.

The wind **roared** through the trees.
The wind **rustled** through the trees.
The wind **murmured** through the trees.

A mob **crashed** through the barricade.
A mob **pushed** against the locked door.
The kindergarten class **skipped** to the playground.

Unless you have a reason to select the general verb, your writing will be more vivid and lively if you choose specific verbs. Such choices are not difficult, although at first they may be a little time-consuming. If, for instance, you look for specific verbs in an unabridged dictionary, you will find over a thousand verbs under the letter S alone. Many other letters are equally or even more abundant in their verbs.

Almost every general verb has numerous specific verbs that vivify its meaning. Test your own knowledge of these specific verbs by finding ten specific verbs each for the words *walk*, *talk*, *look*, and *love*.

If you examine good writing carefully, you will discover that such writing is made vigorous and convincing by the selection of specific verbs. When Thomas Jefferson wrote the Declaration of Independence in 1776, he wanted to convince the many colonists yet undecided that breaking away from England was a good idea. Therefore, he chose strong, specific verbs to state how much a tyrant George III was.

He has **plundered** our seas, **ravaged** our coasts, **burned** our towns, and **destroyed** the lives of our people.

Had Jefferson been a careless writer, he might have written something like this:

He has **disturbed** our seas and our coasts, **messed up** our towns, and **didn't do** our people any good either.

The unconvinced colonists probably would have remained unconvinced. Their response would probably have been "Who cares?"

A primary responsibility of the writer is to make such choices so that readers *do* care. One of those choices is to use specific verbs.

EXERCISE 2F: SPECIFIC VERBS

In the following narrative paragraphs underline the specific verbs that you consider well chosen and circle those that you think could be improved.

On the torture scale, bamboo wedges methodically driven under each fingernail is second only to dressing my four-year-old daughter for church. Deciding what to wear was the beginning of round one. I have always considered a dress appropriate for church. She, on the other hand, chose turquoise shorts, a purple sweater, patent leather shoes, a kelly green sweatband, and her Wendy's Jazz Cap. Thus began the de-humanization of a mother. I pleaded, I bribed, and I threatened her with bodily harm. Finally, after 30 minutes, I broke her down. She agreed to wear her red dress.

The bell just rang for round two! She immediately started her "I bet I can push mommy over the edge" dance. This dance consisted of running around the room, gyrating her hips, and waving her arms in a wild frenzy. The "dance" terminated when she threw herself on her bed, stomach first, kicking her feet wildly in the air. Not letting her get the best of me, I seized the opportunity presented by her vulnerable position. I leaped on the bed, placed my knee into the small of her back and bore down gently, but firmly. Rendering her immobile, I put on her underpants. Round two was over.

Round three began as soon as she spied me going into her closet for the dress. She immediately assumed the "over-the-head-clothing" stance. Her arms became welded to the side of her torso. I began to beg and grovel at her feet, but still she remained rigid and immovable. I did the only thing left to do. I began to pry first one arm, and then the other, away from her body and into her dress. Thus ended round three. Only her socks and shoes were left.

The bell just rang in round four. I have yet to see my child's face while putting on her socks. When she sees a pair of socks, she is off and running. The race was on. I was in hot pursuit, trying to catch a foot in mid-air. I had the socks in position. I lunged. Score one! I lunged again. Score two! the socks were on her feet. The "shoe technique" is definitely an art. As my daughter continued her retreat, I placed her shoes in strategic locations on the floor. When she came around for the second lap, she inadvertently placed first one foot, and then the other, into her shoes. Victory, at last! The "she-devil" is ready for church.

Now we are ready to hear the minister preach, as always, about the fires of hell and eternal damnation. My definition has changed considerably since my daughter's fourth birthday. Thousands and thousands of naked four-year-olds lined up waiting for me to dress them for church—now that is eternal damnation!

Maggie Henson
(Student)

SPECIFIC NOUNS AND MODIFIERS

As you become more experienced in the process of writing, you will realize that what you say and the way you say it will depend on what you mean. For instance, most of the time you will choose specific nouns and modifiers because they will enable you to be more precise. However, there will be occasional times, when you will prefer not to be specific. Suppose that you are at a picnic, and a luxurious lunch has been spread out on the table. Suddenly a cat jumps up among the plates.

"Quick, somebody," you shout. "Chase that cat away from the table!"

You don't need to be specific about that cat. It makes no difference if the cat is orange or gray, if it is a purebred Angora or a stray. The only communication you are interested in making is to shoo the cat away.

But for the greater number of times, you do wish to be specific because the specific makes your writing clear, and brief, and vigorous. No matter how vague and general your word choice is, you will probably convey some idea of what you mean. Yet ten different readers might get ten different meanings. If your writing is no clearer than this, you have failed to communicate your idea. Usually you want your reader to share your image with you. For this, you need to be specific.

My new cat is all white with slightly pink ears.

When the nouns you use can be interpreted in more than one way, then they are too general. Look at the following example:

Major Cunningham uses **drugs.**

In this sentence, the noun **drugs** is too general. One reader might picture Major Cunningham taking insulin for his diabetes, another might see him smoking marijuana, another might assume that he is popping amphetamines, and still another might conclude that he is shooting heroin every day. The reader doesn't know what kind of drugs the major is taking or how often he is taking them.

Now look at another example:

Mr. Magillacuddy has a **problem.**

This sentence could be interpreted in a number of ways. Maybe Mr. Magillacuddy's problem is only a temporary financial setback—a cut in pay. Maybe he has a serious medical problem, an incurable disease, or maybe his "problem" is that Mrs. Magillacuddy is driving him crazy.

You can clarify the meaning of each of these sentences by

1. Making the noun more specific.
2. Adding specific modifiers:
   a. Adjectives—to modify nouns or pronouns.
   b. Adverbs—to modify verbs, adjectives, or other adverbs.

For example:

Major Cunningham takes **amphetamines daily.** [specific noun and adverb]
Mr. Magillacuddy has had a **devastating financial setback** [specific adjectives and specific noun]; he lost his job.

Notice that in each of these sentences the modifiers as well as the nouns are specific. You can't make a noun specific and then add just any adjective or adverb. For example, if you say that Major Cunningham took amphetamines **regularly,** you are not necessarily saying that he took them every day. You are just saying that he took them at regular intervals—maybe every few hours, maybe every day, maybe every other day. Likewise, if you say that Mr. Magillacuddy has a **bad** problem or a **serious** financial problem, you are not telling the reader that his problem is so bad that it really devastates him.

The illustration below lists general nouns that have been made specific. Notice how you can make nouns more specific by asking yourself a series of questions. Take the word *document*, for example:

What kind   *a legal*
of document?   *document*
                      What kind of
                      legal document?   *a will*
                                  Whose will?   *Uncle Joe's will*
                                  What kind of
                                  will?   *a million*
                                                            dollars
                                                            to each
                                                            of us

There will be rare times when you will not want to be specific or at least not totally specific; you will occasionally want to be general because you wish to refer to a broad range of things or ideas rather than to the narrowed word. Usually, however, you will want to move as far as possible to the specific.

GENERAL ──────────────────────────────────→ SPECIFIC

dog	hunting dog	hound	bassett hound	my bassett, Eclipse
container	glass container	a bottle	a wine bottle	a tapering green Rhine wine bottle
suit	formal suit	a tuxedo	a colorful tuxedo	a mint-green tuxedo, wrinkled and torn
experience	childhood experience	an accident	a bad accident	a fatal automobile accident
executive	business executive	a vice-president	an oil company vice-president	the energetic, articulate vice-president of Mayhem Oil Company

EXERCISE 2G: SPECIFIC NOUNS

Write four increasingly specific words for each of the following nouns.

1. vehicle _____ _____ _____ _____

2. building _____ _____ _____ _____

3. food _____ _____ _____ _____

4. individual _____ _____ _____ _____

5. job _____ _____ _____ _____

6. game _____ _____ _____ _____

7. criminal _____ _____ _____ _____

8. makeup _____ _____ _____ _____

9. water _____ _____ _____ _____

10. medicine _____ _____ _____ _____

SPECIFIC MODIFIERS

Avoid overused adjectives, such as *nice, pretty, interesting, worthwhile, rewarding, thrilling, wonderful,* and overused adverbs such as *very, actually, really, terribly.* Also avoid stringing a lot of adjectives or adverbs together in one sentence. Don't overdo modifiers.

In almost every instance, vague modifiers can be replaced by more specific ones.

> A *nice* house might be cozy, charming, comfortable, neat, or well-constructed.
> A *pretty* girl might be graceful, elegant, dainty, striking, stunning, or provocative.
> An *interesting* scene might be curious, revealing, absorbing, fascinating, or eyecatching.
> A *very dumb* answer might be described as irrelevant, naive, ignorant, or stupid.
> A *very serious* injury might be grave, critical, dangerous, or crippling.
> A *really cold* day might be icy, frigid, numbing, paralyzing, or bone-chilling.
> A *terribly hot* day might be sweltering, sizzling, scorching, broiling, blistering, blazing, or hellish.

Always try to select the word that conveys the precise meaning you intend.

EXERCISE 2H: SPECIFIC ADJECTIVES

Supply the sentences below with specific adjectives.

1. Our day at the beach was a _____, _____ disaster.

2. We planned to have an early breakfast at Jake and Mary's new house, but it was over-run with _____ carpenters.

3. We tried a restaurant along the road, but its food was _____, its service _____, its atmosphere _____.

4. Katie's _____ pup yapped; Jane's _____ girl was car sick; Lynn's _____ boyfriend never drove _____ miles an hour.

5. When we finally got to the beach, the weather had turned _____, with a _____ temperature and _____ clouds.

6. The _____ lunch basket overturned into the

_____ sand and that _____ pup jumped into the

_____ contents.

7. Jake tried to rescue Mary's _____, _____ pie, but _____ succeeded in dropping _____, _____ basket. Mary burst into _____ tears.

8. Two of the men stumped off to the _____ snack shack and returned with a couple of _____ sacks of _____ hamburgers.

9. No sooner had we started to eat this _____ substitute for our _____ lunch than a _____ rain started.

10. Totally _____, we trotted off to the cars only to find that the wimp's car had a _____ tire. As an outing, that day was _____.

EXERCISE 2I: SPECIFIC ADVERBS

Insert a specific modifier in the blanks in the following sentences. Remember, the more specific and vivid the modifier, the clearer the meaning.

1. Jeffrey showed the president _____ respect.

2. Professor Gonzales gave a _____ argument for making Ecology 101 a required subject.

3. Geraldo smoked _____.

4. The new game was so _____ competitive that the students decided to play it _____.

5. The car was _____ designed.

6. Although she is over fifty, Chen's mother is always _____ dressed.

7. My boss _____ awarded me the prize for employee of the month.

8. Ernie was _____ polite to the policeman who stopped him.

9. His plan was _____ designed to find out why there is so much cruelty in our prisons.

10. Chan ran _____ to the police call box in the corner.

CHAPTER 3

Describing

To describe means "to picture with words." When you describe you enable your readers to get a sensory impression in their minds. It need not be visual although the sense of sight is the one most frequently used. Impressions may also be made by any of your other senses—sound, touch, smell, or taste, even the kinetic sense of your muscles and viscera moving, or your skin crawling.

You select details from any one or several of your senses to form a *central impression* for your readers to "see." For example, your central impression, made up of sensory details, of the retired policeman at the school crossing is that he is patient and pleasant, whereas his occasional young replacement is brusque and surly. As an example of place, if you are conveying the sound of the school gym when the score is tied during the big game, this certainly varies from the sound of that gym half an hour after the home team has lost and the only person remaining is a maintenance worker dejectedly sweeping the bleachers.

Your central impression becomes the attitude of your thesis statement. The thesis statement will not be a factual observation of what your senses "see"; it will be your interpretation of what those senses see.

Description becomes effective when it makes readers see what you see and feel what you feel. You can't do that just by telling your readers; you must get them to experience, through your words, what you have experienced. Your aim in descriptive writing is to create vivid images in the minds of readers that make your sensory experiences come alive.

DESCRIPTION AS A HELP TO OTHER WRITING

Although description is one of the four major types of writing (the others are narration, exposition, and persuasion/argumentation), seldom does description stand alone in an entire essay. It is more often written to help convey the meaning of the other types of writing. In narration, for example, description is used to give the setting in which the action takes place. It is also used to make the reader see the characters and understand their actions in the story. Although description seldom stands alone, it is of vital importance in showing both places and people. Through description, you recreate for your reader a sensory experience of a place or of a person that you have already experienced, either in life or in imagination. Your description gives vividness to the story you're telling.

Perhaps you wish to tell about a summer romance at a camp where you worked one summer. You might set the stage with a description like this:

> My first morning as a counselor at Camp Tingle began at 6 A.M. with a dip in the lake. Although directly overhead the sky was already bright blue, the high pines that rimmed the lake kept the sun from the round lake's surface. The lake looked almost black and motionless. Only the smallest ripples inched up and fell back on the dark brown sand and rounded pebbles of the beach. It looked primeval, beyond time. Then, suddenly, sixty yelling children rushed from the woodland paths to throw themselves into the lake. The yells changed to screams as the icy, spring-fed water stung their bodies still warm from bed. I followed them more slowly, but they were right. The only bearable way was to jump in. Gasping, but in my best crawl, I crossed the lake and came halfway back again. I rolled over to float a minute before I joined the shouting, splashing children. How beautiful it is, I thought, and with a shiver, how exhilarating.

There you are in a beautiful and exhilarating setting—all ready for a summer love.

In exposition, which is explaining something to your reader, you will also often want to use description to help you. Particularly if you are trying to explain something abstract, it is helpful to show your readers what your abstraction stands for. Simply stated, abstract is the opposite of concrete. If something is abstract, then you can't see it or touch it or smell it or hear it or taste it. In other words, you can't picture it. For example, you can't picture loyalty, but you can picture the old hound trudging after the town drunk. Thus, through description, the abstract becomes concrete. Suppose, for a psychology class, you are writing a paper about the problems of the elderly. You decide to narrow it to the problem of the loneliness of old people. You obviously can't just say, "Old people are often lonely." However, you might describe your neighbor across the street:

> Mary Carter is a round little dumpling of a woman, who at 79 is far and away the oldest resident of our neighborhood. Her face is as round as her figure, with a network of fine, soft lines around her mouth, lines that cosmetic ads call "smile" lines or "laugh" lines. Mary does smile a lot, but somehow her blue eyes contradict her mouth. They dart glances to every face, looking for warmth, not just tolerance. Since she doesn't have anyone at home to talk to (except for a parakeet who will probably make the *Guinness Book of Records* for the longest silence in bird-dom) and since the neighbors are too busy to talk to her often, when she does get someone to talk to, she talks a lot. If you meet her on the street, she always stops you. If you try to back away from her, she holds onto your wrist or even a button on your coat. She just hates to let you go.
>
> Of course, she really wants to see her son. He's what she talks about most. He does come about once a month. But every day she hopes he's coming. Every day about 5:30 she peeks around her little house to see that everything's neat. She usually bakes a few cookies or brownies, for he always likes something sweet. But she's a realist, too; she just bakes a few, for somehow, brownies aren't very good when you're alone.

Now if you multiply Mary Carter by thousands, you have your abstraction. Mary Carter dramatizes your subject, the loneliness of old people. Description, the selection of a few vivid details to help the reader see what you see and feel what you feel, is of vital importance in most writing.

ORGANIZATION

STEPS IN WRITING A DESCRIPTION

Learning how to describe is not difficult if you follow this four-step process:

Step 1. Be observant.

Step 2. Form a central impression (this will be the basis of your thesis sentence).

Step 3. Select specific, concrete details to support your thesis statement.

Step 4. Determine how your details will be organized.

Observation

Good description begins with close observation. If you are to get your reader to see what you see and feel what you feel, you must first of all be a keen observer. Nothing will aid your description more than a keen eye for detail.

Note the contrast in the following brief descriptive passages:

VAGUE:

Jake was an interesting fellow about twenty years old. He seemed to have a lot of interest in his studies. Anyway, he sort of stared at the professor.

SPECIFIC AND CONCRETE:

Jake would stand out in any classroom. His sharp eyes peered from under iron rims, sending darts of eagerness and suspicion directly toward his opponent, the professor.

VAGUE:

The garage was kind of sloppy and overcrowded. There didn't seem to be any particular place for anything.

SPECIFIC AND CONCRETE:

Above the bench at the rear, nuts and bolts and screws and clamps and sockets overflowed from broken drawers and cubbyholes and overturned boxes. Along both walls, snow tires and bald tires, rusted rims and broken springs and shackles, bicycle parts and battered garden tools spilled out onto a floor black with grease.

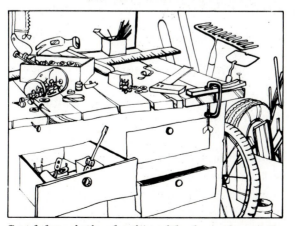

Good description begins with close observation.

VAGUE:

The landowner, Mr. Larz, sat in his car with the door open and leisurely relit his cigar. Then he told us to go back to work.

SPECIFIC AND CONCRETE:

The landowner, Mr. Larz, sat framed in the open door of his green Chrysler, parked in the shade of a live oak. His stubby legs scarcely reached the dirt, and his heavy paunch strained against a brass zipper that bulged into the sunlight. Wiping a drool of tobacco juice from the corner of his mouth with the back of his hand, he scraped the burnt end of the chewed cigar stump against the door frame. Then he leaned backward to fish a battered Zippo lighter from his front pocket and leaned forward again to light the cigar stub. "Aw right, boys," he said, "let's go back to work."

VAGUE:

Mrs. Pelluzzi's garden was neat and orderly. She grew a variety of vegetables and took good care of everything.

SPECIFIC AND CONCRETE:

Not one weed was allowed to live in Mrs. Pelluzzi's garden, and every plant was kept in its place. Swiss chard and onions and peppers grew in precisely spaced rows, and flat-headed cabbages, both white and purple, marched across the garden in perfect ranks. Pole beans climbed their neat teepees, the tomatoes pressed against chicken-wire hoops, and even the boisterous zucchini dared to travel just so far and no farther.

As you can see from these examples, it takes more than vague statements to get your reader to visualize what you describe. You've got to make a direct appeal to your reader's senses and emotions, and you do that best through careful observation of specific details.

The Central Impression

Have you ever walked into a room and thought, "How dreary. I don't want to stay here very long"? Or upon entering a room have you immediately thought, "What a happy place this is"? These thoughts are central impressions, the overall atmosphere of a place.

When you meet a person for the first time, you often form an immediate impression:

Boy, is Mark clean-cut; my parents would approve of him.

I think I'll like Pablo; he looks like a nice guy.

Cindy's very sweet, and she's smart, too.

Mimi's a lot of fun, I'll bet.

You may also remember having seen a quiet farm slumbering in the February cold, and thought, "This is the most peaceful place I've ever seen"—another central impression.

The central impression becomes the attitude of your descriptive essay.

Subject	Attitude
basement den	dreary
mother's kitchen	happy
Mark	clean-cut
Pablo	nice guy
farm	peaceful

Now, having both subject and attitude, you are ready to create your thesis statement. Perhaps you wish to tell your reader why that farm seemed so peaceful to you. You recall the scene in detail and come up with this:

> Backed against the protecting hillside and flanked by its sturdy barns, the farmhouse, with its yellow lamplight shining through the dank February twilight, looked like a safe, warm haven.

Your mind constantly gathers details that you perceive through your senses and then generalizes these details into a central impression. Because your mind works so quickly, you often do not consciously know **why** you get the impression you did from the person, place, or thing that you observed. You must think back or reflect on the details that form that impression or feeling.

Selection of Details

Suppose you want to write an essay about a place that meant a lot to you when you were a child. You remember that when you were twelve your family moved into a big old house you really loved. The very best thing about it was an unused room in the basement which your parents said you could have for your "den."

Filled with twelve-year-old enthusiasm, you pelted down the cellar steps for your first view of **your** den. You still remember the shock of your first impression—that room was so dreary you could have cried. You jot down a list of the details of that dismal room:

> dark grey cement floor
> bookshelves in bright blue, red, and yellow lining one wall
> dirt-streaked windows that let in little light
> golden shafts of sunlight piercing the gloom

discarded living room furniture faded into a dull brown
a rickety brown table with legs of unequal length
a dusty glass table lamp with a stained shade that cut out most of the
     bulb light
a handsome open fireplace clogged with ashes
a crusted, discolored brass floor lamp with a naked bulb
an old threadbare carpet whose pattern could no longer be seen
dust in the corners
well-proportioned window seat with ragged cushions
cobwebs between the ceiling rafters
a dank, musty smell
a smell of mildew or just age coming from the overstuffed couch and
     chair
stale cigarette smoke
the damp, clammy air
drafts sneaking through the windows
sound of water dripping in the laundry room
creaking in the rafters when someone walked upstairs

Checking over these details, you realize that a few of them don't
support the first impression you want to make—that the room was
dreary. You go through the list again striking out those details that
don't support your central impression of *dreariness*.

dark grey cement floor
~~bookshelves in bright blue, red, and yellow lining one wall~~
dirt-streaked windows that let in little light
~~golden shafts of sunlight piercing the gloom~~
discarded living room furniture faded into a dull brown
a rickety brown table with legs of unequal length
a dusty glass table lamp with a stained shade that cut out most of the
     bulb light
~~a handsome open fireplace clogged with ashes~~
a crusted, discolored brass floor lamp with a naked bulb
an old threadbare carpet whose pattern could no longer be seen
dust in the corners
~~well-proportioned window seat with ragged cushions~~
cobwebs between the ceiling rafters
a dank, musty smell
a smell of mildew or just age coming from the overstuffed couch and
     chair
stale cigarette smoke
the damp, clammy air
drafts sneaking through the windows
sound of water dripping in the laundry room
creaking in the rafters when someone walked upstairs

The description of your first impression might be this:

> Although it soon became the best loved room of my childhood, all I felt when I first saw my basement den was disappointment because it was so dreary. In the little light that struggled through the dirt-streaked windows, the dark grey cement floor seemed to disappear in the dusty corners. The unpainted cement block walls faded away in that dim light. I smelled their clammy dankness rather than saw them. The blackened crossbeams of the ceiling made a grid draped with strings and shreds of cobwebs. The dampness was emphasized by the drip, drip, drip of the faucets in the laundry room. My first thought was that this would make a better den for a bear than a kid.

You might go on to another paragraph beginning:

> But if the room itself was depressing, the furniture was even worse.

You would then go on to support the central impression in that topic sentence. These two paragraphs would act as an introduction to the main section of your essay: the appearance of the loved den *after* you got rid of the dreariness. You would have two descriptions, a "before" and an "after" description.

Writing description is not difficult. Actually your brain has sifted and selected details and formed a central impression without your consciously doing anything. To write a good description, you need only to recall the central impression, and then go back to the source of the impression and find the details that inspired it.

For example, suppose you were describing the drill instructor you had in the Marines. You might begin with just a list of physical characteristics, a strictly literal, matter-of-fact description:

> My drill instructor in the Marines was a short, husky man, about five feet, six inches tall, weighing about 200 pounds. He had a big head and a wide neck, and his short legs seemed out of proportion to the rest of his body. He had dark brown eyes and short-cropped hair and a number of wrinkles in his forehead. . . .

So far your reader has no central impression of your drill instructor. He can't form a clear image in his mind. Besides, he is probably so bored that he has lost all interest in reading the rest of your paper. If, on the other hand, you had begun your paper by saying,

"My drill instructor in the Marines always reminded me of a bulldog," then your reader would have a clear picture in his mind.

Your descriptive details would mean something. Read the following details and see how they gradually add up to the central impression:

> He was a sawed-off, husky-looking guy with an abnormally short pair of legs supporting a five-foot, six-inch, 200-pound frame.
>
> He had an oversized head and a neck so wide that his head seemed to be sitting directly on his shoulders. The only time I noticed his neck was during a fit of rage when his veins bulged out so far, I thought that they were going to burst.
>
> The first time I looked at him, my eyes immediately focused on his vicious-looking face.
>
> The deep, leathery creases in his forehead hung down over his cold, dark eyes in such a way that it would have been physically impossible for him to change his ferocious countenance.
>
> His pudgy, flattened nose seemed perfectly suited to the rest of his bulldog face.

> He wore a permanent scowl. His mouth drooped so low that his sagging jowls scraped his collar.
>
> He could absolutely terrorize his men by simply looking them straight in the eye and snarling. All they could see was a savage bulldog on the verge of attack. Even the short bristly hairs on his head stood at attention when he barked out his commands.

Now the physical characteristics of the drill instructor mean something because each of them helps to create the picture of a bulldog. Instead of an unrelated list of physical features, you now have a coherent group of details leading to a specific central impression. Notice that the image of the bulldog was formed not just by what you saw, but also by what you heard and what you felt. For example, you **heard** the drill instructor *snarling* and *barking* out his commands, and you **felt** the *leathery* creases in his forehead along with his *bristly* hair and his *cold*, dark eyes. By observing what you hear, feel, and smell, as well as what you see, you will make your descriptions clearer and more interesting.

Sometimes writers try to improve their descriptions by adding modifiers (mostly adjectives) to their details, but adding modifiers without providing the reader with a clear central impression will not give you a good description. You will still have nothing but a list of meaningless details. For example, suppose your descriptive essay began like this:

> My drill instructor was a short, squatty, sawed-off looking guy with a huge, oversized head and a broad, wide neck. He had cold, dark chocolate-brown eyes and a wide, flattened, pudgy, scrunched up nose.

You have more modifiers, but you still don't have a central impression of the drill instructor—not until the details are related to the image of a bulldog.

Organization of Details

Once you have determined your central impression, you need to choose some definite principle of organizing your details. Then stick to it. Often, the best principle is that of visual order, the pattern that the eye would naturally follow. In describing a person, you might go from head to foot, or vice versa. In describing a particular scene, you might describe the details from left to right, from right to left, from near to far, or from far to near. You could, of course, start with a central feature or characteristic and then gradually expand the view to include the surrounding details needed to round out the picture.

Quite often you may need to establish a fixed point from which the object or scene is being observed. Let us say, for example, that you are observing a carnival in the town square from a fourth-floor window. Once having established this point of observation, you must be consistent. Don't suddenly shift from the fourth-floor vantage point to a ground-level view. You simply do not shift the point of view without a good reason. In an extended description, of course, you may have good reason to view the same object or scene from different points of view at different times. The important thing is that you take your reader with you by indicating clearly these shifts in point of view.

If, for example, you were describing that "dreary" basement room, you would need to tell the readers where each piece of furniture sits and where the windows are, if they are to get a clear picture of the room. You have your choice as to where to start, but once you do so, you must keep to that direction so that the readers can follow you.

In the following descriptive passage note how the man is described from a fixed point as he moves toward the observer.

> If you see Hank walking toward you, the first thing that hits you is the sheer size of the boy. Even at six-foot-two, he doesn't appear tall, just big. As he moves toward you, you can't help but notice how coordinated he is; his step is light, like that of a dancer or like the athlete he is. He doesn't wear muscle shirts or leave his shirt open to the waist, but as he nears, you can see well-defined muscles in his arms and shoulders. He doesn't try to flaunt or hide his terrific build, and, up close, his genuine smile and his hesitant manner make you forget his size. He's a beautiful teddy bear.

Don't be content to write "Tim was scrawny and hyper, and I could see this as he approached." Instead, **describe:** "Tim jerked and moved both his hands and head spasmodically as he neared the bench where I sat. At five-foot-two and 110 pounds, he looked emaciated, but it was obvious that his mind raced and his limbs reacted. When he reached me, his eyes darted from side to side and I wanted to grab his hands to keep them from flying off in all directions. His quivering voice was so intense I wanted to say, "Hey, Tim, it's not that important."

Not only must your details be organized and lively, but they must also be unified. Choose only details that point to your central impression. Rule out all irrelevant or contradictory details. Suppose that your thesis sentence says "Willi Hipple is an **utterly grotesque** little man." You would not then go on to describe him as having a strong, straight frame and finely chiseled features. If you say that "Lake Louise is a **jewel in a wilderness setting,**" then going on to describe discarded beer cans floating in an oil slick would be totally inconsistent.

Tone

Tone, as it is in every type of writing, is important in description, for it is tone that establishes your attitude toward your subject. After you have determined what your subject is to be and the audience you are going to address, you must decide what your attitude will be toward your subject. Are you going to take it seriously or are you going to laugh about it? Are you going to be sentimental or satirical? How do you feel about it? For example, the essay about Mary Carter (p. 82) has a definite attitude of compassion for lonely and loving old ladies. An entirely different attitude is expressed in the student essay about the dog in Chapter 4; here the attitude is joking about the author's frustration in controlling his pet. Your tone can be anything that you feel and want to communicate about your subject.

Geoffrey Chaucer, in the *Canterbury Tales*, described pilgrims on their way to Canterbury. Because he wanted his readers to be able to visualize his characters, he described each one so that they not only could be seen but would also evoke an emotional effect. That is, the readers feel some emotional attitude for each pilgrim. They think: the Knight is a good man; the Squire is a little foolish but young and sweet; the Wife of Bath is somewhat rowdy but self-sufficient and courageous.

Of the Knight, Chaucer observed, ". . . much distinguished, he never yet a boorish thing had said in all his life to any, come what might; he was a true, a perfect, gentle knight."

In such brief descriptions, Chaucer lets us see his characters and get a feeling for them. He describes the teenage wife in "The Miller's Tale" thus: ". . . she would skip or play some game or other, like any kid or calf behind its mother. Skittish she was and jolly as a colt, tall as a mast and upright as an arrow. She was a daisy, oh, a lolly-pop."

Chaucer's readers are never in doubt about how he felt or wanted us to feel about his various characters.

INTRODUCTION

As for overall pattern of organization, your descriptive essay will have the same beginning, middle, and end as your previous essays. Your introduction should serve to capture your reader's interest and lead up to your **thesis sentence.** Your thesis statement should clearly establish the **central impression**—the controlling idea to which everything else in the essay should relate.

Suppose you have just come back from a trip to Vienna, and you want to convey your central impression of those magical two weeks. You might write something like this:

FRANZ JOSEPH'S ELEVATOR

For years I had wanted to go to Vienna. As the song says, Vienna was the city of my dreams. But when I finally got there, I was so excited I stumbled on the train steps and sprained my ankle. So, my sightseeing started on crutches. The first night I went to the opera, where a kindhearted usher, taking pity on me for my third balcony seat, said, "We do have an elevator; it's very special, but I'll take you up in it." I was grateful until I saw the elevator. Then I was ecstatic. That elevator had been the Emperor Franz Joseph's. And I was riding in it. That elevator came to stand for all Vienna to me. It was spacious and well-proportioned, but, above all, I remember the colors: scarlet, and white, and gold—now that I look back, the symbol of Vienna.

....

Your subject is Vienna. Your controlling idea is that the elevator with its elegant scarlet, white, and gold came to symbolize the beauty of Vienna.

BODY

The body of your essay must provide the specific details to support your central impression. Frequently, each paragraph in the body will deal with one specific aspect of your subject. The important thing is that all contribute to the one central impression.

One distinction that you must keep clearly in mind is the difference between **telling about** and **showing.** General statements just tell about; if you are to show, you must use concrete details that create an image in the mind of the reader. The heart and soul of good descriptive writing is showing. The difference between telling and showing, illustrated throughout this chapter, is crucial in developing a good description.

General Statements (Telling About)	**Concrete Details (Showing)**
It was a long twisting road with high trees on each side. At the bottom of a long hill, there was a small river with a cement bridge over it. The square cement sides of the bridge made the road too narrow for two cars to pass.	Winding through tall birches and poplars, the mottled blacktop snaked its way downhill to the river. At the bottom, a straight stretch of tarmac wedged between blunt and ugly cement abutments on either side of a short bridge that arched across the bubbling river.

Note how the general statements that **tell about** are dull and lifeless. To **show** your reader, you must use vivid, active language. For instance, note the contrast in verbs used in the two passages: *was . . . was . . . made* versus *snaked . . . wedged . . . arched.*

Another important element in developing a good description is **selection,** discussed earlier in the chapter. You could never include every minute detail of a given scene; if you tried to, you'd probably end up with a mass of meaningless details. You miss the whole point of good description if you don't strictly follow the process of selection. You must select only those details that support your central impression and ruthlessly weed out details that do not.

Finally, throughout the body of your essay you must provide a sense of movement, which takes your reader with you as you show the scene unfolding. The primary movement is visual; let your eyes and the eyes of your reader scan the picture from far to near, from near to far, from left to right, from head to toe, or from the top of the hill to the bottom. Along the way, you need to provide smooth transition from one paragraph to another. Here, too, the most natural way is visual: "Down along the water's edge, . . . Across the narrow bridge, . . . Up the steep side of the ravine, . . . Looking out from the narrow attic window, . . . From his gleaming shoes to the razor crease in his trousers, . . . Around the smooth oval of her face, . . ."

CONCLUSION

As a counterpart to the introduction, the conclusion serves to sum up all of the details and reinforce your central impression. Together with the introduction, it provides a frame for your picture.

Carefully note how the details in the body of the following essay support the central impression:

THE OLD PLACE

In the back of everyone's mind, I suspect, there is a picture of one particular spot that holds a special meaning. As for me, although maybe the lines of the image have softened and what was there gets blurred with what might have been, I know I'll never forget the old farmhouse where I lived until I was sixteen. Yet whenever I try to picture the old place in my mind today, I experience strangely mixed feelings of delight and melancholy.

The narrow farmhouse, wrapped in brownish Insulbrick, seems to lean toward a steep hillside at the bottom end of a lopsided valley. My earliest memories surround the old house and go in and out through the banging screen door, but the images are all fragmented—just bits and pieces of a thousand things. I remember rusty feathers flying in one long squawk and the swirling red fury of the rooster whose fiery beak drove

I try to picture the old place.

me screaming to the house. I remember the lamp-post stanchions of the brass bed in the attic when my brother and I used to pull the patchwork quilts up over our ears in winter. I remember the mud flying from the fat black lugs of the rear tires as I first drove the "doodlebug," our homemade tractor. I recall the snow scudding up over the hood of the old Dodge pickup as I bucked through to the main road. Best of all, I remember those country meals we ate at the massive butcher-block table in the kitchen: sizzling fried pork and crisp home-fries, glowing fresh ham riveted with cloves, platters of sleek new potatoes sprinkled with parsley, flecked scones and pancakes hot from the iron griddle, with raspberry and strawberry and wild plum preserves. I can hear again the family chatter around the loaded table and see my father lean forward with arms akimbo to carve a haunch of beef.

I recall, too, the mournful soughing of the wind in the pines at night, the dead silence that followed a February snowstorm, the long wait for the first signs of spring, and the bleached gravel road that wound over the hills to the world at large. But the world had its own way of intruding: it kept cutting pieces out of the picture. Hard pressed for cash when my sister went to nursing school, my dad sold off a chunk of hardscrabble pasture, which soon became a gravel pit with dump trucks groveling in and out. Little Star Lake, which gleamed through the tops of the hemlocks down behind the house, was bought by a resort developer and quickly sprouted trailers and squat summer cottages. The old farmhouse itself seemed to lean more heavily toward the hillside and shrink a little farther into the ground. Finally, worn down by years of grinding toil, my mother kept urging my dad to sell out and move to the city.

When the screen door had banged for the final time, my dad handed me the keys, and I drove my folks down the white gravel road that my sister and my brothers had traveled, one by one. Sometimes I think, now, about going back to see the old place. I could drive there in two hours. But I won't. Maybe it is just foolish sentiment, but I want to keep in my mind a picture of the old place, not exactly the way it was but the way I want it to remain.

Note how specific details and visual images help to convey both a picture and a mood. Note, too, how the observer moves into and then away from the scene. And it is not just a static picture: the screen door bangs, the rooster swirls in furious motion, the mud flies, and the pickup bucks through the snow.

Here is a student essay of description, in which the writer carefully chose his details to convey his sense of fear.

FEAR

Fear can take many forms. We all have experienced at least one of them at some time in our lives. There is the fear of height and the fear of death, the fear of closed-in places and the fear of the dark, just to name a few. When I think of fear, I remember a little town in South Carolina called Yemassee, where I first experienced lasting fear.

When we left the train that dark, humid night in December, all we could see was the single dim light that hung on the depot platform. A sickly sweet odor filled the air, and the stillness was deafening. The only thing that moved was the fading lights on the rear of the train. The station was in dire need of repair, the windows and doors were boarded shut, and the whole building shook when anyone moved. There was a feeling of apprehension in the air, and the men milling around and talking only seemed to make it worse. The humidity made our clothes stick to our bodies, but the little drops of sweat were ice cold as they ran down our spines. The longer we waited the less talk there was, and everyone began to wonder why we had been abandoned.

Then it happened. Just as the tension reached its peak, a voice shouted at us, "You girls have five seconds to get on that bus!" Out of nowhere appeared the biggest, most sinister looking man I have ever seen. His Smokey Bear hat was pulled down over his face and hid everything but his mouth, which spewed forth some of the vilest profanity ever heard on this earth. His uniform creases looked as though a person could cut his finger on them, and his brass buckles gleamed. He moved with the grace of a leopard with his muscles bunched as though ready to spring. The man, the depot, and the night seemed to work in perfect harmony to create an almost overpowering feeling of fear.

As the bus started to move away, I looked back at the depot. The drill instructor had disappeared. Silence returned. The dim light swayed in the sultry breeze. Nothing moved on the desolate platform, nor would until the next group of young men came on their way to Parris Island and Marine Corps boot camp.

Mark Custer
(Student)

During World War II, one of the most loved and admired war correspondents was Ernie Pyle, who covered both European and Pacific theaters of war and who reported on the more human-interest stories of both fighting men and civilians caught in war zones. Because his dispatches, which were read by hundreds of thousands of Americans daily, were universal in appeal, they have been reprinted in a volume titled *Ernie's War*. Here is a bit of Ernie's compassionate description.

A TUBE STATION [an English subway station]

London, January 29, 1941

It was not until I went down seventy feet into the bowels of the Liverpool Street tube and saw humanity sprawled there in childlike helplessness that my heart first jumped and my throat caught.

I know I must have stopped suddenly and drawn back.

I know I must have said to myself, "Oh my God!"

* * *

On benches on each side, as though sitting or lying on a long streetcar seat, were the people, hundreds of them. And as we walked, they stretched into thousands.

Many of these people were old—wretched and worn old people who had never known many of the good things of life and who were now winding up their days on this earth in desperate discomfort.

They were the bundled-up, patched-up people with lined

faces that we have seen for years sitting dumbly in waiting lines at our own relief offices at home.

* * *

It was the old people who seemed so tragic. Think of yourself at seventy or eighty, full of pain and the dim memories of a lifetime that has probably all been bleak. And then think of yourself now, traveling at dusk every night to a subway station, wrapping your ragged overcoat around your old shoulders and sitting on a wooden bench with your back against a curved steel wall. Sitting there all night, in nodding and fitful sleep.

Think of that as your destiny—every night, every night from now on.

Ernie Pyle
(War Correspondent)

PITFALLS TO AVOID

1. Don't clutter your description with strings of repetitious adjectives. "A long, hot, sultry, dragged-out, stifling day" could better be described as "an endless day of oppressive heat" or "a merciless day of stifling heat."

2. Don't use vague or ambiguous wording in your thesis sentence. For example: "The old house was kind of a queer place" does not create a clear central impression. You would have a better thesis sentence if you said, "The old house was filled with curious remnants of the past," or "In the old house, time seemed to have stopped."

3. Don't try to cover the whole waterfront. Limit the area and focus on a specific subject; then try to work in more revealing detail. Don't try to describe all of Florida. Limit yourself to Disney World. Even then, don't try to describe all of Disney World. Limit yourself to the entrance to Fantasy Land.

4. Don't shift from description to a long recital of your personal reaction. For example: "It was a beautiful old mansion. I couldn't help wondering what my mother would think of it. She always did like those old houses with turrets."

5. Don't jump unexpectedly to a new point of observation. For example: "The great stone mansion loomed beyond the iron gates. From the mountaintop it would look like a toy fortress." Instead, open those iron gates and take your reader with you every step of the way.

6. Don't tack on a nebulous conclusion, such as "So that is what the old place was like. It had its good points and its bad points. I guess I kind of miss it, so I like to think of it once in a while." A

conclusion such as that does nothing except drain your essay of whatever vitality it had.

Write a descriptive essay on one of the following topics.

People

Your boss
Your childhood friend
Your college friend
Your football coach
Your enemy
The five-year-old next door
The woman at the supermarket checkout
  counter
The police officer who helps youngsters
  cross the street
The voice on the phone at your school
The gas station attendant
Your confidant
Your counselor
A waiter or waitress
An athlete
An entertainer
Your husband or wife
Your mother or father
Your grandmother or grandfather
Your brother or sister
Your doctor or dentist
Your high school principal
Your teacher
Your teammate
Your boyfriend or girlfriend
Your neighbor

Places

An army barracks
A crowded club room
A quiet park
A busy airport
A busy shopping mall
A school cafeteria
A principal's office
A hospital delivery room
An emergency room
An unemployment office
A doctor's waiting room
An empty auditorium
A department store at
  holiday time
A downtown street
A kindergarten classroom
A playground
A tenement house
A souvenir drawer or box
A crowded auditorium
A closet or locker
Your grandmother's attic
Your bedroom
Your kitchen
Your backyard
Your favorite vacation spot

TECHNIQUES OF CLEAR WRITING

COORDINATION AND SUBORDINATION

By choosing to use a coordinate clause or a subordinate clause, you choose which of two precise relationships you wish to point out. When you put two ideas into coordinating clauses, you are saying that these two ideas are of equal importance to you. You identify your clause as coordinate because you introduce it with a coordinate conjunction. (A conjunction is simply a part of speech that joins things together.)

There are only seven coordinating conjunctions, so they are easy to remember—**and, but, or, for, nor, so, yet.** All other conjunctions are subordinating. For example, suppose you want to say that you enjoy playing two sports equally well. You might say, "I love playing baseball, but I have as much fun playing soccer." Or you might say, "I love playing baseball, and I enjoy soccer as much." The use of **and** and **but** in these two sentences clearly shows that you want to give both of these ideas similar emphasis.

If you choose to emphasize one idea over another, then you will use one independent clause and one dependent clause, linking the two together with a subordinating conjunction. An independent clause expresses a complete thought; a dependent clause expresses less than a complete thought.

The most common subordinating conjunctions are **after, although, as if, because, before, if, since, than, that, unless, until, when, whenever, whether, wherever, while.**

Independent Clause	**Coordinating Conjunction**	**Independent Clause**
I love baseball	and	I enjoy soccer

Independent Clause	**Subordinating Conjunction**	**Dependent Clause**
I prefer baseball	although	I enjoy soccer

You can, of course, if you wish, place the dependent clause at the beginning of the sentence. It makes no difference where in the sentence it is; the subordinating conjunction tells which is the dependent clause. The dependent clause is less important than the independent clause because it will not stand alone as a sentence.

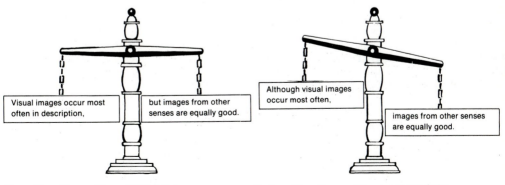

Coordination—Equal Weight   **Subordination—Unequal Weight**

Look at the following sentences:

JANE:
Although I hate to cook, I love to give dinner parties.

MARY:
Although I love to give dinner parties, I hate to cook.

Who will have dinner parties?

JACK:
Even though I love to fish, I have no time for it.

JIM:
Even though I have no time for it, I love to fish.

Who will probably go fishing?

BILL:
I study a lot because I am a good student.

TONY:
I am a good student because I study a lot.

Which makes more sense?

All these examples illustrate the difference between coordination and subordination. When ideas have the same degree of importance, they are *coordinate;* when one idea is less important than the other, then one is *subordinate* to the other. It's easy to remember the difference between **co**ordination and **sub**ordination because *co* means equal and *sub* means under or less. Therefore, when you are connecting two clauses of **equal** weight, you connect them with a **co**ordinate conjunction. When you are connecting a **less important** clause (incomplete thought) to a more important clause (complete thought), then you connect them with a **sub**ordinate conjunction.

Both types of conjunctions are used to show how one part of a sentence relates to another part. Once you know when to use coordinate conjunctions and when to use subordinate conjunctions, you have to make sure that you are using the right ones. Look at each group of conjunctions separately and note the relationship suggested by each individual conjunction:

COORDINATE CONJUNCTIONS

And calls for an additional statement
But calls for a contrast
For calls for a reason
Nor calls for another negative statement
Or calls for an alternative
So calls for an effect
Yet calls for a contrast

SUBORDINATE CONJUNCTIONS

After shows time
Although implies a contrast
As if sets a condition
As long as sets a condition
As soon as shows time
Because gives a reason
Before shows time
Even though implies a contrast
If sets a condition
Since gives a reason
Unless sets a condition
Until shows time
When shows time
Whenever shows time
Wherever shows place
While shows time

Using the right conjunctions is important. If you don't, your sentences won't make much sense. What follows are examples of faulty coordination and faulty subordination.

ILLOGICAL COORDINATION:

FAULTY:
I love show songs, and I'm bored with other popular music.

IMPROVED:
Although I love show songs, I'm bored with other popular music.

or

Although I'm bored with other popular music, I love show songs.

FAULTY:
You hurt my feelings, **yet** I'm going to leave.

IMPROVED:
You hurt my feelings, **so** I'm going to leave.
Because you hurt my feelings, I'm going to leave.

ILLOGICAL SUBORDINATION:

FAULTY:
While I spilled coffee on my pants, I cancelled my job interview.

IMPROVED:
After I spilled coffee on my pants, I cancelled my job interview.
Since I spilled coffee on my pants, I cancelled my job interview.

FAULTY:
Before you say you love me, I will not marry you.

IMPROVED:
Unless you say you love me, I will not marry you.
Until you say you love me, I will not marry you.

A Note on Punctuation

When two independent clauses are connected with a coordinate conjunction, place a comma **before** the conjunction.

[*Independent clause*], **but** [*independent clause*].

When you join two independent clauses without a coordinate conjunction, place a semicolon between the clauses.

[*Independent clause*]; [*independent clause*].

NOTE: The semicolon should be used only when the two ideas are closely related. If they are not, make two sentences.

When a sentence begins with a subordinate clause, place a comma after the clause (as we just did in this sentence).

[*Dependent clause*], [*independent clause*].

If the subordinate clause comes at the end of the sentence, do **not** insert any punctuation before the clause, as in the example below:

Don't use a comma **if the subordinate clause comes at the end of a sentence.**

EXERCISE 3A: PUNCTUATION

Correct the punctuation of the following sentences. (Do not add periods or capital letters.)

1. Geraldo has many favorite TV shows, one of them is *20/20*.

   _____

2. Because the Penguins have Mario Lemieux they now are challenging the leaders of the Patrick Division of hockey.

   _____

   _____

3. I love to watch old movies, because they remind me of another time.

_____

_____

4. Some people think professional wrestling is disgusting champion wrestlers make a lot of money.

_____

_____

5. Although I love chocolate I realize it is not good for me it hurts me in many ways.

_____

_____

6. Traveling is great fun and very educational but it is also quite tiring.

_____

_____

7. If I ever get a chance to travel I will visit Greece first.

_____

8. Courtesy doesn't have to be learned by reading the authorities it really consists of having empathy for the other person.

_____

_____

9. Winning is good but competing is better.

_____

_____

10. His speech teacher appreciates Juan's efforts so he never misses her class.

_____

_____

11. When he got the flu George called the doctor the nurse said the doctor would call when she returned.

_____

_____

12. The motion picture *African Queen* is great it evokes our patriotism and our admiration.

_____

_____

13. Because of the value system in the United States we have few poets and philosophers we have many people aspiring to become doctors and lawyers.

_____

_____

14. Since Martin had to stay at school to wait for his ride he decided to spend some time in the library to work on his research paper.

_____

_____

15. Although Richard won a scholarship he felt he was ill-prepared for college for he had trouble expressing himself in both speech and writing.

_____

_____

_____

EXERCISE 3B: FAULTY COORDINATION

The following sentences are examples of faulty coordination. Improve each sentence by inserting a better coordinate conjunction or replacing the coordinate conjunction with a subordinate conjunction to put the less important idea in a subordinate clause.

1. I really enjoy Robert Ludlum's novels, and I read them as soon as they come out.
2. Basketball is a strenuous sport, but players should not eat a heavy meal before they start a game.
3. Ashley had seen pictures of the Statue of Liberty many times, and she never realized how big it really was until she visited there.
4. Kelly is a great swimmer, and her main interest this year seems to be track.
5. I love the commercials that feature the dog Alex, and he really is a good actor.
6. Statistics say that the average American spends one year looking for misplaced objects, and I've spent more time than that already, and I'm only twenty-three years old!
7. Billy Joe Carstine fell into the bushes, and we all laughed.
8. Marion is hoping for a football scholarship, but he prepares for all his classes every day.
9. About a ton of hazardous waste is produced in the U.S. every year for every American, but we have to find a way to dispose of it safely and efficiently.

10. The horse was very small, and she carried the 250 pound man effortlessly.

RELATIVE PRONOUNS
(Who, Whom, Which, That)

Using relative pronouns—**who, whom, which, that**—is a subtle but effective way of showing what idea you think is more important and which you think is less important in your sentence. These relative pronouns act as the subjects of dependent clauses. As their name indicates, these dependent clauses have less emphasis than do independent clauses.

For instance, suppose you had written this: "Stephen Henderson was a well-known singer. He married my aunt." Your reader would not know which idea you considered more important. But if you wrote, "Stephen Henderson, who was a well-known singer, married my aunt," you would have made it clear the marriage is what you are more interested in. Or, if you reversed it and wrote, "Stephen Henderson, who married my aunt, was a well-known singer," it would be clear that you are emphasizing him as a singer.

You decide where you want to put the emphasis, but make sure your readers know where you are putting it.

NOTE: It is usually preferable when writing about people to use **who,** rather than **that** or **which.** When you are writing about things, there is seldom a need to distinguish between the use of **that** or **which.**

EXERCISE 3C: COMBINING SENTENCES

In the following sets of sentences, relationships are not made clear. Combine each set, using who, whom, that, *or* which, *to establish a main idea and a dependent one.*

1. She joined the Navy in 1988. She had been eager to join since high school.

_____

_____

2. The instructor failed to meet his class. He had been hurt in an automobile accident.

_____

_____

3. The writer's new book was a sentimental love story. He almost always wrote comedies.

_____

_____

4. Sara Allgood was a star of the Abbey Theater. William Butler Yeats wrote a play for her.

_____

_____

5. The antique car was a Rolls. It was in bad shape.

_____

_____

6. The class cheered the speech. It pleased everyone in the audience.

_____

_____

7. Last week's speech had been a disappointment. It had not been well researched.

_____

_____

8. The student lounge is a cheerful place. The administration furnished it well and maintains it carefully.

_____

_____

9. The new condominiums are selling rapidly. They are reasonably priced and soundly constructed.

_____

_____

10. The steps to the swimming pool are crumbling. They are made of ceramic tile.

_____

_____

WORD POWER

ELIMINATING DEADWOOD AND REDUNDANCIES

One reason for the lack of liveliness and vitality in the writing of beginners is excess verbiage. Students use too many words to express their ideas. They repeat; they use ten words where two would do. There are various reasons for these types of errors:

1. A fear that the reader will not understand their first explanation.
2. A lack of vocabulary (and an aversion to searching for the exact word).
3. A desire to reach a specified number of words assigned by the instructor.
4. A lack of knowledge of the subject (and an aversion to searching for more information).
5. A lack of careful editing and rewriting.

Actually, the last item is the most important for you to remember. It doesn't really matter how many excess words you have in your first draft; nobody sees that. You should go over your essays carefully, eliminating all unnecessary words and phrases.

You can eliminate unnecessary words many ways. Here are a few:

1. Use a precise word rather than a string of modifiers:

   The large white dog with black spots [7 words]
   The Dalmatian [2 words]
   The second-year physical science course [6 words]
   Physics II [2 words]

2. Reduce a clause to a phrase whenever possible:

   The house which was on the corner [7 words]
   The house on the corner [5 words]

   Or reduce a phrase to a word:

   The corner house [3 words]

   Or, if the information is unnecessary, leave it out completely. If it isn't necessary to say where the house is situated, don't mention it.

   The house [2 words]

3. Avoid phrases that merely add words, not meaning:

Due to the fact that [5 words]
Because [1 word]
In the event that [4 words]
If [1 word]
In view of the fact that [6 words]
Since [1 word]

4. Don't be timid. If it is important to your purpose to say something unpleasant, say it without trying to disguise its unpleasantness.

It seems to me, although of course this is only my opinion, that the decision of the chairman was not very well thought out, nor did it consider the solutions that had been carefully worked out over the first six months.

Say, "The chairperson was mistaken" or wrong or stupid or whatever you really mean.

5. Don't be repetitious or redundant:

Young juveniles
Youths
7 A.M. in the morning
7 A.M.
He will apply for and try to get a job in accounting.
He will apply **for an accounting job.**

6. Avoid negatives where possible.

Our cafeteria does not serve good food. [7 words]
Our cafeteria **serves poor food.** [5 words]

7. Use the active voice.

The test was taken by him. [6 words]
He took the test. [4 words]

EXERCISE 3D: CONCISENESS

Revise each of the following sentences to eliminate excess words.

1. The test for the driver's license was given by a police officer.

_____

2. Andrew did not pass the first test given in biology.

_____

3. The car that Charlene has is very expensive and costly.

_____

4. In my opinion, the gravy that Stan served had lumps in it.

_____

5. The restaurant called Murray's which is on the corner of 5th and Main serves food that is really good.

_____

6. My parents do not like the woman that I married.

_____

7. The book that Fran likes best of all the books she has ever read is *Atlas Shrugged* which was written by Ayn Rand.

_____

8. The certificate that hangs on the wall in Geraldine's office is her diploma from Penn State.

_____

9. Will did not fail to make a reservation for a room in the Holiday Inn in Orlando.

_____

10. Michael stuffed and jammed the articles into the bag that was designed to carry books.

_____

_____

EXERCISE 3E: CONCISENESS

The following sentences are wordy. Revise them to eliminate redundancies and deadwood.

1. In case you decide to change your mind and do something else, will you please tell me and let me know so that I can also make new plans and arrange to do something else, too.

_____

_____

2. I would like to share with you and report on the rumor that I heard on the grapevine about the possible information that there is perhaps a potential cutback in employees.

_____

_____

3. In considering this aspect of the situation that maybe there will be a possible chance of a decrease to reduce the number of

employees, we ought to be warned and make ready in case there is a cutback and fewer people will remain on the payroll.

_____

_____

4. This novel reverts back to the twenties and repeats again the repetitious clichés of that period-in-time's morals and ethics.

_____

_____

5. It was whispered to me on the quiet that our representative would not always stand up for and protect our interests and the things we wanted to gain.

_____

_____

6. As a rule it usually happens that a first-semester course when you are just beginning to study a subject is made up entirely and almost all together of the vocabulary of that subject.

_____

_____

7. In his biography of Walt Whitman, the author who wrote the book discusses Whitman's life and writings, but he pays more attention to his life and does not emphasize his work.

_____

_____

8. I was so tired and fatigued that I could not complete my home-work or finish my assignments; I was unprepared and not ready for the oral quiz which we had to recite.

_____

_____

9. The book that Robert read was a play written by an author whose name was Marc Connelly who wrote plays in the thirties and forties. Connelly's play was called *The Green Pastures* and it was based on a collection of short stories titled *Ol' Man Adam an' His Chillun* which had been written earlier.

_____

_____

10. The short summary of the book only told in brief form the main points of the plot and introduced the characters so we could have some beginning recognition of what they were like and

how they would be likely to act when we saw them in greater depth.

USING ABSTRACT WORDS OR CONCRETE WORDS

Another choice you need to make in your writing is between an abstract word and a concrete word. **Abstract** and **concrete** words are somewhat like general and specific words, but not totally so. As was said earlier in this chapter, the general terms refer to broader ideas. For example:

General	Specific
College	Harvard
city	Chicago
football team	Cleveland Browns
short distance	ten feet

An abstract term usually is rather general, but, in addition, the abstract term appeals to intellectual understanding whereas concrete terms appeal to the senses—**sight, sound, smell, touch,** and **taste.**

Abstract	Concrete
colorful	purple and pink dots
noisy	banging drums
soft	goose feathers
smooth and hard	polished oak
seasoned	salted and peppered

One of the ways we can make an abstract term a concrete image is to place it in a setting of time or space.

The sugar maple in my side yard glowed in its autumn reds and yellows.

Compare the following pairs of statements:

VAGUE AND ABSTRACT:
The foundry was a dirty place to work.

CONCRETE:
The black grime of the foundry grated its way into every pore, and six

showers couldn't get the grit out of your scalp and eyebrows or the creases of your midriff.

VAGUE AND ABSTRACT:
The man in front of the carnival tent had a harsh voice.

CONCRETE:
The carnival barker at the sideshow ground out his spiel in a gravelly voice.

Thus, being concrete appeals to the senses as well as to the intellect. You **show** the reader, not just tell him or her. If you write, "When I had to give my first speech, I was terrified," you are appealing to the reader's intellect, her memory, perhaps of herself in a similar situation. You are being concrete if you write: "When the emcee introduced me, I felt I couldn't get up; my legs didn't seem to be a part of my body. My mouth and lips were dry, but the palms of my hands were so wet that the notecards they held were limp and the writing on them smeared. I felt a prickling sensation at the back of my head, and I wondered if my hair were standing on end."

Show the reader how nervous you were.

Here are more examples:

General	Specific	Concrete
a dog	a beagle puppy	A beagle puppy tripping over his own feet as he runs to greet us
sounds	sounds of food cooking	the sizzling of the bacon, the plop-plop of coffee perking
prison	Alcatraz	the high stone walls atop the barren rock in the middle of the bay

dirt	grit	the grit crackling under our shoes on the old wooden porch
cold air	50° below zero air	the bitter air that froze the spittle on our lips and frosted our eyebrows and stiffened our hair
heavyweight boxer	Mike Tyson	Mike Tyson, a slugging machine

A writer chooses concrete and specific words to stimulate the reader to visualize. If the writer's choice of words is concrete, most readers will automatically respond with an image. Even commonplace descriptions evoke some sensory experience:

The full moon in a cloudless sky   [re-creates sight]

The sting of the icy shower   [re-creates touch]

The squeak of the chalk on the blackboard   [re-creates sound]

Gingerbread baking   [re-creates smell]

The first sip of a cold beer   [re-creates taste]

The sense of motion can be conveyed by a verb: One rabbit *escaped;* another was *seized* in the hound's gaping jaws.

EXERCISE 3F: CONCRETE WORDS

Revise the following sentences to replace the vague and abstract terms with·concrete wording. (Use your dictionary, your thesaurus, and your imagination.)

1. I had a good evening because all the people were nice.

   _____

2. Michelle collected old cars and fixed them up beautifully.

   _____

3. The towns in the river valley suffered economically.

   _____

4. I was very interested in *To Kill a Mockingbird* because it seemed to me to be like *Intruder in the Dust.*

   _____

   _____

5. I thought both stories were good because they were so interesting.

   _____

6. The garbage dump at the seashore can be spotted a long way off.

_____

7. There is no way to tell you how I feel.

_____

8. He has always been emotional.

_____

9. This has been an unusually depressing day.

_____

10. Joyce is my idea of an intellectual.

_____

EXERCISE 3G: SUPPLYING SPECIFIC DETAILS

Rewrite three of the numbered statements below in specific terms, inventing specific details to develop the general statements. EXAMPLE: When we got up in the morning, we saw all over the neighborhood the signs of last night's storm.

When the thunder woke me at 5 A.M., I saw that my baby brother was already awake. We watched as the trailing edge of the storm passed over our street. We looked at the way the road was darker than usual, darkened by a film of water. Next door, our neighbors had a valley behind their house. Already it was beginning to overflow with fog and mist. It looked like a huge soup bowl that had been slightly overfilled.

Jay Bauer
(Student)

1. The shelves were stacked with many kinds of books.

_____

2. The wagon track through the fields was lined with wild flowers.

_____

3. The modern kitchen was well equipped for a cook.

_____

4. The children at the party were all dressed in their fanciest clothes.

_____

5. Douglas was always doing things that made him seem untrustworthy.

_____

6. Every time Sean began to work on his novel, his thoughts wandered off to unrelated topics.

_____

7. Carol's den bulged with evidence of her many projects.

_____

8. Veronica was distressed by the many expenses she faced as a homeowner.

_____

9. The audience at the football game reacted with a variety of responses.

_____

10. The lovely antique cloth was almost totally covered with platters and dishes of party food.

_____

C H A P T E R 4

Explaining With Examples

Probably the most frequent way we learn is through examples. Certainly one of the most frequent ways by which we support our ideas is through examples. As a very young child, there must have been many times when you said to your mother things like: "Johnny is a bad boy." If your mother didn't look convinced, you went on to bolster your argument with examples, saying, "He pinched the dog; he broke my good car; he hit me on the nose." In your four-year-old mind, these examples proved your case.

Later, in grade school, your arithmetic teacher, in trying to explain division to you, would probably have used several methods of explanation, including definition. "Division is the operation of determining how many times one quantity is contained in another." But definition alone would have left you confused. To understand how to do division problems, you would have had to see examples.

Examples are indispensable in learning. It's almost impossible for you to understand general concepts until you are given specific examples. Chapters 1 through 3 of this book contain over 100 specific examples that were included to help you understand the concepts. General terms such as **central impression** or **consistent**

point of view or **subordination** should have become clearer to you after you saw these concepts illustrated with examples.

Examples are used in all fields. For instance, the psychologist and the sociologist use the case study to show the reader such things as the psychotic personality or the environment of the ghetto child. In building the case study of Bob P., the psychologist might include:

> The paranoid personality sees enemies everywhere. For example, Bob thinks the clerk at the supermarket is watching him suspiciously. He feels she suspects him of shoplifting.

In explaining the inner city, the sociologist might include:

> The ghetto child lives in a prison. For example, Paco has never been more than five blocks from his home. There are no visible walls, but the invisible ones are there. He says that he feels he is different when he leaves his own "turf."

In the physical sciences, the chemist and physicist will cite examples of their own experiments and experiments of others to prove their hypotheses. Sportswriters use examples to illustrate their statements. Notice that examples can serve both of these purposes; they can **illustrate** or **prove.** If the chemist reports the findings of several different scientists in different areas and at different times and they got the same results from a given experiment, she has proved a point. Sportswriters, on the other hand, generally are working with theses that cannot be proved:

> Steve Carlson is the best pitcher in baseball.
> Joe Louis was the world's greatest heavyweight boxer.
> The New York Rangers are the toughest team in hockey.

Nothing could **prove** these statements, but they could be illustrated or supported by examples.

Really, it is hard to think of a subject that examples will not clarify. They can make the difficult easier to understand; they can make the abstract concrete; they can make the academic personal.

Explaining through examples is one of the most effective ways to support your controlling idea. The technique of explaining with examples is closely related to narration. The difference is that narration expands one example into a full story, whereas in explaining with examples you use several brief narratives. Like telling a story, giving examples seems to be a natural way of proving your point to someone else because that is usually the way you arrive at your own conclusion. Through certain experiences you have had or events you have witnessed, you form a generalization. The generalization becomes your thesis sentence, the abstract statement that unifies your essay. When you want to prove your generalization to others, show them the examples that led to your conclusion.

Because using examples is one of the most natural and effective ways of proving your point, you use it every day in speaking with your friends.

You Say: Boy, I had a lousy day.

Friend: How's that?

You: Well, first of all, I got up late and didn't have time for breakfast. I decided to pick up something at McDonald's and eat it in the car on the way to school. I got an Egg McMuffin, and when I took my first bite, the egg slipped out and slid down my sweater. Now I have egg stains on my new sweater.

Friend: That is a bad start.

You: That's not all. When I got to my first class—late, of course—I found out the teacher was giving a pop quiz. I flunked it, I'm sure, because for the first time all semester I didn't do the homework.

Friend: Wow!

You: That's not the worst of it. When I saw my girl, she really snubbed me. I had forgotten that I was supposed to pick her up this morning.

Friend: Wow! You did have a bad day.

The three little episodes you related to your friend are examples, and you proved your point by using them.

ORGANIZATION

WHAT MAKES GOOD EXAMPLES

To be good, the examples that you choose must be

1. Specific
2. Relevant
3. Typical

Specific Examples

As in all good writing, your details, in this case your examples, must be specific. General statements usually do not prove your point. **For example** (notice how often *for example* comes up), if you were trying to prove that you had "a lousy day," the following examples wouldn't work very well because they are too general to be interesting:

I made a mess of breakfast.

I flunked a quiz.

I forgot my girlfriend.

Suppose you were writing a paper about individuals who changed history but whose names are largely forgotten. As examples, you might cite the following people:

William Morton, the man who introduced the use of anesthesia in surgery

Eadweard Muybridge, the father of motion pictures

Howard Aiken, the man who designed the first computer

Margaret Sanger, the woman who started the birth control movement in the United States

You could then expand each example in a paragraph and give your reader more details about each person's achievements. However, if you developed your thesis by referring to these examples,

A dentist from Massachusetts

An amateur photographer from California

A graduate student from Harvard

An influential writer from America

you would not be providing your reader with good illustrations. Each one is too general. You have to be more specific if you want your readers to understand you.

Relevant Examples

In addition to being specific, your examples must also be *relevant;* that is, they must pertain precisely to your controlling idea. If you say "Car buyers need to be alert to the deceptive practices employed by some dealers," then specific examples of those "deceptive practices" would help your reader to understand exactly what you mean. If, however, you proceeded to cite examples of the tricks that people play when they go to trade in their cars, those examples would not provide relevant support.

If, for example, in your paper about some of the most important yet least known men in history, you cited Abraham Lincoln, Albert Einstein, and Adolf Hitler, you would not be giving your reader good examples. They would be specific, but they would not be relevant. These three men certainly changed people's lives, but they are not exactly forgotten names in history. These examples deal with the topic in general (important persons in history), but they do not pertain to your specific comment on that topic—that the names of some of the most influential figures in history are practically unknown.

Here is a paragrah that makes use of relevant examples:

> The work of great writers, which we often accept as being natural and spontaneous, is more often, in fact, the result of painstaking rewriting and revision. Ernest Hemingway, for example, is said to have rewritten the final chapter of *Farewell to Arms* more than forty times, and portions of *The Old Man and the Sea* were rewritten at least thirty times. Walt Whitman wrote forty versions of the opening line of "Out of the Cradle Endlessly Rocking," and the poet Dylan Thomas rewrote some of his lines as many as seventy times before his work was published. Popular novelist Margery Allingham thus described the care she takes with her writing. "I write every paragraph four times: once to get my meaning down, once to put in everything I left out, once to take out everything that seems unnecessary, and once to make the whole thing sound as if I had only just thought of it." The list of examples could go on and on; writers by the score have spent years in rewriting and revising their work before it ever got published. Gustave Flaubert, author of *Madame Bovary*, once wrote to George Sand: "You have no notion what it is to sit out an entire day with your head between your hands beating your unfortunate brain for a word."

Typical Examples

As well as being specific and relevant, good examples are *typical*. You cannot use an extraordinary circumstance to **prove** a point. If your examples are to provide effective support, they must be typical.

If you say "I don't like history," you cannot support your point by using an atypical example such as:

> We had a substitute teacher in history today, and he just droned on and on about the Wars of the Roses, and I didn't understand a thing he said.

This would **not** be an example of the regular history class because usually you don't have a substitute teacher.

Or, if you say "It's easy to make good grades at this school," an example such as this would **not** do:

> My oldest brother, who has an I.Q. of 160, made straight A's his freshman year here.

Your brother would not be an example of a typical student, even at Harvard.

You are not likely to convince an intelligent reader that most great writers were drug addicts by citing the fact that Edgar Allen Poe took laudanum and that Thomas DeQuincey was an opium eater. And only a naive reader would believe that all Iranians are camel drivers or goat herders, no matter how many examples of primitive tribesmen you present. Intelligent readers would recognize that the examples you offer are simply not typical.

Make sure that all your examples are specific, relevant, and typical.

INTRODUCTION

An *introduction* has two important purposes:

1. to arouse interest in the reader
2. to set the tone of the essay

To arouse interest, you might use a relevant incident, a startling fact or statistic, or any of the other devices discussed in Chapter 1. To set the tone, you want to choose a style that will indicate what your attitude is going to be—factual, serious, sentimental, humorous, or whatever.

In a joking essay, *The Ant as a Fraud,* Mark Twain pretends to take the ant's endeavors terribly seriously.

His introduction: "In the Black Forest, I saw an ant go through this performance with a dead spider of fully ten times his own weight."

DEVELOPMENT

Twain's *development,* which is made up of three parts, continues with the same joking style—characteristic of much of Mark Twain's work—by pretending great seriousness.

Twain uses three different methods to develop his essay, description, comparison, and examples. But no matter how his development changes, his tone remains the same.

Development A: Description

The spider was not quite dead, but too far gone to resist. He had a round body the size of a pea. The little ant—observing that I was noticing—turned him on his back, sunk his fangs into his throat, lifted him in the air, and started off vigorously with him, stumbling over little pebbles, stepping on the spider's legs and tripping himself up, dragging him backwards, shoving him bodily ahead, dragging him up stones six inches high instead of going around them, climbing weeds twenty times his own height and jumping from their summits,—and finally leaving him in the middle of the road to be confiscated by any other fool of an ant that wanted him.

Development B: Comparison

I measured the ground which this ass traversed, and arrived at the conclusion that what he had accomplished inside of twenty minutes would constitute some such job as this, relatively speaking, for a man; to wit: to strap two eight-hundred pound horses together, carry them eighteen hundred feet, mainly over (not around) boulders averaging six feet high, and in the course of the journey climb up and jump from one precipice like Niagara, and three steeples each a hundred and twenty feet high, and then put the horses down, in an exposed place, without anybody to watch them, and go off to indulge in some other idiotic miracle for vanity's sake.

Development C: Examples

Science has recently discovered that the ant does not lay up anything for winter use. This will knock him out of literature, to some extent. He does not work, except when people are looking. . . . This amounts to deception, and will injure him for the Sunday Schools. He has not judgment enough to know what is good to eat from what isn't. This amounts to ignorance, and will impair the world's respect for him. He cannot stroll around a stump and find his way home again. This amounts to idiocy, and once the damaging fact is established, thoughtful people will cease to look up to him, the sentimental will cease to fondle him. His vaunted industry is but a vanity and of no effect because he never gets home with anything he starts with. . . .

CONCLUSION

It is strange beyond comprehension that so manifest a humbug as the ant has been able to fool so many nations and keep it up so many ages without being found out.

Notice that Twain does not conclude his essay with his examples but returns to the broader idea of the introduction.

You want to keep in mind that the essay has three distinct parts: **introduction, body, conclusion.**

THE ORDERING OF EXAMPLES: CLIMACTIC ORDER

In an essay making use of examples, the details that make up the body are the examples you have selected. Like all selections of details, your chosen examples must be presented in some logical and consistent order. As the author, you decide what that order is. However, just as chronological order is most effective for narrative, and spatial order is most effective for description, climactic order usually works best for examples. In climactic order, you start with the example that is least important and work up to a final example, saving the example that you think is the most important for last.

Sometimes two principles of order are at work. In the conversation of the boy who had a bad day, the examples followed both a time order and a climactic order. You recall that he began with dropping his Egg McMuffin, went on to flunk a quiz, and ended up quarreling with his girlfriend. This is a sequence in time, of course, but there is a feeling that his quarrel with his girlfriend looms larger than his earlier problems. Indeed, because climactic order is so conventional, readers assume the thing placed last is meant to be understood as the most important.

In the following student paragraph, notice how the writer has moved in an orderly fashion from the disadvantages that bother her least, through those that are increasingly bothersome, to her ultimate frustrations of the goodnight kiss:

A short stature is a disadvantage to a teenage girl. She often finds that she has been mistaken for a child; consequently, she receives menus reserved for loyal customers age twelve and under, is refused the right to ride elaborate amusement rides without a parent or guardian, and, to the shocked embarrassment of her date, is admitted to theaters at children's rates. Another disadvantage of being a short teen turns up during clothes shopping. Although the length and fit of a preadolescent style may suit her build, the Junior Petite selection is more appealing to her fashion sense. Thus, the short teen spends endless hours in search of a perfect fit only to settle for a garment in need of hemming and other minor repairs. Another disadvantage bedevils the short teen—the need for short dates. The availability of short males is limited; therefore, the short girl is left to cope with an array of tall, ungainly dates. These dates are often trouble! For example, if the couple wants to go to a dance, the girl, to increase her height, usually dons high-heeled shoes. Since many of the styles were never intended for the dance scene, they are soon kicked off, leaving the situation worse than before. Another problem arises when the couple slow-dances. The girl finds herself making eye contact with her partner's stomach and trying, in vain, to wrap her arms around his neck. The traditional good-night kiss also poses a problem for the mismatched couple. After contorting his long frame into various uncomfortable positions, the tall male resorts either to lifting his short date a few inches off the ground or stepping down from the porch to kiss his short date while she stands two steps above him. For a teenage girl, short height's a hindrance!

Jackie Kunzmann
(Student)

EXAMPLES AS A HELP TO OTHER WRITING

Examples, as you have seen, are an end in themselves. If chosen well, they are an excellent way to explain. In addition, they can be a tremendous help in other, more complex, types of writing. In defining, for example, examples are a frequent help. If you look back to the beginning of this chapter you will see examples used in this way to help in the definition of mathematical division.

Suppose you want to write an essay about odd characters you have known. You narrow your subject to your Uncle Joe. (You remember Uncle Joe. He's the one in Chapter 2 with the generous will.) Since, among other things, you want to talk about Uncle Joe's collection of limericks, you decide to define a limerick. A limerick, your handbook says, is a "popular type of jingle verse dealing with the peculiarities of people and written in five lines. The first, second, and fifth lines, which have three metrical feet, rhyme. The third and fourth lines, each with two metrical feet, also rhyme."

There's the definition, but you don't find it much help except for that bit about peculiarities, which is Uncle Joe, all right. If you're going to get the idea across, you'll have to give an example of a limerick. You find that even the handbook uses an example by Edward Lear to clarify its definition.

> There was an Old man of the Dee
> Who was sadly annoyed by a Flea;
> When he said, "I will scratch it!"
> They gave him a hatchet
> Which grieved that Old Man of the Dee.

With an example, the definition of the limerick is much clearer. However, the example doesn't give the sense of Uncle Joe's rather gamey sense of humor. How, then, will you convey that? You choose another example, this time explaining that it shows the bawdy humor that characterizes most limericks and pleases Uncle Joe. (What limerick would you use?)

Regardless of your subject or the length of the essay, one of the key methods of development is through the use of examples. No matter what the main pattern of development might be, you may need examples to make your ideas clear and show your reader what you mean.

Here is an essay by a student supporting his amusing and unconventional thesis with examples. This is a use of examples for their own sake.

....

MAN'S BEST FRIEND?

....

These days, large amounts of money are spent on dog training. Obedience schools flourish, spreading the notion that a dog can actually be trained. Owners enroll their dogs in these schools expecting a mutt to be transformed into a poised, obedient servant. I have no illusions concerning this matter; I believe the dog trains the owner. My dog has trained me perfectly.

For example, whenever I give my dog a bath, which she totally dislikes, she does everything in her power to make the experience as unpleasant for me as possible. She squirms, shakes, and splashes, anything to get me wet, short of grabbing me and pulling me into the tub. I usually end up with the bath, and she ends up gloating over my injured pride. Consequently, she doesn't get a bath unless it is absolutely necessary.

She is loath to get a bath, but she is never reluctant to ride in the car; she will go anywhere, anytime. She loves riding in the car so much that she has devised a scheme for taking a ride even though I am not going anywhere. She jumps into the car and sits, oblivious to my attempts at coaxing her out. If I try to grab her and drag her out, she growls and snaps at me. She will get out only after I have taken her for a ride, even if it is just a spin around the block.

I have learned to live with the truth; my dog is the owner of a very obedient human being.

Ron Alberti
(Student)

....

Although the next student essay is also lighthearted, it uses examples to support a broader controlling idea than the preceding essay.

....
A BALL OF CONFUSION
....

Academic enlightenment has led me to everyday bewilderment. Having recently returned to the classroom after a twenty-year absence, I have discovered that my classes require many new and varied ways of thinking. Unlike the jobs I have held where thought was a one-dimensional process, academic discipline requires more abstract and multifaceted modes of thought.

Upon entering a classroom last week, I was confronted with a nonfunctional pencil sharpener. Until three weeks ago, I would have considered this to be a minor annoyance and not have given it a second thought. Now, however, I must decide upon an academic perspective from which to view this glitch in the scholastic system. If I perceive it though the eyes of English Composition, I must judge the subject (pencil sharpener) to have a bad attitude. Simple enough, but wait. What would sociology have to say about the dysfunctional subject; probably that it symbolizes a lack of quality and funding in lower socio-economic higher education. Biology, of course, would contend the sharpening device was simply a loser in the evolutionary war; it was unfit and did not deserve to survive and breed others like it. My mathematical mind wonders if this event falls within the parameters of a standard deviation? What laws of probability are involved here? Is there a formula to give the percentage of breakdowns, by month, in a particular classroom? Worse yet, wasn't I supposed to memorize that formula? Regrettably, history has two conflicting views. The historically liberal commentary on this low tech failure might be: the military industrial complex draws away our best scientific minds to make war, not better pencil sharpeners. Conservatives would naturally assume the sharpener was broken by lower-class vandals bent on trashing our entire system of government. Psychology, I am sure, would find a myriad of sexual connotations in the interaction between sharpener and sharpenee.

As I sit here trying to sort out the true philosophical meaning of the mechanically disturbed pencil sharpener, I decide to indulge in group therapy. Turning on the radio, I hear the "Temptations," a group skilled in audio therapy, diagnose me as a "Ball of Confusion."

Bob Pfeiffer
(Student)
....

PITFALLS TO AVOID

1. Don't forget that you need to provide the transitions which show the relationship between the examples and the main points of your essay. Examples alone are not going to be effective unless your reader clearly sees the connection between the general statements and the examples that illustrate them.

2. Don't stack the cards by giving a series of biased examples. Suppose you want to show that college is worthwhile. If the only examples you cite are those of successful graduates holding high-paying jobs, you are not apt to convince a fair-minded reader.

3. Don't select nontypical examples to support your thesis. Even a large number of exceptional cases will not prove your generalization.

4. Don't just give general examples. Name names, give numbers, provide who, where, when.

5. Don't make the mistake of cramming your essay with nothing but reams of factual details and statistics. Your main job is to interpret the facts and offer examples that clearly show what you mean.

SUGGESTED TOPICS

Select a topic from the following list or choose a subject on which you have some knowledge or experience and write an essay developed by examples. Make sure your topic is narrow enough to be proved.

1. My father's sense of humor
2. Parental punishments
3. Embarrassing experiences
4. Sympathetic employers
5. Practical jokes
6. Strange neighbors
7. Strange partners
8. Amusing characters
9. Funny sayings
10. Exercises in futility
11. Announcers' bloopers
12. Television absurdities
13. Famous women in history
14. Ghosts and goblins
15. Human characteristics in animals
16. Ways people dance
17. Blind dates
18. Misleading ads
19. Techniques in getting a date
20. Controversial heroes
21. Contradictions in terms
22. Great children's stories
23. Comic strips with a message
24. Political dirty tricks
25. Myths in American history

26. Teachers' idiosyncracies
27. Children's punishments of parents
28. Part-time jobs
29. Unusual pets
30. Ridiculous clothing fads
31. Funny incidents in church
32. Odd hobbies
33. Annoying commercials
34. Disappointments
35. Famous fumbles
36. Famous cowards
37. Close calls
38. Famous couples
39. Extrasensory perception
40. Animal characteristics in people
41. Humor in commercials
42. Rip-offs
43. Cults
44. Movie heroes
45. Movie villains
46. Literary styles
47. Violence in fairy tales
48. "Real life" comic strips
49. Unfair test techniques
50. Having more than one boyfriend

TECHNIQUES OF CLEAR WRITING

AGREEMENT

Two kinds of agreement are necessary to make your sentences clear. The first is *subject–verb agreement*; the second is *pronoun–antecedent agreement*. Although these names may seem a bit bulky, the rules are simple.

Subject–Verb

The basic principle of subject–verb agreement is this:

A subject and a verb must agree in person and number.

There are *three persons:* first, second, and third. There are *two numbers:* singular and plural. *First* person refers to the person speaking, pronouns being *I* (singular) or *we* (plural). *Second* person refers to the person spoken to: *you* (singular) and *you* (plural). *Third* person refers to the person spoken about: *he, she, it* (singular) and *they* (plural).

Number says whether the persons involved are *singular* or *plural*: singular numbers are *I, you, he/she/it;* plural numbers are *we, you,* and *they.*

Person	Number		Person	Number	
First person	singular	*I*	First person	plural	*we*

| Second person | singular | *you* | Second person | plural | *you* |
| Third person | singular | *he, she, it* | Third person | plural | *they* |

I am hungry   **We are** hungry
You are hungry   **You are** hungry
He is hungry   **They are** hungry

I have a new car   **We have** a new car
You have a new car   **You have** a new car
He has a new car   **They have** a new car

(**To be** and **to have** are not only frequently used alone, but they are also used as auxillary verbs in the compound tenses.)

to be

I am singing   **We are** singing
You are singing   **You are** singing
He is singing   **They are** singing

to have
I have sung   **We have** sung
You have sung   **You have** sung
He has sung   **They have** sung

Except in the irregular verbs **to be** and **to have** and in the third person singular of the **present** tense of other verbs, agreement is consistent. The forms of the verbs do not change. **The addition of the -s in the third person singular, however, is very important.**

It is also important in forming the negative contraction of the third person singular of the verb *to do*.

	Singular	**Contraction**	**Plural**	**Contraction**
First Person	I do not	I don't	We do not	We don't
Second Person	You do not	You don't	You do not	You don't
Third Person	He does not	He doesn't	They do not	They don't

Rules Regarding Subject—Verb Agreement

1. A singular subject has a singular verb.

   The **man bicycles** to work.

2. A plural subject has a plural verb.

   The **men bicycle** to work.
   The **rules are** forgotten.

3. A verb that comes before the subject also agrees with the subject.

There **were** two **dogs** in the yard.
On the shelf **are** three **textbooks.**

4. Two or more singular subjects joined by *and* have a plural verb

The **teacher and** the **student are** working together.
John, Mary, and Beth practice daily.

unless the combined persons or things are regarded as a unit.

The **bow and arrow was** the weapon of the Indian.
Forty-five dollars seems like a high price for that sweater.
The **Congress is** in session.

5. Compound subjects connected by *or, but,* or *nor* take a singular verb if the subjects are singular.

The **director or her assistant chooses** the cast.

If the subjects are plural, the verb must be plural.

Not the **supervisors but** the **workers determine** the work load.

If one subject is singular and one is plural, the verb agrees with the nearer subject.

The **instructor or** the **students collect** the assignments.
The **students or** the **instructor collects** the assignments.

6. The following pronouns take a singular verb:

anybody	anybody
anything	somebody
nobody	someone
each	either
neither	one

All these pronouns have a singular sense; that is, you have a feeling that only a **single** thing is referred to. However, you must remember that, even though they sound as if they are plural,

everyone   everybody

also take a singular verb.

7. No matter what comes between subject and verb, only the subject influences the verb.

a. Modifiers like:

as well as	in addition to
together with	accompanied by

do **not** take the place of *and.* Therefore, they do not form a compound subject.

My **father,** as well as his sisters, **is** a singer. [singular subject, singular verb]

My **dog,** accompanied by all her pups, **was** in the show. [singular subject, singular verb]

My **parents,** in addition to my grandfather, **are** coming for graduation. [plural subject, plural verb]

b. Prepositional phrases like

to the skies	by the walls	for the summer months
of the city	with the family	between the hedges

are also only modifiers of the subject and do not influence the verb.

The **cost** to the students **is** fair. [singular subject, singular verb]

A **crate** of oranges **was** delivered from Florida. [singular subject, singular verb]

Pronoun-Antecedent

The basic principle of pronoun-antecedent agreement is this:
A pronoun must agree with its antecedent; that is, with the noun to which it refers.

When the **burglar** saw the police car approaching, **he** dropped **his** gun and ran.

When the **burglars** saw the police car approaching, **they** dropped **their** guns and ran.

1. Not every pronoun has an antecedent.

It is very cold today.
It is a long way from Boston to Phoenix.

Here, the *it* has no antecedent and needs none.

2. If the antecedent is singular, the pronoun must be singular. Remember that *everyone, someone,* and similar pronouns (listed in item 6 in the subject–verb rules above) are all singular.

Everybody is willing to do **her** (or **his**) share.
Everyone has forgotten to bring **his** notes.
Each of the girls has **her** own car.

3. When two antecedents are joined by *either . . . or, neither . . . nor, not only . . . but also, both . . . and,* the pronoun must agree with the nearer of the two antecedents.

Neither the coach nor the **players** have lost **their** enthusiasm.
Neither the players nor the **coach** has lost **his** enthusiasm.
Not only the three brothers but the **sister** has had **her** education cut short.
Either George's sisters or **he** will lose **his** chance to go to college.

NOTE: A relative pronoun (*who, which, that,* etc.) should also agree with the nearer of two antecedents.

Sylvia loves everything and **everybody who** is connected with the theater.
She adores everybody and **everything that** is associated with acting.

4. A collective noun used as an antecedent usually requires a singular pronoun.

The **team** had made up **its** own schedule for practice.
The **jury** had arrived at **its** verdict.
The **company** has changed **its** policy.
The **group** was free to choose **its** own meeting place.

An exception exists: when emphasis is on the individuals who "make up" the body referred to by a collective noun, plural pronouns (and verb forms) are used.

The **crowd** always express **their** disapproval in various ways: **some shout insults, some cheer, and some toss overripe vegetables.**

Here, the members of the crowd were acting individually. Often, you can avoid problems by just saying *members of,* as in the following:

The **members of** the orchestra were taking **their** seats.
The **members of** the group were divided in **their** loyalties.

5. The pronouns *who, which,* and *that* may be singular or plural depending on the antecedent. All the following examples are correct:

She is one of those girls who **are** always giggling.
[*Who* is plural because it has a plural antecedent, *girls;* therefore, the verb must be plural.]
The girl who **draws** the winning number will go on the tour. [Since *girl* is singular, *who* is singular.]
Filling out tax forms is one of those tasks that **are** often delayed until the last moment.
He lives on one of those streets that **are** down by the river.
He lives on a street that **is** close to the river.

NOTE: When you have "the only one of . . . ," then the singular verb is used:

She is the only one of the girls who **is** going on the tour.
This is the only one of the books that **was** damaged in the fire.

6. Avoid using indefinite *they* and *it.*

FAULTY:
In Louisiana **they** could produce a lot more sugar cane.

IMPROVED:
Louisiana growers could produce a lot more sugar cane.

FAULTY:
In the garden book **it** says you should plant the bulbs in October.

IMPROVED:
The garden book says you should plant the bulbs in October.

7. With few exceptions, a pronoun should clearly refer to a definite antecedent. If your reader cannot immediately see what the pronoun refers to, then you need to reword the sentence.

FAULTY:
Teddy told his dad that **he** had a flat tire.

CLEAR:
Teddy told his dad, "You've got a flat tire."
Teddy told his dad, "I've got a flat tire."
Teddy told his dad that the Chevy had a flat tire.

FAULTY:
The two pitchers were from Junction High **who** led the league in shutouts.

CLEAR:
The two pitchers who led the league in shutouts were from Junction High.

FAULTY:
When the puppy crawled into the cat's box, **it** hissed and scratched sand in his eyes.

CLEAR:
When the puppy crawled into the cat's box, the cat hissed and scratched sand in the puppy's eyes.

FAULTY:
The lawyer must talk to her client in everyday language since her knowledge of the law is limited.

CLEAR:
Since her client's knowledge of the law is limited, the lawyer must talk to him in everyday language.

FAULTY:
Christopher has deliberately broken almost all his toys, and this is what worries his mother.

CLEAR:
Christopher has deliberately broken almost all his toys, and this destructive behavior worries his mother.

EXERCISE 4A: AGREEMENT

Correct any faulty agreement by revising the following sentences. If the sentence is correct, put a C on the line.

1. Arlene's teacher told her she would be going to the oratory contest in November.

_____

_____

2. Sometimes he cheats on tests, and this, somehow, has infected the whole class.

_____

_____

3. The professor asked me one of those ethical questions which are always hard to answer.

_____

_____

4. Paula is the only one of the students who are scholarly.

_____

_____

5. Each of the persons in the choir can read music, and they all have beautiful voices.

_____

_____

6. Everything that was needed for all of the Scouts to attend the Jubilee were donated by local merchants.

_____

_____

7. As upsetting as it was at the time, the benefits we gained from watching the autopsy were many.

_____

_____

8. He gave up the hope of losing weight because it required diet and exercise which they hated.

_____

_____

9. Manuel wanted to visit Mexico, so he saved his money, worked two jobs, and learned to ride a motorcycle which he would ride there; this helped him to make the trip.

_____

_____

10. When the man saw the burglar, he ran.

_____

_____

EXERCISE 4B: AGREEMENT

Correct any faulty agreement by revising the following sentences. If the sentence is correct, put a C on the line.

1. Neither my mother nor her sisters is going to come for the celebration.

_____

2. In the syllabus, it says that the final examination is on May 22.

_____

3. The two wrestlers were champions who represented the college fraternities.

_____

4. The class reached their decision and announced its verdict.

_____

5. My parents, accompanied by my best friend, is coming for my graduation.

_____

6. The reports of the officers are hard to understand because they were hurried.

_____

7. In the garage are the collection of skateboards.

_____

8. The Senate are convened as are the House of Representatives.

_____

9. Everybody is eager to help their committee win the prize.

_____

10. Jill is one of those students who always have a good excuse for missing class.

_____

WORD POWER

PRONOUNS AS SUBJECTS AND OBJECTS

There are six pronouns that have forms that differ depending on whether they are used as subject or as object of the sentence:

Subject	Object
I	me
he	him
they	them
we	us
she	her
who, whoever	whom, whomever

If the subject of a sentence is a pronoun, you need to be careful to use the subject form:

Jake and I [*not* me] offered to help Fred.
Mary and I [*not* me] believe in exercising three times a week.

In sidewalk English you often hear something like this: "Jeff and me was called into the office." Such sentences contain a compound error: the *me* should be *I* (subject), and the *was* should be *were* because the subject (**Jeff and I**) is plural.

If a pronoun is the object of a verb or preposition, the object form must be used:

They invited him and **me** [not *I*] to the party.
The gift was intended for Julie and **me** [not *I*].
With **whom** [not *who*] did you discuss your problem?
Those **whom** [not *who*] we invited should be here by seven-thirty.
The history professor made both of us, Jake and **me** [not *I*], write a paper on the French Revolution.
Between you and **me** [not *I*], he is badly mistaken about the cost of owning a car.
Knowing Beth and **me** [not *I*] as well as he does, I'm surprised that he didn't call us.

In pronoun–noun combinations such as "we husbands" or "us wives," the pronoun form will depend on how the noun is used in the sentence. If the noun is used as a subject, then you must use the subject form of the pronoun:

> **We husbands** are actually benefiting from the women's liberation movement.

If the noun is used as an object, then you must use the object form of the pronoun:

> The women's liberation movement has opened a lot of doors for **us wives.**

NOTE: Despite the frequent use of *who* instead of *whom* in informal speech, written English still calls for the use of *whom* or *whomever* in objective constructions:

> **Whom** are you expecting?
> From **whom** do you expect to receive this money?
> He's a man in **whom** I once had great faith.
> Energy costs will continue to rise, no matter **whom** we elect.
> Herman Melville was a man **whom** the critics had ignored.
> She is a young woman who tells her problems to **whomever** she happens to meet.
> We can appoint **whomever** we choose.

Watch out for the form in which the pronoun is the subject of the verb that follows:

> The article offers good advice to **whoever** has money to invest. [*Whoever* is the subject of *has.*]
> There is little doubt about **who** financed his political campaign. [*Who* is the subject of *financed.*]
> Gill asked Ruby **who** she thought should be elected. [*Who* is the subject of *should be elected.*]

In a good many constructions, *that* may be used in place of the more formal *whom* or *whomever.*

> He was the sort of man **whom/that** his neighbors scarcely noticed.
> The colonists were determined to oppose **whomever/anyone that** the governor appointed.

In addition to the subject and object forms of verbs, there are the forms made by adding *-self* or *-selves*, such as *myself, himself, themselves.* These forms have two uses. First, they may show that the subject and the object are the same, as in "He hurt himself." In this case it is called a *reflexive* form. Second, the form may be used for emphasis, as in "My mother herself told me." In this case it is called an *intensive* form. These forms should be used **only** in these two ways.

FAULTY:
My wife and myself visited Chautauqua last week.

CORRECT:
My wife and I visited Chautauqua last week.

FAULTY:
The Ambersons invited Jerry and myself to the party.

CORRECT:
The Ambersons invited Jerry and me to the party.

EXERCISE 4C: PRONOUNS

In each of the following sentences, circle the form of the pronoun that completes the sentence correctly.

1. The doctor told both of us, George and (I, me) to start exercising.
2. Among the three of us, Betty, Jim, and (I, me), we ate fourteen hot dogs.
3. The ski instructor and (I, me) disagreed about the proper way to stop.
4. Between (we, us) Democrats, there is no question as to what is right.
5. Charlie asked (who, whom) is calling the shots here.
6. (We, Us) married students know why we're here.
7. Josh and (I, me) used to drive the rabbi wild with our questions.
8. Fidel taught Che and (I, me) the principles of agrarianism.
9. "Who blocked that end?" asked the coach. "It was (I, me)," replied the left tackle, who was an English major.
10. "(Who, Whom) asked the question I couldn't answer yesterday," said the dean.
11. (Whoever, Whomever) reads this book will benefit from it.
12. (Who, Whom) do you wish to nominate for student body president?
13. In the last election, many people could not decide (who, whom) was the better candidate.

14. Diana asked my boyfriend and (I, me, myself) to head the committee.
15. High schools offer education to (whoever, whomever) desires a degree.

TENSE

Because the verb is the most important part of the sentence, it is important to know how to use verbs properly. The verb not only tells the reader what specific action is taking place, it also tells **when** the action is taking place. Every time you use a verb in a sentence, you are using a specific tense. *Tense* means "time"—the time of the action of the verb. For example:

PRESENT:
Anthony calls Michele every day.

PAST:
Anthony called Michele yesterday.

FUTURE:
Anthony will call Michele tomorrow.

The sentences above illustrate the major divisions in time—the simple past, present, and future tenses. Most people are so familiar with these basic tenses that they use them automatically. In fact, some people think that these are the only tenses in the English language. However, you will realize that you can't communicate with anyone very long in just the simple present, past, and future tenses.

Present-Tense Agreement

In spite of their familiarity, present and past tenses present some problems.

In the present tense, the form (the spelling) of the verb changes **only** in the third person singular.

	Singular	**Plural**
First person	I know	We know
Second person	You know	You know
Third person	He knows	They know

To fail to put the *-s* ending on the third person singular or to put it on any other verb form is generally considered a serious error in mechanics.

-ed Endings

The simple past tense of regular verbs is formed by adding -ed to the present tense, as in *walked, talked, carried.*

There are two other ways in which -ed is used in forming verbs, the perfect tenses and verb forms in the passive voice.

The Three Uses of -ed in Regular Verbs

1. The simple past tense	I **walked** the dog.
2. All perfect tenses	The dog **has walked** here before.
	The dog **had walked** here before he got hurt.
	The dog **will have walked** here for three years by February.
3. Passive voice	The dog **is walked** here every day.
	The dog **was walked** here yesterday.
	The dog **will be walked** here tomorrow
	The dog **has been** walked here every day for a year.
	The dog **had been walked** here until the highway was built.
	The dog **will have been walked** here for three years by next Thursday.

Compound Tenses

Perfect and progressive tenses show variations of time within the past, present, and future tenses.

Perfect Tenses

The past perfect tense is used for an action completed in the past, before some other action:

The salesperson insisted that she **had talked** to my husband.

The present perfect tense is used for an action in the past that is continuing:

I **have talked** to him repeatedly about his drinking problem.

The future perfect tense is used when the action will be completed at some point in the future:

On February 1 we **shall have been married** for fifty years.

Progressive Tenses

The present progressive is used for an ongoing action in the present:

The SAT scores at Wimbleton High School **are rising.**

The past progressive tense is used for an ongoing action in the past:

The SAT scores at Wimbleton High School **were rising.**

The future progressive is used for an ongoing action in the future:

The SAT scores at Wimbleton High School **will be rising.**

Being Consistent

The most important thing to remember about tense is that you must be consistent. You cannot randomly shift from one tense to another. For example, if you were telling a story about what happened to you on your vacation last summer, you would stay in the past tense. If, on the other hand, you were explaining the difference between your German Shepherd and your Irish Setter, you would stay in the present tense. There will be times, of course, when you have to move to a different tense. If, for example, you were contrasting the driving habits of your old boyfriend with those of your new boyfriend, the part of your paper about your old boyfriend would be written in the past tense, and the part about your new boyfriend would be written in the present tense. You should not move to a different tense, however, unless you have a good reason, so proofread your papers carefully and make sure that your writing contains no unnecessary shifts in tense.

EXERCISE 4D: SHIFTS IN TENSE

In the following essay, some of the verb forms have been changed to make the essay inconsistent in tense. Read the narrative carefully and correct all of the needless shifts in tense.

....

THE WHITE NILE

....

Topic Sentence

Mutesa, the young king of Buganda, was a savage and bloodthirsty monster.

Body

Hardly a day went by without some victim being executed at his command, and this is done wilfully, casually, almost as a kind of game. A page will neglect to have closed or opened a door, and at once, at a sign from Mutesa, they would have been taken away, screaming, to have their heads lopped off. A roll of drums obliterates the cries of their death-throes. Nothing that W. S. Gilbert was about to invent with his Lord High Executioner in *The Mikado*, nothing in the behavior of the raving Red Queen in *Alice's Adventures in Wonderland*, is more fantastic than the scenes that have occurred whenever Mutesa holds a court, the only differences being that these scenes were hideously and monstrously real. Torture by burning alive, the mutilation of victims by cutting off their hands, ears, and feet, the burial of living wives with their dead husbands—all these things were taken as a matter of course. This was more than a simple blood-lust; Mutesa crushed out life in the same way as a child stepped on an insect, never for an instant thinking of the consequences, or experiencing a moment's pity for the pain he had inflicted. He felt no pain, except his own.

Concluding Sentence

He, and all the people about him at his court, give the impression of playing at life, of living with an air of mad make-believe.

Alan Morehead

....

EXERCISE 4E: VERB TENSES

Use the following verbs in two sentences, putting the verb in a different tense in each sentence.

(live) **1.** Present perfect _____

Present progressive _____

(hate) **2.** Present _____

Future perfect _____

(teach) **3.** Past progressive _____

Present perfect _____

(stay) **4.** Present _____

Future perfect _____

(be) **5.** Future perfect _____

Present perfect progressive _____

(call) **6.** Past perfect _____

Present perfect progressive _____

(promise) **7.** Present perfect _____

Past perfect _____

(cough) **8.** Present perfect progressive _____

Future perfect _____

(hurry) **9.** Past _____

Past progressive _____

(jump) **10.** Past perfect progressive _____

Past perfect _____

IRREGULAR VERBS

Some of the irregularities in the mechanics of English are holdovers from the long history of the language. They are vestiges of language spoken by our ancestors hundreds, even thousands of years ago. Among these remains are the so-called *irregular verbs.*

As you have just seen, the regular verbs have four principal parts:

1. Present form   I talk, he talks
2. Present participle   talk*ing*
3. Past tense   talk*ed*
4. Past participle   talk*ed*

The past participle is the same form as the past tense but is used in combination with various forms of **have.**

I have talk**ed**
She had talk**ed**
We shall have talk**ed**

Irregular verbs do not conform to this pattern. Although there are only a hundred or so irregular verbs in the language, they are important enough that you should memorize their forms. Fortunately, most of them are so well-known that the forms come to you almost automatically.

Notice the changing forms in some of the most common irregular verbs. The changes, incidentally, occur only in past tense and in the past participle; the present participle always is made by adding *-ing*.

Present	Past	Past and Past Participle
begin	began	(have) begun
blow	blew	(have) blown
break	broke	(have) broken
bring	brought	(have) brought
choose	chose	(have) chosen
come	came	(have) come
dig	dug	(have) dug
do	did	(have) done
eat	ate	(have) eaten
fly	flew	(have) flown
go	went	(have) gone
rise	rose	(have) risen
see	saw	(have) seen
sing	sang	(have) sung
write	wrote	(have) written

If you are ever unsure of the *principal parts* of a verb, your dictionary will give you the forms.

A few verbs offer you a choice of two acceptable forms:

He dived (dove) off the high board.
They lighted (lit) cigarettes as soon as possible.
The boat sank (sunk) in five feet of water.

Some few verbs use different forms of the same principal part to show a difference in meaning:

The stockings were *hung* by the chimney with care.

BUT

The murderer was *hanged.*
The sun *shone* brightly.

BUT

The halls were cleaned and *shined.*

Special Cases

To Be

Be is a verb we cannot do without. However, as one scholar pointed out, it is a "badly mixed up verb"; it is the most irregular of all verbs.

Present	**Past**
I am	I was
you are	you were
he, she, it is	he, she, it was
we are	we were
you are	you were
they are	they were

Present Participle	**Past Participle**
being	(have) been

Confusing Forms

Some pairs of verbs have forms similar enough to be confusing.

Lie, lay, lain means that someone or something is somewhere, usually stretched out. (The combined form *lie down* is the same.)

> The man *lies* in the hammock.
> The dog *lay* in the shade.
> We all should have *lain* down.

Lay, laid, laid means that somebody has put something somewhere. You can test the correctness of your form by seeing if *put* can be substituted.

> I always *lay* my keys there.
> He *laid* his overcoat on the chair.
> He had *laid* his tools on the porch.

Sit, sat, sat means that someone is seated. (*Sit down* follows the same pattern.)

> She *sits* at her desk.
> They *sat* before the fire.
> We have *sat* here waiting for hours.

Set, set, set is usually another substitute for *put*, along with *lay*. The few exceptions to this sense include *the sun* **sets,** *the bird* **set,** *the cement has* **set.** Otherwise, *set* is a transitive verb (a verb that takes an object, or completer).

> I *set* the cat down outside the door.
> He *set* the luggage on the rack.
> They have *set* their burdens down.

Rise, rose, risen means to get up.

I *rise* at seven.
They *rose* quickly.
She has *risen*.

Raise, raised, raised means to lift up.

I *raise* the roof when I'm mad.
I *raised* the flag at school.
I have *raised* my hand every day in class.

EXERCISE 4F: CORRECT TENSE OF VERBS

Insert the correct form of the verb to the left in each of the blanks.

(walk)   **1.** Valerie _____ four miles every day. She _____ this many miles a day for six months. By next month, she _____ one thousand miles.

(read)   **2.** Sam _____ constantly. Last week he _____ three books by Robert Ludlum.

(discover)   **3.** Yesterday he _____ that what he _____ last week was worthless.

(lie)   **4.** After exercising I like to _____ on the sofa. After the hike last Wednesday, I _____ there for three hours.

(wear)   **5.** Donald _____ beautiful clothes, but he _____ that outfit three times this week.

(lay)   **6.** I _____ my keys on the table a minute ago, I thought, but they're not there. I must _____ them somewhere else.

(make)   **7.** Kathleen _____ a million dollars before she was thirty. Still, she _____ an enormous effort to earn more.

(wake)   **8.** The dog _____ me this morning at 6:00 a.m. He usually _____ me at 8:00 a.m., but he _____ me as early as 5:00 a.m.

(sit)   **9.** Gary _____ at a table with five girls every day in sociology class. He _____ there yesterday. Actually he _____ there all semester.

(work)   **10.** He _____ at McDonald's. He _____ till 11:00 p.m. last night. By next Thursday, he _____ there two years.

EXERCISE 4G: IRREGULAR VERBS

*In each of the following groups of sentences, fill in the first blank with the correct form of the **third person singular of the present tense,** the second blank with the **past tense,** and the third with the **past participle** following some form of have.*

(rise) **1.** The student _____ at seven. Yesterday she overslept and _____ at nine o'clock. She _____ late for several days.

(lie) **2.** The dog _____ under the porch. He _____ there all day long. He _____ so long that he must be sick.

(be) **3.** The boy _____ on the telephone. He _____ on the phone every day last week. He _____ on the phone daily for many weeks.

(do) **4.** The announcer _____ his work well. He _____ his work well in his old job. He _____ his telethons particularly well.

(choose) **5.** The city _____ a new master of ceremonies every Fouth of July. It _____ a woman last year. It _____ excellent representatives every year.

(sink) **6.** The pond _____ in the winter months. It _____ two feet last winter. It _____ almost that much every winter for the past five years.

(come) **7.** The chairperson _____ early to the meetings. She _____ unusually early to the last meeting. She _____ early to prepare the agenda.

(lay) **8.** _____ the tickets on the desk. You _____ them there the past week. You _____ always _____ them there.

(see) **9.** I _____ the spring flowers. I _____ them in the garden. I _____ them for several days.

(write) **10.** He _____ to his Marine wife every day. He _____ to her twice last Thursday. He _____ to her faithfully ever since she went on active duty.

C H A P T E R 5

Process

THE PROCESS THEME

Process, as a writing term, can be understood with either one of two emphases. In the more traditional sense, process is a way of writing that explains how you do something—the steps you follow to do something, to create something, to understand something. For example, you might want to explain how to build a brick barbecue in your backyard, or to trace the method you use to write an economics paper, or to record the hibernation patterns of bears. No matter what your subject matter, you will want to list the steps from beginning to end, making sure that (1) all the steps are included, (2) they are in proper, logical order, (3) each one is clear, and (4) they end with the finished product.

THE PROCESS PAPER

Process is a basic form of exposition, which itself means explanation. It is closely allied with several other modes of development— with narrative, for instance, because it exists in time and, therefore, the incidents or steps often take place in a logical, chronological order. (After all, you would scarcely ice the cake before mixing the batter.)

Process is also related to division and classification because the steps are divided units. If we are sticking with our cake as a simple example, we might divide our classifications or the process to these:

Assembling the ingredients

Mixing the batter

Baking the cake

Making the frosting

Taking baked cake from oven and cooling

Frosting the cake

No matter how simple or complex, the process must follow a logical order from first to last, with meaningful classifications of the steps.

ORGANIZATION

Most often, the organization of the process paper follows standard expository organization—introduction with thesis statement; body that supports thesis statement; conclusion.

Introduction: Usually brief, the introduction identifies the process, which is the subject, and tells the purpose of explaining it. The thesis statement should include both of these and may be the entire introduction. If not, the thesis statement should be the last sentence in the introduction (or possibly the first sentence in the following paragraph).

Body: As in every essay, the body is the support of the thesis statement. Here you decide upon the main steps of your process and determine that they are, first, in the right order, and, second, that they are as clearly and simply stated as possible. For every major step, make sure you have as many supporting steps as necessary and that they are in the correct order.

Conclusion: Like the introduction, the conclusion to the process paper will probably be brief. Having told what to do, the paper generally concludes, in effect, "Here it is!" and implies the value and significance of knowing it. For example, if you watched the Julia Child cooking program on television, you know that in the last minute she whisked the dish off the stove into the dining room, saying *bon appetit.* The obvious value of her cooking process was the fine meal to follow.

In the following essay, which contains a final twist, a student explains the correct way to mount a horse.

THE RIDER'S COURAGE

He was black as ebony and his eyes blazed with a wild fury. He beckoned me with his magnificent and intimidating beauty. Terror filled my heart, but still I could not take my eyes off him. I knew at once this was the horse that I had to ride. The thought of mounting him filled me with apprehension: my heart was racing, my palms were sweating, and my knees began to buckle beneath me. Gaining control of my senses, I recalled the basic steps necessary to execute not only a safe but also a graceful mount. Slowly and carefully I approached the stallion from his left side. Swiftly I grabbed the reins and pulled them taut. This quick and precise action let the horse know I was in charge of the situation, although unbeknownst to him, I did have my doubts. With reins in my right hand I took hold of the saddle horn. In one swift action, I put my left foot into the left stirrup, shifted my weight from my right foot to my left foot, I swung my right leg over his back side and into the right stirrup. Now I was firmly planted in the saddle. To reinforce to the horse, as well as myself, that I was the fearless leader of this duet, I gave the reins an authoritative tug. There remained only the final and most crucial step to complete this, thus far, successful mounting. Sweatbeads began to form on my brow, because failure to execute this final action correctly could result in my falling off the horse and being trampled by his enormous hooves. While holding the reins taut in my right hand, I slowly and carefully leaned forward in the saddle; with my cheek barely brushing his mane I reached out with my left hand and dropped the quarter into the slot. Three minutes of ecstasy! Tally-ho!

Maggie Henson
(Student)

The following student essay explains the process of gaining the respect of very young sports enthusiasts.

OUR FUTURE AND OUR PAST

"I believe that children are our future
Teach them well and let them lead the way
Show them all the beauty they possess inside

Give them a sense of pride
To make it easier
Let the children's laughter
Remind us how we used to be"
—Whitney Houston, "The Greatest Love of All"

The lyrics of Whitney Houston provide an apt, although somewhat unusual, coaching philosophy for those who practice the trade in baseball's humblest vineyard, the six to nine-year olds. Little League coach, the mere phrase ignites ghastly images of pot-bellied, egomaniacal practitioners of the discredited art of vicarious living, along with its complementary mindset of victory at all cost. While this stereotype is all too often true, the hollow and transient thrill of victory cannot match the enduring admiration, respect, and love a coach can *earn* from his or her players through the donation of time, attention, and concern. For someone willing to forego egocentric goals, coach can become a synonym for friend, confidant, instructor, and parent of boys and girls that one could wish for as one's own.

You see, baseball, far from being an end in itself, spreads its branches skyward towards the loftier goals of player maturity, independence, self-esteem, and personal growth. To be successful at this more unconventional method of coaching, age regression is imperative. As an adult, the youthful emotions of insecurity, endless daydreaming, tentative flights from the parental nest, and peer group participation are sometimes hard to empathize with, but empathy, not baseball expertise or a "winning attitude," is the quintessential coaching virtue, for it, above all else, enables the coach to focus his attention and concern on that which benefits his players the most.

For a typical seven-year-old, pressure is trying to perform an uncertain skill with "millions of people" in the bleachers. Cruel fate is: the batter hitting the ball to you while you are engrossed in picking dandelions, or your shoe falling off as you scurry towards first base in celebration of your first hit. Confusion reigns supreme, as the umpire calls, "Strike three," and you didn't even swing the bat. Disappointment comes in the guise of a strikeout versus the Darth Vader of the first grade. The agony of defeat pays a visit when the opponent's winning margin is higher than you are able to count. Uncertainty strikes home when you must ask your coach, "Did we start the real game yet?" and it is already the second inning. To a coach, these endless disasters provide ample opportunity to intangibly (a kind word) or tangibly (a trip to the Dairy Queen) demonstrate support for your players in their time of travail.

Reinforcing their positive accomplishments, patiently demonstrating for the fifty-third time the proper way to field a ground ball, and assuaging a battered self-image are the dues a coach must pay to *merit* respect on a seven-year-old's terms. This respect, in turn, *grants the coach the privilege* of sharing in their unfettered joy, enthusiasm, sense of pride, and openness. Dante's last concentric ring does not contain a heart so hardened that he could not feel a child's excitement as he launches a "home run" that rolls every inch of fifty feet from home plate.

More importantly, in becoming a friend, rather than an authority figure, your ideals concerning fair play, respect for others' feelings, and kindness are sown on fertile and receptive minds. You hope the players will come to share the belief that in all of life's trials, only your effort, not victory, can be a constant. On a less philosophical plane, if the children's laughter and spontaneity do not elicit memories of simpler pleasures unencumbered by adult motives and world-weariness, coaching at this unskilled playing level is not your niche in life. Thus baseball, taken as a metaphor for life, provides a splendid opportunity to inculcate boys and girls with values that extend far beyond the green and white geometric configuration of the diamond. Not Vince Lombardi's famous dictum, "Winning isn't everything, it's the only thing," but Whitney Houston's appropriately titled "The Greatest Love of All" should guide Little League coaches.

Bob Pfieffer
(Student)

EXERCISE 5A

Make an outline in which you list the steps in the process of choosing a dog for a family pet. Make sure the outline includes all the choices that are involved in adding this new member to your family.

EXERCISE 5B

Write a thesis statement for a serious essay on "How to Study for a Test" or "How to Answer an Essay Question." Refer to the Prologue and to the epilogue on writing an essay exam if you need additional information.

EXERCISE 5C

Write an introduction to a playful essay on assembling toys.

TECHNIQUES OF CLEAR WRITING

PREPARING THE FINAL DRAFT

There are *three processes* you basically should follow after writing your first draft and before turning in your final draft. These processes are *revising, rewriting,* and *editing.* Although these overlap somewhat, they are three separate processes. *Revising* is improving the overall product, checking your ideas, your organization, and your content. *Rewriting* consists of sharpening your sentences and selecting better words—more eloquent or more precise ones. *Editing* makes sure you have corrected all your errors, both in your writing and in your mechanics.

REVISING

Outline: Revision

A good and quick way to start your revision is to make a sentence outline of your draft, beginning with your thesis statement and following with the topic sentences of each subsequent paragraph. Ask yourself if this outline presents your idea in a unified, consistent, coherent process from beginning to end.

Consider the following student outline and its revision.

Thesis: I Hate Speech Class
A. I hate being called on all the time.
B. I hate to criticize other people, and I used to hate their criticizing me until I noticed most of the criticism was good.
C. I hated the classroom exercises until lately when I discovered I'm pretty good at them.
D. Most of all, I hate giving speeches because I get so nervous although I find now I can control the nervousness, turn it into energy.

If these are the topic sentences in the body of *your* paragraph, obviously your thesis statement must be changed.

Perhaps a more fitting thesis statement would be one of the following: "I like speech class," or "Speech class has been good for me," or "Because, like most people, I feared public speaking, I resisted taking the course for as long as I could, but, because it was required for my major, I enrolled and to my surprise, found it to be one of the most useful and rewarding courses I've ever taken."

Introduction: Revision

After you have completed your first draft, allow it to "cool" for at least a day before you start to revise, so that you can be objective about it.

As you look at it objectively, you may find that you have drifted from your announced thesis statement or have not sufficiently supported it. If so, you must either rewrite your thesis statement to cover the body of your paper or alter the body to follow the thesis statement. Whichever you do will be determined by your purpose.

Ask yourself whether you gave a clear statement of your subject and attitude. Will it create interest or arouse curiosity? Does it lead clearly into discussion of your topic?

Here you must entice your reader to read your work and establish the tone of your essay. Are you going to be deadly serious or funny? Are you going to be sarcastic or straightforward? Thus, you establish the purpose and tone in your introduction. You might use either of the following examples depending on your purpose.

> Butterflies in the stomach, sweating hands, dry mouth, shaking legs—you must give a speech! Sky diving off Mount Everest or swimming in the Bermuda Triangle seems preferable. Why?
>
> Why is fear of public speaking the number one fear in the United States? Why do we fear it more than we fear flying or more than we fear activities that actually are dangerous?

Body: Revision

Does everything in the body support your attitude and pertain to your subject? If not, delete or rewrite or place the material in an informational footnote.

Conclusion: Revision

This is your last chance to make your point with your reader, so make it strong and clear. The conclusion reemphasizes your thesis without simply repeating it. Ideally, it advances your thought and expresses it in vivid and clear language.

> So, speaking in public is easy. It's just like driving a car—scary at first, and just pure pleasure after you've mastered it.

or

> Students usually dread taking a speech course, but they end up enjoying the class and benefiting from what they've learned academically, socially, personally, and, most of all perhaps, economically.

WORD POWER

REWRITING

Rewriting is done to make your subject as clear and your style as enjoyable as possible for your reader. Rewriting is concerned not with the large structures of your writing but with the smaller elements like the sentences and the words. It is here in the rewriting process that you will work on such things as *sentence variety, levels of usage, word choice,* and *word order.*

Sentence Variety

Sentences come in many varieties. They are of different types and lengths; they have different purposes and styles. Varying your sentences makes your writing more enjoyable for your readers. Using just one sentence pattern can make any writing dull.

For a complete analysis of sentence variety, see the Techniques of Clear Writing section in Chapter 9.

Levels of Usage

The four basic levels of usage are formal, standard, colloquial, and substandard. Of these, the *formal* level is reserved for speaking or writing on occasions of great importance—usually political, academic, or religious. The *substandard* level is not acceptable usage in any circumstances. The *standard* is the level of language for almost all of your writing and for a great part of your speech. The *colloquial* level is used for highly informal, intimate, slangy conversation among friends and acquaintances.

You will find an expanded discussion of levels of usage in the Word Power section in Chapter 8 on Combining Methods of Development.

Word Choice

Throughout this book many considerations have been given to the selection of the correct nouns and verbs in your writing. But word choice is not confined just to subjects and verbs: Every word in a sentence can affect the meaning. The adjective, for example, is very important. Is the girl across the room *lovely, pretty,* or *exotic?* Is your grandfather *foul-tempered, cranky,* or *testy?* The adverb, too, can make a big difference. Is the book's heroine moving *languidly* or *sorrowfully?* Does its hero speak *brusquely* or *tersely?* Nor can you ignore the "little" words. Notice the difference the conjunction makes:

> She could have been a great skier, **and** she loved to bowl.
> She could have been a great skier, **but** she loved to bowl.

or

> He was a charming man, **and** he was popular.
> He was a charming man, **so** he was popular.

You should try to avoid the carelessness that permits you to substitute **and** when another conjunction makes your meaning clearer. Don't say "I got a refund on my taxes, *and* I had a party" if you mean, "I got a refund on my taxes, *so* I had a party," or "I got a refund on my taxes, *but* I had a party." The second example shows a cause-and-effect relationship. The third implies your refund money was spent on the party.

Right and wrong in word choice depends upon your purpose. Indeed, in writing as a process you recognize that there is no right or wrong except as it clarifies or muddies your purpose. How do your meanings change as your words change?

EXERCISE 5D: STYLE

Go back and read the two student essays in the rhetoric section of this chapter (pp. 150–152). Notice the difference in tone, formality, and style. What specific things make the styles so different?

Word Order

One of the things you have to decide upon as you consider the words in your sentence is *word order*. How you arrange the words in your sentence is fairly inflexible because the nature of the English language itself determines meaning, first, by the order of words and, second, by the use of prepositions.

In many languages other than English—Latin, for example—meaning is determined by the inflected form of the words—that is, their spelling—and their word order makes no difference.

Latin—inflected	Translation
Johannes amat Mariam.	John loves Mary.
Amat Johannes Mariam.	John loves Mary.
Mariam amat Johannes.	John loves Mary.

But in English, which has few inflections, word order usually establishes meaning. In English when you try to change word order, you say something else.

English—uninflected

John loves Mary.	(Isn't that nice.)
Loves John Mary.	(What did you say?)
Mary loves John.	(And he loves her? How *very* nice.)

Essentially, in English, the standard sentence is subject–verb–object. The modifying words, phrases, and clauses are placed as closely as possible to the words being modified. Thus,

The cat caught the mouse.
The *gray* cat *easily* caught the *frightened* mouse.
The *gray and black* cat *easily and swiftly* caught the mouse *who had been injured.*

However, you do have some freedom in arranging the order of your words *if your purpose demands it.* If you wish to emphasize a word you may put it first. For example:

I have never seen that.
That I have never seen.
Never have I seen that.

Phrases, too, are fairly easy to change in place. As in this example,

He was far from home, lonely and friendless.
Lonely and friendless, he was far from home.

Although you may experiment with changes in word order, the most important element is restraint. Excessive use of the unusual word order is tiresome. No matter how you change the words, or even how much, you must make certain that you have a purpose for change and that the change advances your purpose.

Prepositions in Word Order

Prepositions seem to be such small and commonplace words that their real significance is often overlooked. *Of, by, for, to, with, since, on, in* seem almost beyond definition. Indeed, you can only successfully define them in the general sense of them all: *prepositions are a class of words that when placed before nouns express such relationships as time, space, possession, intention, accompaniment.*

Yet these little words are an essential structure of the English language. They supplant the relatively cumbersome *inflection* of many other languages and of the earlier English language itself. As you saw in the example about "John loves Mary" on page 156, the forms (the spellings) of words vary to convey their meaning. In Latin, for example, there are five *cases*, different forms to express different meaning. In Old English, there were seven cases for nouns. Other parts of speech vary in form also in inflected languages, so English users owe much to the little preposition for the relative ease of their language.

A few inflected forms are extant from Old English to the present day. *Who* is the inflected form for the subject; *whom* is the inflected form for the object; *whose* is the inflected form for the case which shows possession. Likewise, personal pronouns inflect cases for subject–object–possessive, such as *she–her–hers* and *they–them—theirs*. Yet these are only a tiny proportion of our words; essentially English is an uninflected language, dependent for its meaning only on word order and prepositions.

Another use of the preposition, although of far less importance than its function in establishing meaning, is its aid in vocabulary building. By combining with some simple verbs, it constructs many new meanings. The following list, for example, is only one of many such verb–preposition combinations. As words, they are good because they are simple, idiomatic (see *Idiom*, p. 209), and understandable by all native English speakers.

Idiom	Meaning
to make a play for	to try to get
to make for	to approach, to attack
to make off	to run away
to make off with	to steal
to make out	to discern, to succeed
to make out with	to kiss (slang)
to make over	to remodel
to make up	to construct, to invent, to reconcile
to make up for	to recompense
to make up to	to try to be friendly

EXERCISE 5E: VERBS AND PREPOSITIONS

Recall five verbs that will combine similarly with prepositions to form new meanings.

1. _____

2. _____

3. _____

4. _____

5. _____

EDITING

Editing probably takes less creative thought than your original writing or your subsequent revising and rewriting. Nevertheless, editing has an importance all its own, for it creates the first impression of your work and, therefore, of you. Both your instructors and your employers, present or future, will react well to writing that is not blotted with mechanical errors. Remember that in a large proportion of your writing, you are asking for something, and usually your success in acquiring, or convincing, or persuading depends on your first impression. If you fail in a first impression, you may not get a chance at anything else. (If you have fully established yourself as a genius and a great person, you may get away with writing inprecisely but even then it is not advisable.)

Here is a sample letter actually received by one of the authors. What would you think of the carelessness of such a job applicant?

Dear sirs,

I heardthat you had a facuty position Im

interested in.   Send me a application   from

Yours truely,

John Loser

Granted that there is much more wrong with that letter than editing alone could remedy; still, the editing is so careless that the writer of it would not get a second chance.

EXERCISE 5F: EDITING

Below is a first draft of a how-to process essay. After studying this chapter, first revise the essay, adding transitional words where necessary, rearranging for clarity, and checking the structure of the essay. One of the ways that you can make your process essay—or any essay—clearer to your reader is by providing signposts. Signposts that you see along the highway tell you how fast it's safe to drive, how the road turns, whether there are railroad tracks ahead, and when to stop. Signposts in your

Signs tell you what to expect, what's ahead.

essay provide readers with important and necessary information. One of the more helpful signposts informs the readers of the order of the steps or the progression of the process. Thus, such words as "First," "Second," "Next," and "Finally" let the reader know exactly when the process moves from one step to the other. For a further discussion of transition, see Chapter 1. Finally, edit the essay below, checking for and correcting all errors.

HOW TO MAKE A CAKE THAT TAKES A FEW MINUTES TO MAKE LOOK LIKE IT TOOK ALL DAY

Most people don't appreciate things that don't take us much time. Also most people don't really appreciate spending hours in the kitchen preparing some delicacy. Therefore, using this deductive reasoning, most people would be interested in learning how to make a treat that takes little time but looks like it takes all day to make.

Here's how to make a quick Easter Basket cake that looks elaborate and time-consuming.

Go to your neighborhood supermarket and buy a box cake, any kind will do. Pick YOUR favorite flavor or the favorite of One you want to empress. While you're there, pick up a can of ready-to-spread icing, some jelly beans and, perhaps, a chocolate bunny or marshmallow chick and a package of coconut and some green food coloring.

Bake the cake according to the directions on the box. Mixing the ingredients takes about five min., baking takes about thirty. Put a few drops of green—or whatever color you desire—dye into a cup of coconut and mix.

When the cake is done and cool, put one layer on the cake plate and ice it, top and sides. With half your can of icing Put the other layer on top and, with a sharp knife, cut a circle about one half inch from the edge of the top layer about one half inch deep. Scoop out the center of the top layer about one half inch deep. It's easier to do if you slash the center with your knife about an inch apart thru the center. Give your kids or your neighbor'es kids this cake. They'll like it, and it's less wasteful.

Fill this scooped out area with your green dyed coconut. Ice the top layer of the cake and—this is one of the things that make it look fancy and time-consuming—shove jelly benas into the icing all around the sides of the cake. And put the chocolate animals and eggs on the dyed cocoanut.

Take a peace of foil, roll it up,. and bend it in the shape of a basket handle. Coil a narrow ribbon around the foil and place a bow on top. Stick the ends into each side of the top of the cake and VOILA! a masterpiece that look like we worked on it for hours. Us it for your centerpiece at Easter dinner and eat it for your Easter Dessert.

You can use this same process for any holiday: birthdays or Saint Patricks day or Forth of July celebrations. All you have to do to make this easy cake suitable is to change the color of the coconut and your side and top decorations. The Stores sell everything nowadays. Bon Appetit!

CHAPTER 6

Comparing and Contrasting

As a method of development, comparison (in the broadest sense, it includes contrast) always has two subjects. You are pointing out similarities (or dissimilarities) in two things. Such comparisons are nearly a constant mental activity. For example, you stop at a friend's house and almost subconsciously you compare and contrast your friend's home to your own. Or you observe that your neighbor has a new lawn tractor; you notice, with a twinge, its superiorities to your own five-year-old mower. You make a new friend at school and think how much he resembles your older brother in looks and personality. All of these observations are either comparison or contrast. When you see similarities—that is *comparison;* when you see dissimilarities—that is *contrast.*

As simple comparisons, the examples just cited are the commonplaces of your daily life, but when you are developing an essay by comparison, you always have a specific purpose in mind. You don't just say, "A is like B" or "A is unlike B." Rather, you indicate your purpose in recounting these likenesses and differences. Customarily, your purpose is to increase your reader's understanding of one of your two subjects. You can more easily understand *A* when you perceive how it is like or unlike *B.*

In *Alice in Wonderland,* Alice goes to a tea party at the Mad Hatter's where he asks her a riddle: "Why is a raven like a writing desk?" After a lot of Wonderland's wandering conversation, Alice says she gives up.

"What," she asks, "is the answer?"

"I haven't the slightest idea," the Hatter replies.

Just as Alice is justifiably annoyed at being asked a riddle with no answer, readers may be irritated by reading a comparison without a point. "What," as Alice asked, "is the purpose of it?"

Comparison/contrast is one of the basic ways for learning something new. You set up a familiar subject and beside it you set up an unfamiliar one. Your readers comprehend the unfamiliar as its points of difference or similarity are made clear by relating them to the familiar. For example, suppose you wish to describe a new male acquaintance. He is, you say, superficially funny, but in a deeper way he is straight and square—much like Bill Cosby. Because your reader has an idea of Bill Cosby, he or she feels a certain understanding of your new acquaintance.

On a more complex level, concepts that you have to learn in school are easier to understand when they are compared or contrasted with something more familiar to you. For example, your history teacher might explain indentured servitude by telling you that it is *like* slavery—a form of temporary slavery.

Fiction writers often use this device to vivify their characters, offsetting them with a *foil,* a character who possesses opposite traits. Thus, the author underscores the stinginess of a Scrooge by showing the open-hearted generosity of Scrooge's nephew. Indeed, the spirit of Dickens's book is a contrast between the old Scrooge and the reformed one. And Huck Finn's realism is best highlighted by contrasting it to Tom Sawyer's romanticism.

In the Dickens example, the necessary purpose is to show the change in Scrooge from a cantankerous old man to a genial gentleman, thus indicating people can and do improve themselves when they see the error of their ways. The effect of the contrast between Huckleberry Finn and Tom Sawyer is to provide a fuller comprehension of both realism and romanticism.

ON WHAT BASIS ARE YOU COMPARING OR CONTRASTING?

To have significance, those things you are comparing must be compared on the same basis. For example, you could compare an egg and a seed on the basis that both of them contain the power to reproduce the parent from which they came. You could also compare both egg and seed on the basis of foodstuffs. But you could not logically compare one feature of the egg, the composition of its yolk, for instance, and another feature of the seed, for example its shape.

Your thesis sentence would be the ideal place in which to point out the basis on which you are comparing the two items or subjects.

Suppose for an English class you decide to contrast two of your favorite short stories. You might have a thesis statement that says, "Although both Mark Twain and Bret Harte are American writers influenced by their experiences in the West, their most important short stories 'The Mysterious Stranger' and 'The Outcasts of Poker Flat' reflect very different outlooks on life." This thesis statement indicates you are going to contrast the two stories. You might point out such differences as Twain's pessimism as opposed to Harte's optimism, and Twain's realistic attitude toward people as contrasted with Harte's sentimental attitude. You could find many more differences, but you give significance to these contrasts on the basis that these men were contemporaries who shared many experiences in their lives which they wrote about. Such a basis of comparison suggests that their work would be similar, not essentially different. Without making such a basis, your thesis statement would say only, "The most important stories of Mark Twain and Bret Harte, "The Mysterious Stranger" and 'The Outcasts of Poker Flat,' are totally different."

Why should it be worthy of comment that two stories are alike or unlike? In this case, considering the two authors' backgrounds, you would expect their stories to be similar; therefore, you have established a basis for making the contrast meaningful.

ORGANIZATION

Once again, your organization will follow the one–two–three development of introduction with thesis statement, body, and conclusion. The comparison–contrast essay, however, requires careful control in the wording of the thesis statement and the development of the body. First of all, you have two subjects rather than the usual one. Furthermore, you must have a clear purpose for the comparison–contrast: You must have a point to make beyond the obvious one of showing likenesses or differences. Providing detailed information on the two subjects is **not** enough. You must make clear to the reader that you are using comparison and contrast **to prove a point.** Telling the reader something that he or she already knows, for example, is pointless. Comparing two items that are obviously

Introduction with Thesis Statement similar (baseball and softball, or two cowboy heroes) or contrasting two items that are obviously different (a car and an airplane, or a steak and a high chair) proves nothing.

An effective thesis statement for a comparison–contrast essay does three things:

1. It names the two subjects being compared or contrasted.
2. It establishes the basis for the comparison or contrast.
3. It indicates what you are trying to demonstrate or prove.

Body You seek to organize the details in the body of the essay in the most effective way to support the purpose indicated in your thesis statement.

TWO BASIC METHODS OF ORGANIZATION

As you have already learned, in all good writing the details are arranged in some sort of logical order. In comparisons and contrasts there are basically two ways to arrange your material:

1. The block method
2. The point-by-point method

Suppose you were contrasting the two greatest generals of the Civil War, Grant and Lee. Using the block method, you would place everything you wanted to say about Grant in one paragraph (one block) and then in the next paragraph (or block) you would put everything you wanted to say about Lee. Arranging the same material point by point, you would discuss each general with respect to one characteristic, one point, and then move on to the next characteristic. You can use either method as long as you are consistent within the paragraph. Don't start with one method and switch to the other within the paragraph.

Let's say you want to develop an essay about two forms of government alien to the United States. You might begin by grouping *contrasting* details under three main headings that establish the basis of the contrast.

Block Method

Thesis Statement.
Although many people in democratic states consider communism and fascism as "bad" forms of government and lump them together, the two systems are actually diametrically opposed in their basic

institutions: who rules, the number one priority, and the prevailing economic system.

A. Communist	**B. Fascist**

1. Who Rules

Oligarchy: a small group of high party officials make the decisions. There is a chair person of this group and often a competition for power within the group.

Dictatorship: one person, the dictator, holds all the power. This person is usually surrounded by a group of individuals to whom power is granted, but they serve at the whim of the dictator who holds all the power.

2. No. 1 Priority

The Masses: according to communist doctrine, everything is done for the good of the masses of people; individuals are unimportant in this form of government.

The State: the country itself is the most important; individuals and the masses are expected to serve the state, and the country.

3. Economic System

Socialistic: the government owns the means of production: the factories and the farms. In true communism, the people (in the form of the government) would also own the means of distribution (wages, salaries, etc.).

Capitalistic: individuals own the means of production but what is produced is determined by state mandate, not the marketplace. The government determines what and how much will be produced.

Interestingly enough, you could also *compare* these two systems.

Point-by-Point Method

Thesis Statement.
While political scientists explain communism as extreme left and fascism as extreme right—opposite ends of the spectrum of government—the nonpolitical individual living under the rule of either type has much in common with the other.

1. People have few rights.
2. They have access to few consumer goods.
3. They have no recourse to justice in the courts.
4. They have no voice in determining their leaders.

In each of these statements you would discuss the two systems, pointing out the similarities.

As in communism and fascism, you could make all your points about communism in one block, then all your points about fascism in an adjoining block.

In the second essay about communism and fascism, for instance, you could explain each basis of comparison or contrast (leadership, priorities, economic system) or (rights, consumer goods, justice, voting privileges) with specific examples, point by point.

A person living in Nazi Germany, one of the best examples of a fascist state, had few rights. A knock on the door at three in the morning could mean the Gestapo was there to arrest someone and drag that person off to some unknown "interrogation center." His or her family would not know where the person was, nor when, if ever, he or she would return. The person's crime could be "making statements against Hitler or the regime," or "listening to the BBC." Those arrested had no defense. Everyone accused was presumed guilty. Young children were taught to spy on their parents and to report any "seditious" actions to the authorities. The word of a six-year-old could send his or her parents, or any individual, to a prison camp or death. There was no appeal. The secret police were not required to prove guilt in court; most "offenders" simply disappeared.

The individual in a communist state also has few rights and no appeals. In Stalinist Russia, people were whisked away to labor camps in Siberia on the basis of rumor and hearsay. Once in the camps, prisoners were subjected to starvation, below-zero temperatures, and arbitrary punishment; their sentences were extended by whim. Stalin once had a man executed because the barking of his dog kept him awake. Prisoners were isolated from family and friends both by physical distance and rules that stated inmates could write home only twice a year. Neither prisoners nor family members had any legal rights to plead their cause. The power of the bureaucrat representing the masses was as absolute as the dictator's.

You must decide which of the two methods you will use in the body of the essay. Remember that in the point-by-point method you compare or contrast the two subjects feature for feature. If you use the block method, you might still discuss the same details, but the organization of your discussion will be different. All of your points about one government will be in one block, then all your points about the other government will be in the next block. Although you discuss the two subjects in separate blocks, you take up similar points about each. Thus the block method is sometimes referred to as the "parallel-order comparison." If you employ parallel order in your development, you are sure to have a clearer and sharper comparison or contrast.

What aspects you choose are up to you, but you must tell the same things about both. You cannot, if you are contrasting cars, deal with the price of one and the performance of the other. Also, your essay must have balance; you cannot give more information on one side than on the other.

In a short essay you usually stick to one method of development, either the point-by-point or block method. In a longer essay, however, you may vary the pattern from paragraph to paragraph. However, you must give systematic and balanced treatment to both subjects.

Conclusion   Because you have **two** subjects instead of one, the comparison—contrast essay calls for careful handling to make the purpose of the essay clear. To describe the two subjects in detail is not enough; you must make the point of your comparison or contrast clear, not leave the reader wondering why you wrote the essay. A good conclusion, then, pulls together the various details of your comparison or contrast and reemphasizes your purpose—to show, for example, that A is more practical than B, that A is more economical than B, or that A is inferior in some respects to B. The conclusion to the essay comparing fascism and communism might read like this:

> So, whether they live in a communist state or a fascist state, individuals are powerless. They cannot vote for or against the dictator or the party leaders. They face shortages of food and clothing and other consumer goods because communist governments stress building industry (capital goods) and fascist governments stress the military (guns over butter). They have few rights because one system stresses the importance of the masses and the other the importance of the state. No matter which of the "opposite" types of governments individuals live in, the effects are the same for ordinary citizens, the common people.

Here is a student essay that contrasts two historical characters.

··

THE DAYS OF WINE AND EMPERORS

··

In the past two hundred years, two men have surveyed the fractious and fragmented vineyard that is Europe and have known the intoxicating exhilaration of being its absolute master. Both were immigrants to their seats of power. Both came legally to power on the pretext of providing stability in the midst of unprecedented chaos. Both used nationalism to uncork the dormant fighting qualities of their countries. Both cultivated battlefield victory by implementing new tactics. Both were ultimately pruned by the sharp shears of a Russian winter. Indeed, Napoleon Bonaparte and Adolph Hitler manifest a similiar historical background. A close examination of their personal lives, their administrative accomplishments, and their historical legacies reveals, however, that Napoleon had the historic effect of a fine wine and Hitler had the impact of a bottle of Tiger Rose, a cheap high followed by a monstrous hangover.

In their character, these men mirrored the traditional image of their adopted nations. Napoleon exemplified the French love of dress, of smart women, of military and political opportunism. Hitler, an Austrian, shared the native German traits of angst, asceticism, austerity, and antagonism.

Nevertheless, their differences were greater. During their respective military successes, Napoleon repeatedly credited victory to his Gallic people and their revolution of 1789. Meanwhile Hitler maintained that Nazi supremacy created the German battlefield glory.

Yet their failures were most telling proofs of each man's character. Realizing that he was tilting at windmills after the Battle of Leipzig, Napoleon abdicated to spare France the ravages of fighting for an impossible dream. By this action, he rewarded those who had served him so loyally. In brutal contrast, Adolf Hitler spent the last days of 1945 in his Berlin bunker issuing vituperative orders for a scorched earth policy for Germany and cursing the German people for being unworthy of his self-proclaimed greatness.

Even though Napoleon and Hitler are best known for their military exploits, their administrative and legislative achievements underscore their differences. The Little General instituted the first mandatory public school system in European history. The Fuhrer's innovation in German education was the re-introduction of the discredited theory of racial purity and Aryan supremacy.

On the legal front, Bonoparte's progressive bent is his establishment of the Napoleonic Code of law. This fiat swept away the antiquated system of justice by class and established the egalitatian principle of "All men are legal equals". On the other hand, Hitler hoisted the regressive banner of martial law, secret police, and persecution.

At most levels of the First Empire, Napoleon introduced the concept of a meritocracy, whereas Hitler counted Nazi loyalty as the highest qualification for office in the Third Reich. Napoleon's policies have been refined to meet the exigencies of the modern world while Hitler's heritage has harvested the grapes of wrath.

Even their last public utterances separate these two meglomaniac dictators who had such great influence on the course of Western Civilization. Napoleon said, "I wish my ashes to rest on the banks of the Seine, in the midst of the French people whom I have loved so much". Hitler, on the other hand, raved, "Our revolution will never be complete until we have dehumanized human beings," and "The German people are not worthy of me . . . let them perish."

By their own words are these two men deified or damned in the judgment of history. Their historical legacies of domestic innovations are more important than their better known military adventures.

Bob Pfeiffer
(student)

PITFALLS TO AVOID

1. Avoid an unbalanced, one-sided comparison. Almost always, you need to give relatively equal space to the two subjects being compared or contrasted. For instance, if you compare a novel with the movie adaptation, you need to provide equal treatment for both the novel and the movie.

2. Avoid seesaw style. You need to use adequate transition so that you don't just jump back and forth from one subject to another in a series of short, choppy sentences.

3. Just showing the differences or similarities between A and B is not enough. Your comparison—contrast essay must serve a useful purpose: to show, for example, that A is superior to B or that B is more practical than A.

4. Watch out for false comparison, that is, a few superficial similarities leading to a false conclusion. If you were to compare the Soviet bureaucracy with the American bureaucracy, no doubt you could find a number of similarities; but you would need to be careful not to ignore fundamental differences, for you might easily arrive at a false conclusion.

5. Don't equivocate: Have a clear point to make, and state it clearly at the outset. If you start your essay with "There are many similarities and differences between the North and the South," that thesis is useless because you fail to take a stand. You leave your reader asking, "So what? What's the point?"

6. Don't state the obvious. Comparing two obviously similar members of the same class or contrasting two obviously different members of the same class is pointless. Your reader will learn nothing.

EXERCISE 6A: BASES OF COMPARING

Put the following sets of items into a class that will indicate their relationships to each other. Express this relationship in a thesis statement for a possible essay developed by comparison–contrast.

Example:

poet, musician
Relationship: Both are artists.
Thesis statement: Through their art, both the poet and the musician attempt to reflect the life around them.

1. Heavy metal, punk rock

Relationship _____

Thesis statement _____

_____

2. An old-fashioned market, a supermarket

Relationship _____

Thesis statement _____

_____

3. Well-dressed twenty years ago, well-dressed today

Relationship _____

Thesis statement _____

_____

4. Today's toys, yesterday's toys

Relationship _____

Thesis statement _____

_____

5. Modern dance, ballet

Relationship _____

Thesis statement _____

_____

6. Portraits, photographs

Relationship _____

Thesis statement _____

_____

7. Football fans, concert enthusiasts

Relationship _____

Thesis statement _____

_____

8. My father, his twin brother (or some appropriate relative)

Relationship _____

Thesis statement _____

_____

9. Reality, TV news

Relationship _____

Thesis statement _____

_____

10. A required course, an elective

Relationship _____

Thesis statement _____

_____

SUGGESTED TOPICS

Choose a subject from the following list or an approved subject of your own and write an essay developed by comparison or contrast.

1. Two athletes
2. Rich people/poor people
3. Two pets
4. Two actors
5. Two friends
6. Two news broadcasters
7. Two writers
8. Heavy metal, punk rock
9. Two jobs
10. Two newspapers
11. Two schools
12. Two relatives
13. Two types of diets
14. Two approaches to coaching
15. Two religions
16. Two ways to discipline children
17. Japanese industrial policy/ U.S. industrial policy
18. Two methods of childbirth
19. Two branches of the service
20. Two types of motorcycles
21. Two attitudes toward death
22. Two types of students
23. Masculinity/Femininity
24. Two types of comedy
25. Two types of architecture
26. Women's rights/then and now
27. Divorce laws/then and now

28. Eating habits yesterday/ today
29. Workers' rights/then and now
30. Telephones old/new
31. Attitudes toward work/then and now
32. Movie-making/then and now
33. The lawyer/the politician
34. Education/then and now
35. Political campaigns/then and now
36. Foreign cars/American cars
37. World War II vets/Vietnam vets
38. College courses 50 years ago/ today
39. Mandatory retirement/ voluntary retirement
40. Single life/married life
41. Computer Scientist/Engineer
42. Book/movie of the book
43. Open-door policy/entrance requirements
44. Practical nurse/registered nurse
45. Old movie theaters/modern cinemas
46. Grandpas/then and now
47. Two mothers-in-law
48. Two ways of dealing with failure
49. Two ways of dealing with success
50. Two presidential styles

TECHNIQUES OF CLEAR WRITING

COMPARISONS WITHIN THE SENTENCE

Because you constantly compare and contrast things, it's important that you know how to do it correctly.

First, you should recognize the three basic degrees of comparison:

Positive:	She was a smart woman.
Comparative:	She was smarter than Saul.
Superlative:	She was the smartest student in the class.

Notice that with most regular adjectives of one syllable you add *-er* if you are comparing one with one and *-est* if you are comparing one with more than one:

Positive	Comparative	Superlative
friendly	friendlier	friendliest
big	bigger	biggest
lonely	lonelier	loneliest
rich	richer	richest
busy	busier	busiest
bright	brighter	brightest

If the adjective has two syllables, you have a choice of *-er* and *-est,* or *more* and *most* (or *less* and *least*).

If the adjective has three or more syllables, you form the comparison with *more* (or *less*) and the superlative with *most* (or *least*).

These rules also apply to the comparison of adverbs.

beautiful	*more* beautiful	*most* beautiful
confusing	*more* confusing	*most* confusing
disturbed	*more* disturbed	*most* disturbed
nervous	*more* nervous	*most* nervous
intelligent	*more* intelligent	*most* intelligent

Watch out for incomplete, confusing, or illogical comparisons as in the following sections.

Incomplete Comparisons

If you remember that a comparison always establishes a relationship between *two* or more items, you can avoid incomplete comparisons such as the following:

INCOMPLETE:
My dog is better. [Better than what?]

CORRECT:
My dog is better than your dog.

INCOMPLETE:
I was so tired. [So tired that what?]

CORRECT:
I was so tired that I couldn't do my homework. (*So* requires a *that* clause, as does *such*.]

INCOMPLETE:
He was as **tall** or **taller** than George.

You would not say "He is as tall than George."
The sentence could be corrected in three ways:

He is as tall as or taller than George.
He is as tall as George or taller [than George].
He is as tall as George, if not taller.

Confusing Comparisons

Some comparisons confuse rather than clarify because they suggest two possible meanings. Always make sure that your reader knows what specific things are being compared. Look at the following examples:

INCORRECT:
I like my dog better than my husband.

Words are left out here, and the result is that the reader doesn't know whether you mean:

> I like my dog better than my husband does.
> I like my dog better than I like my husband.

The wording does make a difference.

Illogical Comparisons

To avoid comparisons that are ridiculous or make no sense at all, you must make sure that the items being compared have a logical basis of comparison. They must belong to the same class of things in order to make the comparison meaningful. Proofread your papers carefully to correct illogical comparisons like these:

> My dog was cheaper than my father.

Surely, the dog was not that cheap! What the writer probably meant was that his dog was "cheaper than his father's dog" or "cheaper than his father's."

> The price of steak here is higher than Texas.

You cannot compare *steak* with *Texas*. What was probably meant was

> The price of steak here is higher than **it is in** Texas.
> Hershel Walker is better than any football player.

Hershel is a football player; how can he be better than himself?

> Hershel Walker is better than any **other** football player.

EXERCISE 6B: CORRECT COMPARISONS

Revise the following sentences to make the comparisons clear and correct.

1. *L.A. Law* is better than any show on TV.

_____

2. He was the better of all the athletes who competed in the decathlon.

_____

3. Sam was so nervous.

_____

4. Tyson is better than any boxer.

_____

5. Dan Rather is as unbiased or more unbiased than Walter Cronkite. _____

6. Jim rated his Chrysler New Yorker as good or better than his wife.

_____

7. Sociology is more interesting than any class.

_____

8. The number of professional athletes from Pennsylvania is larger than Texas.

_____

9. Between Hershel Walker and Tim Worley, Walker will be the most outstanding.

_____

10. On the basketball court, Brian's arms look longer than a gorilla.

_____

11. Rosetta's pies are bigger and better and tastier.

_____

12. When I started teaching, my pay was lower than a paper boy.

_____

13. Oz pop tastes better and costs less.

_____

14. I wouldn't bet that my next car costs even more.

_____

15. Soames couldn't tempt Samantha because her fiance was as gifted or more gifted than Soames was.

WORD POWER

METAPHOR: A SPECIAL TYPE OF COMPARISON

Metaphor is a type of comparison, special in several ways.

1. It almost always compares; it almost never contrasts. In a famous poem, Christina Rosetti uses the metaphor "My heart is like a singing bird." The poet means that she is so happy that she feels as if her heart were a singing bird. This makes good, if not literal, sense. But if she contrasted the image to, say, "My heart is not like a singing bird", her image would be so obvious as to be senseless.

2. Metaphor is not a literal or actual comparison; it is imaginative, where one subject is known and literal, whereas the second subject is unfamiliar and only suggestive of meaning. Consider, for example, the comparison in the title of Bach's hymn "A Mighty Fortress Is Our God." Here *fortress* is a term for a tangible thing, one that can be perceived through the five senses, but *God* is a term for an intangible concept that can be appreciated only through faith.

3. Metaphor need not be based on a comparison of two totally unlike things such as *fortress* and *God*. A statement also becomes metaphorical when the meaning of the first subject is "extended", that is, the meaning of the word stretches to mean other things. For example, the word *jaws* indicated originally only the hinged, bony structure at the bottom of the facial skeleton. Then the word extended to ideas *resembling* the first meaning: the jaws of gorge, the jaws of death. It also has a slang meaning based on a function of the jaw, to jaw in the sense of to jabber.

The great majority of words have one or more extended meanings. Indeed, language normally grows by metaphorical extension of meanings. Notice, for instance, how many very simple words have extended to other meanings: the *eye* of a needle or a potato or a storm, the *toe* of a boot, the *foot* of a mountain or a tree or a page, the *leg* of a table, the *heel* of a loaf of bread, the *bed* of a river or of flowers, the *head* and *foot* of a bed and of a flight of stairs. The extended meaning is a "resemblance."

The History and Importance of Metaphor

Metaphor goes back at least to the ancient Greeks. The word means a "transferring", a "carrying across" of ideas. Aristotle said that "to employ metaphors happily and effectively" was the greatest skill in writing, and, to do so, it was necessary "to have an eye for resemblances."

Modern scholarship confirms Aristotle's belief in the function and importance of metaphor. A great contemporary scholar, I. A. Richards, says, "We all live and speak only through 'our eye for resemblances.' As individuals we gain our command of metaphor just as we learn whatever else makes us distinctively human." Thus ancient and modern scholarship unite in their thinking that the uses of metaphor are basic to human intelligence.

Metaphor is not merely a device to make writing effective and attractive, like a medal on a tunic or a frill on a shirt. Many metaphors do provide illustration; almost all intensify emotion. When Robert Burns wished to say how very homesick he felt, he intensified his emotion by metaphor:

> *My heart's in the highlands,*
> *My heart is not here.*
> *My heart's in the highlands*
> *'a chasing the deer,*
> *'a chasing the wild deer,*
> *And following the roe,*
> *My heart's in the highlands,*
> *Wherever I go.*

Here is an excellent metaphor of illustration by Mark Twain:

First and general subject	We should be careful to get out of an experience only the wisdom that is in it - and stop there,
Illustration	lest we be like the cat that sits on a hot stove lid. She will never sit down on a hot stove lid again - and that is well, but also she will never sit down on a cold one.

Metaphor as intensification of emotion and as illustration is important, but in its essential function, it is much more than that. It has been called "the matrix of thought" when we recognize the resemblances of things. *It is thinking itself when we arrive at a new idea made up of our subjects one and two.*

The importance of metaphor is revealed when it is observed that metaphor is contained in all usage except the abstractions of science. It has been seriously maintained that a writer cannot get through three sentences without using metaphor. Of course, in scientific writing, communication does not even require language but can show meaning in such notations as $2 + 2 = 4$ or $E = MC^2$.

In all other writing—fiction, poetry, drama, political addresses, sermons, lectures, articles, letters (especially love letters), essays, metaphor is a primary device of expression. It is no mere decoration nor addition but an essential tool for interpreting experience.

MIXED METAPHORS

Some metaphors are dubbed "mixed" or "confused" because the two subjects are so unlike that there can be no reasonable similarity between them. Such unlike subjects from totally disparate categories usually make your metaphors absurd, although readers with a taste for hilarity may laugh a lot.

Metaphors are of two types, slightly different in form: The *implied* ("You are my sunshine"), which says that *A* is *B,* and the *explicit,* which says that *A* is like *B* ("My love is like a red, red rose"). The implied metaphor, in which the first subject is assumed but not expressed, is dangerous for unwary writers, for it is extremely easy for anyone to "mix" incongruous images. Here are a handful, most of them from well-known people:

1. The sacred cows have come home to roost with a vengeance.
2. That's a very hard blow to swallow.
3. Don't sit there like a sore thumb.
4. It's as easy as falling off a piece of cake.
5. It's time to swallow the bullet.
6. I was so surprised that you could have knocked me over with a fender.
7. He was a very astute politician with both ears glued to the grindstone.
8. That guy's out to butter his own nest.
9. You can take Mohammed to the mountain, but you can't make him drink.
10. Mr. Speaker, I smell a rat. I see it floating in the air; and if it is not nipped in the bud, it will burst forth into a terrible conflagration that will deluge the world. (This gem has lasted since 1801 when a Member of Parliament announced it. Since then many delighted readers have enjoyed this multiple error in mixed metaphor.)

EXERICSE 6C: MIXED METAPHORS

In the preceding list of mixed metaphors, identify the two incongruous elements in each example. Also, determine the implied first subject.

Example

He's like a duck out of water.

Since you don't know the context of the above example, you don't know why "he" is in an embarrassing situation. But he obviously is. However, the metaphor is mixed because a duck out of water is almost as capable as a duck in water. It's the *fish* out of water that is in desperate straits.

Mixed metaphors result when metaphorical terms from two different sources are combined in one half of the comparison, one subject. As you have noticed, the effect of this is usually incongruity and absurdity. Occasionally, however, the effect is superb. For example, Hamlet, reflecting on suicide, muses whether he should "take up arms against a sea of troubles,/ And by opposing end them." When poetry is this good even thoughtful readers pay no attention to mixed metaphor. However, you had best make sure that you write as well as Shakespeare before you try it.

ANALOGIES AND METAPHORS

Both analogies and metaphors are nonliteral comparisons. In everyday usage they seem almost synonymous, yet they have differences that are helpful to understand. The *analogy* is based on science; the *metaphor* on imagination. The analogy is arrived at by reason; the metaphor by intuition. The analogy is judged good or weak by its validity; the metaphor by its perceived truth.

If in science and philosophy when you are comparing two things, you notice that qualities *a,b,c,d* and *e* are alike, you may *assume by analogy* that qualities *f* and *g* are also alike. However, in writing, the comparison grows more flexible and, in practice, the distinction between analogy and metaphor is difficult to make.

A traditional example to explain analogy in this freer sense is this: "Knowledge is to the mind what light is to the eye." That is, knowledge, which is *enlightment,* is light to the mind just as physical light is light to the eye.

There is even a formula to express an analogy. It is stated a:b::c:?. The relationship of *a* is to *b* as the relationship of *c* is to *some unknown,* which unknown, you, in writing your analogy, will explain. For instance, pup:dog::boy:man; or painter:art::novelist:fiction.

War and football obviously fall into separate categories, but the game of football resembles the "game" of war. Both a coach and a general talk in terms of victory and defeat. Both use blitzes and secret weapons and front-line reinforcements to plan offensive and defensive strategies. Both train their players to defend the flanks and crush the opposition.

EXAMPLES OF EXTENDED ANALOGY

In his book *Physics for Technicians,* Ernest Zebrowski simplifies a difficult concept (the radioactive decay process) by comparing it to a more understandable analogy.

> There is still one thing we have to add to get a complete picture of the radioactive decay process. We might start with a question: If the heavy radioactive nuclei are constantly disintegrating into simpler nuclei, how do we explain the presence of any heavy radioactive substances in nature? Why haven't they all disintegrated?
>
> The answer is that most of them have. Only a relative few can be found in the earth's crust. These naturally occurring radioactive nuclei are unstable, to be sure, but they are not as unstable as the other radioactive nuclei that have long since disappeared from nature. We might envision the process as follows: suppose we have a flat table and a pile of coins containing 100 nickels, 100 dimes, and 100 pennies. We stand all of these coins on their edges, not too close together, and we leave the room. Of course, the coins are in an unstable position, but the dimes are more unstable than the pennies, which in turn are more unstable than the nickels. If we return to the room a few hours later, we might find that a large number of dimes have fallen over. A smaller number of pennies will have toppled, and very few nickels. If left alone for a few days, all the dimes may have fallen while a majority of nickels still stand. The coins on the table are very similar to what happens in a mixture of three different radioactive substances. The most unstable substance decays very quickly, while the others decay at slower rates.

Among literary examples, there are many allegories, parables, and fables. In these forms there are close resemblances between the first and second subjects. Consider the pleasing fable from Aesop about the City Mouse and the Country Mouse.

> Once upon a time a Country Mouse invited his old friend in the city to visit him in the country. The City Mouse accepted the invitation. To honor his friend's visit, the Country Mouse

served all of his stored up food———dried peas, corn, cheese-parings, and nuts. But the City Mouse had tastes far fancier than such things.

He exclaimed to his friend, "How can you bear to live in such a dismal place as this! You are living like a toad in a hole! You are wasting your time here. We must make the most of life. A mouse, you know, does not live forever. Come with me and I'll show you real life."

Overwhelmed by his friend, the Country Mouse agreed and they set off for the City. They crept stealthily into the outskirts late in the evening and reached the City Mouse's home close to midnight. It was beautiful—simply splendid!

On the dining table there were the remains of a great feast with plenty of the choicest foods. Now it was the turn of the City Mouse to play host, so he served his friend with all the delicious delicacies—cavier and smoked salmon and rare roast beef. The Country Mouse made himself quite at home and nibbled on all the good things, thinking how lucky he was to be made welcome by his friend.

Suddenly, just as he was musing with contempt on his old life, the door banged open and the party goers returned. Both frightened mice leaped from the table and cowered in the nearest corner. When finally the mice dared to peak out, they were almost captured by a resident cat.

In the middle of the night, when at last all was quiet, the Country Mouse stole out of their hiding place and bade the City Mouse good-by. "Thank you, my friend, but I must go home. This fine life suits some very well. Nevertheless, I prefer a simple life without worries. I cannot live even a splendid life if it is filled with fear." And he set off cheerfully for the country.

WE ARE KILLING THE EARTH

We, the human beings on the planet Earth, should be the custodians of the planet, taking care of it and handing it on to future generations. Much like caring parents watch over and nurture their babies, we must watch over and nurture earth. Instead, we are killing the planet we depend upon for our own lives. If we were parents and earth were our child, we would certainly be jailed for child abuse. However, because it will take a long time before we complete the murder, people today are unaware, unconcerned. In many ways, the planet is like a baby. Like a baby it cannot talk; it cannot tell us what is wrong, what hurts. We have to look for signs, clues as to what is wrong. If a baby screams, or throws up or flails about or is restless or listless, a diligent parent realizes something is wrong and searches for the cause. Likewise the planet has shown symptoms. There have been devastating forest fires: 1.38 million of Yellowstone National Park's 2.2 million acres burned despite the efforts of 10,000 firefighters from all over the nation; 18 million acres of the Soviet Chinese border were destroyed; an area of Amazon rain forest the size of Nebraska was charred. Last summer was the hottest and driest since the dust bowl. Farmers in the U.S. lost $15 billion in unharvestable crops. The Ohio River, ordinarily a third of a mile wide, dwindled to less than 30 yards, forcing barges to travel single file in lines 100 miles long. Hurricane Gilbert, which lashed Mexico and Texas, had winds that reached 175 miles per hour and the lowest barometric pressure ever recorded in this hemisphere. Hurricane Joan smashed into Latin America leaving 300,000 homeless. Are the caretakers of the planet looking for a cause?

If the diligent parent finds that the baby's temperature has risen above normal, he calls a doctor and follows orders. He may give the baby antibiotics, aspirin, or cool baths, depending on what the doctor has deemed the cause of the temperature because he knows there can be serious consequences to a high fever. Earth has a temperature; there is a global warming (the Greenhouse Effect). If the temperature continues to rise, which the National Society of Sciences predicts, by the year 2100 the grain belts of the world in Asia and North America could no longer produce grain, and the world would face starvation. Also, according to Carl Sagan, all the coastal cities on the planet would be flooded. What is the cause of this rise in temperature? We know the cause; it is the burning of coal, oil, and natural gas, which produces carbon dioxide. Are we cutting back on the use of the fuels? No. One cure is to plant trees; they ingest carbon dioxide and exude oxygen. What are we doing? We are "permitting the destruction worldwide, of an acre of forest every second."

What if a parent poisoned a son or a daughter, not with something quick and violent like strychnine, but a little at a time—just slow doses of poison that damaged parts of the body: the stomach, the kidneys, the lungs. That's what the custodians of the planet are doing. The ozone layer, which protects us from the dangerous rays of the sun, is being destroyed by industrial chemicals. Over half of Germany's forests are dying from acid rain as are the forests and lakes of our own Northeast. Deforestation in India and Nepal caused the flood in

Bangladesh that killed thousands and left over 25 million homeless.

Ten percent of our rivers are heavily polluted and over a billion urban human beings breathe heavily polluted air. And here it comes together. The custodians of the planet are, as they kill the planet, killing their children at the same time. As the child breathes the poisoned air and drinks the poisoned water, goes hungry because the grain belt has been destroyed, moves inland because the coastal cities are flooded, faces death from the sun's deadly rays and the storms and floods and other disasters caused by decades of abuse, the child will surely die.

EXERCISE 6D: METAPHORS AND ANALOGIES

Here are some well-known metaphors and analogies from famous poets. Read them carefully to determine what each writer wanted to explain. Notice that the final quotation, number 10, is an "extended metaphor" in which one element of the metaphor occurs in each stanza.

1. "You were that all to me, love, for which my heart did pine,
   A green isle in the sea, love, a fountain and a shrine . . . "

   Edgar Allen Poe

2. "The birthday of my life is come,
   Because my love has come to me."

   Christina Rossetti

3. "Home is the hunter, home from the hill.
   And the sailor home from the sea."

   Robert Louis Stevenson

4. ". . . . All the world's a stage,
   And all the men and women merely players. . . . "

   Shakespeare

5. " 'Tis with our judgments as with our watches, none goes just alike, yet each believes his own."

   Alexander Pope

6. "Think of the storm roaming the sky uneasily like a dog looking for a place to sleep in, listen to it growling."

   Elizabeth Bishop

7. "Fair as a star, when only one
   Is shining in the sky."

   William Wordsworth

8. "How far that little candle throws its beam!
   So shines a good deed in a naughty world."

   Shakespeare

9. "He was like the cock who thought the sun had risen to hear him crow."

George Eliot

10. "Does the road wind up-hill all the way?
Yes, to the very end.
Will the day's journey take the whole long day?
From morn to night, my friend.

But is there for the night a resting-place?
A roof for when the slow dark hours begin.
May not the darkness hide it from my face?
You cannot miss that inn.

Shall I meet other wayfarers at night?
Those who have gone before.
Then must I knock, or call when just in sight?
They will not keep you waiting at that door.

Shall I find comfort, travel-sore and weak?
Of labour you shall find the sum.
Will there be beds for me and all who seek?
Yes, beds for all who come.

Christina Rossetti

CHAPTER 7

Dividing and Classifying

In the last chapter it was said that comparison was so natural a process that it was a characteristic of our humanity. That is equally true of our process of dividing and classifying; it too is a natural mental activity. It is a human need to create *order* out of the disorder, the *chaos* that surrounds us.

DIVISION AND CLASSIFICATION

Classification is a basic way of organizing knowledge. It is a filing system. However, it is a filing system with a difference: each *class* within the *classification system* is united by the qualities that make up that class. For example, suppose you have the class boats; that class is not made up of one boat after another in an entire parade of boats. The class boat is made up of boatness, the qualities that characterize boats; it does not consist of individual boats. The qualities that constitute boatness define the class boats. In a more technical sense, you might define a class as a number of significant characteristics that all members of the class share. *Significant characteristics* raise another aspect of classifying—your audience. For instance, suppose you were trying to identify the class of trees. The significant characteristics of *tree* would vary with your audience. What would be the significant characteristics of the tree to (a) a landscape gardner, (b) a forester, (c) a botanist, (d) a cabinet maker, (e) an environmentalist?

GROUPINGS BECOME INCREASINGLY NARROWED AND SPECIALIZED

Without the ability to *divide and classify* information, nothing would make sense because nothing would be organized, nothing would be categorized, nothing would reveal its relationship to anything else. Indeed, one of the first things you learned to do as an infant was to organize what you were learning, break it down (divide it), and place it in specific categories (classify it).

Probably one of the first things you ever noticed was that some few faces were familiar and pleasant to you, while all the others were unfamiliar and possibly threatening. Later, your infant brain would distinguish among tastes and smells and sounds. When you were recognizing sounds, you might have first distinguished between human sounds and mechanical sounds:

Human Sounds	Mechanical Sounds
crying	cars
talking	train whistles
laughing	planes
shouting	bells
singing	musical instruments

As you grew older, you learned that each sound could be broken down further. For example, you learned to classify different kinds of musical instruments; you learned to distinguish a drum from a horn and a horn from a piano. As an adult, you divide and classify more complex information, but you are still doing basically the same thing you did as an infant when you were learning to distinguish one sound from another:

1. Dividing information into parts
2. Classifying those parts by placing them in logical categories

Our first attempts at dividing and classifying are crude, and the lines of division may be blurred, as when a child classifies all dogs as big, middle-sized, and puppies. Later, division and classification become more complex; dogs, for example, are seen to be divided in various types and classified according to a variety of characteristics.

Finally, you have the specific and exacting kind of classification used by professionals in every branch of science.

Geologists, for instance, divide geologic time into five vast eras, the Archeozoic, the Proterozoic, the Paleozoic, the Mesozoic, and the Cenozoic. They also divide time itself into three classifications: sideral time, or time measured by the stars; solar time, or time measured by the sun; historic time, or time measurable by humanity's existence. All of these classifications can be subdivided. For example, geologists divide rocks into two primary classes—bedrock and overmantle, bedrock is the solid rock and overmantle is the broken rock and sand that usually lie on the surface of the earth. The broken rock can again be subdivided into three classes. These subdivisions can go on and on.

Such scientific classification is totally comprehensive. For example, when a biologist classifies animals, **every** creature in the entire animal kingdom is considered. Nonscientific classifications, which are called "literary" or informal, do not try to be all-inclusive. Nevertheless, their aim is the same. They clarify complexity by showing it classification by classification and subdivision by subdivision. They bring order out of chaos.

Poets as well as scientists use classification. For example, almost every creation story tells how the creator made the world by dividing chaos into parts and identifying, through classification, each part. Here is the poet Ovid explaining the Roman version of creation. Notice how he portrays the creator making an understandable and livable world by breaking down chaos, where everything is confusedly mixed together, into its parts:

....

THE CREATION
....

Before the ocean was, or earth, or heaven,
Nature was all alike, a shapelessness,
Chaos, so-called, all rude and lumpy matter
Nothing but bulk, inert, in whose confusion
Discordant atoms warred: there was no sun
To light the universe; there was no moon
With slender silver crescents filling slowly;
No earth hung balanced in surrounding air;
No sea reached far along the fringe of shore.
Land, to be sure, there was, and air, and ocean,
But land on which no man could stand, and water
No man could swim in, air no man could breathe.

Till God, or kindlier Nature,
Settled all argument, and separated

Heaven from earth, water from land, our air
From the high stratosphere.
So things evolved, and out of blind confusion
Found each its place, bound in eternal order.

Whatever god it was, who out of chaos
Brought order to the universe, and gave it
Division, subdivision, he molded earth,
In the beginning, into a great globe,
Even on every side, and bade the waters
To spread and rise, under the rushing winds.

These boundaries given,
Behold, the stars, long hidden under darkness,
Broke through and shone, all over the spangled heaven,
Their home forever, and the gods lived there,
And shining fish were given the waves for dwelling
And beasts the earth, and birds the moving air.

Rolfe Humphries
(Translator)

Many ideas that you might consider good possible subjects require you to divide them into more easily handled smaller parts. For example, if you decide to write your essay on "Liars I Have Known," you might divide your topic into four types. The first type is the liars who are afraid of the consequences of something they have or haven't done. The second type deals in untruth to impress the audience with how important he or she is. The third type is the polite lie: "Your speech was brilliant, boss," or "That's a fine old car, son." The final type tells the lie simply to make the story funnier; they will never let the truth interfere with a good story.

You must be sure that you have used a single principle for your division. If you say, "There are four basic sleeping positions, each of which gives a clue to the sleeper's personality," then it would not be correct, for example, to include in your division of sleeping positions "those who dream," because those who dream could sleep in any of the given positions.

If you were to write an essay on the Olympics, you might begin by dividing the general subject into smaller parts or divisions, such as Individual Sports, Paired Sports, and Team Sports. Then you could develop each part systematically by classifying individual, paired, and team sports according to the skills needed, the method of judging the participants, or whatever one classifying principle best suits your purpose.

Just think for a moment about the many ways recipes can

be—and are—divided and classified. Suppose you are newly married and have been given the task of cooking for friends. Your family has given you 1,000 tried and true recipes. You are profoundly grateful to them, but you realize that, if the recipes are to help you, they will have to be organized. You cannot go through 1,000 recipes every time you must prepare a meal.

You decide to divide the recipes into breakfast, lunch, and dinner. You find you have one breakfast recipe (seasoned scrambled eggs), three possible lunch recipes, and 996 dinner dishes. As you begin to look into the possibilities, you see that there are hundreds, perhaps thousands, of ways recipes can be classified. Here are a few:

length of time needed to prepare: days, hours, minutes

food groups: protein, carbohydrates, sugars, starches

courses: appetizers, soups, salads, entrees, desserts

temperature: hot, room temperature, cold, frozen

origin: European, Asian, South American, African, American

cost: expensive, moderate, inexpensive

types: meats, vegetables, breads, fruits, fish, fowl, eggs

number of people: the two of us, small dinner party, large buffet

All of these can be subdivided, of course. Meats can be divided into beef, veal, lamb, pork, ham, bacon, mutton, internal meats, and game. Even game can be further divided. *Game:* rabbit, deer, bear.

Of course, if there is a dieter in the family, you will also classify your recipes as

high caloric, medium caloric, low caloric

If there is a health problem, you might also classify your meals as

high cholesterol, medium cholesterol, low cholesterol

or

high fat, medium fat, low fat

or

high salt, medium salt, low salt

Maybe the most important classification is *dishes I really like, dishes I like a little, dishes I hate.*

You could think of many many other ways to classify these recipes. Some people might use amount of time it takes to clean up after the meal or how good the dish *looks.*

As you can see, dividing and classifying is a necessary skill, and it is used constantly in our everyday lives.

ORGANIZATION

Like all the other types of writing we have studied, division and classification is organized on the three-part structure of (1) introduction and thesis statement, (2) the developed body of the essay, and (3) the conclusion.

Division and classification, as a mode of writing, is a purposeful grouping of things, activities, or ideas. If the process is to be of any significant meaning, you must divide and classify according to some sensible ruling principle. This ruling principle will be expressed in your thesis statement. Suppose you have decided to write about animals. You might divide them, *at the first stage*, into wild and domestic animals. These classes are far too large to write about, so you choose a narrower class and move *to the second stage* of classification; among domestic animals you choose between work animals and pets. This classification still is too broad so you change again into *the third stage*—pets. Among this class you have primarily dogs, cats, birds, fish, and other water creatures. From these you might select dogs to write about, creating *a fourth stage*, and then breeds of dogs, which is your *fifth stage.* Thus, your classifying system would look like this:

Stage 1—Wild Animals . . . Domestic Animals

Stage 2—Work Animals . . . Pets

Stage 3—Cats, Dogs, Birds, Fish

Stage 4—Working Dogs, Hunting Dogs, Toys

Stage 5—Hounds, Terriers, Spaniels, Retrievers

Dividing and classifying, thus, is not just dividing into two subjects (because that is comparison and contrast) but is a series of classifications. You can enter the system *at any stage;* perhaps you have determined to start your essay with stage five. Your thesis statement might read something like this: "Of the dozens of types of hunting dogs in America, four breeds are the most popular." Then you go on to explain why the four chosen breeds are the best. As you do that, breed by breed for all four, you develop the body of your paper.

You have only one consideration in this classifying system: you must be certain that you are classifying on only one principle. You could not justify putting a breed of hunting cats among your dogs.

You keep things simple for your readers by providing transitions between the classes in your system and among the classes in each stage.

Suppose that you have been reading about hostages seized by terrorists and you decide that hostages might be a good subject to write about. Now there are many possible approaches to that subject, but assume that you decide to concentrate on what happens to the people who are held hostage. After giving the subject a little thought, you might decide to further limit your discussion to those who are held for prolonged periods—not just for an hour or two, but for weeks or months.

After more reading and thinking about hostages held by terrorist groups, you might find that you have a good many notes which could look like this:

1. Helpless and dependent
2. Threat of violence and death hanging over
3. Physical wearing down—weight loss, etc.
4. Agony of uncertainty—at hands of the desperate and unpredictable
5. Existing ailments made worse
6. Confinement and restricted movement taking a toll
7. May develop deep-seated illness (infections, heart and circulation trouble, etc.)
8. Cut off from friends, family, and rest of society—lacking their love and support
9. Effect on health for rest of life
10. Suffer from "flashbacks"—agonizing nightmares, etc.

To bring some semblance of order to your random notes, you might first of all divide them into two groups: (1) physical effects, and (2) mental effects of being held captive.

Then you could start sorting out your notes according to these two main divisions:

A. Physical effects of prolonged confinement
   1. Effects of close confinement and restricted physical activity
   2. Physical deterioration that sets in
   3. Existing ailments made worse by confinement
   4. Deep-seated illnesses that develop from stress
   5. Physical effect continuing after release

B. Psychological effects of prolonged confinement
 1. Continuing fear of violence and death
 2. Agonizing uncertainty of a fate unknown
 3. Utter helplessness, isolation, and dependence
 4. Complete separation from family, friends, and society
 5. Torment of flashbacks following release

Note that each point has been refined and sharpened as you progressed.

What you have done up to this point is to **divide** your subject into two parts according to separate but related bases—physical and mental. Further, you have **classified** these physical and mental effects in a fairly systematic way.

Introduction Because everything changes as it moves, you may find it necessary to change the order of certain points as you develop your essay. The important thing is that you have a track to run on, a sensible plan for developing your essay. What you need to do now is to define your purpose. What is it that you want to prove or demonstrate with the information you have gathered? Perhaps you would like your reader to understand the various types of physical punishment and mental torture that hostages undergo. If so, you might use an introduction such as this:

> Over the past decade, more than forty attacks have been made on diplomatic missions in various parts of the world. To terrorists and guerrillas of whatever stripe, American embassies and diplomatic missions seem inviting targets, for Americans make valuable hostages. Sometimes the hostages, whether embassy personnel or American business people seized for ransom, are released after brief periods of negotiations; but some have been held for weeks, months, or years. Those are the ones who suffer most. During their long periods of captivity, hostages are frequently subjected to various types of physical punishment and mental torment.

Body The body of this essay would be developed by explaining each type of physical and psychological effect of prolonged confinement.

In most essays developed by division and classification, the logical order of arrangement is **climactic.** Having established your main divisions or classifications, you arrange them in the order of increasing importance.

You should never take your reader's interest for granted, and arranging the material in the body of your essay in the order of increasing importance helps to ensure continued interest. Whether you are writing about toadstools or atomic warheads, you create a sense of climax by building from the least dramatic to the most dramatic illustration. If you save the most vivid and dramatic part until last, then the reader will follow you to the climax and may be convinced.

Conclusion   Your essay should not end with one division, class, or type. What you need is a brief conclusion that repeats the ruling principle in your thesis statement and leaves that idea clear in the mind of your reader.

Here is an essay that uses division and classification as its major method of development.

....

THE DAILY HERO

....

Literature has one characteristic that is always present. That element may differ; it may vary; it may change so much that you may not recognize its identity without scanning it closely. Nevertheless, literature is unified by one essential quality; literature always has a hero; its essential characteristic is heroism. That heroism may be embodied in a person or in a concept or in both. Usually, however, the hero is a *person who stands for the idea*, the concept that the author wants to present. For example, Hester Prynne and Huckleberry Finn are characters who act in their own stories, but they also go beyond their stories to represent qualities in all of us; in a way, they symbolize us. They are symbols of us because they represent the best that is in us.

The definition of heroism entails two qualities: first, the heroes undergo and suffer through the same things in life that we all do, but, second, although they are recognizably the same, they and their lives seem larger than that of everyday. Their sufferings, their mistakes, even their wrong-doings seem larger and more intense than ours. And when they overcome these, their successes, based on their virtues, also seem larger. They *seem* larger because they *are* larger: The hero's shortcomings are never mean or petty or cheap; his good qualities are always courageous and generous and honest.

Almost all old literature has characters who fit this description, and they come from different classes of literature—from ancient Greek drama, from the plays of Shakespeare and the other Elizabethans, from the Scandinavian sagas, from the romances of the Middle Ages like King Arthur's, from the witty heroes of intelligence of the Restoration aristocracy—these are only a few.

From all of these classifications of literature, the characters can be again classified as to kinds of heroes. For example, there is the hero as a soldier, like Achilles in Greek epic and myth; there is the hero of integrity, like Antigone; there is the hero who càn cope in all practical matters, like Odysseus, also from Homer's epics; and another type of thinker as hero, Hamlet. There is the hero as lover, like Tristram in the stories of King Arthur. Even Arthur himself and his knight Lancelot are heroes as lovers although Arthur is also hero as king and as warrior, and Lancelot is also hero as friend and as warrior. Cyrano de Bergerac, from 20th-century French drama, is a hero as soldier, as friend, as poet, and above all as lover.

Many other kinds of heroes exist, but perhaps the ones who appear most often and most convincingly are these three—the hero as soldier, the hero as intellectual and practical thinker, and the hero as lover. One other classification is important—the anti-hero. This classification divides into two parts: the anti-hero as villain and the anti-hero as twerp.

The hero as villain has most of the attributes of the real hero, but he is totally self-centered and doesn't care whom he hurts or even destroys. Shakespeare's Richard III is such a villain-hero. (When such a villain is played by an attractive actor, the audience has a hard time not loving the villain because of his hero-like qualities.) All of these heroes stand for a group of some kind—nation, clan, race, or faction for whom they will risk disaster and death. The hero is not only a symbol for us but represents us to the death.

When we come to the subclassification of the anti-hero as wimp, we are encountering an extremely modern character and idea. The modern age does not tend to produce heroic characters. Indeed, one noted critic maintains modern times cannot visualize a modern hero because our time does not believe that any hero can be. Our age, he says, reflects in its literature only people and concepts that it can believe in. Heroes and heroism are dreams that have passed.

Arthur Miller, a distinguished and popular playwright, denies this vigorously. In his play *Death of a Salesman*, he presents his idea of a modern hero, who is a wimp struggling against the staggering odds of his commonplace life. Even his name speaks of his status; he is no Siegfried nor Roland nor Galahad. His name is a babyfied version of a common name and a symbol of his standing "on the totem pole"—Willie Loman. Here is our poor little hero as wimp, who fights back as manfully as he can.

However, the hero does exist in modern times; indeed a variety of heroes appears daily to approximately 70 percent of the vast newspaper-reading public in the comic strips. There is even one comic-strip hero accurately based on the Arthurian romances of the Middle Ages; Prince Valiant is correctly drawn and his adventures precisely told, following the age-old stories of the romancers.

Although Prince Valiant is alone in his class, there are several other typically heroic characters in modern dress. For example, *Judge Parker* and *Rex Morgan, M.D.*, are leaders of the people, as their titles show, and, like Odysseus, lead through the high level of their social standing, their morality, and their practical and professional wisdom. There is another hero of this type who is modern because she is a woman character and, even though of the type of Parker and Morgan, she lacks the implications of their professionalism and is wise through her sound common sense and her human experience. She is *Mary Worth*.

Despite the long-running success of these more or less traditional heroes, the typical heroes of the funny papers are modern wimps in their infinite variety. The wimps are heroes because they accept the extraordinary yet commonplace activities of their commonplace lives with endurance and a wry humor that adds up to grace.

Beetle Baily is the soldier as wimp hero, the butt of all the jokes and misadventures of a peace-time army. Nevertheless, he endures, sometimes wins a point in his life-long quarrel with Fate embodied as Sarge. General Halftrack is a variation on the wimp soldier who wins somewhat less sympathy because his high rank underscores his feeble incompetencies. Yet even he is a nice little man doing the best he can.

The modern thinker-hero is well represented by the assorted characters who alternately take the hero's role in *Doonesbury*. Here, because the hero varies from person to person, it is really the cartoonist's *thinking* that is the hero: it is an attack against what he considers the evils and absurdities of society, especially politics. His "enemies," thus, may be important or trivial, but his attack is always sharp.

In a recent Sunday strip, for example, his beak-nosed, mustached creation is interviewing Dan Quayle for radio. The figure of Quayle is drawn with nothing between the earphones where his head should be except one large feather. Three panels are devoted to Quayle's inability to quote the Golden Rule. Stupidity in public officials is treated lightly, but the meaning of the strip is serious. The hero is not joking.

The importance of the idea in *Doonesbury* rather than the

character is obvious because most readers don't even know the characters by name. With every new idea considered, another member of the cast steps forward to take over the leading role. This character is not individualized because the point of the satire is the thing that matters.

The hero as lover differs greatly from his great predecessors. Only Cathy among comic strip characters is at the age and stage of romance. The old writers treated romance as serious, capable of joy but usually tragic in the end. Love was wonderful beyond all things but thwarted, unrequited, and frequently ending with early death of one or both. Love in marriage was mentioned only as background or as competition.

With modern Cathy, the hero-lover's major emotion is frustration, never joy. And no wonder, for her wimp boyfriend is pure wimp, unequal to her in spirit, vitality, and hopefulness. Nevertheless, she is heroic in her perseverance to obtain a more loving world, even though we are amused by her continued and recognizable frustrations.

The frustrated hero-lover shows up by the dozens in comic strips dealing with family life, ranging from the fifty-year-old *Blondie* to the new one-panel cartoon, *The Lockhorns*. Love is almost unidentifiable in these strips, but the characters are faithful, caring, and tolerant even if sometimes irascible. Their troubles are small but many, but, underneath it all, they endure with laughter.

In modern literature we have many heroes, no matter what pessimistic critics may say. Among them, the daily heroes of the comic strips brighten a few minutes of our daily lives.

Questions for Discussion

1. Discuss the structure of the preceding essay. What is the basic two-part division? Outline the division and classification of both parts.
2. What is the basic point of the essay? Do you agree with it?
3. Do you agree with the critic who says that our time is not heroic, or do you support the idea that the "little man" can be a hero? Support your answer.
4. Name a person that you consider a modern-day hero in or out of the comic strips. Support your nomination in a short paragraph.
5. Do a division and classification outline of your favorite comic strips. You may use the hero as the basis of your classification or use some other unifying topic of your choice.

1. Avoid either-or categories: Not all politicians are liberal or conservative; not all restaurants are good or bad. Any such division is faulty because it leaves out some members of the classification system. (If there are only two, it is comparison or contrast.)

2. Avoid overlapping categories. If you were discussing foods, for example, a classification such as meat, fish, poultry, and veal would be defective. Veal is a type of meat and therefore not a separate category.

3. Don't be vague; be specific as to what your classification will cover. Within that narrowed classification, include all members.

4. Avoid trying to cover too many categories for a short essay. You couldn't hope adequately to cover all types of music in one short essay. Often, what you need to do is narrow your focus; you might, for example, discuss the types of dance music that are popular today.

5. Avoid meaningless classification. Just dividing your subject into parts does not necessarily provide a useful classification. Just saying that people can be divided into the young, old, and middle-aged doesn't mean anything unless you have a clear purpose in mind and explain that purpose to your reader.

6. Don't forget to provide the transitions necessary to take your reader with you. Try to provide smooth transition as you move your discussion from one division or category to another.

EXERCISE 7A: CLASSIFYING

Classify the following sets of items in two ways, each on a different basis.

1. Books on a student's desk

    Stephen King's *Pet Sematary*
    Introduction to Sociology
    Research Writing Seminar
    Agatha Christie, *Murder on the Orient Express*
    German II
    James Michener's *Space*
    Advanced Fiction
    Algebra I
    Shakespeare's Sonnets
    Eighteenth-Century Poetry
    Learning to Speak in Public
    Issac Asimov's *The Martian Chronicles*
    Western Civilization I

2. Words and Phrases

Multifarious
hunk (a guy)
spitball
you know
ancillary
parsimonious
eloquence
pushy
cheap
circumstances
cool it
aforementioned

EXERCISE 7B: CLASSIFYING

Classify in five ways the students in your classroom.

SUGGESTED TOPICS

Write an essay of division and classification using one of the following topics or an approved topic of your own choosing.

1. Hairstyles
2. Picnics
3. Politicians
4. Banks
5. Sun glasses
6. Bosses
7. Parents
8. Alibis
9. Fads
10. College classes
11. Geographical areas of the U.S.
12. Activities for sick children
13. Promotions
14. Penalties for cheating
15. Penalties for crime
16. Portraits
17. Jokes
18. Motives
19. Criminals
20. Textbooks
21. Local police officers
22. Student occupations
23. Singers
24. Dancers
25. Speech patterns in the U.S.
26. Architecture
27. Movies
28. People who shouldn't marry
29. Music
30. Courses I enjoy
31. Newspapers
32. Talk-show hosts
33. Neighborhoods near you
34. Forests
35. Poets
36. Frustrations
37. Successes
38. Adult toys

39. Symbols
40. Dreams
41. Actors
42. Bicycles
43. Furniture styles
44. Alarm clocks

45. Eye contact
46. Intelligence
47. Storms
48. Stupidity
49. Childhood illnesses
50. Photographs

TECHNIQUES OF CLEAR WRITING

CLARITY THROUGH EMPHASIS

For effective writing you need to emphasize the important points. Your thoughts must be cogent but also well placed in your sentences.

Emphasis Through Placement Within the Sentence

In the following examples, notice how you can emphasize a point by changing its position in the sentence. Note in particular that it is more effective to place a point that deserves emphasis at the beginning or end of a sentence than to place it in the middle:

> The president and congress received ominous messages from abroad; they worked through the night; they knew that war threatened.
>
> The president and congress, having received ominous messages from abroad and knowing that war threatened, worked through the night.
>
> The president and congress, working through the night and receiving ominous messages from abroad, knew that war threatened.

All the sentences above give you the same information; however, they do not give you the same feeling. In the first sentence all the items of information are as equally emphasized as possible for they are all in equal, independent clauses, even though one is somewhat emphasized by being made last. In the second sentence, the two more important ideas are buried in the middle of the sentence. In the third sentence, the two lesser ideas are buried, and the most important is put in the last, the most important, position.

Abraham Lincoln, who is known as The Great Emancipator, is the best-loved person in American history.

Abraham Lincoln, who is the best-loved person in American history, is known as The Great Emancipator.

Note that the first sentence emphasizes Lincoln's place in the heart of Americans. The second sentence emphasizes his role in freeing the slaves.

In some sentences there is no correct or incorrect order; the right order is the one that emphasizes what the writer wants to emphasize. Look at the following sentences.

Othello, whose tragic flaw was impulsiveness, was tricked into disaster by his lieutenant.

Othello, tricked into disaster by his lieutenant, was tragically flawed by impulsiveness.

Tragically flawed by impulsiveness, Othello was tricked into disaster by his lieutenant.

The first sentence emphasizes the disaster; the second sentence emphasizes the impulsiveness. The third sentence makes the disaster somewhat stronger but makes the impulsiveness strong too, for no element of the sentence is buried; each is given an important position in the sentence.

Emphasis Through Position in Clauses

The most important idea in a sentence should be in the main clause; less important ideas should be subordinated.

INCORRECT:
I was walking home from school when I saw the accident occur.

CORRECT:
As I was walking home from school, I saw the accident.

INCORRECT:
When he learned he had won the Nobel Prize, Ralph Bunche was having dinner with some friends.

CORRECT:
While having dinner with his friends, Ralph Bunche learned that he had won the Nobel Prize.

Emphasis Through Forceful Expression

The most obvious way to make your point emphatic is through forceful statement. Emerson advised, "Say what you have to say in words as hard as bullets." Writers find that using strong words to make a blunt, straightforward statement is often the most emphatic way to express profound convictions. Such a statement also gains emphasis through brevity. "War is hell," for example, is more emphatic than "War is a terrible act of voilence that creates misery and pain."

Repeating a point or a word also lends emphasis, but it is usually emotional emphasis. You make it clear that you *care* about something or someone if you said it more than once. "This was my last chance—my very last." Notice also how much more compelling it is to repeat a name than to say it just once. In the opera *Pagliacci*, the clown sings his heartbroken aria "Marta, Marta". In a Robert Burns' poem, an old wife speaks of her lifelong affection for John Anderson, "John Anderson, my jo, John, my John." And King David, mourning his dead son, cries out, "Oh, Absalom, Absalom, my son Absalom, my son, my son"!

Emphasis Within the Essay

Emphasis within the essay works the same way as emphasis within the sentence: the strongest positions are first and last, at the beginning of your essay and the end of your essay. Usually, saving the best for last is the most effective way of developing an essay. Your most convincing argument, your most important detail, your most interesting point, the idea you will leave in the reader's mind—that is what you put last. Then you are using climactic order; your details build to a climax as your discussion progresses from your least important point to your most important point. For example, if you were writing a paper on Pap Finn's treatment of Huck in *The Adventures of Huckleberry Finn*, you might decide to include the following points: (1) he tried to take his money from him, (2) in a bout with the DT's, he tried to kill him, (3) he beat him regularly, and (4) he refused to allow Huck to go to school. However, your paper wouldn't be very effective unless you arranged your points in climactic order:

1. He refused to allow Huck to go to school.
2. He tried to take his money from him.
3. He beat him regularly.
4. In a bout with the DT's, he tried to kill him.

Faulty Emphasis

Emphasis in your writing requires that you be precise. For instance, if you decided that you would achieve emphasis through forceful statement, you would have to be careful to select the most important thing to be forceful about. You would feel silly being forceful about something trivial. You would also have to limit your forcefulness to a very few, important statements. An essay loaded with strong, blunt statements would lose effectiveness because it would make you sound rude or quarrelsome.

Another type of faulty emphasis is the careless use of superlatives. If everything is marvelous, phenomenal, beautiful, fantastic, terrible, awful, or horrifying, then there is no distinction being made between the emphatic and the nonemphatic. Hysterical punctuation also weakens emphasis. Control your use of exclamation points, capital letters, dots, dashes, and underlining. Indeed, control is the key to emphasis. Remember, emphasizing too much will result in emphasizing nothing.

EXERCISE 7C: DECIDING WHAT TO EMPHASIZE

The correct placement of words in a sentence depends on what you want to emphasize:

a. Sick with nervousness, the student started his exam.
b. The student, sick with nervousness, started his exam.
c. The student started his exam sick with nervousness.

or

d. The student, starting his exam, was sick with nervousness.
e. The student was sick with nervousness as he started his exam.
f. As he started his exam, the student was sick with nervousness.

In the first three sentences, the emphasis is placed on "starting his exam" because that idea is placed in the independent clause. The first sentence is probably the most effective placement with a strong phrase first and an even stronger one last. The second sentence tends toward weakness because the phrase "sick with nervousness" is buried in the middle of the sentence. In the third, the weaker phrase is placed in the stronger position.

In the second set of sentences, the emphasis is placed on "sick with nervousness," for it is in the independent clause. In the first sentence, that idea is buried; in the second the most important idea is not placed in the stronger position. The third sentence is probably the most effectively arranged.

Nevertheless, you choose the placing of words because you know what you want to say.

Discuss the emphasis in each of the following sentences. Then choose the most effective word placement.

1. **a.** Pompeii was buried under thirty feet of ash and lava.
   b. Buried under thirty feet of ash and lava was Pompeii.
   c. Thirty feet of ash and lava buried Pomepii.

2. **a.** Of course, the coach was disappointed.
   b. The coach, of course, was disappointed.
   c. The coach was disappointed, of course.

3. **a.** All hope is gone for rescuing the survivors.
   b. For rescuing the survivors all hope is gone.
   c. Gone is all hope for rescuing the survivors.

4. **a.** Prince Krayobv, his kingdom gone, his parents cruelly murdered, his own wretched body torn and bleeding, plotted his revenge.
   b. Prince Krayobv plotted his revenge, his kingdom gone, his parents cruelly murdered, his own wretched body torn and bleeding.
   c. His kingdom gone, his parents, cruelly murdered, his own wretched body torn and bleeding, Prince Krayobv plotted his revenge.

5. **a.** Elsie, timid and quiet, argues well when she is excited.
   b. Timid and quiet, Elsie argues well when she is excited.
   c. Although she is timid and quiet, Elsie argues well when she is excited.

6. **a.** The troops were notified that they would start on maneuvers as soon as darkness fell.
   b. As soon as darkness fell, the troops were notified they would start on maneuvers.
   c. They would start on maneuvers as soon as darkness fell, the troops were notified.

7. **a.** He committed a serious error in plagarizing his term paper.
   b. Plagarizing his term paper was a serious error.
   c. In plagarizing, his term paper, he committed a serious error.

8. **a.** Hearing the answer, the police officers became furious.
   b. The police officers, hearing the answer, became furious.
   c. The police officers became furious when they heard the answer.

9. **a.** Our leader is dead.
   b. Dead is our leader.
   c. Dead, dead is our leader.

10. **a.** First, they won the game.
    b. They won the first game.
    c. They won the game first.

11. **a.** Trapped in the sweltering, crocodile-infested swamp, Tom surrendered.
    b. Tom surrendered because he was trapped in the sweltering, crocodile-infested swamp.
    c. Tom, surrounded in the sweltering, crocodile-infested swamp, surrendered.

12. **a.** Dealing with police corruption, *The Big Easy* is an enlightening movie.
    b. *The Big Easy,* an enlightening movie, deals with police corruption.
    c. *The Big Easy* is an enlightening movie that deals with police corruption.

REVISING FOR ECONOMY AND PRECISION

You have already learned that to write well you must be concise and precise. Good writing depends on strong, active verbs and precise nouns and modifiers. It also demands that you avoid unnecessary *to be* verbs, fuzzy generalizations, jargon, clichés, repetitions, and wordiness. However, knowing the rules and applying them are two different matters. To write concisely and precisely takes careful revision.

In a first draft, a student wrote: "Our history teacher is a very good person when it comes to making decisions based on the principles of a democratic society."

In revising, she first took out the *very.* (A statement is usually weakened, not strengthened, by *very.*) *Person* added nothing, so she took it out. Then she realized that *principles of a democratic society* was so broad that it had almost no meaning. Also, she wanted to avoid *is* and replace it with a stronger verb. She recognized that *when it comes to making* was wordy. Her first revision read: "Our history teacher makes decisions on the basis of democratic principles." But she then realized that *decisions* and *basis of democratic principles* were too general. She revised again. "Our history teacher reaches decisions democratically." This final revision cut twenty-two words to six, six words that said something.

When you are revising to make your writing concise and precise, you must consider your sentences as in the example above. You must also consider the paragraph. Are you avoiding repeating yourself? Are you eliminating unnecessary words or phrases? Are you combining elements that go together? Are you reducing clauses to phrases and phrases to single words? (Review the checklist in Chapter 4.)

EXERCISE 7D: REVISING FOR ECONOMY AND PRECISION

The following paragraph is a wordy rewriting of a precise and concise paragraph about plagiarism. The thirty-four numbered and italicized items can be made more concise or even eliminated. After you have read the paragraph, rewrite it for conciseness. You will find clues, comments, and suggestions for your rewrite in the list that follows the paragraph.

Plagiarism is [1]*a kind of burglary* [2]*except that it is done* in academic work and literary writings. [3]*It is like taking things* [4]*that really belong to some other person* but [5]*not recognizing their ownership and* [6]*treating their academic findings and their writings* [7]*as if they belonged to the person who is plagiarizing.* Some [8]*types of* plagiarism [9]*come about as the result of* [10]*pure, straightforward* [11]*failure to be honest;* students, because they think maybe they [12]*have too much to do,* or maybe they are [13]*the type who don't like to work much,* or maybe they [14]*aren't very good at studying and getting their work done,* copy [15]*things printed in books and magazines and newspapers* or even copy [16]*things that other students may have done.* [17]*Of course,* they [18]*really* know [19]*that what they are doing is* [20]*morally wrong,* but [21]*in spite of this, they do it anyway* and they hope that they will not be found out [22]*by the instructor.* [23]*Students who do this kind of plagiarizing* are [24]*really* criminals, [25]*though of course not a criminal like a murderer or a bank robber.* Students [26]*like this* [27]*do not deserve to be treated with respect by society,* because society, [28]*by and large,* [29]*does not approve of* criminals. The [30]*greatest number of examples of plagiarism,* however, [31]*does not so much grow out of* [32]*not being honest* as it does from [33]*a failure of being mature* [34]*in an intellectual way.*

1. Useless general phrase since the second clause indicates the specific kind of burglary.
2. Can be reduced to two adjectives modifying burglary.
3. It isn't "like" taking things it *is* taking things.
4. Reduce clause to phrase.
5. Unnecessary because of second following phrase.
6. Combine.
7. Put 4, 5, and 6 into an appositional phrase following burglary.
8. Unnecessary.
9. Reduce to verb.

10. Wrong connotation to modify dishonest; choose one adjective with correct feeling for dishonesty.
11. Reduce to one word.
12. Reduce to one word.
13. Reduce to one word.
14. Reduce to one word.
15. Combine.
16. Reduce to phrase.
17. Unnecessary transition.
18. Unnecessary.
19. Replace with personal pronoun.
20. Unnecessary modifier.
21. Unnecessary.
22. Unnecessary.
23. Use only the personal pronoun.
24. Unnecessary.
25. Replace with one word modifying criminal, meaning "an unimportant criminal."
26. Unnecessary and vague, Identify "Students" more precisely.
27. Eliminate negative and condense.
28. Unnecessary.
29. Avoid negative forms; find an antonym.
30. Substitute a one-word modifier of plagiarism.
31. Find a more precise verb.
32. Use one noun, a positive, not a negative, form.
33. Find a one-word, positive form.
34. Reduce to a single adjective modifying the form you find for item 33.

After you have revised this paragraph, ask your teacher to show you a copy of the original.

EXERCISE 7E: REVISING FOR ECONOMY AND PRECISION

The following essay is repetitious and wordy. Revise it to turn it into a clear, concise essay.

From all my years of growing up in my school days, there are three times that I will always remember because of the feeling of happiness and accomplishment I felt. The first thing I will remember is being elected to and getting on student council. The second is my first date and the sensational feeling I had inside of myself because it was with a boy I had liked for a long time. The third thing I will always remember is the night I graduated from high school and how proud I felt of the accomplishment I had achieved. The reason I will remember these three events is because each of these feelings were feelings I had never experienced before and that is why I will always cherish them and keep them in my memories forever.

The first thing I will always remember is getting elected to student council because it was a great honor in our school and one that was highly respected. I never really expected to win the election, but my friends and my favorite teacher whom I like more than any of the others urged and coaxed me to become a candidate and run. The reason I never really expected to win was because the opposing candidate I was running against was a student who was the most popular and best-liked student in the whole class. Once I was a candidate, however, I wrote up a platform which contained all the principles and plans on which I would base all the aspects of being a student council member. I made a speech which I delivered at an assembly of the whole school the day before election. The next day was election day, and I was surprised to learn when the votes were tallied up and counted that I had won by a sizable margin of seventeen votes. I had won a triumph over the most popular student in the class.

The second thing I will always remember is my first date and the sensational feeling I had inside of myself and my happiness since it was with that very same boy I had beaten for student council, a boy that I had liked for a long time. He came up to me in the library where I was and asked if he could speak to me because he had something to ask me. He sat down and asked if I was busy Friday night because he wanted me to go to a dance the school was sponsoring; with a gleam in my eyes, I accepted. Friday night, he arrived at my house at seven-thirty, and our first date had begun. While at the dance, we danced to all but four dances. As always, time flew by and at eleven the dance was over. After the dance was over, we stopped for hamburgers; then he brought me home. It will be a date I will never forget because of the feeling of joy I felt.

The third thing I will always remember is the night I graduated from high school and how proud I felt of the accomplishment I had made. The night before graduation, my grandparents came from Pittsburgh to see the ceremony of graduation. We left to go on to the high school auditorium where my parents and relatives would go to see graduation. When we arrived, the auditorium was beautifully decorated with Boston ferns and filled with the proud parents of the students who would be graduating. The graduates lined up in a long line and the school band began to play march music. After we reached the stage and listened to several speeches, it was time to receive our diplomas. When the ceremony was over and it was time for the graduates to exit the stage, I suddenly realized how proud I felt of the accomplishment I had made because I had graduated in the top third of my class.

In closing, the things that I will always remember, the things that gave me a feeling of accomplishment and joy are getting elected to the student council, getting my first date, and graduating from high school. The reason I will remember these three events is that each of these feelings were feelings I had never experienced before and that is why I will always cherish them and keep them in my memories forever.

WORD POWER

IDIOM

Idiom refers to the characteristic way in which people put together the words of a language. Every language has its natural idioms; people put words together in a certain way to express a particular idea or feeling. These combinations of words may, in the literal sense, be illogical, untranslatable, and even ungrammatical. But idioms grow out of the language and come to have an existence of their own. English has thousands of these peculiar combinations of words. Consider the following examples involving the one word, *heart:*

He's got heart.
She's all heart.
My heart's in the Highlands.

Her heart's in the right place.
His heart was in his mouth.
She didn't have the heart to tell him.
She wore her heart on her sleeve.
We had a real heart-to-heart talk.
I am heartsick at losing my home.

Welcome from the bottom of my heart.
Thomas Paine gave heart to the American Revolution.

They live in the heart of New York City.
Her heart is set on getting a diploma.
We must not lose heart.
He took the rebuke to heart.
She lost her heart to Paris.

He was a scoundrel at heart
You have a heart of stone.
She loved them with all her heart.
I know that hard-hearted villain's story by heart.
Sit there to your heart's content.
Eat your heart out.

For each of hundreds of common verbs such as *do, get, cut, set, hit, put, see, push, pull, take, make,* there are dozens of idiomatic expressions.

She wore her heart on her sleeve.   **She's all heart.**

If you have ever studied a foreign language, you remember that you had to memorize lists of idioms. Idioms, in any language, must be memorized. You can't just figure out their meanings, because they don't follow any rules. Despite this, idiomatic usage is valuable in that it offers quick, precise communication among most native speakers of a language. Such phrases as *come in handy, make no bones about it,* and *do away with* convey rather complicated ideas quickly and clearly.

For the few times when you do have trouble with idioms, there are two solutions. The long-run solution is to make yourself aware of how idioms are used by educated speakers and writers. The immediate solution is to consult your dictionary. The problem generally concerns what preposition should follow what verb, as in such phrases as *make up, make up for, make after, make much of, make out with.* You will find that most dictionaries will give you directions about this under the entry for the verb, in this case *make.*

CLICHÉS AND TRITE EXPRESSIONS

You don't always have time to think before you speak. As a result, you sometimes say the first thing that comes into your head. Once you start to do that, you sometimes load your conversation with trite, overworked expressions. Suppose, for example, that you were listening to the following conversation:

MARTHA: So . . . what's up, George?
GEORGE: Oh, I'm just doin' my own thing.
MARTHA: Yeah? Cool!
GEORGE: Ya' know, Martha, you ought to start doin' your own thing, somewhere down the road.

MARTHA: Yeah . . . I know where you're comin' from, George.
GEORGE: Well, hang in there, Martha.

Once you see George and Martha's words written down in black and white, you can see how meaningless their conversation becomes. For example, what did George mean when he said, "I'm just doin' my own thing? He could have been planning to get married or quit his job. The truth is that you don't know what he means. Unfortunately, students who depend on such trite, overworked expressions when they talk are just reinforcing a bad habit—**lazy thinking.** If they don't take the time to say exactly what they mean, then they probably won't take the time to **write** exactly what they mean. In other words, meaningless talk turns into meaningless writing. Look at another example—a typical conversation between two students:

JULIO: What happened?
LOUISE: Well, there was this really weird guy, O.K.? And he was tailgating me, ya' know, like all the way to the turnpike, O.K.? So, when I got on to the turnpike, O.K.? Like he's still following me, ya' know? So then, like I really started to panic. I was shaking like a leaf. So at the first rest stop I saw, O.K.? I pulled off, O.K.? And I like pretend that I'm going to stop, O.K.? I was trying to like act as cool as possible, ya' know, but inside I was like really scared stiff, ya' know? So anyway, I slowed the car down to like ten miles per hour, O.K.? And kept looking for anything that resembled a police car, ya' know? Finally, I spotted one, O.K.? And as soon as the guy saw me heading toward the police car, O.K.? He took off, like a bat out of hell. Boy, I was like really relieved, ya' know? I couldn't believe my eyes. I mean like I could have hugged that police officer, ya' know?

If you ever find yourself talking like Louise, watch out. In this reply to Julio's question, Louise used a meaningless word or phrase twenty-five times. Boring and meaningless as this is in speech, such meaningless words and ready-made phrases are even more objectionable in writing. These phrases are often referred to as clichés. A *cliché* is any stale, worn-out expression that has been used so often that it clarifies nothing for the reader and tends to put the reader to sleep.

Clichés are one of those mistakes that are made for a good reason. Everyone hopes to write with clarity and sparkle, and so people use metaphors that can add brightness to their writing. Unfortunately, clichés are overused metaphors, which are called "dead" or "dying" metaphors because they retain no sense of the imaginative comparison of a living metaphor. Instead of enlivening your writing they deaden it. Contrast, for example, the melancholy but vivid metaphor "The heart of another is always a dark forest" with any of the clichés in the following list. These clichés, like all others, were once bright but have since been dulled into plain commonplaces by years of constant usage.

Notice that clichés are always in the form of a metaphor: dirty *as* a pig, cheeks rosy *as* an apple, cheaper *than* dirt, richer *than* Croesus. Although clichés sometimes appear like an adjective and a noun, *paper thin,* for example, they indicate *thin as paper.*

Even if you do not have time to think up a good metaphor, don't settle for a cliché. Remember that words, precisely chosen, can be colorful and imaginative as well as clear. The word *snow,* for instance, creates a vivid image whereas the phrase *white as snow* does not.

List of Clichés and Trite Expressions

Ugly as sin
Pretty as a picture
Fresh as a daisy
Red as a beet
Old as the hills
Sober as a judge
Mad as a hornet
Sly as a fox
Dumb as a doorknob
Quiet as a mouse
Black as night
Smart as a whip
Crazy as a loon
Quick as a wink
Slow as a turtle
Stiff as a board
Cross as a bear
Phony as a three-dollar bill
Honest as the day is long
As much fun as a barrel of
monkeys
Funny as a crutch
White as a sheet
Snow white
True blue
Pitch black
Sky high
Sparkling clean
Crystal clear
Dirt cheap

Happy as a lark
Soft as silk
Hard as a rock
Warm as toast
Cold as ice
Skinny as a rail
Big as a bear
Filthy rich
Like pulling teeth
Like a fish out of water
Like a bump on a log
Like finding a needle in a haystack
Like a hot potato
When hell freezes over
When push comes to shove
Between a rock and a hard place
The bottom line
Working one's fingers to the bone
Day in and day out
One in a million

Blowing one's own horn
Come up smelling like a rose
Variety is the spice of life
Stand up and be counted
Giving the best years of one's life
Not wrapped too tight
Raining cats and dogs
Costing an arm and a leg
On a roll

EXERCISE 7F: CLICHÉS

Replace the italicized clichés and trite expressions in the following sentences with more original and exact wording.

1. Pedro was as *cool as a cucumber* as he accepted the award.
2. Although he could *swim like a fish*, he was a *bull in a china shop* on shore.
3. *Absence makes the heart grow fonder.*
4. Skiing is not *my cup of tea.*
5. At the divorce trial, Pepita said she had given Raoul *the best years of her life.*
6. Raoul said, "*Every dog has his day*" when the divorce was granted.
7. My two daughters are *as different as night and day.*
8. *When my ship comes* in, I'll give you *diamonds and pearls.*
9. Peter *worked like a beaver*, but Jeffrey was *hot as a firecracker.*
10. Fifi was *cute as a button*, but *dumb as an ox.*
11. I have no sympathy for him: I think he is *as guilty as sin.*
12. Of course you can come to the picnic—*the more the merrier.*
13. *Out of sight, out of mind.*
14. *You can't tell a book by its cover.*
15. There is no use worrying about that; *it's water over the dam.*
16. *The grass is always greener on the other side of the fence.*
17. It's hotter *than the hinges of hell.*
18. It's great *weather for ducks.*
19. I'm between the *devil and the deep blue sea.*
20. I know her *like I know the palm of my hand.*

CHAPTER 8

Combining Methods of Development

In all the methods of writing previously discussed and practiced, you have concentrated on one method at a time. In each of the following chapters of this text, you may develop your thesis by any *combination of methods* that pleases you. You may choose any methods (narration, description, examples, comparison and contrast, classifying) and any of the methods you have yet to study (defining, causation, persuasion) and work them into a unified essay.

ADVANTAGES OF COMBINING DIFFERENT METHODS OF DEVELOPMENT

To combine a number of methods is really a more usual type of organization than focusing on any single method, especially for essays of four or more paragraphs. A combination frequently has these advantages: It is easier for the writer, who only has his or her subject and not the method to consider: it is more interesting for readers who have a variety of methods to please them.

If, for example, you are writing an essay on Italy today, you might begin with description:

> In Italy the sun still rises early over the shimmering Adriatic and glistens over the red tile roofs and yellow walls of the clustered buildings. The roads that twist and turn suddenly feel hot through the soles of your shoes. Olive trees two thousand years old, their roots a labyrinth of twisted legs, still bear fruit. Medieval walled towns throw shadows down the sides of the cliffs they rest upon.

go on to examples:

> Italy today is not Rome of yesterday, but the evidence of ancient Rome is everywhere. Remains of the ancient aqueducts that brought water to the city still stand. Buses that take tourists to and from the airport ride on the original Appian Way and enter the city through gates two thousand years old.

use comparison–contrast:

> The old and the new coexist in Italy. A modern eight-lane highway veers left to skirt the ancient ruins of the 110-foot-high Coliseum. New Mercedes scenic-cruiser buses edge through the ancient gates and over roads build for chariots and ox-carts. The walls of the giant Circus Maximus hold back the chic condominums and modern department stores of the growing city. The Tiber still winds through the city as it did centuries ago, but now it's so polluted with industrial waste that a mouthful of its water can be fatal.

or use a short narrative or anecdote:

> The Italian temper is volatile but not physical. Once I saw a driver, held up momentarily by another driver stopping to pick up a passenger, leap from his car and rush up to the offending vehicle. Screaming and waving his arms, he challenged the driver of the first car. This driver also got out of his car, and the two screamed at each other, arms waving threateningly. I thought I was about to witness a murder—or mayhem at least. However, the passenger arrived and got into the first car. When this happened, the two drivers returned to their own vehicles and left. They were whistling as they drove off.

For the assignments throughout the rest of this book, choose whatever combination of methods you feel will best develop your thesis.

The following lighthearted satire on summer reading is a fine example of an essay developed by a combination of methods. The author, Dave Barry, begins with an introduction that classifies four activities. He goes on to describe the three classes he is rejecting and the library in which are housed the books comprising his summer reading. He classifies again, this time the types of summer reading available now. He then develops those by heavily descriptive narration. His conclusion returns precisely to his introduction: that he is frightened by a narrative whether told or read.

....

THE IDEAL SUMMER BOOKS: HUGE, SCARY, AND WATERPROOF

....

Introduction

Classification —four options

Reasons for deleting option 1— sports

Reasons for deleting option 2— nature

I came to love summer reading back in the 1950's, when I spent my summers at a camp located in Dutchess County right near a New York State mental hospital. We campers had four major activity options: sports, nature, crafts and reading. I ruled out sports, which consisted primarily of swimming in a lake filled with a murky, dark-green waterlike substance. You couldn't see what was in there, but you knew it was hostile.

I tried nature briefly, but in those days it contained an enormous amount of dirt. I learned this on overnight camping trips on which we slept in bedrolls that we made ourselves by folding three blankets together in a special secret out-doorsman's way such that when you climbed inside them, they instantly disassembled into three random blankets. So when night fell, we campers would be basically lying on the ground, forming an attractive buffet-style display for the mosquitoes and getting dirt everywhere, including under our eyelids. Meanwhile our counselor—who at the time seemed to be a wise and caring human being, but who I now realize was actually a teen-ager—would tell us traditional bedtime camping stories about homicidal ax-wielding maniacs who had escaped that very day from the mental hospital and were probably creeping around in the woods at that very moment. Then we'd all enjoy a relaxing three to five minutes of sleep while we waited for dawn.

Reasons for deleting option 3— crafts

After nature I tried crafts. The main craft item that boy campers produced was an authentic Indian tom-tom, which we made in the authentic Indian manner by stretching pieces of rubber over the ends of industrial-size lima-bean cans. This camp bought lima beans by the metric ton, so we had plenty of raw material, the problem being that—you have probably noticed this in your own life—unless you are involved in an actual tribal war, there is only so much you can do with a tom-tom. You beat it a few hundred times, and the thrill is gone.

Choosing
option 4—
reading.
Description of
library

So finally I took up summer reading. Although the camp "library" was really nothing more than a musty old storeroom, it contained one of the nation's largest independently owned collections of bats. This made the book-selection process quite exciting: you'd dart into the library with one arm held over your head, snatch a book pretty much at random, then dart back out to see what you had. If you were lucky, it was from the Tom Swift or Hardy Boys series. Sometimes you'd get a Nancy Drew, and then of course you had to throw it back.

Description of
favorite books

My favorite stories were the ones about Tom Swift, the boy science genius who flew his own biplane and could communicate via wireless radio. I knew these stories were dated, but I liked them anyway. I liked the idea of a boy who was free to spend his time harnessing the amazing powers of magnetism if he felt like it, with nobody to tell him that he had to sleep in the dirt. And so for several summers, while the other campers were out learning valuable lore such as how to determine your location by noting where the moss grows on a tree, I was reading about how Tom Swift wowed his chums with his electric runabout. Ever since then I have viewed summer reading as an important way to avoid accomplishing anything useful.

Concluding
sentence of
introductory
content and
topic sentence
for main
thesis:
practical hints
for summer

Speaking of useful: over the years I've picked up some practical hints that can help you decide which books to take along on your vacation. Probably the most important question to ask yourself is: Do you have small children? If the answer is yes, your best bet is to take along a book that has been hailed by the critics as "waterproof." Because the book will definitely get wet. *Everything* will get wet. Even if you're not vacationing at the beach. Your children will see to that. Attracting moisture is an instinctive ability that small children have, given to them by nature so that they do not gradually become immobilized by a three-inch crust of dried Zoo-Roni. You could release an 18-month-old child in the Gobi Desert, hundreds of miles from any known water supply, and within minutes that child would somehow become soaked to the skin.

Reading
waterproof
books

"But," you ask, "are there any waterproof books currently available?" Fortunately, the answer is yes. Unfortunately, they are mostly about marine life. My 8-year-old son has one, entitled, "Guide to Corals and Fishes" (the waterproof edition, by Idaz and Jerry Greenberg; available wherever snorkeling supplies are sold), which he frequently reads underwater, although this is not necessary. I've read parts of it myself, and although I feel it's fairly weak on character development, the plot has an appealing symmetry, with a lengthy middle section about cute and harmless creatures nicely framed by a beginning section about creatures that could bite your legs right off and a closing section about creatures that could poison you. "If stung, consult a doctor" is a good example of the lean, no-nonsense prose you'll find throughout this book.

Reading large size books

If water resistance is not a factor in your vacation-reading decision, you'll want to go with size. The ideal summer book is the size of a major appliance, a book that can't get lost in the sand, a book that won't suddenly run out of words on you when you're far from civilization. I personally prefer techno-thrillers, as epitomized by Tom Clancy's *Hunt for Red October*, a book so detailed and technically accurate that by the time you're done reading it you can actually build your own nuclear submarine. Techno-thrillers also tend to heighten your geopolitical awareness by giving you a realistic picture of what modern, high-tech warfare would be like if everything actually worked, as opposed to in real life, where highly sophisticated multimillion-dollar bombers have been known to crash because they encountered unforseen pelicans. For some reason, whenever I read a techno-thriller, the name that keeps popping into my mind is: Tom Swift.

Types of summer reading-narration

Type 1—techno-thrillers Examples and description

Type 2—sweeping sagas

Another extremely large kind of book for your summer vacation pleasure is what we in the book-blurb business call the "sweeping saga"—a book that follows the activities of every single member of a large, attractive, star-crossed family from approximately the dawn of time until the Reagan Administration; a book with so many characters that by the time you get to page 537 you have no idea who all these people are, but you don't dare go back to try to find out because you're only a third of the way through and you have already invested more time reading this book than you spent in all your undergraduate classes combined, and you are determined to finish the damn thing even if it means refusing to go back to work and ultimately losing your job.

Type 3—Gothic horror

If you want guaranteed excitement in your summer reading, you should buy a book by Stephen King or some similar author, the kind of book that we in the business call "novels of Gothic horror" because we are reluctant to come right out and call them "novels wherein people's brains are occasionally eaten by snakes." You can identify these novels easily because the covers usually depict attractive children whose eyes are glowing like beer signs. This is, of course, a well-known symptom of demonic possession, but it usually takes the characters in the novel hundreds of pages to figure it out. They're always saying things like, "I don't understand it! Aunt Louise was hacked into pieces the size of Wheat Chex, and yet there was nobody in the room with her except young Jason here! Jason, stop shining your eyes in my face!"

Concluding paragraph— returns to fear. Repeat of frights of his youth.

What I especially like about Gothic horror novels is the mood they create. You could be reading on the front porch of a peaceful country cabin, surrounded by the glories of nature, but after you read 50 pages of Stephen King, even the squirrels will seem menacing. I tend to read these books with my eyes all squinched up to prevent scary words from suddenly leaping into my brain, but it never works: I end up lying awake for half the night. It reminds me of my youth.*

*Dave Barry, a humor columnist for the *Miami Herald*, won a Pulitzer Prize in 1988.

PITFALLS TO AVOID

1. Don't forget that even with a combination of methods, you still will need your basic three-part structure of introduction, body, and conclusion. The body will be made up of the various methods.
2. Don't use your first method as your introduction. Your introduction should include a few sentences to interest your reader and a thesis statement general enough to be supported by all the methods of development you use.
3. Don't confuse your reader by starting one method of development and switching to another without completing the first.
4. Don't risk losing your reader by failing to supply transitions.
5. Don't rely on the number of methods used to make your point. Each method should be complete in itself.
6. Don't conclude your essay with the conclusion of your final method; return to your thesis idea.

TECHNIQUES OF CLEAR WRITING

PARALLEL WORDING

Parallel wording is a technique that makes your writing more coherent, more interesting, and more emphatic. No good writer can do without it. It means that you state similar (parallel) ideas with similar (parallel) wording. (See Chapter 1, p. 35–36). For example, in the first sentence of this paragraph you were told that parallel wording enhances your writing in three ways: by making it **more coherent, more interesting,** and **more emphatic.** Each idea is similar in the sense that each indicates a quality of good writing, and each idea is equally important. Each then is parallel and thus requires parallel wording. You can state these ideas with words, phrases, or clauses, as long as you make them parallel. For example:

WORDS

Parallel wording is a technique that enhances your writing through **coherence, interest,** and **emphasis.**

PHRASES

Parallel wording is a technique that you can use to **make your writing more coherent, to make it more interesting,** and **to make it more emphatic.**

Notice how this sentence is weakened when the parallel wording is removed:

Parallel wording is a technique that makes your writing more coherent, adding interest, and you can make your writing emphatic with parallelism.

As you can see, with parallel wording your sentences are strong, precise, and clear. In addition, parallelism makes them eloquent and easy to remember. (In that last sentence, there is the word *eloquent* and the phrase *easy to remember.* If that were changed to be parallel—for instance, *eloquent* and *memorable*—you probably would consider it a better sentence.)

Because parallelism often results in eloquence, many great writers use it frequently. Shakespeare, for one, employed it many times for important concepts, and those concepts tend to be memorable. Look at some of his most famous quotations to see how they lose effectiveness when they are no longer parallel.

PARALLEL:

To be or not **to be:** that is the question.   *Hamlet*

NONPARALLEL:

To be or not to exist: that is the question.

PARALLEL:

I come **to bury** Caesar, not **to praise** him.   *Julius Caesar*

NONPARALLEL:

I come to bury Caesar, having no intention of praising him.

PARALLEL:
Friends, Romans, Countrymen, lend me your ears.   *Julius Caesar*

NONPARALLEL:
Friends, people whose heritage is Roman, men of this great country, lend me your ears.

PARALLEL:
I am a Jew. **Hath not a Jew** eyes? **Hath not a Jew** hands, organs, dimensions, senses, affections, passions? . . . **If you prick us, do we not** bleed? **If you tickle us, do we not** laugh? **If you poison us, do we not** die? and **if you wrong us, shall we not** revenge?   *The Merchant of Venice*

NONPARALLEL:
I am a Jew. Hath not a Jew eyes? Doesn't a member of the Jewish race have hands, organs, dimensions, senses, affections, passions? . . . If you prick us, don't we bleed? We laugh when you tickle us, don't we? Suppose you poison us; do you not think that we would die? And how about wronging us? Wouldn't we try to get revenge?

PARALLEL:
All the world's a stage,
And **all the men and women** merely players.
They have **their exits** and **their entrances.**   *As You Like It*

NONPARALLEL:
All the world's a stage,
And men and women are merely players.
They have their exits and entrances are theirs too.

PARALLEL:
A horse! A horse! my kingdom for a horse!   *Richard III*

NONPARALLEL:
A horse! An equestrian animal! I'd give my kingdom for such a steed!

Aside from the basic technique of parallelism of putting similar ideas in similar grammatical structures, there are several other minor tricks to smooth out or strengthen your sentences in parallel ways. For example, in such phrases as **not only** . . . **but also, neither** . . . **nor, either** . . . **or,** and **both** . . . **and,** you emphasize the parallelism by putting those phrases as close as possible to the words that you wish to make parallel.

    For example:

FAULTY:
The gym team not only has been victorious as a team but also as individual gymnasts.

IMPROVED:
The team has been victorious not only as a team but also as individual gymnasts.

FAULTY:

The demerits not only were disappointing to the coach but to the sponsors also.

IMPROVED:

The demerits were disappointing not only to the coach but also to the sponsors.

NOTE: You never want to force ideas into a parallel structure if those ideas are not parallel. For instance, you would not say, "Suku was happy-go-lucky, cheerful, and a member of the chess club." Nor would you say, "The psychology class held four special sessions for review, took two field trips, and found the instructor amusing."

EXERCISE 8A: PARALLELISM

Revise the following sentences to eliminate faults in parallelism.

1. Manuel was a good student, conscientious, imaginative, and he worked hard.

   _____

2. The cast not only were skillful in acting but were more than competent as singers and dancers also.

   _____

3. The tax rebate neither aided the renters nor were the home-owners helped.

   _____

4. She should try for the promotion for both her own good and because it would be good for the business.

   _____

5. The book had an exciting plot, lovable characters and was on the best-seller list for three months.

   _____

6. In the secretarial class, the instructor advised the students to dress conservatively, wearing dark colors, and to avoid personal business in business hours.

   _____

7. To study for an exam, the student should review his class notes, his textbook should be reread with possible questions being asked, and comparing ideas with other students.

   _____

Suppose, for example, that you select the number 378; that gives you "utilitarian resolution role." If you select 826, that gives you "responsive clientele competencies." Almost any three-digit number will give you a phrase that sounds impressive but says nothing.

EXERCISE 8B: GOBBLEDYGOOK AND JARGON

Gobbledygook is often an attempt to make someone or something more important than they are. Rewrite the following sentences to eliminate the inflated language and make the message clear.

EXAMPLE:
One must prioritize one's time in order to achieve maximum effort on the most pressing of one's obligations.

TRANSLATION:
Do the most important jobs first.

1. We will need everyone's input on expected expenditures for the upcoming dance extravaganza. Until this data is compiled, we have only ballpark figures which do not facilitate accurate plan making.

   _____

   _____

2. The professor evaluated the products of the extensive efforts of the sophomore class to critique Virginia Woolf.

   _____

   _____

3. Due to the occurrence of inclement weather, a decision was made by the administrative authorities of the college to cancel all pre-noon classes.

   _____

   _____

4. Your child is lacking competency in some subject areas due to the absence of motivational skills concerning work done outside the institution.

   _____

   _____

5. In the case of Avi, who is critical, there are circumstances that indicate his medical situation is serious.

   _____

   _____

6. The hoopsters of Hoop-la College debut tonight to fire the open-ing gun of the hardwood circuit.

_____

_____

7. The instructional personnel of our institution of higher learning are frustrated because budgetary limitations make their innovative proposals infeasible.

_____

_____

8. The utilization of computer technology will facilitate the re-trieval of information from our data bank.

_____

_____

9. Hopefully, all employees are urged to extinguish illumination and other energy-consuming facilities when departing the premises for the night.

_____

_____

10. The student's achievement scores negated the decision to accel-erate her with the others in her peer group.

_____

_____

Euphemisms

Euphemisms are mild, pleasant-sounding words used to hide the blunt truth and perhaps unpleasant facts of life. Poor people are "the underprivileged" or "the lower income brackets." Old people are "golden agers" or "senior citizens." Dead people are referred to as "the deceased" or "the dearly departed"; they never die, they just "pass away."

Not all euphemisms are harmful or deceptive, but they can become a little ridiculous, as when garbage collectors become "sani-tary engineers," barbers become "hair stylists" or "tonsorial artists," prison guards become "correctional officers," and rat catchers be-come "rodent control operators."

A multitude of crimes punishable by law hide behind such euphemisms as "indiscretion," "misconduct," "delinquency," "inti-macy," "indecency," "misappropriation," or "negligence." Euphemisms become vicious distortions of language and meaning when brutal aggression becomes "liberation," forced labor becomes "re-education," and shooting civilians is called "pacification." Because direct and straightforward language best delivers clear, undistorted messages, it makes sense to avoid euphemisms altogether.

Synonyms

You may have noticed that all the choices discussed in this section have been choices among synonyms, words that mean almost the same thing. The English language is rich in synonyms, so you have ample resources from which to choose words that make distinctions on the basis of connotation, usage, abstraction or concreteness, generalization or specificity.

Notice the distinctions made among the synonyms for the word *sign* in the *American Heritage Dictionary:*

> Synonyms: *sign, badge, mark, token, indication, symptom, note.* These nouns are compared as they denote outward evidence of something. *Sign,* the most general, can mean virtually any [kind of objective evidence]. *Badge* usually refers to something worn that denotes membership in a group, or rank, achievement, or condition: *Her mink coat was a badge of success. Mark* can refer to a personal characteristic or indication of character: *Intolerance is the mark of a bigot.* It can also denote evidence of an experience: *Poverty had left its mark on him. Token* usually refers to a symbol, pledge, or proof of something intangible: *a token of affection. Indication* refers to evidence of a condition. *Symptom* suggests visible evidence of an adverse condition, such as a disease. *Note* applies to a distinguishing characteristic or feature: *the note of mysticism in his novels.*

EXERCISE 8C: SYNONYMS AND THE DISTINCTIONS AMONG THEM

Using a good, modern, unabridged dictionary (or, ideally, the Oxford English Dictionary*) look up the synonyms for the following words. Can the synonyms be used interchangeably? Notice the differences you see among them.*

1. courtesy
2. cry
3. mischievous
4. reckless
5. appeal

EXERCISE 8D: SYNONYMS TO BE DISTINGUISHED AMONG

Among the following groups of words, the essential meaning in each group is similar, but each word is somewhat different from every other word in its group. Without using a dictionary, tell what differences you see among these words.

Example: Wit, humor, comedy, farce. Wit is a keen perception of clever ideas and the apt expression of them. Humor is cheerful sense of the amusing circumstances of life. Comedy, most often associated with drama, is lighthearted and amusing in theme and character and ends happily. Farce is light and humorous drama in which the fun consists of twists of plot rather than in character development.

1. Moral, upright, honest, virtuous
2. Like, love, fondness, affection
3. Goodbye, adieu, farewell, so long. (Hello, good day, hi, how are you?)
4. Grief, sorrow, regret, misery
5. Power, strength, capability, capacity

REVIEW OF RULES REGARDING GOOD DICTION

1. Choose the simple word over the long word if the simpler word says what you mean.
2. Choose the precise and concise word to eliminate wordiness.
3. Choose a fresh comparison over a worn-out phrase. If you can't think of an original comparison, choose plain, direct statements rather than clichés.
4. Choose reasonable statements rather than excessive statements of enthusiasm or disapproval. ("Cedar Point Amusement Park is the greatest place in the world for anyone to spend a vacation.")
5. Choose reasonable statements rather than preaching. ("Young people must respect their parents.")
6. Choose a standard word rather than the in-group language of jargon, unless you are writing to an in-group.
7. Choose vigorous action verbs to improve the clarity and force of your writing.

Franklin P. Adams, a popular writer of humorous verse (what is the distinction between verse and poetry?), wrote a poem addressed to a thesaurus. As you read the poem, observe that scarcely any two of the synonyms could replace each other if the poem were not meant as a joke.

To a Thesaurus

O precious codex, volume, tome,
Book, writing, compilation, work
Attend the while,
A jest, a jape, a quip, a quirk.

For I would pen, engross, indite,
Transcribe, set forth, compose, address,
Record, submit—yea, even write
An ode, an elegy to bless—

To bless, set store by, celebrate,
Approve, esteem, endow with soul,
Commend, acclaim, appreciate,
Immortalize, laud, praise, extol

Without thy help, recruit, support,
Opitulation, furtherance,
Assistance, rescue, aid, resort,
Favour, sustention and advance?

Alas! alack! and well-a-day!
My case would then be dour and sad,
Likewise distressing, dismal, grey,
Pathetic, mournful, dreary, bad.

Though I could keep this up all day,
This lyric, elegiac song,
Meseems hath come the time to say
Farewell! Adieu! Good-bye! So long!

CHAPTER 9

Defining

THE NEED FOR DEFINITION

"What do you mean?"
"What does that question *really* mean?"
"What does the instructor mean by those rules?"
"What does that point in the textbook mean?"

Perhaps some form of this question is more frequently asked than any other. Everyone has a continual and imperative need for definition if the world is to be understandable at all. To take the correct action, to do a good job, to understand each other and even ourselves, we must be able to define the words and the terms that we use to communicate with. Yet words have many different meanings; people have different interpretations of words and ideas; and people mean different things when they use the same words. If, for example, you ask twenty people to define the word *liberal* you'll probably be surprised at the number of different answers you'll get.

In everyday situations we see the confusion created by the failure to define terms. For instance, the dictionary defines *liberal* as "broad-minded," "ample," and "unconfined," among other meanings. But the implications of these meanings are so wide that to communicate clearly, you must define (limit) the word to your meaning. If not, you have Uncle Fritz, who thinks Genghis Khan and Attila the Hun were "liberals" and Aunt Petulia, who thinks that any woman who wears slacks is a "liberal."

Many people say that there is no possibility of discussing politics or religion without quarreling. Because politics and religion are essentially controversial subjects, it is particularly important to have all basic terms fully defined. Even then, of course, disagreement can arise, but it will be sensible disagreement and not a confused argument about disparate points of view. The word *define* means to set limits to a subject, just as you might build a fence about something as if to say "this is what I'm talking about, this and no more."

All definitions, whether limited or extended, must have two characteristics to be a definition; they must be *necessary* and *sufficient.* Suppose you consider what is perhaps the most famous definition ever made—Aristotle's definition of man as "a rational animal." Both words, *rational* and *animal* are necessary to define *man,* or human, but the two words are sufficient; nothing else is required.

The Limited Definition

Whatever the subject of your essay or its method of development, you may need to provide at least a limited definition of key terms. A *limited* definition enables you to clarify briefly by setting limits to your ideas. For example, a limited definition of *democracy* might be as brief as this: A democracy is a form of government in which power is vested in the people who execute it under freely elected agents.

The Extended Definition

In an *extended* definition, on the other hand, the defining discussion of democracy might well run to pages, as it does in Crevecoeur's famous essay, *"What Is Democracy?"* Many words need a paragraph, an essay, or even a book to define them adequately. Words such as *civil disobedience, loyalty, peace, freedom, liberty, wealth, education,* and *art* are examples of words that require extended definitions.

An extended definition offers the opportunity to explore the full meaning of a term. It gives you a chance to go beyond a general definition and explore the implications and possibilities of meaning. If you start with a basic definition, you can expand it in a variety of ways. You may develop your extended definition through one method; however, you will usually find that a combination of methods works best.

Synonym

Extended example

Comparison

Examples

Courage is resistance to fear, mastery of fear—not absence of fear. Except a creature be part coward it is not a compliment to say it is brave; it is merely a loose misapplication of the word. Consider the flea!—incomparably the bravest of all the creatures of God, if ignorance of fear were courage. Whether you are asleep or awake he will attack you, caring nothing for the fact that in bulk and strength you are to him as are the massed armies of the earth to a suckling child; he lives both day and night and all days and nights in the very lap of peril and the immediate presence of death, and yet is no more afraid than is the man who walks the streets of a city that was threatened by an earthquake ten centuries before. When we speak of Clive, Nelson, and Putnam as men who "didn't know what fear was," we ought always to add the flea—and put him at the head of the procession.

Mark Twain

Concrete and Abstract Terms

The distinction between concrete and abstract terms is a key element in definition, as earlier chapters indicated. *Concrete* terms refer to and give a name to some physical thing; they refer to something that can be seen, touched, measured, or weighed. *Abstract* terms, however, give a name to or put a label on certain intellectual and emotional concepts. Thus, the task of defining abstract terms is more complex. Terms such as *integrity, truth, justice,* and *patriotism* have nothing concrete to refer to. Thus, no two people have exactly the same concept of such words.

It is these abstract terms that cause a great deal of difficulty in communication. One individual's idea of patriotism, for example, may be comprised of many intangibles such as religious beliefs, family attitudes, the course of recent events, and the individual's outlook. When you must use abstract terms, you can make them clear by providing relevent, concrete examples.

METHODS OF DEFINITION

Formal Definition

A formal definition follows a fixed form that usually provides the clearest short definition. This form always includes three parts:

Terms to Be Defined	General Classification	Differentiating Detail
pronghorn	an animal of the antelope family	three feet at shoulder, horns split and 15 inches long, a ruminant of N. American plains
awe	a feeling of reverence or admiration	extremely powerful, produced by sense of the grand or sublime
adverb	one of the seven parts of speech	modifiers of verbs, adjectives, other adverbs; expressing time, place, manner, degree
morale	moral and mental condition of a person or group	concerned with cheer, confidence, self-reliance
philosophy	an academic discipline within the liberal arts	deals with the rational investigation of being and knowledge
harpsichord	keyboard instrument	precursor of piano, in which strings are plucked, not struck
ambulance	wheeled vehicle	equipped for transporting sick or injured people
sonnet	lyric poem	made up of 14 lines of iambic pentameter in one of two rhyme schemes, English or Italian
alarmist	an excitable person	who exaggerates dangers, foretells calamities and disasters
to define	a transitive verb	sets limits to boundaries, usually in order to set forth the meaning of a word

NOTE: A formal definition may include unfamiliar terms, but it always mentions them so you can also look them up, and so have a complete definition. For example, notice the terms *iambic pentameter* in sonnet.

Here are some guidelines for making your formal definitions complete and precise. Formal definition almost guarantees your clarity of thought.

1. Adhere to the form: term to be defined; general classification; differentiating details.
2. Place the term in a class, choosing the smallest appropriate class. A manatee could be placed in the class of animal, but much differentiating detail would be needed because the class is not sufficiently limited. When you place the manatee in a class of "plant-eating aquatic mammals," you have narrowed the class to take a first step toward definition.
3. Your definition must take into account every differentiating detail that is necessary. If you define a drill as "a tool for boring holes in wood," you have failed to account for drills used to bore holes in rock, masonry, metal, etc.
4. Your definition must exclude everything that does not logically belong to the term being defined. If you define manatee as "a gentle creature of the sea" or "a member of an endangered species," you have failed to exclude other gentle sea creatures or members of endangered species.
5. By following the pattern of formal definition, you avoid creating a circular definition, the kind of definition that just repeats the term to be defined in slightly different words: "An earache is a pain in the ear." So are circular definitions.

Defining by Synonyms

One of the easiest and fastest ways to explain the meaning of a word is to define with synonyms, words that mean something similar to the words you are defining. This technique is particularly useful when you are defining a term that may be unfamiliar to your reader. For example, suppose your personnel manager has sent you the résumés of three applicants for a job in your company. On each of the résumés she has written one word. The words are *querulous, obstreperous,* and *affable.* Unless you have precise knowledge of what these words mean, you have only a foggy notion of which applicant impressed the personnel director favorably. A quick check with the dictionary can supply you with synonyms:

querulous: whining, complaining, finicky

obstreperous: noisy, unruly, biosterous

affable: pleasant, amiable, helpful, agreeable

Now you can make an intelligent decision on whom you will interview or hire.

When you define with synonyms, you must bear two things in mind. First, the word supplied as a synonym must be a simpler word than the term to be defined. Second, the grammatical form of both words must be the same. Notice that the synonyms for *querulous*, *obstreperous*, and *propitious* are all simpler words of the same grammatical form (adjective) as the words defined. For example:

> *to osculate* (a difficult term) means "*to kiss*" (a simpler term)

NOT

> *to kiss* means "to osculate"

And, making sure to use the same part of speech,

> *to osculate* means "to kiss"

NOT

> *to osculate* means "kissing"

Defining by Word Origin

One of the most obvious, yet often overlooked, methods of clarifying the meaning of a term is to examine the origin of the term. For example, the word *sabotage* means "the intentional destruction of materials, machines, or some productive process." The meaning of the term becomes quite clear when you learn that *sabotage* comes from the French word *sabot*, meaning "shoe," and that it was coined during the French Revolution when the workers "sabotaged" French factories by throwing their shoes into the machinery. Once you learn how and when the word *sabotage* became part of the English language, you not only have a clearer understanding of the word, but you are also less likely to forget the meaning of the word because the picture of French peasants throwing their shoes into factory machinery will always flash into your mind every time you see the word.

Put the boot to it.

Looking up the origin of a word also reminds you that language is constantly changing, with old words gaining new meanings and new words being born. The word *chauvinist*, for example, was never used before 1815. It was coined as a result of the fanatic loyalty of a French soldier, Nicholas Chauvin, to Napoleon. Thus, *chauvinism* has come to mean blind attachment to something, such as one's beliefs or, as it is commonly used today, one's sex. The word *boycott* is another word that has a relatively recent origin, and it also originated from a person's name. In the 1880's, during the struggle between British landowners and Irish tenant farmers, a man by the name of Captain Charles Boycott was hired to collect the rent from the farmers on a large estate in County Mayo. The impoverished Irish peasants, however, got together and decided to ostracize Captain Boycott by ignoring him and refusing to pay.

You cannot depend exclusively on word origin for a sound definition because the meanings of words do change with time. Today, for example, the word *sabotage* does not always refer to the destruction of material objects. It often refers to a more subtle means of obstruction such as interfering with a presidential candidate's campaign strategy. The meaning of the word *boycott* has also undergone some change. Although it still means "refusal to deal with someone," *boycott* today is usually used to refer to a ban on particular goods, such as the embargo of Iraqi oil or the boycott of the Olympics in 1980. Use word origin in your definition essay only if the word's origin or history helps the reader to understand the meaning that you wish to convey.

Defining by Examples

Examples are a most effective way to define. As you learned in Chapter 4, examples can always aid understanding by supplying illustrations. Perhaps you want to know exactly what an *anecdote* is. How does it differ from other kinds of short fiction?

In the *Little, Brown Book of Anecdotes,* the editor explains the literary form of the anecdote as a very brief narrative on a biographical basis with comic overtones, usually with the comic point expressed in dialogue. The remainder of the book is made up of anecdotes about a multitude of characters alphabetically listed. These anecdotes serve as examples.

In an essay defining anecdotes, you might use the editor's explanation as your thesis statement and follow that by quoting a few anecdotes as examples. For instance:

Lord Castleross, an Irish nobleman and newspaper executive, was visiting in the United States and was invited to a golf match. A very avid golfer approached him to ask, "And what is your handicap, Lord Castleross?" "Drink and debauchery," he answered sadly but truly.

***

Sir Thomas Beecham, a great orchestral conductor, noticed in the lobby of an English hotel an attractive woman who seemed familiar to him but whom he really could not recall. As he paused to talk to her, he vaguely remembered that she had a brother. Hoping for a clue, he asked her how her brother was and if he was still working at the same job. "Oh, he's very well," she answered, "and still king."

Examples such as these would illustrate and support your thesis statement.

Defining by Comparison and Contrast

You may define one term by comparing or contrasting its meaning with that of another term. You might define a liberal by showing how his or her views differ from those of a conservative. Comparison and contrast is especially useful in defining closely related terms. For instance, *tragedy* and *misfortune* are closely related terms, yet not every misfortune is a tragedy. By means of comparison and contrast, you could show the frequently ignored distinction between these two terms. Specifically, although news reports often refer to events of the day—a fire, an auto accident, an explosion— as being tragic, tragedy, at least in its traditional meaning, always involves a tragic flaw or moral weakness on the part of a central character.

Defining by Division and Classification

A useful method of defining a complex term is to divide and classify the various aspects of its meaning. If you wanted to discuss the economic classes in the United States, you might divide people into various groups, such as the very rich, the affluent professionals, the middle-income workers, the working poor, and the indigent. You might then proceed to classify the members of a particular group. For example, the indigent might be classified to include the disabled workers, the physically handicapped, the mentally unfit, the emotionally disturbed, and the socially maladjusted.

Defining by Negation

Defining by negation means that you supply no definition of any sort. You do not give a synonym, nor compare and contrast, nor define by etymology or examples. When you explain by negation, you clarify something by saying what it is not. You might say of a *ghost* that it is not a real person; it has no physical qualifications. Metaphorically, you might say that someone who has no possibility of succeeding "doesn't have a ghost of a chance." Having given a negative description of your meaning, your definition, when it does come, arrives with great weight of meaning. Look how effectively Shakespeare uses negation in one of his sonnets:

True love, he says, will admit neither obstacles nor change. "Love is not love which alters when it alteration finds."

EXERCISE 9A: FORMAL DEFINITION

Using an up-to-date desk dictionary, construct a formal definition of each of the following terms.

(epicure) **1.** _____

(lachrymose) **2.** _____

(rhetoric) **3.** _____

(strobe light) **4.** _____

(vernacular) **5.** _____

(to hector) **6.** _____

(gabardine) **7.** _____

(abacus) **8.** _____

(to nuzzle) **9.** _____

(rhumba) **10.** _____

Notice how the following essay makes use of several methods of definition:

··

WHAT IS A DISASTER?

··

What is a disaster? We Americans tend to use this word, as we do most words, loosely. We say things like, "My date last night was a disaster," when we mean we were bored; or, "My day at work was a disaster" when we don't think we accomplished as much as we had planned. We say, "This morning was a disaster; my car wouldn't start, and I was late to school." These might be misfortunes, mistakes, or mishaps, but they are not disasters.

Negation

Disasters can be natural, like an earthquake, a flood, or

Division and classification

tornado; or man-made like the space shuttle explosion, the Pan Am crash over Scotland, or the chemical pollution of Love Canal. Man-made disasters can be accidental, like the chemical spill at Bhopal, India, or planned like the Japanese attack on Pearl Harbor. Pearl Harbor was a disaster for the U.S., but it was purposeful on the part of the Japanese and a triumph for them in 1941.

Formal definition

Example

A disaster is a happening that causes great harm; it implies great destruction or damage; it is ruinous. The oil spill at Valdez, Alaska, was a disaster. It caused great harm to wildlife, to the economy of the area, to the beauty of one of the last unspoiled places on our planet. The destruction was great and the damage is likely irreversible. Two hundred miles south of Valdez, the salmon in the spawning area are contaminated; there are no snails in the rocks on beaches. Dead eagles and other sea birds along with sea otters are creating more pollution as their oil-soaked remains are burned; their crime? they were at the wrong place at the wrong time. Fishermen have lost $400,000,000 so far; many will not be able to make the payments and will lose their boats, their livelihood. No one won at Valdez; there was no triumph, no gain, just tremendous loss to everyone on the planet. And everyone on earth lost one of the few places on earth that was still unspoiled.

Contrast

Perhaps to understand the extent of the disaster, one must visualize Prince William Sound before and after.

Description

Before, majestic snow-capped mountains tower over the rocky beaches and pristine waters that make up the Sound. Playful otters frolic on the beaches and float on their backs in the lapping water. Eagles soar above as sea birds swoop in for fish or stalk the shores. Fish abound as did fishermen who had made their living there for 110 years. It is a paradise, a last frontier; it is what the United States was before industry and pollution destroyed many of the natural wonders.

Narration

Suddenly, into these idyllic surroundings, comes disaster. A ship as big as a large hotel hits a rock and *eleven million gallons* of viscous crude oil pour into the water and on to the beaches. Everything, water, rocks, vegetation is covered with black, sticky, deadly oil. The vegetation dies quickly; rocks are permanently stained even after extensive cleaning—some with chemicals that may have destroyed even more of the environment.

Description

How much wildlife died we will never know, but volunteers, when they got there, found sea otters with their luxurious fur matted with the thick viscous oil. Birds, their undersides coated with the gooey crude oil, were unable to extract themselves from the ooze. They died along with untold numbers of fish as volunteers tried to scrub the glue-like mess from the ones fortunate enough to be caught. The heavy fur and heavy feathers that protected the otters and the birds from the cold waters of the Sound meant doom when the waters were coated with sticky, stubborn crude oil. The oil saturated feathers and fur; the once friendly habitat became fatal. Many more fish and fowl and animals will die slowly along the 700 miles of coastline.

Example

A disaster is permanent. People still wonder about and visit the ruins of Pompeii. When the volcano erupted there, the city was destroyed; people died as they sat at their tables. Today, there is no Pompeii, only ruins. Prince William Sound may also be dead. While the rocks on the beaches have been scrubbed and most of the surface oil removed, the oil, as it disintegrated, has sifted down to the bottom of the Sound. As it

Ultimate effect

infects the bottom of the ecosystem, Prince William Sound may be dying. If the basis of the delicate system is gone, soon all will be gone as each higher stage feeds on the lower. The highest stage, the people who gain their livelihood from Prince William Sound's largess, the fishermen will be gone too. A disaster is all bad, all ruin, devastation for everyone.

Cause and effect

What causes disasters? The eruption of Mt. Vesuvius caused the destruction of Pompeii. The sliding of two continental plates caused the earthquake in San Francisco. What caused the disaster at Valdez? Some say a drunken captain was the cause, but that explanation is both questionable and simplistic. A human-made disaster usually has multiple causes. Why wasn't the ship monitored by Coast Guard radar which could have told the *Valdez* that she was off course. Why wasn't Exxon ready for a possible disaster? Why was the staff of a huge tanker reduced to twenty men when earlier forty men staffed smaller ships? Can every crew member be expected to be alert and ready when working twelve to fourteen hours a day? The ship apparently responded slowly to an order for hard-right-rudder. Was this because the helmsman used a counter-rudder maneuver to slow the swing? Or is a ship this size just too big to maneuver quickly?

Conclusion

Whatever the cause, the oil spill at Valdez was a disaster. Not a misfortune, not a tragedy, but a disaster. We, the world, have lost another natural treasure. It is now tainted, spoiled by humans, the greatest spoiler of them all.

ORGANIZATION

As in all the other essays you are writing, the basic organization remains the three-fold structure: introduction—body—conclusion.

INTRODUCTION

The main purpose of the introduction is to bring sharply into focus the term you intend to define. Your thesis sentence differs from a general definition in one significant respect: a thesis sentence presents a specific attitude toward the term. Is the term commonly misunderstood? In what way? What do you consider to be the most important aspect of its meaning? Why do you attach a certain meaning to this term? Do your ideas and associations differ from the generally accepted meaning of the term?

These questions show why the thesis sentence for your definition essay must be carefully worded and why your attitude must be carefully narrowed and made very specific. A thesis sentence such as "Wealth has many meanings" is too obvious and too general to spark the reader's interest. A better thesis sentence might be: "At every stage in life, we know what wealth is, but it is never the same in any two stages."

BODY

Any combination of methods may be used in developing the body of your definition. In defining *prejudice,* for example, you might classify different types of prejudice according to their origin: prejudice resulting from ignorance, prejudice resulting from environment, and prejudice resulting from deprivation. Having explained these different types of prejudice, you might then use examples from various sources or anecdotes from personal experience to show how people's actions reveal their prejudices. Further, you might use statistics to show how prejudice affects income, promotion, and entry into certain professions. In defining *poverty,* you might use figures to show how the official poverty level has changed over the past ten years. You might also compare a rich person's definition of poverty as "an all-encompassing hardship" with a poor person's statement that "it's like being in hell with your back broke."

Or if you are going to define *psychopaths,* you can't just say that

Obsession can produce magnificent results.

"psychopaths are people who are different from ordinary, normal people." This is vague and dull. A better introduction might begin with a quotation from Robert Lindner's *Must You Conform?:* "There walk among us men and women who are in but not of our world." Such a sentence might attract the attention of your reader and lead to a more specific thesis sentence: "These men and women are the conscienceless, explosive, unreasoning, and often unrecognized psychopaths who menace society."

After you have introduced your essay with a sentence or two to get the interest of the reader, write your thesis sentence, making sure that it is clear and specific. For example, consider the following introduction to an essay on obsession:

> According to the general definition of the word, obsession strongly suggests an abnormal preoccupation with a fixed idea. It carries with it a notion of abnormal and neurotic behavior as a result of thinking that is definitely lopsided and usually somewhat sick. What is often ignored, however, is that obsession can be a marvelous thing—the focal point around which all of the individual's talents and energies are marshaled. Obsession can produce magnificent results when it serves one great purpose in life, whether that purpose be to write beautiful poetry, carve great monuments, or just build a better mousetrap.

This essay could be effectively developed with telling examples of people whose obsessions drove them to achieve their aims in life.

CONCLUSION

An effective method of concluding an extended definition is to summarize briefly your discussion and then restate the essential meaning of the term. Try to pull together the various aspects of meaning you have discussed, and then conclude with a clear statement that points up the essence of the term's meaning as you interpret it. An apt quotation might serve your purpose, but more often you conclude by restating your thesis sentence. For example, the essay on obsession might be brought to a conclusion with a restatement of the thesis: "Obsession can drive humans to great heights and leave everything else—the baseness, the folly, the anguish—forgotten in the presence of their achievement."

Here is one student's definition of marriage:

....
A LESSON WELL LEARNED
....

"For better, for worse, for richer, for poorer, in sickness and in health. Till death do us part and I do." As the minister pronounced us husband and wife, I smiled knowingly to myself. I was seventeen years old and my image of marriage was a fairy tale in which I would be queen in my own little castle, a dream in which all was bliss and excitement and independence. At seventeen, I knew it all, especially what the word *marriage* meant—or so I thought. After four years of marriage and two years of divorce, I now know what the word *marriage* means. Marriage is a commitment between two people that involves love, sharing, compromise, and acceptance of one another.

The word *marriage*, to me, cannot be defined in a dictionary. The dictionary definition of marriage is (1) the legal union of a man with a woman for life, and (2) the formal declaration or contract by which act a man and a woman join in wedlock. Those definitions are very cold and broad. A dictionary definition just does not include the implication of emotional involvement—a serious mistake, as I've found out.

The emotional involvement of marriage happens gradually. The first step in this process is the change in self-image which usually occurs during the honeymoon. The introduction of the mate as "Mrs. So and So" or "my husband" brings the realization to the newly married couple that they are no longer two separate people, but united and committed to each other. Responsibilities, as well as obligations, are realized as part of the marriage. The couple begin to know each other, accept one another, and share each other's happiness as well as disappointments. Only through living with one another, through seeing each other's faults and accepting that no one is perfect, and compromising when necessary can a couple achieve the emotional commitment necessary for a marriage to succeed.

For a marriage to succeed, it must not include certain qualities. Jealousy, for one, cannot exist. For example, when I was married, both my husband and I were extremely jealous. Anything more than a fleeting glance in another person's direction would plummet the other into a jealous rage. Jealousy cannot see and would invariably lead into a long, drawn-out verbal battle. Coupled with the plight of jealousy comes the curse of mistrust. For example, one day my father became very ill. Upon learning this from my distressed Mom, I hurriedly dressed and left without leaving a note or calling my husband at work. As it turned out, my Dad was admitted to the hospital in serious condition. As upset as I was, I totally forgot to call my husband to explain the situation. When I returned home very late that night, he was seeing red—he was sure I was cheating. We exchanged angry, hurtful words, which only increased my distress. After spending the night on the couch, he awoke with a clearer head. He apologized to me, but it was too late—the damage had been done. These qualities can certainly be detrimental to a marriage.

Now that I'm an old lady of twenty-four, my conception of marriage has changed considerably. I realize fully the commitment involved in the process of learning to accept, share, and love another person. I've learned that to be married is hard work, but that it is something definitely worth working for. And last, had I known at seventeen what I know now, I would have realized that neither of us were ready for the commitment of marriage.

Bonnie Shamrock
(Student)

PITFALLS TO AVOID

1. Avoid such vague commonplaces as "Love means different things to different people." Such statements do not help to define but rather arouse a vast indifference. Your reaction to statements like this is "So what?" That is your clue that your expression is boring and vapid.
2. Don't try to list every meaning of the term. You are writing an essay, not making a catalog. What you need is a specific attitude concerning the significance of the term; that is what you need to develop.
3. Don't let your discussion drift so that you end up discussing something unrelated to the term you are supposed to be defining.

Repeating the term (or recognizable synonyms) at frequent intervals will help you stay on the track and help to keep the thesis before your reader.

4. Avoid starting with such threadbare phrases as "According to my dictionaries. . . . " Consult the most complete and up-to-date dictionaries you can get your hands on, but don't just quote these dictionaries. Try to get a firm grasp of the meaning and then express it in your own words.

5. Avoid vague and sloppy definition. Use specific examples and concrete details to make your meaning clear and vivid.

6. Remember that you almost undoubtedly need to use several methods to make your extended definition clear and complete. Negation, for example, is useful in eliminating areas of meaning that do not apply, but negation alone will not provide a complete definition.

EXERCISE 9B: METHODS OF DEFINITION

Identify the method or methods of definition used in each of the following:

_____ 1. *Oddball* is a slang term for an eccentric or unconventional person.

_____ 2. *Loquacious* means talkative.

_____ 3. A movie *star* is someone like Dustin Hoffman, Laurence Olivier, and Angelica Houston.

_____ 4. *Hari-kiri* is a Japanese ceremonial suicide committed by ripping open the abdomen with a knife.

_____ 5. *Dysentery* is not a pain in the stomach; it is not nausea. It is an infection of the lower digestive tract producing pain, fever, and severe diarrhea.

_____ 6. *Ancillary:* auxiliary or accessory; from *ancilla,* a young serving maid in a Latin household.

_____ 7. *Betrayal:* (a) treachery or disloyalty; (b) the exhibition or revelation of a fault; (c) deception; (d) unfulfillment of one's better self; seduction and desertion of a person.

_____ 8. *Mores:* Mores are important sociological folkways that are accepted without question and that embody the fundamental moral views of a group.

_____ 9. *Persona:* A persona is not a human being nor is it a physical or legal personality. It is a critical and literary term to describe a public and assumed role in a play or novel.

_____ 10. *Tête-à-tête:* A *tête-à-tête* is a term taken from French meaning a conversation between two people.

EXERCISE 9C: INADEQUATE DEFINITION

Read the following definitions and explain why they are inadequate. Then write a correct definition of the italicized term.

1. A *tambourine* is a musical instrument.

_____

2. A *puppet* is a marionette.

_____

3. *Magnanimity* is the quality of being magnanimous.

_____

4. An *apron* is a protective covering.

_____

5. A *patronymic* is a middle name.

_____

6. The *string section* is an important part of an orchestra.

_____

7. A *tricycle* is a three-wheeled machine for transportation which is made of metal, is steered by handlebars with a bell on them, and usually has tires made of hard rubber.

_____

8. *Sociology* is one of the social sciences.

_____

9. *Laughter* is a kind of convulsion that some people have when they think something is funny.

_____

10. *Sorrow* is a feeling you have when you feel sorry for something.

_____

SUGGESTED TOPICS

Write an extended definition on one of the following topics.

1. A bigot	**6.** A perfectionist	**11.** An egomaniac
2. An intellectual	**7.** A parasite	**12.** An artist
3. A chauvinist	**8.** A humanitarian	**13.** A misogynist
4. An optimist	**9.** An alcoholic	**14.** A nonconformist
5. A pessimist	**10.** A workaholic	**15.** A sadist

16. A lie	**28.** Propaganda	**40.** Ambition
17. An educator	**29.** Marriage	**41.** Slander
18. A mercenary	**30.** Charisma	**42.** Common sense
19. A friend	**31.** Heaven	**43.** Learning
20. An acquaintance	**32.** Hell	**44.** Freedom
21. A mother	**33.** Courage	**45.** Guilt
22. A father	**34.** Wealth	**46.** Victory
23. A student	**35.** Happiness	**47.** Failure
24. A war crime	**36.** Greed	**48.** Morality
25. A fair price	**37.** Honesty	**49.** Immorality
26. Academic freedom	**38.** Success	**50.** Romantic love
27. Power	**39.** Trust	

TECHNIQUES OF CLEAR WRITING

SENTENCE VARIETY

A traditional definition says that "A sentence is a group of words containing a subject and a verb and expressing at least one complete thought." But a sentence is only fully defined when you consider the various types of sentences there are. When you write, or rewrite, for sentence variety, you make your sentences more enjoyable for your reader.

One obvious variation is length. (You might be interested in knowing that the length of the average sentence in a doctoral dissertation is 22 to 24 words.) In spoken English, sentences tend to be short. The point in rewriting is to vary your sentences; frequently the type of sentence will determine the approximate length.

To study the types of sentences, you need, as in so many other definitions, to turn to classification.

Classification A: On the Basis of Function

1. Statements   Declarative sentences
2. Questions   Interrogative sentences
3. Commands   Imperative sentences
4. Exclamations   Exclamatory sentences

These classes are almost self-explanatory.

A declarative sentence is a simple statement.

You will be at the dance; I'll see you there.

An interrogative sentence is a question.

> Will you be at the dance? Will I see you there?

An imperative sentence is a command.

> Be at the dance—or else.

An exclamatory sentence denotes an emotion like surprise or excitement.

> You *will* be at the dance! I thought you were going away.

Some ideas will not work in all four forms, but most will work in three. Notice how punctuation helps to express the meaning, just as tone of voice does in speech. The exclamation point, in particular, gives emphasis. (Don't use more than one; it sounds hysterical.)

DECLARATIVE:
You are lucky.

INTERROGATIVE:
Are you lucky?

IMPERATIVE:
Be lucky!

EXCLAMATORY:
You *are* lucky!

Classification B: On the Basis of Grammar

1. Simple
2. Compound
3. Complex
4. Compound–Complex

The *simple sentence* has one subject–verb combination, although it can have compound subjects or verbs.

> The *book was* depressing.

> The *book* and the *movie were* both depressing.

> The *book saddened* me but *enlightened* me.

The *simple* sentence is used effectively to express a simple thought. You never want a sentence to be more elaborate than the thought it conveys. The simple sentence is also effective to express strong emotion, for its simplicity lends it strength. A strong statement should not be weakened by qualifiers. You would scarcely say, "Because you have a fast car, a big allowance, curly hair, a darling smile, and a good sense of humor, I love you." When you want to indicate that you're in love, the simple "I love you" is more effective.

The *compound sentence* is made of two or more independent clauses linked together with a coordinating conjunction (*and, but, or, nor, for, so,* or *yet*). These sentences are effective when you wish to present several ideas that are equal in importance: *He loved his parents, he respected his teachers, and he enjoyed his friends.*

    S   V   S   V

The *book was* depressing and enlightening, but the *movie was* just depressing.

The *complex sentence* has one independent clause (sentence) and one or more dependent clauses (not a complete sentence). This type of sentence allows the writer to show various relationships between ideas in the sentence, primarily that one idea is more important than the others. Experienced writers use it about 70 percent of the time. You, too, should use it frequently to highlight your important ideas.

> Although the book was depressing and enlightening, the movie was just depressing.

> or

> Although the movie was just depressing, the book was depressing and enlightening.

The dependent clause is introduced by a subordinating conjunction. The subordinating conjunction you choose is important because it shows the relationship of the subordinate clause to the main clause. The subordinating conjunctions can show various relationships and precise distinctions in meaning. Note the difference made in the following sentences by changing the subordinating conjunctions.

Although she loved her husband, she decided to divorce him.
Because she loved her husband, she decided to divorce him.

As its name suggests, the *compound-complex sentence* combines a *compound* sentence (two simple sentences) with a *complex* sentence (one or more dependent clauses).

Compound: I called my dog, and he came running.
Complex: When I called my dog, he came running.
Compound-Complex: When I called my dog, he came running, and he refused to leave me.

The compound-complex sentence is effective when you want to show relationships among several ideas that are so closely associated that you wish to combine all of them in one sentence.

Although the book was depressing and enlightening, the movie was just depressing, but the message was clear in both.

Classification C: On the Basis of Rhetoric

1. Loose
2. Periodic
3. Balanced
4. Antithetical

Periodic and Loose Sentences

The *loose sentence* is the most common type of sentence. Loose sentences give the message first, then add details. *Periodic sentences* withhold the ending of the sentence, putting the details between the subject and the predicate.

LOOSE:
Chief Freshwater watched his braves die at the hands of the white man's cavalry, well equipped and fresh while his braves had few weapons and were underfed and dead tired.

PERIODIC:
Chief Freshwater, watching as his tired and ill-equipped braves faced the white man's fresh and well-equipped cavalry, cried out as his men died.

Periodic sentences are dramatic and should be used only when the subject is dramatic. The following would be anticlimactic and ludicrous.

> While Sandra cowered in her room, terrified and incoherent, her clothes drenched with sweat, her face stained with tears, it rained.

Because the loose sentence is the type that seems most natural in English, you should choose it for most of the more commonplace things you write. Sometimes you will choose to put a subordinate idea both before and after the main clause. You might say, "Having sold her business, rented her house, put her furniture in storage, and said goodbye to her friends, Deirdre sailed to the Fiji Islands, a trip she had always wanted to take." The most important idea is in the weakest position, but it remains the strongest idea because it is in the independent clause. The loose sentence, as its name suggests, is not rigid in its form.

On the other hand, the *periodic sentence* is fixed in form. It does not complete its meaning until the very end of the sentence. All subordinate ideas come first. Since the strongest position in any writing—whether it be a sentence or longer—is the end, when you wish to be forceful, you choose the periodic sentence. The concluding clause of the periodic sentence has the double importance of being last and being independent: *Having sold her house, rented her business, put her furniture in storage, and said goodbye to her friends,* **Deirdre at last set sail for the Fiji Islands.** An effective periodic sentence builds to a climax and so creates a dramatic suspense.

The *balanced sentence* you are already familiar with as parallel structure. In both the sentences about Deirdre, everything that she did before sailing was presented in parallel form. The parallelism of the balanced sentence is a good choice, when you wish to emphasize that your points are of equal value. For example, *The voyage out was smooth and placid; the voyage back was calm and serene.*

The *antithetical sentence* is another familiar type. It is the balanced sentence, but with an additional characteristic: the parts of the parallelism are alike in structure but opposed in meaning.

> With malice toward none, with charity toward all
> I struggled daily to restore his sanity; I succeeded only in destroying my tranquility.

Like the balanced sentence, the antithetical should be chosen to make strong points.

The good essay uses a variety of sentence patterns. Such variety, however, should not be strained for. If there are no dramatic points in your essay, do not include any periodic sentences. It would be ludicrous to postpone the ending of such a sentence as this one: *When the blizzards rage outside, when the wind howls through the trees ripping off branches, and when the temperatures reach fifty below zero, I usually stay inside.*

If you work conscientiously on getting the right kind of sentence for each idea, the variety will come of itself.

EXERCISE 9D: IDENTIFYING SENTENCE TYPES

In the blank line farthest to the left, indicate whether the sentence is (a) simple, (b) compound, (c) complex, or (d) compound-complex. On the blank line next to it, indicate whether the sentence is (e) declarative, (f) interrogative, (g) exclamatory, or (h) imperative.

_____ _____ **1.** There is something awesome about the Pyramids.

_____ _____ **2.** Is it their size or is it their age, or the setting out in the desert?

_____ _____ **3.** Actually, they're not really out in the middle of the desert; they're actually right in a city, Cairo.

_____ _____ **4.** Incongruously, a golf course, complete with plush green fairways and inviting shade trees, stands just across the street; and a modern hotel sits close by.

_____ _____ **5.** The camels that you ride to the Pyramids exit their stables and lope up a four-lane paved highway, make a sharp left, and you're there—about a one-block ride.

_____ _____ **6.** Nevertheless, once there, you forget the bustling city just around the bend, and gaze in amazement at the towering structures.

_____ _____ **7.** The material that once covered the structures has long since worn away except at the very top, leaving the massive, crumbling stones exposed.

_____ _____ **8.** What a sight they are: massive, towering, ancient!

_____ _____ **9.** If you are daring, you can climb up the structures; the boulders form steps, large steps, but climbable.

_____ _____ **10.** But there are no railings, and you have to come down, too; it's better just to look, in awe, at what ancient man was able to conceive and build.

EXERCISE 9E: CHANGING SENTENCE FORM

Change all the sentences in Exercise 9d to another form, and identify the new form. For example, change simple sentences to complex; compound sentences to complex; and compound-complex to complex. Use your imagination and your skills. Make your sentences better than the original sentences.

EXERCISE 9F: WRITING PERIODIC SENTENCES

Periodic sentences are dramatic and compeling. Write three periodic sentences, choosing appropriate subject matter for each; then write them as loose sentences and be ready to discuss the differences in the two. Let your imagination soar as you concoct scenarios suitable to the exciting periodic sentence.

_____

_____

_____

_____

_____

Using all simple sentences makes your essay seem babyish. Remember your first-grade reader? "See Dick. See Dick run." Dull, dull, dull. Even gruesome stories can seem dull if your sentences lack variety. Notice the monotony of the following passage:

> The Mexican police made a gruesome discovery last week. They had been investigating a drug-smuggling operation. They found evidence of satanism or voodoo practicing. They found corpses of fourteen males. These victims had been mutilated. Some had been slashed with knives. Some had their hearts ripped out. One had his eyes gouged out. Some had ears, nipples, and testicles removed. One had his head cut off. A twenty-one-year-old American student was one of the victims. They also found a roasted human brain in a pot. They found a container with human hair and a goat's head and parts of a chicken. The perpetrators believed in human sacrifice. They thought it would protect them.

Combining sentences, making some compound and some complex, and varying the length of your sentences add sophistication

and interest to your essays. Adding descriptive adjectives and adverbs also helps.

EXERCISE 9G: REWRITING A PARAGRAPH

Rewrite the paragraph on the discoveries of the Mexican police, varying sentence type and length. Also, feel free to add modifiers to clarify and intensify the ideas.

WORD POWER

THE DICTIONARY

The first people to speak any form of English were known as the Anglo-Saxons and they lived in England almost 1,500 years ago. The language they spoke, now called Old English, was a strong, flexible language with a large vocabulary. The Anglo-Saxons, conscious and proud of their vocabulary, called it their "word horde," which implies that they considered their vocabulary the treasure it is, for the words speakers know are the tools with which they think. Every-one's thinking is limited by the words one has to think with.

As protection for the treasure of words, languages today depend upon the dictionary. The dictionary, the best known of reference works, lists the words of a language, supplies much information about each word, and provides its users with standards for usage.

How the Dictionary Can Be Most Helpful

In Defining

You probably use your dictionary most often to find what a word means. When you look up the definition, however, don't just settle for the first meaning the dictionary gives you. Having spent the time to look the word up, read the entire entry because the more you learn, the less you will forget.

In most dictionaries the first meaning given is the oldest and thus the primary meaning. For instance, if you look up the word *red*, you find that its first definition pertains to the specific color, but if you read on, you find that its extended meaning indicates *revolutionary* and, more specifically, communistic because of the red color of many revolutionary banners. Since language grows and enriches itself through extended meanings, it is important to read all of them. Take, for example, even so common an adjective as *tame.* Its first or primary meaning is "changed from wildness to domesticity." But its extended meanings go far beyond that to indicate "naturally gentle and unafraid; submissive; fawning; docile; insipid; flat; sluggish; languid." As you consider how *tame* can mean all of these things, you increase your awareness, not just of one word but of several, and so you build your vocabulary.

Just reading the dictionary can be interesting as well as informative. If, for instance, your eye wanders across the page from *tame*, you might spot the word *taleteller* and notice that it has two diverse meanings. Its earlier sense means an oral narrator, but its secondary sense has a connotation of disapproval, for it means a gossip. The closely similar word *talebearer*, however, has only the connotatively disapproving sense of a gossip. **Looking up words to find their various meanings is one of the very best ways to increase your language awareness, which is imperative for good writing.**

Good dictionaries will usually give you synonyms (and sometimes antonyms) of words being defined. Since there are no exact synonyms, when a word has a number of synonyms, the dictionary frequently distinguishes among them so you can use them precisely. For example, the *American Heritage Dictionary* defines *passion* as "any powerful emotion or appetite, such as love, joy, hatred, anger, or greed." After a full discussion it concludes:

> *synonyms: passion, fervor, enthusiasm, zeal, ardor.*
> These all denote strong feeling, either sustained or passing, for or about something or somebody. *Passion* is a deep, overwhelming feeling or emotion. When directed toward a person, it usually connotes love as well as sexual desire, although it can also refer to hostile emotions such as anger and hatred. Used lightly, it suggests an avid interest, as in a hobby: *a passion for gardening. Fervor* is a highly intense, sustained emotional state, frequently (like *passion*) with a potential loss of control implied: *he fought with fervor.* Quite different is *enthusiasm*, which reflects excitement and responsiveness to more specific or concrete things. *Zeal*, sometimes reflecting strong, forceful devotion to a specific cause, expresses a driving attraction to something which grows out of motivation or attitude: *zeal for the project. Ardor* can be for a cause but commonly connotes a warm, rapturous feeling directed toward persons.

In Pronunciation and Spelling

The same care that you give to meanings should also be given to the forms of words. First, what is meant by "forms of words"? Essentially, the form of a word is its spelling, possible variants in spelling (for example, *dialog* and *dialogue*), variations between British spellings and American spellings (*theatre* and *theater*), variations in number (*mouse, mice*), and variations in gender (*goose, gander*). Forms can refer to the various parts of speech a word may take: noun forms, adjective forms, adverb forms, verb forms. Form also shows the principal parts of verbs when they are irregular. When you are attentive to the forms of words, you improve both your pronunciation and spelling, for these two skills help each other. If you are sure of the sound of a word, you probably can spell it correctly and vice versa. However, if you still need help, most dictionaries have not only a guide to pronunciation at the bottom of each page but also sections which give rules for pronunciation and for spelling.

In Usage

Usage refers to the habitual or customary way in which the speakers and writers of a language employ it. Good modern dictionaries will identify for you the accepted usages of a word: standard, colloquial, slang, or subliterate; currently being used, old-fashioned, or no longer used at all.

In Western culture the first important dictionary was that of the eighteenth-century French Academy, which, as well as giving meanings for words, laid down rules for grammar and usage. It was what is now known as a "prescriptive" dictionary, a rule giver. It is widely admired because it was early and comprehensive; it is widely ignored because rules change and no longer apply. All languages that are still spoken and written are "living" languages, and all living things change. Wise dictionary makers today avoid writing a rule-making dictionary; instead, they write dictionaries that are "descriptive," that is, that describe what people do as they use language.

The dictionary that is usually considered the first important one in English is Dr. Samuel Johnson's, published in 1755. Dr. Johnson had announced that he hoped his dictionary would "refine and purify" the English language. However, long before the end of the seven years it took him to make his dictionary, he found that a living language could not be pinned down with rules. The best a lexicographer could do was to describe the language as used by the best writers and speakers.

The "descriptive" approach to dictionary making has been the most influential since Dr. Johnson. In spite of this, however, during the nineteenth century, especially in America, the dictionary was considered a rule giver, and, as such, almost sacred. People would intone "The dictionary says, . . . " and give a rule. You probably have heard someone say smugly, "*Ain't* isn't in the dictionary." Perhaps it isn't in every dictionary, but it is in modern dictionaries because it is in the language. The *American Heritage Dictionary* has this to say about it:

> **ain't.** Nonstandard. Contraction of am not. Also extended in use to mean are not, is not, has not, and have not. . . . Unacceptable in writing . . . according to ninety-nine percent of the Usage Panel [a group of one hundred respected professional writers who advised the lexicographers on usage] and unacceptable in speech to eighty-four percent. . . .

This partial quotation is typical of the advice on usage given in good contemporary dictionaries. They describe how and by whom the word is used. When you know this about a word, you have a basis for choosing exactly the right word for your purpose.

In Miscellaneous Aids

The larger dictionaries usually contain a table of contents telling what other information is available beyond that given for each entry. *Webster's New International*, for instance, includes sections on new words and their sources and a comprehensive history of the English language. The appendices include abbreviations, census figures, forms of address (how to speak or write to a bishop or a U.S. senator, for example), an alphabetized list of short biographies, an alphabetized list of towns, cities, rivers, mountains, and other geographic information. There are also pages of pictures of such things as coins, flags, airplanes, bridges, famous buildings, dogs, wildflowers, and military insignia. Like the pages of other unabridged dictionaries, this dictionary's more than three thousand pages is a hoard of knowledge.

Types of Dictionaries

Unabridged Dictionaries

The principle source for complete information on words is an *unabridged* dictionary. For example, *Webster's Third New International Dictionary of the English Language*, found in many college libraries, has 450,000 entries (pocket dictionaries usually have no more than 50,000). In addition, the *Third International* offers complete definitions and ample illustrations of the various uses of words. If you want an even more exhaustive history of a word, your best source would be *The Oxford English Dictionary* (O.E.D.). This scholarly, multivolume dictionary provides the most comprehensive historical study of English words and illustrates in great detail the changes in meaning many words have undergone since they first appeared in the language. Other unabridged dictionaries, such as *The Random House Dictionary of the English Language* (260,000 entries), are more limited in scope but more permissive than the O.E.D., especially with respect to current American usage. Although unabridged dictionaries may not be practical for everyday use, you should become familiar with them so that you know where to turn when you encounter a word not included in an abridged dictionary and when you want detailed information about a word.

Pocket Dictionaries

Pocket dictionaries are generally inadequate for college use. Frequently, you may find that the word you need is not listed or the definition that is offered is unsufficient. Furthermore, the pocket dictionaries generally do not provide the advice on usage or the examples you may need to understand the full range of a word's use and meaning.

Desk Dictionaries

A good, up-to-date desk dictionary is your best bet for everyday use. Look for one that has 100,000 or more entries, and be sure to check for a recent copyright date. Many abridged dictionaries are available; any selection from the following list of popular editions would serve you well:

The American Heritage Dictionary of the English Language. 2nd ed. Boston: Houghton Mifflin, Boston, 1983.

Funk & Wagnall's New Comprehensive Dictionary of the English Language. Chicago: Ferguson, 1987.

Random House College Dictionary. Rev. ed. New York: McKay, 1989.

Webster's Ninth New Collegiate Dictionary. Springfield, Mass: Merriam-Webster, Inc., 1989.

Webster's New World Dictionary of the American Language. Rev. ed. New York: Warner Books, 1990.

Tips on Increasing Your Vocabulary

The English language is one of the greatest tools for thinking that exists, and one of the reasons for its greatness is that it is so vast. Its extent can't even be measured, but linguists agree that there are at least a million words in the English language vocabulary. You can share in the power of your language by increasing the words you understand and use.

1. Look at the *context* in which an unfamiliar word appears. You frequently have some notion of its meaning from the way it is

used and the meanings of its neighboring words. Suppose you saw a headline like this: "John Adams, long-time philanthropist, gives city schools $2,000,000." You might intelligently guess that a philanthropist is generous with his or her money. (This doesn't always work: Try *redoubtable,* as in "The redoubtable Mr. Adams." The *doubt* in that word throws off your guess, instead of giving you a clue.)

2. Look up the word. In the first instance your guess would have been fairly accurate, for the dictionary defines *philanthropist* as a person who has an affection for all mankind, which is manifested in donations of money, property, or work to specific groups of people or society in general.

3. Take note of the word's origin. The word *philanthropist* comes from two Greek roots: *phila* which means love and *anthro* which means man or mankind.

4. As soon as you learn a new word, start using it. Check its pronunciation in the dictionary (fi·lan'/·thro·pe), say it several times, and write it in several sentences. You will quickly make it yours. Once it is yours, you will be surprised at how often this "unfamiliar" word pops up.

EXERCISE 9H: DICTIONARY DEFINITIONS

The following words frequently appear on vocabulary tests and lists of words that college freshmen should know. For each, complete the following process:

1. Carefully check each word on the list.
2. Unless you are certain that you know the meaning, circle the word.
3. Look up the meaning of each circled word in a modern desk dictionary.
4. After reading the complete dictionary entry, close the dictionary and write your own brief definition.

1. morose	11. tacit	21. entourage	31. expunge
2. sidle	12. disburse	22. eschew	32. volition
3. arable	13. wry	23. prerogative	33. scurrilous
4. desultory	14. dither	24. lucid	34. wheedle
5. ubiquitous	15. declaim	25. heinous	35. surfeit
6. sedate	16. adroit	26. innate	36. verdant
7. congenital	17. strident	27. venal	37. sham
8. temerity	18. extirpate	28. myriad	38. officious
9. simile	19. strew	29. congenial	39. veracity
10. purport	20. configuration	30. docile	40. qualm

41. secular	**46.** perverse	**51.** trundle	**56.** nurture
42. reticence	**47.** flaccid	**52.** acrimony	**57.** upbraid
43. litigation	**48.** marital	**53.** consternation	**58.** rancor
44. travesty	**49.** regale	**54.** pernicious	**59.** portend
45. intrinsic	**50.** vestige	**55.** maxim	**60.** cogent

EXERCISE 9I: ROOTS

In a good desk dictionary, look up the following words to see how each is related to the Latin word scribo, *"to write."*

1. describe	**6.** prescribe	**11.** nondescript
2. descriptive	**7.** subscribe	**12.** proscribe
3. indescribable	**8.** scribble	**13.** inscribe
4. manuscript	**9.** ascribe	**14.** scribe
5. postscript	**10.** conscript	**15.** scrip

DENOTATION AND CONNOTATION

A mortician never handles a *corpse*, he prepares a *body* or *patient*. This business is carried on in a preparation-room or operating-room, and when it is achieved the patient is put into a casket and stored in the resposing-room or slumber-room of the funeral-home. On the day of the funeral he or she is moved to the chapel therein for the last exorcism, and then hauled to the cemetery in a funeral-car or casket-coach. The old-time *shroud* is now a *negligee* or *slumber-shirt* or *slumber-robe*, the mortician's *worktruck* is an *ambulance*, and the *cemetery* is fast becoming a *memorial park*.

H. L. Mencken

By studying the italicized words in the passage above, you will see that some words have similar meanings but evoke very different responses. Take the words *body* and *corpse*, for example. Although one can be used as a synonym for the other, *corpse* creates a much more negative feeling than *body* because you associate *corpse* with death. These two words illustrate the difference between *denotation*—the literal meaning of a word— and *connotation*—the feelings or impressions that a word calls up. Knowing the dictionary definition of a word (the denotative meaning) is not enough; you must also be aware of what the word **connotes**. Otherwise, you may use wrong words and mislead the reader.

Denotation

Denotation is the "dictionary meaning" of a word, which means you can look up the word to find out what thing or idea that word points to or denotes. There are several levels of these literal meanings. The first words you ever knew simply denoted things (*teddy bear, cup, cookie*) or actions (*play, fall, cry*) or people (*mother, father, baby*). Since you could actually point to or act out these things, you didn't need other words to explain them.

As you grew older, you learned words that pointed to more complex types of meaning, things that were not really present to be pointed to (last summer's romance, tomorrow's date). As you learned more, you could denote things that never were, like a mermaid or Jack the Giant Killer. You can denote a **class** of things or people, like the tall ships or the faculty. You can denote a generalization, like dreams, or an abstraction, like love. But in all of these word choices, you are still referring to the core meaning, the denotation. Denotative language is objective. It is used when your purpose is to convey factual information, avoiding subjective attitudes and judgments.

Connotation

Whereas denotation points out core meanings giving you information, *connotation* gives you the emotional atmosphere that surrounds these words. Connotation suggests how the writer feels about that information and how he or she wants you to feel about it. Connotative language is subjective. It is used when your purpose is to arouse emotion—fear, hope, enthusiasm.

Connotations arise from the associations that accompany a word. Over years, centuries perhaps, writers have used certain words to express approval or disapproval. These long associations temper feelings about the word. A word that has strong connotations makes the reader feel approval or disapproval, perhaps not even recognizing the reason for such feelings. Suppose, for example, you needed some professional service. Wouldn't you choose someone described as a lawyer rather than a shyster, a surgeon rather than a sawbones, a veterinarian rather than a horse doctor? In each case, the pairs of words might have been applied to the same person, but you probably would not employ a professional whom you thought of as a shyster or sawbones or horse doctor.

New York Times columnist William Safire gives both the connotative and denotative meanings of words to clarify his interpretations of "Washington talk":

media: a slightly sinister or clinical word for the "the press," often intended to carry a manipulative or mechanical connotation
moratorium: stems from the Latin for "delay" but has a more majestic connotation.

Notice how wide a range of meaning is covered by a denotation and its connotation.

Denotation	Connotation	
	Approving	**Disapproving**
shy	reserved	backward
popular prices	economical	cheap
gluttony	overindulgence	piggishness
businessman or business woman	executive	fat cat
educated	well-read	academic

EXERCISE 9J: SUPPLYING DENOTATION AND CONOTATION

Denotation	Approving	Disapproving
1. Child	_____	_____
2. _____	delicious	_____
3. _____	_____	ugly
4. _____	Amusing	_____
5. Talkative	_____	_____
6. _____	_____	to gossip
7. Pessimist	_____	_____
8. Realist	_____	_____
9. _____	_____	whiner
10. _____	magnanimous	_____

EXERCISE 9K: SUPPLYING FAVORABLE CONNOTATION

Place the words in order in each of the following sets, beginning with the word with the least favorable connotation and ending with the word with the most favorable connotation.

1. Stout, portly, chubby, obese, plump, corpulent, rotund

_____

2. Insane, crazy, mentally ill, deranged, mad

_____

3. Faithless, false, disloyal, traitorous, treacherous

_____

4. Chance, fortune, luck, hazard, hap, accident

_____

5. A lie, a falsehood, a fib, an exaggeration, a prevarication

_____

6. Infidel, freethinker, heathen, pagan, unbeliever

_____

7. Horse, steed, nag, thoroughbred, charger, hayburner

_____

8. Inform, brainwash, instruct, persuade, indoctrinate

_____

9. Quiet, still, noiseless, soundless

_____

10. Studious, bookish, intellectual, grind, egghead

_____

EXERCISE 9L: SUPPLYING THE BEST CONNOTATION

Although the denotative meaning of these words is similar, the connotative meaning is different. Of the choices in parentheses, circle the word you should use on each occasion. Then, explain why each word you choose has the best connotation.

1. You tell your boss that her remark was (funny/ridiculous/humorous/witty/ludicrous).

_____

2. You also tell her that you were disappointed with your paycheck because you had (assumed/presumed/banked on/expected/hoped for) a raise.

_____

3. You tell your mother that her Thanksgiving dinner was (tasty/palatable/edible/delicious).

_____

4. You say your father is (firm/strict/stern/unyielding).

_____

5. Your colleague impresses you as being (playful/trifling/funny/jesting).

_____

6. You compliment your instructor on his lecture, saying it was (loquacious/eloquent/garrulous/fluent).

_____

7. You tell your friend that she is (parsimonious/thrifty/stingy/miserly/pennypinching).

_____

8. You refer to the gift you bought your brother as (inexpensive/cheap/a bargain/economical/worth little).

_____

9. You tell your friend that the cousin you want her to go on a blind date with is (skinny/slim/emaciated/slender/lean/lanky).

_____

10. The manager (rejected/turned down/spurned/disallowed) your suggestion.

_____

C H A P T E R   10

Cause and Effect

Person One: Why?

Person Two: Because.

Person One: Because *why?*

That seemingly childish question-and-answer sequence is one of the most frequent and demanding of human situations. Human beings seem to have a built-in need to know *why.* From the time we could first talk, we have wanted to know *why.* Our questions may be trivial. (Why is there no milk for the coffee?) They may be bitterly important. (Why doesn't she love me any more? Why didn't I get that job I'd been promised?)

We need to know the reason *why.* We assume something is responsible; we seek the *causal relationship* between the situation now and something in the past. Things "don't just happen," we say. Everything must have a cause. We seek for the cause through a process called *causal analysis.*

Understanding the causes of some event or situation is one of our most important abilities, for this enables us to prevent future bad situations and to strive for future good ones, or at least to predict and prepare for what is to come.

Cause really includes all the factors that make some result occur. However, if all these factors were given in respose to "why," the questioner probably would not stay for an answer. Moreover, all the factors may not be known or understood. Consequently, one or just a few are singled out as being "the cause."

When you identify something as "the cause" you must be sure that it is both a **necessary** and a **sufficient** cause. When you say that A is a *necessary cause* of B, you are saying that B must always occur when A does. If A does not occur, then B will not occur. Also, to be a *sufficient cause* of B, A must be significant enough to cause B to happen. By applying the basic definition that *cause* is the *necessary and sufficient condition* producing an event, you can avoid many errors in reasoning about causes and their effects.

Every cause has an effect, we assume, and every effect has a cause. The problem is to find the relationship between the two, which is sometimes too exceedingly complex for practical analysis. In the story "I Want to Know Why" the boy hero *could* not know why; his psychology was not mature enough. But in simpler situations we can perceive the causal relationship, and it comforts us and reassures us. Even in these, however, we must analyze with great care.

SUFFICIENT CAUSE/ CONTRIBUTING CAUSE

Sometimes an error in cause and effect comes about through mistaking a *contributing* cause for *sufficient* cause. A *contributing* cause helps to bring about a specific event, but it is not enough in itself to be the sole cause of the effect. For example, to say that Germany lost World War II because the nation ran out of gasoline does give a contributing cause, but it is minor compared with more significant reasons, such as the decimation of the German armies by the Russian winter, the stubborn resistance of the RAF, and the successful bombing raids on German industrial centers.

Causal analysis works in two directions. You may start with the situation as it is and go back in time to discover why. Or you may start at the cause and go forward in time to see what effect some action will have. In other words, you may reason from cause to effect or from effect to cause.

If you had spent most of your time improving your skills for your new job and neglecting your school work by cutting your classes and doing no homework, this could logically be the cause for lower grades in school, or, equally logically, it could be the cause for success at work (cause to effect). If, on the other hand, you were

greatly surprised to see your lowered grade report, you might well reason that this effect was the result of your neglect of school (effect to cause).

When you move from such obvious examples to more remote events, however, you quickly see that accurate cause-and-effect reasoning can become a complex problem. Why did Lee Harvey Oswald kill President Kennedy? Was there any one cause for his action? Does anyone know for certain all of the possible causes and effects?

As you try to analyze the causes or effects of complex situations, you need to guard against seizing upon the first explanation that comes to mind and supposing that you have solved the problem. Much faulty reasoning about cause and effect results from the tendency to oversimplify. Most events involving human beings have multiple causes. Suppose you read in the paper, ICY ROAD CAUSES FATAL CRASH. That headline implies a simple cause-and-effect relationship, but the reality may be far more complex. The driver may have been driving too fast for the weather conditions, or may have overslept and been rushing to work, or may have been driving on bald tires; the possibilities go on and on. The point is that the icy road by itself is not **sufficient** to explain the fatal crash. Did every car that traveled that road crash? Were other motorists killed at the same spot?

ENOUGH INFORMATION

Careful reasoning demands sufficient information to establish a clear connection between cause and effect, yet all too often people rush to conclusions without adequate information. Could the explosion of a hydrogen bomb at Bikini Atoll cause a drought in Nebraska or floods in Arkansas? A surprising number of people blamed local weather conditions on the testing of atomic weapons, and some still do. Is the price of pork chops the result of having a Democrat or a Republican in the White House? Surprisingly, some people will blame the president if prices go up—unless it was their favorite who was elected. If you are to write a good paper, you must have—or find—enough information to provide necessary and sufficient cause or to project probable effects.

NARROWED TOPIC

To discuss the causes and effects of major events intelligently, you need to narrow the range of your analysis and set careful limits to your discussion. If you tried to explain why Germany was defeated in World War II, for instance, you could spend half a lifetime investigating various causes. If, however, you carefully limited the discussion to the major reasons why the German air force, the Luftwaffe, failed to win the Battle of Britain, you would have a far better chance of presenting a persuasive argument based upon cause and effect. Keep in mind, too, that in cause-and-effect reasoning you are dealing in probabilities. You can seldom be certain that your explanation is the only possible one, so you need to reason carefully from well-established facts to a conclusion that will appeal to intelligent readers.

ANALYZING CAUSES

Causal analysis is one of the great tools of logical thinking; an essay using this method should be logically organized and thoroughly developed. Inadequate preparation can lead to an erroneous conclusion. Let's take a quick look at the two methods of causal analysis: (1) **find the cause,** and (2) **project the effects.**

FINDING THE CAUSE

Why did Henry fail the test?
He was sick the night before.
Before you can assume that this was the cause of the failure, you must investigate further.
Did he fail any other tests?
Yes, he failed two other tests. Was he sick the night before each one?

Perhaps the quick answer was not the right one. Unless he failed only those three tests and his health was bad before each one, and you can eliminate all other possible causes for his failure, you probably have not established a cause-and-effect relationship.

Upon further investigation, you may discover more information: (1) Henry attends class irregularly; (2) he spends less than two hours per week studying for the class; (3) he missed three lab sessions; (4) his homework is seldom done, and when it is done, it is often late and incomplete; and (5) he takes few notes and is inattentive during class.

As your investigation proceeds, you see that being sick is not the whole answer to Henry's failing the test. Your investigation has also led you to more fundamental reasons for the failure. There are often larger, basic reasons for a situation than you see at first:

Henry doesn't really care about school.

Henry has a lackadaisical attitude about all work.

His study habits are poor.

He really doesn't want to be in college; he wants to be a mechanic.

Projecting the effect will not be difficult once you have discovered this information:

PROJECTING THE EFFECT

Henry will probably flunk out of school.

In **projecting the effect** of any situation, make sure that your prediction is logical. Show step by step, without omission, what effect will logically come from what cause or causes. In projecting Henry's fate, you have little difficulty in showing the underlying causes. To be convincing, however, you must **show** them, not just leap over them to the projected effect.

In projecting the effects of more complicated conditions, you have to be even more careful. What are the probable effects of certain chemical pollutants in drinking water? If a state spends little money on education, what effect does that have on SAT scores or graduation percentages?

The process here is still one of reasoning from the known to the unknown, but predicting future effects on the basis of known causes is hazardous at best. You can be fairly safe, of course, when the predicted effect is based upon some natural law or established scientific principle. For example, we know that water will boil at 212° F, and we know the effects of mercury poisoning. But predicting what effect a state's expenditures on education may have on SAT scores or graduation rates is far less certain.

There are too many unknowns, too many possible causes and effects, to make any prediction with a high degree of probability. When the evidence will support nothing more than a reasonable guess, say so.

In causal analysis that moves from cause to effects, the cause need not always be in the present and the effects in the future. You might want to identify causes of present or even past effects. The interpretation of history, for example, depends on an analysis of cause and effects that are all in the past.

THE CHAIN OF CAUSE AND EFFECT

When you follow the logical process to establish a sound cause-and-effect relationship, you frequently encounter a cause-and-effect series or chain of events. What you need to do then is to take the chain apart and examine the relationship between each link. Sometimes you reason from cause to effect and other times you must reason from effect to cause. Furthermore, what may be the effect in one link may become the cause in the next link. For example, if severe malnutrition impairs a child's mental development, then the result, deficient intelligence, could become the cause of later effects, such as the inability to find gainful employment. Thus it is often necessary to reason through an extensive chain of causes and effects step by step.

More often than not, your search for causes begins only after something has gone wrong and you are faced with a problem. If you are to solve the problem and perhaps prevent similar occurrences in the future, you must analyze the evidence carefully and take into consideration all of the possible causes. When the FAA sends out a team to investigate an airplane crash, the investigators examine every shred of evidence in an effort to determine the cause of the crash, and, if possible, to prevent similar accidents in the future. Working from the **known,** the physical evidence, they try to find the **unknown,** the probable cause. If they can definitely determine the cause to be a fault in the aircraft design, for example, then design changes can be made in order to reduce the chance of a similar accident in the future. Investigating plane crashes, of course, is a job for experts, but when you are presented with a complex problem, you need to examine the evidence with the same kind of thoroughness and persistence.

ORGANIZATION

INTRODUCTION

The introduction should draw attention to and focus upon the controlling idea of your essay. An apt quotation, a striking example, or a brief anecdote may serve to capture your reader's interest and focus it on the point you want to make. Then your thesis sentence should clearly state the controlling idea of your essay, one based upon cause-and-effect reasoning.

Frequently, your thesis sentence will state that *A* is the cause of *B*, imply that *B* is the result of *A*, or indicate some continuation of causes and effects.

Note the following introduction:

Men shed their sickness in books. (D.H. Lawrence)

The novelist meant that many great writers solved in their writings the problems that haunted their minds and psyches. Indeed, almost everyone does it to some extent. Did you ever write a letter which you never mailed, and probably never really intended to mail? Did you ever write a love poem you knew you would not deliver? You were "just getting it off your chest," you may have told yourself.

Even some great writers were obsessed by painful ideas and emotions. *They wrote because they had to; they had to explain the unexplainable and to comfort themselves; their writing was both obsession and cure for obsession.*

BODY

The body of the essay may combine several methods and make use of various types of support, such as examples or brief case histories, comparison or analogy, statistical evidence or authoritative quotations. The only genuine restriction is that the materials presented in the body must provide clear and relevant support for your thesis sentence.

To support the thesis about great writers, for example, you could develop the body of the essay by showing the cause-and-effect relationship between their traumatic experiences and their work.

The following outline suggests main points in the possible development of such an essay:

1. Charles Dickens's finest work came directly out of the miseries of his childhood.
2. James Joyce's *Ulysses* seems to reflect every slight and every wound he suffered in his childhood and youth.
3. Alexander Solzhenitzyn's work bears the stamp of one who survived the frozen hell of Soviet labor camps.
4. Dylan Thomas in his work warred against his own lack of self-esteem.
5. Mark Twain, who "laughed so that he would not cry," suffered bitterly from melancholia acquired in his early life.

Notice that these five points are examples: each author's experience develops the point made in the thesis statement that writing was both obsession and therapy. Each example involves tracing an effect back to its cause identified in the thesis statement.

CONCLUSION

The conclusion that will serve you best is one that briefly pulls together the main points of your essay and reinforces your controlling idea. For the essay outlined here, the following might provide a fitting conclusion:

....

For many great writers, their sensitivity and talent are motivated by their interior wounds. They have to write because that is the means of self-salvation. Sometimes they write with faint—or no—hope of being published; most writers are volumnious letter writers. Faulkner penned a beautiful little romance, hand-written and hand-decorated and bound, for the woman he loved and who rejected him for ten years.

He never intended it for publication and it never was until after his death and the woman's when her grandson had it published. For Faulkner, it was relief from his pain. His is an unusual case. Nevertheless, many writers transmute their personal pain into art.

....

The essay below has a clear three-part organization. Notice how the author leads up to her main idea and then states her thesis clearly in the last sentence of her introduction. Note, also, that the introduction and the conclusion are relatively short compared with the body of the essay, where the main idea is developed. In this essay, the thesis statement is supported mainly with specific examples.

THE DECLINE OF QUALITY

Introduction

    A question that puzzles me is why inexpensive things must be made ugly. . . . I have heard it suggested that raucous colors and hideous decoration are meant to distract the purchaser's eye from shoddy workmanship, but since that only results in a remedy worse than the disease, it cannot be the whole explanation. . . . I do not see why the presumption cannot be made the other way: that the consumer would respond to good design rather than junk. The answer will doubtless be that when this experiment has been tried, the mass of consumers failed to respond. **For this failure, I believe, two institutions of our culture are largely to blame: education and advertising.**

Thesis statement

Body

Cause A

    We have some superb schools, public and private, in this country but the dominant tendency, once again, is non-Q. **Education for the majority has slipped to a level undemanding of effort,** satisfied with the least, lacking respect for its own values, and actually teaching very little. We read in the press that, despite the anxious concern and experiments of educators, college entrance scores are sinking and the national rate of schoolchildren reading at below-grade levels hovers at 50 percent. The common tendency is to blame television, and while I suppose that the two-minute attention span it fosters, and the passive involvement of the viewer, must negatively affect the learning process, I suspect something more basic is at fault.

Examples

    That something, I believe, lies in the new *attitudes* toward both teaching and learning. Schoolchildren are not taught to work. Homework is frivolous or absent. The idea has grown that learning must be fun; students must study what they like; therefore courses have largely become elective. Work is left to the highly motivated, and failure for the others does not matter because, owing to certain socially concerned but ill-conceived rules, students in many school systems cannot be flunked.

Examples

    Further, one becomes aware through occasional glimpses into *curriculums,* that subject matter makes increasing concessions to junk. Where are the summer reading lists and book reports of former years? A high school student of my ac-

Examples

quaintance in affluent suburbia was recently assigned by his English teacher, no less, to watch television for a week and keep a record on 3-by-5 index cards of what he had seen. . . . How will the young become acquainted with quality if they are not exposed to it? . . .

Cause B

   Advertising augments the condition. From infancy to adulthood, advertising is the air Americans breathe, the information we absorb, almost without knowing it. It floods our mind with pictures of perfection and goals of happiness easy to attain. Face cream will banish age, decaffeinated coffee will

Examples

banish nerves, floor wax will bring in the neighbors for a cheery bridge game or gossip, grandchildren will love you if your disposition improves with the right laxative, storekeepers and pharmacists overflow with sound avuncular advice, the right beer endows you with hearty masculine identity, and almost any-

Examples

thing from deodorants to cigarettes, toothpaste, hair shampoo and lately even antacids will bring on love affairs, usually on horseback or on a beach. Moreover, all the people engaged in these delights are beautiful. Dare I suggest that this is not the true world? We are feeding on foolery, of which a steady diet, for those who feed on little else, cannot help but leave a certain fuzziness of perceptions. . . .

Conclusion

   I cannot believe we shall founder under the rising tide of incompetence and trash. . . . Although I know we have already grown accustomed to less beauty, less elegance, less excellence, . . . yet perversely I have confidence in the competence and excellence of the best among us. . . . If incompetence does not kill us first, quality will continue the combat against numbers. It will not win, but it will provide a refuge for the trash-beleaguered. It will supply scattered beauty, pride in accomplishment, the charm of fine things. . . . As long as people exist, some will always strive for the best; some will attain it.

Barbara Tuchman

TRACING A COMPLEX CAUSE-AND EFFECT RELATIONSHIP

In the following essay, Stan Sinberg presents a spoofing effect of memory and ponders the cause of it. He gives various amusing examples of the effect of his memory and suggests a cause that also amuses even though psychologists would deny it.

SOMETIMES YOUR MIND RUNS OUT OF HANGERS

Say your closet was so packed to the rafters with old knickers and clip-on ties from when you were a child that whenever you bought new clothes you had to throw out something else. And suppose what you had to discard was your new $250 suit, rather than the shorts you hadn't worn since you were 5. You'd think that was pretty stupid, wouldn't you? You'd wonder why you just couldn't throw out the old, useless clothes instead, right? Well, then. Welcome to the wonderful world of the brain.

This is how *my* brain operates, anyway. Childhood trivia that serves no purpose whatsoever remains eternally embedded in my memory banks. Things I *need* to know, though, unfortunately get tossed out almost immediately. For instance:

I still remember the phone number we had when I was 4 years old: CYpress 3-2804 (back then we used letters). There is no reason on earth to remember this number. I haven't dialed it in 30 years. It's not like I could call it in a pinch and my mother would send money. Yet remember it I do. At the same time, I recently met a woman who gave me her number on the run. Not having a pen, I repeated the number over and over on the way home. Halfway there I ran into a friend, started talking and by the time I got home, the number, and the woman, were gone forever. If only her number were CYpress 3-2804.

When I was in second grade and nearsighted and vain, I memorized the bottom line of the school eye chart, so that I wouldn't have to wear glasses. I escaped that ordeal, but I *still remember the entire bottom line!* Why? Am I afraid I'm going to find myself back in that same second-grade classroom to have my eyes tested?

Speaking of school, not only can I tell you the name of everybody in my first-grade class, I can tell you where they sat. *Where they sat!* I can only assume I'm storing this vital information in case we ever have a 40th-anniversary reunion and start fighting over the seating arrangements. Just don't ask me where I put the traffic summons I got yesterday, because I have no idea.

I don't follow baseball anymore. I couldn't name you five players on either the Mets or the Yankees, my purported home teams. Yet I can rattle off the names, positions and batting averages of the entire 1961 New York Yankees club without batting an eye. Conceivably this might prove useful one day, although I've yet to have anyone ask me, "Hey, what *was* Tony

Kubek's batting average in 1961 anyway?" I tried bringing it up in conversation once, but it seemed forced.

My brain holds onto a veritable encyclopedia of useless information. Sometimes I watch the game show "Jeopardy." Unlike some viewers who pride themselves on knowing the answers (the questions, really), it *bothers* me that my head is filled with so much trivia.

"It was the 33rd state admitted to the Union," Alex says, and I push my imaginary button and call out "What was Oregon?"

"He was Herman of Herman's Hermits." I shout out "Who was Peter Noone?" when all along I know the correct question is "Who cares?"

How do I know this stuff? Why do I know this stuff? I haven't thought about the ratification of states since I was 12. Yet I answer with the same certainty as though I'd learned it yesterday.

That's the problem, of course. It wasn't yesterday. If it were yesterday, I probably wouldn't remember it. I read *The New York Times*, and 20 minutes later it's forgotten. I meet someone named Pat, and only a mnemonic device wherein I picture her with a slab of butter pasted on her nose helps me recall her name. I read a 500-page novel like *Crime and Punishment*, and two weeks later I'm summarizing it as "This story about a guy who commits a murder and gives himself away."

This almost Proustian recall of the details of my early life would be actually charming if I didn't suspect that it's precisely because of my remembering this early stuff that I don't remember current facts. Like that crammed closet that runs out of room, my brain doesn't seem to have any space left for new information. When something new goes in, something else is expunged. Unfortunately, it's usually the knowledge that's just arrived that gets the heave-ho. The junk that's been sitting unused for 30-some odd years—that stays.

Sometimes this becomes embarrassing. I was at a party recently where everyone had to tell a joke. This was mortifying, because the "joke retainer" portion of my brain is apparently full, leaving me incapable of remembering new ones I hear. Completely at a loss, I was reduced to asking incredulous party-goers, "Why did the moron throw the clock out the window?" Richard Katz told it to me when I was 6.

Can you name all the state capitals? I can. I memorized them in fifth grade. But don't expect me to point out Nicaragua or Afghanistan on a map, because the "Geographical Locations That Aren't Within a Half-Hour of My House" section of my cerebrum is filled with the likes of Jefferson City (Mo.) and Frankfort (Tenn.).

The bottom line, I fear, is I learned too much when I was young. My head is completely filled up. It's not my fault. By reading today's newspaper I've been exposed to more information than people in the 19th century got in a lifetime. Human brains, once big enough for the world, are no longer up to the task: They're 10M hard-drives in a 40M hard-drive world. Or, as my grandfather might've said, regarding my grandmother's shopping habits, "The clothes keep comin', but there ain't no more hangers to put 'em on."

Sorry, French. I'll never learn you. Too bad, new investment techniques, you won't be staying long. Kevin Saunders (second seat, fourth row) got there first.

(Stan Sinberg is a New York writer and entertainer.)

Questions for Discussion

1. Explain the basic analogy of Sinberg's essay.
2. Is there any useless information *you* are carrying around in your mind?
3. What do the types of information Sinberg keeps in his brain have in common?
4. Point out all the places where Sinberg supports his analogy.
5. Why is the essay funny?
6. How does the author excuse himself from blame?
7. Do you agree with Sinberg's analogy? What would be a more accurate analogy than that of the closet?

EXERCISE 10A: SUFFICIENT CAUSE/CONTRIBUTING CAUSE

Each of the sentences below contains a cause-and-effect relationship. Study each sentence carefully, and see if it contains a sufficient cause or a contributing cause. Mark S (sufficient) or C (contributing). Be prepared to defend your decisions.

_____ 1. SAT scores are dropping in the United States because students are more interested in fun than in education.

_____ 2. Teenagers keep their rooms messy because they know it frustrates their parents.

_____ 3. People are watching more TV today because the programs are better.

_____ 4. Asian students in the United States get higher grades and win more scholarships because they give education a higher priority in their lives than American students do.

_____ **5.** The dumping of steel by foreign nations has killed the steel industry in the United States.

_____ **6.** High school students carry their lunch to school because they don't like the food served in cafeterias.

_____ **7.** The water on the road froze because the temperature dropped below 32°F.

_____ **8.** Carl broke his toe because he missed the football and kicked a rock instead.

_____ **9.** Senator Pluto won the election because he spent more money than any of his competitors.

_____ **10.** The Steelers won four Super Bowls because they had a good coach.

_____ **11.** Smoking causes cancer.

_____ **12.** Sonia makes good grades because she does her homework every night.

_____ **13.** My grandmother died because she was seventy-eight.

_____ **14.** Chevrolets are very popular cars because Americans are tired of foreign cars.

_____ **15.** The American economy is being wrecked by the greediness of unions.

_____ **16.** Maria did not get good grades because she had a job.

_____ **17.** Vice-president Quayle is not popular because he is a rich man.

_____ **18.** Kenneth has a headache because he played tennis in the sun.

_____ **19.** Tim didn't get a promotion because people thought he was snobbish.

_____ **20.** I flunked the math exam because the problems were hard.

ANALOGY

In the chapter on comparison and contrast you learned about analogy as a special method of comparing two things that really had no conventional basis for comparison—a girl with a red rose, a boss with a snake in the grass. Likewise, when Shakespeare wrote a sonnet beginning "Shall I compare thee to a summer's day," he only meant to **suggest** that his beloved was warm, beautiful, satisfying. He did not expect his reader to extend the comparison to include sweat, sunburn, and bugs. Such comparisons are known as *figurative analogies.*

In *War and Remembrance,* Herman Wouk offers a vivid figurative analogy to suggest the meaning of the term *extremism.* It is by no means realistic or literally true, but it is highly suggestive of the meaning of this very abstract term.

Extremism is the universal tuberculosis of modern society: a world infection of resentment and hatred generated by rapid change and the breakdown of old values. In the stabler nations, the tubercles are sealed off in scar tissue, and these are the harmless lunatic movements. In times of social disorder, depression, war, or revolution, the germs can break forth and infect the nation. This happened in Germany (in the 1930s and early 40s). It could happen anywhere, even in the United States.

Although vivid figurative analogy can enlarge your readers' understanding of your point without being complete or literally true, you **cannot** substitute figurative analogy for sound cause-and-effect reasoning.

However, analogy can be used to support a cause-and-effect argument when it is limited to a careful comparison of relationships.

If you wish to use analogy as a support of your cause-and-effect thesis statement, you must choose your analogy on the following logical grounds:

1. To support a conclusion, an analogy must have a number of important likenesses that are relevant to the comparison you wish to make.
2. To support a conclusion, an analogy must have no important differences that are relevant to the comparison you wish to make.

For example, much medical research is based on the physiological likeness between human beings and laboratory animals such as rats. In the laboratory the researcher experiments upon numbers of rats until he thinks he can make a sound generalization about the reaction of rats. Then, by analogy, he says that men and rats are essentially the same in the area being tested and have no essential differences in that area; thus, the reaction found in rats will probably be found in human beings. For instance, in determining whether or not the caffeine in the coffee drunk by pregnant women can harm unborn children, experimenters are giving doses of caffeine to pregnant rats to test the ultimate possibility of its having harmful effects on human beings.

Reasoning by analogy is one of the most common ways of thinking. Everyone attempts to understand new problems by comparing them to problems already solved. It seems to be almost a natural way of thinking. You notice a pattern of similarities between one thing and another, and, from that observation, you assume that the pattern can be extended. When you reason by analogy, you observe that two things have a number of characteristics in common and no essential characteristics that differ. Analogy **suggests** to you that these two things are probably alike in still more characteristics. The key word here is *probably*.

George Bernard Shaw, arguing for the need for prison reform in his day, attempts to support his conclusion by analogy. The Prison Commissioners, Shaw said, aimed at **punishment and reform** for criminals. Such a double aim was a contradiction, because, says Shaw:

> Now , if you are to punish a man retributively, you must injure him. If you are to reform him, you must improve him. And men are not improved by injuries. To propose to punish and reform people by the same operation is exactly as if you were to take a man suffering from pneumonia, and attempt to combine punitive and curative treatment. Arguing that a man with pneumonia is a danger to the community, and that he need not catch it if he takes proper care of his health, you resolve that he shall have a severe lesson, both to punish him for his negligence and pulmonary weakness and to deter others from following his example. You therefore strip him naked, and in that condition stand him all night in the snow. But as you admit the duty of restoring him to health if possible, and discharging him with sound lungs, you engage a doctor to superintend the punishment and administer cough lozenges, made as unpleasant to the taste as possible so as not to pamper the culprit. A Board of Commissioners ordering such treatment would prove thereby that either they were imbeciles or else they were hotly in earnest about punishing the patient and not in the least in earnest about curing him.
>
> When our Prison Commissioners pretend to combine punishment with moral reformation they are in the same dilemma.

Note that, because what Shaw has to say about the man with pneumonia is so convincing, you are liable to accept his analogy that a prisoner is like the pneumonia patient. Bearing in mind the standards that must be applied to an analogy to make it a support for a conclusion, determine whether Shaw has only a persuasive figurative analogy or one that is a sound support for a conclusion. (An analogy, remember, must have many important likenesses and no important differences within the areas being compared.)

PITFALLS TO AVOID

1. Don't oversimplify. Remember that many events have multiple causes, so don't settle for the first explanation that comes to mind.
2. Avoid the post-hoc fallacy. Make sure that you are not attributing a cause-effect relationship to a mere coincidence. Remember, just because *A* happened before *B* does not mean that *A* *caused B.*
3. Don't confuse a contributing cause with a sufficient cause. If the cause is not enough in itself to bring about a specific event, then it is only a contributing cause.
4. Don't use two items for an analogy that have only a few superficial likenesses. If you are using an analogy to support a cause-effect thesis, make sure that the two things being compared have a number of *important* characteristics in common and *no* essential characteristics that differ. Also, remember that you can't use an analogy to *prove* a cause-effect thesis—only to *support* a cause-effect thesis.
5. Above all, don't form any conclusion without adequate information.

SUGGESTED TOPICS FOR A CAUSE AND EFFECT ESSAY

1. Sex and salary
2. Handguns and homicide
3. Neighborhood crime watches and decrease in crimes
4. Happiness and psychic energy
5. Drug addiction and crime
6. Mouth cancer and tobacco chewing
7. Fertilizer and crop yield
8. Stress and heart disease
9. Exercise and weight loss or gain
10. Casual drug use and the drug problem
11. Artificial sweeteners and disease
12. Catalytic converters and exhaust pollution
13. Age and sexism
14. Television violence and youthful crime
15. Computer technology and unemployment
16. Broken homes and juvenile delinquency
17. Financial problems and teenage divorces
18. Childhood experiences and adult phobias

19. Supply and demand
20. Pride and quality of product
21. Economic needs and career choice
22. Political oppression and revolution
23. Writing ability and earning power
24. Idle time and depression
25. Physical appearance and personality
26. High labor costs (or high management costs) and industrial collapse
27. Skin color and income
28. Physical health and mental health
29. Car size and safety
30. Age of drivers and number of accidents
31. Radiation and genetic damage
32. Pornography and sex crimes
33. Quality and price
34. Formal education and earning power
35. Height and managerial success
36. Proficiency in language and success
37. Age and value systems
38. Peer pressure and aspirations
39. Peer pressure and use of drugs
40. Grades and popularity
41. Personality and style of dress
42. Laughter and mental health
43. American foreign policy and treatment of American tourists
44. Diet and cancer
45. Homelife and success in school
46. Advertising and consumer buying habits
47. Freedom of expression and capitalism
48. Reading level and grades
49. Dress codes and classroom behavior
50. Prenatal nutrition and child development

TECHNIQUES OF CLEAR WRITING

ELIMINATING SENTENCE ERRORS

You want to make your writing as clear and easy to understand as possible. Your reader should not have to reread your sentences and labor to figure out what you are trying to say. (Most readers won't bother.)

Punctuation Errors

Fragments   One of the most common errors in sentence structure is really an error in punctuation: *the sentence fragment.* When a group of words that does not include a complete subject and predicate is ended by a period, you have a fragment. A fragment, you will recall, consists of detached elements that should be joined either to the preceding or to the following sentence.

INCORRECT:
Filled with old newspapers, rags, and trash from basement to attic. The home was a firetrap.

CORRECT:
Filled with old newspapers, rags, and trash from basement to attic, the home was a firetrap.
The home, filled with old newspapers, rags, and trash from basement to attic, was a firetrap.

INCORRECT:
The principal could get nothing done. Especially with the telephone ringing constantly and disgruntled parents barging into his office.

CORRECT:
The principal could get nothing done, especially with the telephone ringing constantly and disgruntled parents barging into his office.

(NOTE: Some incomplete sentences are permissible ["What did they gain? Nothing!"], but you should avoid their use except in dialogue or for special effects.)

Comma Splices and Fused Sentences   Closely related to the fragment are sentence errors also stemming from punctuation—the *fused sentence* and the *run-on* (or *comma splice*) *sentence.* Both have two independent clauses. The run-on sentence has a comma. Both can be corrected in several ways.

INCORRECT:
The road was steep, stony, and rutted [no punctuation or a comma] it was almost impassable.

CORRECT:
Two sentences: The road was steep, stony, and rutted. It was almost impassable.
Use of a semicolon: The road was steep, stony, and rutted; it was almost impassable.

Use of a comma and a coordinating conjunction (*and, but, or, for, nor, so, yet*): The road was steep, stony, and rutted, so it was almost impassable.

Reducing one independent clause to a subordinate clause: Since [or because] the road was steep, stony, and rutted, it was almost impassable.

EXERCISE 10B: PUNCTUATING SENTENCES

By adding whatever additional punctuation or wording is needed, revise all incorrect sentences to eliminate fragments, comma splices, and fused sentences. If the sentence is already correct, write C beside the number.

1. The New England beaches in winter are starkly beautiful; their outlines are clear and strong, but their colors are muted and misty.
2. The middle class suffers most from economic depression they get little or no help from government subsidies.
3. Particularly pleasant in the bright days of September and October.
4. *The Song of the South* is a fine old movie for children. Retelling the tales of Uncle Remus.
5. Trying to determine which foods are really good for you. It doubles your shopping time.
6. Sir Laurence Olivier the greatest actor of our time.
7. Although they were intelligent and studied long hours.
8. Hoping to hear from Gladys and wishing hard for her good luck.
9. George and Alma playing down the ninth fairway hoping for a winning score on their favorite hole.
10. Millard Fillmore was obscure as presidents go but he is well known for one important historical first he had the first White House bathtub installed.
11. Cleaning otters after the Valdez oil spill was costly it took nine people three hours to clean one otter.
12. TV newscasters are getting expensive Diane Sawyer is being paid a reported 1.6 million per year by ABC and over ten more news stars earn more than a million a year.
13. Having a career to handle and a family to support and wanting some of the good things life has to offer.
14. Mary Higgins Clark is one of my favorite authors every story she writes is suspenseful, hard to put down—even at four in the morning.
15. Though they toured the ruins of the Acropolis, and traveled through the plains of Marathon, and climbed the mountains at Delphi.
16. Having watched the movie *Big* and realizing the difference in thinking between a thirteen-year-old and a thirty-year-old.
17. The award-winning novel *War and Remembrance* vivifies the era of the Nazi regime from its start in the late 1930s to its demise in 1945.

18. Chris saw a racehorse shot at the track last Thursday, now he refuses to go to the races.
19. I read that bacon is full of carcinogens, now I eat ham for breakfast.
20. Planning a wedding in Minneapolis when you live in Dallas and work in Yuma.
21. The rich and famous of this world, living in luxury while street people strip garbage cans for food.
22. To drive a car and not use a seat belt.
23. Just to relax in a deck chair passing some of the most scenic sights on earth.
24. A teacher, old enough to retire, who simply enjoys interacting with the students in the classroom, and hates the paperwork.
25. Nursing is a great profession. But a lot of hard work.

Structural Errors

Mixed and Illogical Constructions

Mixed, or illogical, construction is a term used to describe a variety of errors that result in sentences that seem to start off in one direction and end up going another.

For example: *The outline for his paper, which Kevin finished last night, will take weeks of research.* This mixed construction can be corrected, as can so many others, by analyzing and correcting the core sentence. (See Core Sentence in Techniques of Clear Writing section in Chapter 2.) It is not the outline that will take weeks; it was finished last night. The entire paper will take weeks of effort.

Another cause for the error of mixed construction is the use of imprecise or ambiguous words. For example: *The advantages that the chairperson discussed at the last meeting will hamper progress.* In almost all situations, advantages will not hamper anything; disadvantages may hamper, but advantages will encourage or promote or facilitate progress.

Although it may seem a minor point, use of phrases such as "is where," "is when," "is because" is a frequent cause of mixed constructions. Moreover, they are awkward and ungrammatical and usually should be avoided. For instance: *When you get to the creek is where you will find the fence takes a bend to the left.* Simply omit *is where* to form a correct sentence.

The errors in mixed construction are many and seem almost individualized. But if you check for correct core sentences, for accurate and unambiguous words, and for the awkward "is where" phrases, you will almost always solve your structural problems.

EXERICSE 10C: MIXED CONSTRUCTIONS

Revise the following sentence to make the wording clear and sensible.

1. His first response to his boss's offer was reluctance.

_____

2. Her graduation is when she is looking forward to a trip to California.

_____

3. I shall leap over the problems in my path.

_____

4. The poet asks if the road always leads uphill.

_____

5. The reason for her award is because she always guards against mistakes.

_____

6. Because it is difficult is why not many students get A's in calculus.

_____

7. The value of the coin, despite some nicks and scratches, he thought was beautiful.

_____

8. All of the things she learned in the class were not on the test.

_____

9. The results of the poll asked how many students preferred pass–fail to A, B, C, D, and F grades.

_____

10. His lack of background in math helped him in choosing a career of his choice.

_____

Dangling Modifiers

A *modifier* is a word, phrase, or clause that describes, clarifies, or narrows another word. For example:

a **tall** building
a **74-story** building
a building **made of Italian marble**

"While reading the paper, my dog . . . "

These modifiers belong next to the word they modify. If a modifier is placed somewhere else, confusion results and clarity is lost. Sometimes the result becomes ludicrous.

> While reading the paper, my dog pestered me to go for a walk. [The dog read the paper?]

If you start the sentence with a participial phrase, the first noun or pronoun after the phrase must be the person or thing the phrase modifies. This is **one way** to correct the dangling modifier.

> While reading the paper, I was disturbed by my dog, who was pestering me to go for a walk.

Another way that such dangling participles can be corrected is by including a subject and changing the participial phrase to a dependent clause:

> While I was reading the paper, my dog was pestering me to go for a walk.

A dangling modifier can be found anywhere in a sentence, but the error is most common when the modifier appears at the beginning of the sentence.

EXERCISE 10D: DANGLING MODIFIERS

Using the examples below as models, correct the dangling modifiers in the following sentences:

INCORRECT:
Having won a stuffed bear, the carnival operators wheedled twelve more dollars from Jake.

CORRECT:
Having won a stuffed bear, Jake was wheedled into spending twelve more dollars by the carnival operators.

INCORRECT:
Being dead tired to start with, the day seemed to stretch into eternity.

CORRECT:
Because I was dead tired to start with, the day seemed to stretch into eternity.

1. Having written the exam, her confidence failed her.

_____

2. Although they had fought the fire all night, the strong wind continued to spread it.

_____

3. Unable to put up with his jealousy and bad temper, her divorce was not unexpected.

_____

4. Weak with laughter, the play had the audience rolling in the aisles.

_____

5. Having washed the dishes, the kitchen looked comfortable and welcoming.

_____

6. After eating a huge meal, my motorcycle seemed to be very bumpy.

_____

7. My leg fell asleep watching the *Jerry Lewis Telethon.*

_____

8. Crying, the plane carrying my best friend flew away.

_____

9. Having discussed the final point, my paper was twenty-three pages long.

_____

10. Having caught a sixty-yard pass, the crowd broke into cheers.

_____

EXERCISE 10E: DANGLING MODIFIERS

Rewrite the following sentences to avoid dangling modifiers.

1. Loaded down with bank notes and laughing merrily, the police chief watched the bank robbers speed away.

_____

2. Having written the letter, her stomach began to growl.

_____

3. My car would not stay on the road with bald tires.

_____

4. The batter missed the ball swinging desperately.

_____

5. I watched the bus pull away sadly, having forgotten my wallet.

_____

6. Laughing heartily, the trained elephants performed for the delighted audience.

_____

7. Red-eyed and sneezing, the goldenrod created misery for many allergic patients.

_____

8. Hopping mad, the man's grocery bill was double what he expected.

_____

9. Having served for ten years on the committee, its purpose was well-known to her.

_____

10. Sad and rejected, the letter gave him no comfort.

_____

11. Making a 99 percent on her test, the teacher congratulated Toniko.

_____

12. While engrossed in reading *War and Peace*, my dog ate my slipper.

_____

13. Leaping high in the air, the ball was just out of reach.

_____

14. Trembling and perspiring, the audience watched Antonio approach the podium.

_____

15. Having cleaned the whole house, my guests called to postpone their visit.

_____

WORD POWER

It Ain't Necessarily So!

A popular American musical has a sprightly character named Sportin' Life who sings a song called "It Ain't Necessarily So." This title shows a healthy attitude toward carelessly accepting a cause-and-effect relationship. Some of the reasons why things carelessly accepted are not "necessarily so" come from language. For instance, one verse of Sportin' Life's song runs:

> *Old Methuselah lived 900 years*
> *Old Methuselah lived 900 years*
> *But who calls that livin'*
> *When no gal will give in*
> *To no man what's 900 years.*

This verse always brought down the house because of its irreverent gaity about the incredible Methuselah. Part of the fun came from a double meaning. The lyrics use the word "livin' " in a sense other than that meant by Methuselah existing to extreme old age. According to Sportin' Life, "livin' " means having a good time—an impossibility he thought, without girls.

Ambiguity and vagueness create difficulties for someone trying to arrive at good cause-and-effect conclusions. Vague and ambiguous words permit many shifts in meaning. For example, if you say,

"The garage *fixed* my car, and the politician *fixed* my ticket," you are equivocating through the multiple meanings of the verb *to fix*. And what is your meaning if you say of someone, "I'm going to give him the business"? Such shifts are fine if your intent, like Sportin' Life's, is to amuse. But if your intent is to support a conclusion, you must choose language that is precise and stable.

EXERCISE 10F: AMBIGUOUS SENTENCES

The following sentences can be understood in more than one way. Rewrite them to convey a single, clear meaning.

1. The lawyer told her client that she couldn't be trusted.

2. Uncle Albert has a heart condition in the hospital and is critical.

3. He cannot be contented because he is retired.

4. This is some party!

5. The Butter and Egg Commission will require all eggs to be stamped with the date they were laid by the farmers.

6. People who drink and drive often get arrested.

7. I took shots when I went to Africa for malaria.

8. Ben's driving instructor told him he was nervous.

9. You can't get a good grade because you attend class.

10. Jacques said the lecture was spectacular.

FALSE IMPLICATIONS

A proverb is usually accepted as wisdom. For example, "A stitch in time saves nine" makes sense by itself and in its implication that it is better to do a job when it needs to be done than to put it off.

However, a number of proverbs are implied analogies that aren't necessarily so; usually the point of such analogies is to blacken someone's reputation. Consider the proverb "Where there's smoke, there's fire." This is pithy and often quoted, so it seems to have authority. Nevertheless, when you consider it, there is no reasonable basis for the comparison of a fire with a reputation. It may well be that smoke does indicate a fire, but that does not support the implication that someone who is gossiped about is at fault. To accept the implied statement because of the correctness of the direct statement is to depend on slogans and repetition instead of clear ideas sensibly discussed.

EXERCISE 10G: IMPLICATIONS

The following sayings all carry implications. Decide what the implications are and if they are "necessarily so." If you are not sure of the meanings of any words, look them up in your dictionary.

1. Music soothes the savage breast.
2. As the twig is bent, the tree inclines.
3. Love me, love my dog.
4. The times make great men.
5. April showers bring May flowers.
6. A fool and his money are soon parted.
7. Penny wise, pound foolish.
8. In for a penny, in for a pound.
9. Don't change horses in the middle of a stream.
10. The man who pays the piper calls the tune.

CONFUSING WORDS

Following are pairs of words that are spelled or pronounced in a similar manner. Check each pair; if you are not sure of the difference in meaning, consult your dictionary.

accede/exceed	cite/site	discreet/discrete
accelerate/exhilarate	coarse/course	dual/duel
accept/except	complement/compliment	eminent/imminent
access/excess	comprehensible/comprehensive	envelop/envelope
all ready/already	conscience/conscious	explicit/implicit
attendance/attendants	continual/continuous	formally/formerly
berth/birth	defective/deficient	forth/fourth
capital/capitol	depreciate/deprecate	ingenious/ingenuous
censor/censure	desirable/desirous	it's/its
cereal/serial	device/devise	know/no

lay/lie
lead/led
leased/least
lend/loan
liable/libel
loose/lose
pain/pane
passed/past
personal/personnel

preceding/proceeding
prescribe/proscribe
principal/principle
quiet/quite
respectfully/respectively
right/rite
secret/secrete
to/too
wait/weight

WORDS AND PHRASES FREQUENTLY MISUSED

Affect/Effect *Affect*, a verb, means "to influence the behavior or outcome." *Effect* is usually a noun, meaning "result"; *effect* can also be a verb meaning "to bring about" or "to produce."

CORRECT:
The choice may *affect* your whole career.

CORRECT:
The *effect* of continued inflation could be disastrous.
Foreign intermediaries helped *effect* the release of the hostages.

Aggravate To *aggravate* means "to worsen or intensify an existing condition"; it should never be used in the sense of "to irritate" or "to annoy."

CORRECT:
Pot smoking *aggravates* heart disease by overstimulating the heart.

CORRECT:
He *irritates* people with his constant complaints.

Alot The only acceptable form is two words, *a lot.*

FAULTY:
She had *alot* of money; she paid cash for a house and *alot* on Cherry Street.

CORRECT:
She had *a lot* of money; she paid cash for a house and *a lot* on Cherry Street.

All of *All* is usually sufficient.

FAULTY:
All of the faculty members were present.

CORRECT:
All the faculty members were present.

Allude/Elude   *Allude* means "to refer to"; *elude* means "to escape."

CORRECT:
Democrats frequently *allude* to the Watergate scandal of the Nixon administration.

CORRECT:
The escaped prisoner was unable to *elude* the pursuing hounds.

Allusion/Illusion   An *allusion* is a reference to something; an *illusion* is a false or deceptive appearance.

CORRECT:
The *allusions* in the speech were to *Gone With The Wind.*

CORRECT:
They create the *illusion* of being confident and successful, but they are terrified of failure.

Bad/Badly   *Bad* is an adjective that describes the subject; *badly* is an adverb.

CORRECT:
I feel *bad* about leaving Centerville.

CORRECT:
Greg was *badly* injured in the accident.

Being as/Being that   Never use these. They are not substitutes for *since* or *because.*

CORRECT:
Since she knew the road, she could get there within an hour. [not *Being as*]

CORRECT:
Because there was an extra set of keys, he could have taken the car. [not *Being that*]

Between/Among *Between* is used with two people or items; *among* is used when there are more than two.

CORRECT:
There is little difference *between* a Pontiac and an Oldsmobile.

CORRECT:
Grading systems vary *among* the Ivy League colleges.

Bunch Use *bunch* when you refer to things that come in clusters; don't use it in place of *group.*

CORRECT:
She selected a huge *bunch* of purple grapes.

CORRECT:
A *group* of young people gathered in front of the hall. [not *bunch*]

Bust/Busted/Bursted There is only one correct form for the principal parts of *burst: burst, burst, burst.*

CORRECT:
Because all the water pipes *burst* last winter—except for the ones that had *burst* the winter before—I installed plastic pipes, which won't *burst* as easily.

Calculate *Calculate* usually refers to a mathematical process, for example, computing costs. It should not be used as a substitute for guess, think, or plan.

CORRECT:
I *guess* that it will be a close election. [not *calculate*]

CORRECT:
I will *calculate* the exact fuel cost for the six months.

Case Expressions like *in the case of* are usually unnecessary.

CORRECT:
That is not true *of* doctors and dentists. [not *in the case of*]

Complected *Complected* should not be used as a substitute for *complexioned.*

CORRECT:
He was redheaded and fair-*complexioned.*

> **Contact** Avoid the use of *contact* both as a noun and a verb; it is vague and overused.

FAULTY:
She has several business *contacts* in New York.

IMPROVED:
She has several business *acquaintances* in New York.

FAULTY:
We will *contact* you in spring.

IMPROVED:
We will *call [telephone, write to, ask about]* you in the spring.

> **Could of/May of/Must of/Would of/Should of** The correct forms are *could have, may have, must have, would have, should have.*

CORRECT:
I *could have* taken the bus. [not *could of*]

> **Enthused** Avoid using *enthused* for *enthusiastic.*

CORRECT:
They were *enthusiastic* over the test results. [not *enthused*]

> **Farther/Further** Use *farther* when distance is involved; use *further* to express the idea of "to a great extent or degree."

CORRECT:
A diesel Volkwagen will take you *farther* for less money than most other cars will.

CORRECT:
Further research is needed before these drugs are marketed.

> **Good/Well** *Good* is an adjective; never use it in place of *well,* an adverb.

CORRECT:
The pumpkin pie looks *good.*

CORRECT:
Michael's new blender works *well.*

CORRECT:
Jose did *well* on the test.

Imply/Infer *Imply* means to suggest; *infer* means to conclude from some evidence or suggestion.

CORRECT:
The speaker seemed to *imply* that we were ignorant of the law.

CORRECT:
We might *infer* that he had a low opinion of our intelligence.

Irregardless The standard form is *regardless.* The negative prefix *ir-* is unnecessary.

CORRECT:
Regardless of the cost, synthetic fuels must be developed.

Kind of/Sort of Use *somewhat* or *rather.*

FAULTY:
The judge's decision in this case seemed *kind of* arbitrary.

CORRECT:
The judge's decision in this case seemed *somewhat* arbitrary.

FAULTY:
He seemed *sort of* upset by George's question.

CORRECT:
He seemed *rather* upset by George's question.

Leave Leave is not a substitute for *let* or *allow.*

CORRECT:
Don't *let* them go before noon. [not *leave*]

CORRECT:
Leave your keys at the service desk.

Liable/Likely *Liable* means legally responsible or exposed to; *likely* means probable.

CORRECT:
They are *likely* to arrive at any time.

CORRECT:
You are *liable* to get a parking fine if you park here.

> **Like** *Like* is a preposition; it should not be used as a substitute for *as if* or *as though*, which are conjunctions.

CORRECT:
Victorians treated children *as if* they were little adults. [not *like*]

> **Literally** *Literally* means "in the strict sense" or "to the letter"; it should never be used figuratively.

FAULTY:
She *literally* died from the heat last August. [Is she dead?]

IMPROVED:
She thought she would die from the heat last August. [Literally speaking, she had nothing more than a sunburn.]

> **Lots of** Do not use *lots of* as a substitute for *many*.

CORRECT:
There were *many* opportunities for advancement. [not *lots of*]

> **Maybe/May be** *Maybe* is an adverb meaning "perhaps"; *may be* is a form of the verb *to be*.

CORRECT:
Maybe they missed the Mayberry exit.

CORRECT:
Detective Shocker *may be* arresting the wrong person.

> **Myself** Avoid the use of *myself* as a substitute for *I* or *me*.

CORRECT:
Mr. Salisbury and *I* were put in charge of the lunch counter. [not *myself*]

CORRECT:
The Steerbusters invited my husband and *me* to the barbecue. [not *myself*]

NOTE: Careful writers limit the use of myself to the reflexive and intensive forms.

REFLEXIVE:
I hurt *myself* by refusing a promotion.

INTENSIVE:
I *myself* saw the vicious dogs attack him.

Number/Amount Use *number* for countable things; use *amount* for things that are measured by volume.

CORRECT:
A large *number* of people had gathered.

CORRECT:
A large *amount* of grain will be shipped to China.

Off of *Off* is sufficient; the *of* is redundant.

CORRECT:
He fell *off* the diving board. [not *off of*]

CORRECT:
Take my name *off* the list. [not *off of*]

Outside of The *of* is redundant.

CORRECT:
Plant the seedlings *outside* the house in May. [not *outside of*]

Real/Really These words are overused and frequently misused; they should be deleted or replaced wherever possible. Often action verbs make strong substitutes for these words in weak adverb constructions.

FAULTY:
It was a *real* pleasant party.

IMPROVED:
It was a *pleasant* party. [or *festive, friendly,* etc.]

FAULTY:
Jack Largemouth did *real* well in the debates.

IMPROVED:
Jack Largemouth spoke convincingly in the debates.

FAULTY:
The debates were *really* difficult for Sam Smallmouth.

IMPROVED:
Sam Smallmouth suffered from stage fright during the debates.

> **Reason is because** *That*, not *because*, is required in this construction.

CORRECT:
The reason she moved is *that* she couldn't get a job in Centerville.

> **Refer back** *Refer* is sufficient; *back* is redundant.

CORRECT:
Refer to the earlier chapters. [not *refer back*]

> **There/Their/They're** *There* means "in that place." *Their* is a possessive. *They're* is a contraction for *they are*.

CORRECT:
They arrived *there* just before dark.

CORRECT:
They unloaded *their* camping equipment.

CORRECT:
They're the kind of people who like to sleep with the grizzly bears.

> **Try and/Go and** Avoid such forms in writing.

CORRECT:
We will *try to* get a good seat. [not *try and*]

CORRECT:
We will *go to* see the second show. [not *go and*]

> **Unique** If something is *unique*, it is the only one of its kind. *Unique* should not be used as a substitute for *unusual* or *extraordinary*, and it should never be modified by *very*, *more*, or *most*. For example, the dress you make for yourself is *unique*, one of a kind; but the dress you buy is *unusual*, not the only one ever made.

FAULTY:
It was a *most unique* opportunity for advancement.

IMPROVED:
It was an *unusual* opportunity for advancement.

Whether or not   *Whether* is sufficient; the *or not* is redundant.

CORRECT:
She wonderd *whether* she should go to the party.

Who/Whom   *Who* and *whoever* are used as subjects of verbs; *whom* and *whomever* are used as objects of verbs and of prepositions.

CORRECT:
They kept asking us *who* we thought would win. [*Who* is the subject of *would win.*]

CORRECT:
The article offers good advice to *whoever* has enough money to invest in real estate. [Whoever is the subject of has.]

EXERCISE 10H: CORRECT WORD CHOICE

Circle the correct word in each of the following sentences.

1. (Its/it's) no wonder that the class is popular; (its/it's) subject is very exciting.
2. (Lay/lie) down on the porch swing while I (lay/lie) our clothes on the bed.
3. They always pay you the most gracious (complements/ compliments).
4. "Our fathers brought (forth/fourth) on this continent a new nation. . . ."
5. Will you please (lend/loan) me your textbook for the next class period?
6. The police officer gave us (implicit/explicit) directions on how to get to the mall; we made it in twenty minutes.
7. The children were (already/all ready) to go trick or treating at seven, but their parents said it was (already/all ready) too dark.
8. They ate the (serial/cereal) while they watched the (serial/ cereal) on TV.
9. His (conscience/conscious) was clear because he was innocent, but he was (conscience/conscious) of the crowd's hostility.

10. She was willing to (lend/loan) a hand, but she considered his contribution a (lend/loan) that they should repay.

EXERCISE 10I: MISUSED WORDS AND PHRASES

Draw a line through each misused word or phrase and write the correct form above it.

1. My parents are invited to every party in the neighborhood. The reason is because they have business contacts everywhere.
2. If I had to choose a favorite between *Rocky I, II, III,* and *IV,* I'd choose *Rocky I.*
3. The professor eluded to a verse from Shakespeare, but the significance alluded the class.
4. Joe felt badly about missing the kick and losing the game; he would try and improve his technique before the next game.
5. Being that Juanita was early for class, she decided to contact her advisor.
6. Sigma Epsilon Chi invited my roommate and myself to pledge, irregardless of our grades.
7. May be I'll go to the dance but I maybe late.
8. "The boys won't leave me alone," said gorgeous Georgia, but she inferred that she liked the attention they gave her.
9. We have to device a method to fix this devise.
10. Their going to present they're plan where there going on their vacation.
11. Will you please try and be on time for the picnic?
12. Martin will go further in his career because he has gone farther as a speaker.
13. Send the directions to Roberta and myself.
14. The child fell off of the gate he was swinging on.
15. May be the concert was cancelled because of the threat of storms.
16. Refer back to last week's correspondence.
17. Can't we have dinner soon? I'm literally starved to death.
18. Her kindness will effect his point of view.
19. They were real enthused about the new gymnastics team.
20. When you get to New York contact me.

CHAPTER 11

Argument and Persuasion

As you have learned in all your classes, each academic discipline has some vocabulary of its own. Perhaps this specialized vocabulary consists of words used only in one specific discipline, such as the word *monism*, which is used only in philosophy. More often, however, the specialized vocabulary is made up of words in common usage that have a more specific and precise meaning in their more narrowed discipline. (For example, ask your drama instructor what a *tragedy* is or your doctor what an *event* is.) Many of the more important words and phrases of argument and persuasion depend upon these particularized definitions.

An argument, far from connoting thrown frying pans or thrown voices, is a reasoned consideration of an idea. An argument is a search for truth, a search to make sense of what we don't understand, to refute what we disbelieve, to plan what we hope for. Argument does not concern things that can be verified or are true by definition, such as Richard the Lionhearted ruled England for ten years or that a pogrom is an organized massacre. Simply looking up the answer resolves such questions. Argument pertains to problems that may be resolved in different ways or questions that may have different plausible answers.

DIFFERENCE BETWEEN ARGUMENT AND PERSUASION

An *argument* is a structure of facts and ideas to reach a conclusion or judgment. Your audience may be only you, yourself, or it may be any number of other people. *Persuasion* aims at using your argument to bring about a wished-for result in your audience. Argument is reasoned and logical; persuasion is emotional or psychological. To study them, argument and persuasion are divided, but in actual practice they work together. That is, argument is the blueprint from which you build your persuasion.

In its simplest form, an argument consists of two parts—*premise* and *conclusion*. The premise is the reason or reasons that support the conclusion, the judgment, we have been led to. In addition, these two parts must be logically related to each other to be arguable. For example, consider this statement: "Since traces of gasoline were found all along the basement walls and a five-gallon gasoline container was hidden in the bushes, police strongly suspected arson." An obvious relationship exists between the traces of gas and the strong suspicion of arson. However, if the police had a strong suspicion of blackmail, there is no observable connection between that and gasoline, and, without that relationship, there is no argument.

Two other types of statements are unarguable. First, a statement of verifiable fact, such as "The Board of Trustees does not meet in August." Second, a statement of personal opinion, such as "I hate rock music."

QUESTIONS PRECEDING THE ARGUMENT

Arguments reflect *assumptions* about the world and life. Everyone makes some assumptions, which are those parts of an argument that strike us as self-evident and sure to be known to and easily accepted by our audience. For example, there is an old line that says no one can argue religion. What underlies this observation are assumptions about one's own religion. A skillful arguer does not outrage the assumptions of his or her audience if the person expects to persuade the audience.

Assumptions like these are nonlogical; their truth is taken on faith by people who hold them. These assumptions are called *a priori premises*, that is, premises *before the fact* of the argument. For example, arguments about abortion are usually fruitless because each side has strong *a priori premises*.

VERBAL SIGNALS OF ARGUMENT

To understand argument fully (and to make it successfully), we rely on common sense and *transitional words and phrases* to signal the relationships of premise and conclusion. Our common sense locates the *thesis* for us; it is the controlling idea of the essay and the conclusion to its main argument.

Transitional words and phrases help us greatly to identify the parts of the argument, the premises and the conclusion. The most frequent transitions that signal premises are:

since   because   if

The most frequent transitions that signal conclusions are:

therefore	consequently	in conclusion
as a result	hence	accordingly
then	thus	so

LOGICAL ARGUMENT AND ERRORS IN LOGIC

Logical argument is a reasoned structure based on common sense, experience, and learning. Nevertheless, faults, called *fallacies*, slip in to invalidate the argument and prevent persuasion.

Common Fallacies

Hasty Generalization

Jumping to conclusions is one of the most dangerous errors made in reasoning. It has ruined friendships, promoted bigotry, destroyed marriages, and even started wars. It has also wreaked havoc on countless numbers of writing assignments and essay tests. The formal name for this type of mistake is *hasty generalization*. For example, suppose you heard the following conversation between two of your neighbors:

HARRY: Don't buy a foreign-made car. You'll be sorry. My son-in-law had one, and he had one problem after another. The carburetor went bad, his brake fluid leaked, and he had to put $300 into transmission repairs. When it wasn't stuck in reverse, it was stalling out. Besides that, the pile of junk rusted out in two years.

CHUCK: Well, my sister bought a foreign-made car, and it runs like a dream. She hasn't had to put one penny into repairs since she bought it. I'm definitely going to buy myself a foreign car.

Neither one of your neighbors has a convincing argument because each of them is jumping to conclusions. Just because **one** foreign-made car is bad doesn't mean that **all** foreign-made cars are bad; likewise, just because **one** foreign-made car is good does not mean that **all** foreign-made cars are good. Each of them is making a hasty generalization about a whole group of cars based on only one example.

Stereotypes

People often rush to unwarranted conclusions when they are forming opinions about other people. Their attitudes toward an entire race or religion is based solely on their attitudes toward one or two members of that race or religion. Thus, *stereotypes* are often formed through ignorance of the first rule of sound reasoning: you can't make a valid general statement about anything based on one or two examples. You, as a reader, should not be so gullible that you can be persuaded by so little evidence, nor should you, as a writer, expect intelligent readers to be persuaded by an argument that fails to examine the evidence adequately before arriving at a conclusion.

The Either-or Fallacy

In an attempt to deal with complex issues they do not fully understand, people often resort to polarized thinking, in which there are only two sides to every issue—good and bad, black and white, right and wrong. Such constant *oversimplification*, known as the *Either-or Fallacy*, lowers the reader's opinion of you as a writer. Watch out for thinking that becomes so polarized that there seem to be only two sides to every issue, that it must be either this way or that way with no alternatives:

> Either we defeat this bill to control handguns or the government will confiscate our hunting rifles.
> Either we let the oil companies make their windfall profits or we freeze to death.

Post Hoc Fallacy

Even worse than reaching a conclusion with just a little evidence is the fallacy of reaching a conclusion without any evidence at all. Sometimes people mistake a mere coincidence for a cause-and-effect relationship. They see that *A* happened before *B*, so they mistakenly assume that *A* caused *B*. This is an error known in logic as *post hoc fallacy* ("after this, therefore because of this"). For example, suppose you see a man in a black jacket hurry into a bank. You notice that he is nervously clutching his briefcase, and a few moments later you hear a siren. You therefore leap to the conclusion that the man in the sinister black jacket has robbed the bank. You have absolutely no evidence to work with—only a suspicion based on coincidence. This is a *post hoc* fallacy.

Circular Reasoning

Another way that people mistakenly reach conclusions without evidence is by engaging in circular reasoning. You have probably met people in your lifetime whom you couldn't understand because they talked in circles. In other words, they kept repeating themselves, periodically inserting a *therefore* or *a so you see* to make you think that they were concluding their argument when actually they were just saying the same thing again in different words. Their argument might have sounded like this:

> Nuclear power is the answer to America's fuel shortage. *Therefore,* nuclear power will solve our energy crisis.

Here, you are given no **reason** to believe that nuclear power is the best answer to America's fuel crisis. In place of evidence, the arguer has presented only a slight rewording of the same idea. Although cause and effect is claimed, no cause is given—only a repetition.

The reasoning in such short examples is so obviously circular that few writers would slip into the error; in more fully developed examples, however, the fallacy is not so easy to spot. Particularly when you are arguing on a subject in which you are emotionally involved or even prejudiced, you may fail to notice that you are guilty of circular reasoning. Notice the circular reasoning in the following example:

> Anyone who has real gumption can certainly succeed in America. If a woman has good sense, she's going to see to it that her talent is not hidden under a bushel and that other people will recognize her ability. Sooner or later, she is going to make her mark, and other people will beat a path to her door. Anybody who has any gumption can get ahead in the good old U.S.A.

Misuse of Authority

The misuse of authority is another common method of distortion. The use of biased or incompetent authorities has become an increasingly popular sales tactic. You need only switch the channel selector on your television a few times to find an example. For instance, how many times have you seen celebrities on a commercial telling you that you should buy a certain automobile? The automobile company has attracted your attention with the sight of a famous personality, but unless he or she is also a skilled mechanic or engineer, there is no good reason why the listener should buy the car being advertised. The authority cited is incompetent.

Even when the authority cited has some special knowledge of the subject being discussed, he or she may be biased on the subject or have a vested interest to protect. If, for example, you cited a statement from the leading members of the American Medical Association to prove that doctors are overworked and underpaid, your evidence would be biased.

False Analogy

Another error in reasoning that misleads the reader is the false analogy. As you learned in Chapter 6, an analogy is a specific form of comparison: finding similarities between two things that are normally classified under different categories. For example, "A football coach is like a general" is a valid analogy because you can draw many parallels between them—strategies, goals, vocabulary, and so on. However, the fallacy occurs when a writer finds just one or two vague similarities between two things and then concludes that the two are alike. Look at the following statement:

> I'm sixteen years old. I'm old enough to drive a car, so I should be old enough to get married without anyone's permission. Therefore, the marriage age should be lowered to sixteen.

This is a false analogy because the responsibilities required of a good driver are different from the responsibilities required of a good husband or wife. You might say that both require maturity, but that is extremely vague. A person can be an excellent driver and still be a totally self-centered, callous, and unreliable person. The analogy might sound good at first, especially to a sixteen-year-old in love, but upon closer examination, you can see that driving a car and marrying are two entirely different matters.

Card Stacking

Card stacking is both a fallacy and a technique of propagandists. By selecting only the evidence supporting an argument, they stack the deck in their favor. This error is particularly dangerous because it is often subtle. The evidence presented could consist of relevant and accurate facts, but those facts may represent only part of the picture, that part supporting the writer's point of view. For example:

> The stock market today is in good shape. Some of the oil company stocks are up 30 percent. Some chemical companies have the highest profits ever.

Some oil company stocks may indeed be up 30 percent, but oil and chemical stocks don't make up the entire stock market. Selecting these stocks and omitting others that are not faring well stacks the deck. It would hardly be accurate to say that the stock market is in "good shape."

The Hidden Assumption

Another error you should watch out for is the hidden assumption. Before you accept any conclusion, you should always make sure that you are aware of the premises on which the argument is based. What is the writer asking you to assume? Look at the following statement:

> Jeannie said that Tuesday is going to be a boring day for her because that's the day she has to talk to the patients in the geriatrics ward.

If you are going to accept Jeannie's conclusion, you must first accept her hidden premise, the assumption on which her argument is based:

HIDDEN PREMISE:
Talking to old people is boring.

STATED PREMISE:
I have to talk to old people.

CONCLUSION:
I am going to be bored.

The hidden premise, of course, is false. Assuming that old people have nothing interesting to say is ridiculous. Thus, Jeannie's conclusion is also invalid because it is based on a hidden assumption that is false.

Misleading Statistics

Even an intelligent reader can often be misled by statistical evidence. Sometimes people are so impressed with numbers that they don't stop to analyze them. Suppose, for example, that the president of your flying fraternity tells you that girls will never make good pilots because 50 percent of the girls in his class failed the final flight exam. Suppose, however, that he conveniently forgot to tell you that there were only *two* girls in his piloting class: one of them failed the test and the other got the highest grade in the class. True, 50 percent did fail because 50 percent of two is one, but the truth is that the figure actually proves nothing. "Fifty percent" simply sounds more impressive than "one." Don't be fooled by arguments like this. Whenever you come across an argument supported with percentages, make sure that you know **exactly** what those percentages refer to: 34 pecent of what? 50 percent of how many?

Figures dealing with averages, even when the figures are accurate, can often be misleading. Suppose, for example, you read an article stating that five prominent American athletes earned an average of $60,000 on the banquet circuit last year. You would naturally assume that **all** these athletes spent a large part of the off season speaking for pay. However, upon closer examination, you might find that the actual figures lead to a substantially different conclusion:

Bruno Baxter	$ 9,000
Terrible Tyler	$ 7,500
Peter Perfection	$288,000
Nancy Nicely	$ 9,000
Rocky Ricketts	$ 16,500

It's true that the average of these five figures is $60,000, but the $288,000 figure is so much higher than the rest that it distorts the average. Many people assume that average means typical, but as you can see, the mathematical average of a series of numbers is sometimes misleading. When you have a very high or low number that distorts the average, a more meaningful figure to give your reader is the median (the number that falls midway between the first and last number) or the mode (the number that appears most often). In this case, both the median and the mode are the same—$9,000. So be careful with statistics. Remember, you can drown in a river whose "average" depth is two inches.

EMOTIONAL ARGUMENT AND ETHICAL VIOLATIONS

Although emotional appeals are sometimes not considered as important as the appeals of logic, the emotional argument is every bit as strong and valuable as the logical. You want and need your audience to *care* about many of the ideas you present. You can help them to care by illustrating your argument by moving, vivid, *accurate* examples. In an emotional appeal you also want your style to be as pleasing as possible. Be courteous to your readers; state your ideas in language as simple and clear as you can make it. Both logical and emotional appeals can, of course, be misused. Unscrupulous persuaders often play upon people's desires and fears for unethical purposes: to encourage prejudice and stereotyped thinking, to stir jealousy and hatred, to instigate irrational action, and to gain blind adherence to fanatical causes.

Your only true defense against deceptive practices is a healthy sense of skepticism. Whenever someone tries to persuade you, you need to ask yourself some sensible questions:

1. Who is trying to prove what? Why?
2. What are the persuader's qualifications? (Does he or she have the necessary training, experience, or relevant expertise?)
3. Are the facts and statistics presented fairly?
4. Does the evidence warrant the conclusion you are to accept?
5. Who stands to gain or lose?

A combination of factual details and emotional appeals can provide a powerful argument. Suppose, for example, that you were a victim of the disastrous 1977 flood in Johnstown, Pennsylvania, a city that was proclaimed "flood-free" in 1943. You are a journalist, and you want to convey the full extent of the horrors of the flood to residents outside the Johnstown area and persuade them to petition the federal authorities for help. You could present them with a factual report of the damages:

> The raging waters traveled through seven counties causing $117 million worth of damage, killing 73 people, and leaving 50,000 others homeless. The total damages were estimated at over $200 million. . . .

These facts alone, however, would not necessarily stir your readers' emotions. They are bombarded with statistical information every day. You would have a far better chance of moving them to action if you appeal to their emotions as well. Imagine how much more impact you would have if you reinforce your factual report with an article like Larry Hudson's in Johnstown's *Tribune-Democrat:*

> There are some things the history books never told us. They just told us it would never happen again. They never told us about the twisted limbs of the victims and the sudden quickening your heart takes when the rubble falls away, and through the mud a body takes form. They never told us that the image of a dead child can penetrate a sleeping mind and shoot you bolt upright in bed.
>
> We never learned from history books about the rubble, the lifted streets and sidewalks turned and tilted into grotesque heaps. . . . And they never told us about the mud. Mud piled higher than your head. Mud that's impossible to walk in. . . . Mud that sticks to your feet, your hands, walls, homes, tires.

Mud that can't be swept away with a broom, but has to be boxed and cajoled into tiny floods until it slops over the doorstep and out into the muddy street to join a river of mud going God knows where.

The history books never told us about the smell. Sewer gas so raw that it burns your eyes and throat. The musty, warm odor of brown water. . . . The smell of death . . . the rotten food, wet paper and wet dogs . . . the smell of yourself. They never told us that boiled water turns dark and tastes much like we all feel.

They never told us how much it would hurt, or about the unwashed bodies, or the psychological thirst that comes when you know water is limited: the vacant stares from the eyes all around you, everywhere.

And the books contained nothing about the way the sun comes up, pouring incongruous warmth upon devastation. Nothing about the birds singing as the dead lay heaped.

Just as fallacies are errors in logic, *propaganda techniques* are delinquencies in ethical behavior. Some of the most frequently used techniques are the following.

Propaganda Techniques

In addition to avoiding the common fallacies, you need to be alert to the techniques of the propagandist and avoid using them in your own writing. A variety of unethical persuasive tactics are often used by the propagandist in an effort to get others to accept arguments without examining the evidence. Among the more frequently used techniques of propaganda are the following.

The Smear Technique

The most common smear technique is one which attacks the person who is proposing an idea rather than attacking the idea itself. The smear technique is often used during the heat of political campaigns. In the 1988 presidential election, for example, Michael Dukakis, the Democratic candidate, was pictured by his opponents as "easy on criminals". One criminal, Willie Horton, had committed a murder while on release from prison. From this, the smear campaign insinuated that, with Dukakis in the White House, murderers would roam freely on our streets. Though Americans fell for this smear campaign, smear tactics often lose more votes than they gain; voters often lose respect for candidates who resort to such tactics. In the same way, you will destroy your credibility with intelligent readers if they discover that you have resorted to smear tactics.

Bandwagon Technique

Some people feel more comfortable going along with the majority (jumping on the bandwagon) rather than standing alone. This pressure to conform, often coupled with the desire to go with a winner, makes some readers susceptible to the bandwagon approach. In some of television's soft drink ads, for example, you are told, in effect, that you should get with it and join the young generation and drink Brand X. The implication is that everybody else is doing it, so you should too. In similar fashion, insurance salespeople and funeral directors sometimes employ the bandwagon approach to persuade you to buy a more expensive insurance policy or a more elaborate casket:

> Almost all our clients are switching to our new Group *B* plan.
>
> We don't sell very many of these models. Most people buy a casket from our deluxe "Rest in Peace" display."

Transfer Technique

Through the transfer technique, the propagandist tries to associate himself and his arguments with people or ideas that already have our respect or admiration, thereby getting us to accept blindly his position. The transfer device frequently makes use of labels and symbols. Some of the worst scoundrels have paraded under the flag of patriotism, and some of the most flagrant violations of human rights have been perpetrated under the guise of national security.

Evading the Issue

Skillful propagandists may find many ways of evading the issue whenever the evidence goes against their arguments. For instance, they may use spurious or irrelevant evidence to mislead the reader. Pointing out how good Secretary so-and-so was to his grandmother provides no evidence of his ability to manage the Social Security system. Spurious arguments frequently focus attention on facts that have little or nothing to do with the central issue. Thus someone may argue that a man or woman who does not play a good game of golf is not fit to be an executive in a prestigious financial institution.

Red Herring Tactic

The red herring tactic is a deliberate attempt to divert attention from the real issue by dragging in a false one. When the unethical persuader knows that his case is weak, he drags in an emotional issue that is designed to mislead the reader. A politician accused of accepting kickbacks from government contracts may try to divert attention by claiming that the investigative agency has persecuted him and his defenseless family. The real issue is whether or not he accepted kickbacks, and the perceptive reader or listener will refuse to be misled by the politician's claim that he is being persecuted.

Questions to Ask Yourself

Check your final argument by asking yourself these questions:

Did I jump to conclusions?
Did I fail to stick to the issues?
Did I neglect to look at **all** sides of the issue?
Did I make too much of a mere coincidence?
Did I ask the reader to assume something that isn't true?
Did I use any misleading statistics?
Did I make any invalid comparisons?
Did I use any biased or unreliable authorities?
Did I back up my generalizations with specific, relevant examples?
Did I leave out any steps in my argument?
Did I attribute a single cause to a complex series of events?
Did I deliberately ignore evidence that didn't support my thesis?

EXERCISE 11A: VALIDITY OF ARGUMENTS

Examine the validity of the following arguments. If any argument is illogical, identify the specific error or errors in reasoning. If the argument contains no fallacies, mark "valid" in the space provided. Watch out for such errors as the following:

Hasty Generalization	Hidden Assumption
Stereotypes	Misleading Statistics
Either-or Fallacy	Smear Technique
Post Hoc Fallacy	Bandwagon Technique
Circular Reasoning	Transfer Technique
Misuse of Authority	Evading the Issue
False Analogy	Red Herring Tactic
Card Stacking	

1. The president of the United States gave a piece of expensive glassware to every foreign head of state that he visited while in office. Therefore, the leader of my sorority has a right to use our contributions to buy expensive gifts for her foreign friends.

2. Don't vote for Janice Jolly for mayor. She fell in love with her

campaign manager and got a divorce after twenty years of marriage.

3. You just lost your job, your hospital bill isn't paid off yet, and you still owe over $1,000 on your charge accounts. This is no time to be thinking about buying a new car.

4. All of the people in your neighborhood must have good jobs if the average home sells for $100,000.

5. Doctors are all the same. The only thing they care about is making money.

6. Why should I take any course outside of my major? I'm not going to be a writer or a historian, so why should I know anything about literature or American history?

7. If the great Chief Sitting Bull were around today, he would tell his tribe that no one can own the land because people die but the land lives on forever. Therefore, you Indians should give up this legal fight to reclaim 50,000 acres of land and let the oil companies use it for exploration.

8. The police found a gun with Professor Fenton's fingerprints on it right beside his body, and the ballistics experts said that it had been fired within the last hour. A psychiatrist has been treating the professor for depression for over a year now, and his wife found a suicide note on his dresser. I guess the students finally got to poor old Mr. Fenton. He just couldn't take the frustrations of teaching any more.

9. Either we put more money into fighting drugs, or we lose a whole generation of kids.

10. Teachers are all the same; they are only interested in their subject, not in the students.

11. People who have suffered from child abuse usually abuse their own children. They punish their children brutally or neglect disciplining at all.

12. As I walked past the National Bank, an alarm sounded, and a woman rushed out of the door. She undoubtedly robbed the bank.

---

13. You must either stop seeing him at all or totally ignore his careless habits.

---

14. People laughed at Henry Ford for saying "History is bunk." I think he was right. History is bunk.

---

15. Families who live in the slums won't work hard.

---

16. All the students in the nine o'clock English class are wimps. They are all trying for A's.

---

17. All the evidence is against Mr. Wiffniff's cheating on his income taxes; his mother and his wife both insist he is kind and polite to everyone.

---

18. We are all switching to Diet Delite. It has fewer calories, less sugar, and is just plain better. Switch with us.

ORGANIZATION

Although there are a great many ways of presenting a persuasive argument, the basic three-part organization will frequently serve you best: (1) You start by taking a clear stand on some issue. (2) You provide specific and detailed support to back up your position. (3) You offer a brief conclusion to wrap up your discussion and reinforce your controlling idea.

In addition to your tried-and-true formula for organization, another thing that adds interest to your essay is the attitude called "the argumentative edge." The argumentative edge can be advantageous in many types of writing but is particularly helpful in persuasion.

The argumentative edge pertains both to style and content. Your style should be vigorous, not bland, creating an attitude of enthusiasm for your side of the argument and an attitude of sturdy disagreement or disparagement for the opposite side. In content, it means that you choose to write about the less popular side of the arguable topic. For example, if your thesis was "don't beat your mother, because it is mean," you would not provoke much of a discussion because the great majority of people would agree with you—but probably not read you. On the other hand, if you choose (with the argumentative edge) a topic such as "Twenty-Two Reasons to Beat Your Mother," you'd gain a lot of attention. Since most of the themes you write are intellectual exercises and not heart-felt convictions, you probably can write on either side; the less popular one is almost always the more interesting.

It is more than a little confusing, at first, to realize that the *introduction* to your essay is the *conclusion* to your argument. The introduction and the conclusion of your essay are both general statements, and as general statements they form the conclusion to your argument. The *body* of your essay is made up of the premises of your argument.

Essay Form	**Argumentative Form**
1. *Introduction*, including generalizing thesis	1. *Conclusion*, drawn evidence that supports it, called *premises*
2. *Body*	2. *Premises*
3. *Conclusion*	3. *Conclusion*

But no matter whether it is your thesis statement or your argumentative conclusion, many times you add interest by making them seem contradictory to popularly held concepts. Consider the following exercise. All five quotations have an argumentative edge.

EXERCISE 11B: UNDERSTANDING THE ARGUMENTATIVE EDGE

The following quotations are from H.L. Mencken. Mencken was a newspaper and magazine editor, a distinguished writer on language, an essayist who was immensely popular in his favorite role as an irreverent cynic and iconoclast. Mencken liked to affront the cherished sentiments of the American people, and he enjoyed outraging readers. On the basis of the great numbers of people who loved his writings, they enjoyed it too. Why? Perhaps because what he said amused them, made them think, and sometimes made them vigorously disagree with him.

1. Equality before the law is probably forever unattainable. It is a noble ideal, but it can never be realized, for what men value in this world is not rights but privileges.

2. Capital punishment has failed in America simply because it has never been tried. If all criminals of a plainly incurable sort were put to death tomorrow, there would be enormously less crime in the next generation.
3. Only a country that is rich and safe can afford to be a democracy, for democracy is the most expensive and nefarious kind of government ever heard of on earth.
4. Why assume glibly that God who presumably created the universe is still running it? It is certainly perfectly conceivable that He may have finished it and then turned it over to lesser gods to operate. In the same way many human institutions are turned over to grossly inferior men. This is true of many universities, and of all great newspapers.
5. Of all the classes of men I dislike, most are those who make their living by talking—actors, clergymen, politicians, and so forth.

QUESTIONS FOR DISCUSSION

Are Mencken's statements arguable, that is, grounds for argument?
How does question 4 differ from the others?
Why does he make this change?
In what way is question 5 different?
What words or phrases in each sentence make them especially argumentative?

INTRODUCTION

The introduction to an essay of persuasion usually presents an issue which the writer wishes the reader to consider. An effective introduction may make use of definition, description, narration, an anecdote, or a pertinent quotation, provided it leads to the central issue. What is important is that you set forth the problem clearly and perhaps indicate a solution.

In writing your persuasive essay, you will look for some attractive or provocative introduction to capture your reader's attention and to lead them up to your thesis statement. This should be a clear and carefully worded sentence or two in which you take a definite stand that you are prepared to support.

BODY

In the body you present both the facts and the logical and emotional appeals to back up your position. You may use comparison, contrast, analogy, statistical evidence, examples, anecdotes, personal experience and observation, or any combination of methods and materials to support your thesis. You need to provide valid evidence to support your stand.

In "Who Makes the Babies?" Paul R. Ehrlich and John P. Holdren develop the body of their essay by several methods. They gather statistical evidence and analyze it to show cause and effect. They say, "Statistically, not only are large families more likely to **be** poor, they are also more likely to **remain** poor." They also use statistics as the basis for a contrast of the average citizen of the United States with the average citizen of India. They say, "—the average American consumes fifty times as much steel—and 300 times as much plastic as the average citizen of India. The ratio of per capita energy consumption . . . for the same two countries is 56 to 1." They also contrast well-to-do and poor Americans. They compare well-to-do black Americans with well-to-do white Americans, saying "Affluent black couples have slightly fewer children than affluent white couples." The authors also use definition as a method to develop concepts like "population control." The body of their essay is a selection of facts and several methods of presenting those facts chosen to make their thesis as persuasive as possible.

Knowing Your Audience

Before you can persuade your audience, you must know as much about it as possible. Are you considering audience members professionally or personally? What is their educational background? What are their interests and amusements? Such questions determine how you will present your argument.

If, for example, you were trying to persuade a group of Christian fundamentalists to contribute to the American Poverty Fund, you might appeal to their desire for eternal salvation by doing the charitable thing. You might base a large part of your argument on biblical quotation:

> The righteous considereth the cause of the poor; but the wicked regardeth not to know it.

> He that giveth unto the poor shall not lack; but he that hideth his eyes shall have many a curse.

If, however, you were appealing to your neighbor, who is a successful banker and an atheist, you would be unlikely to persuade him to give to the American Poverty Fund lest he burn in hell. Instead of presenting your appeal from a strictly theological standpoint, you might appeal to his well-known humanitarianism and to his fiscal responsibility to his company in earning tax credits and good-will in public relations.

Presenting the Evidence

If you hope to persuade intelligent readers that your argument is sound, you must demonstrate thorough and accurate knowledge of your subject. There is no substitute for a careful study of the subject and a thorough investigation of all the pertinent facts before you begin to write. Careful presentation of accurate factual support is essential to your credibility. Careless statements or exaggerated claims may lead your reader to distrust your argument from the outset. You can't afford to be careless with the facts and just hope that your reader won't know the difference. A single misstatement regarding a significant fact may destroy your credibility. If, for example, you were to claim that handguns are responsible for 75,000 homicides in the United States each year, any knowledgeable reader would see that your claim is grossly exaggerated and would have reason to doubt whether **any** of your statements can be relied upon.

Acknowledging Your Sources

In presenting a persuasive argument, you must frequently rely on printed sources for facts, statistics, and the testimony of experts to support your opinion. Whenever you use quoted material or statements of fact and opinion other than your own, you must clearly identify your source, either within the text of your paper or in footnotes. Usually, if the references are few and brief, they can be inserted, within parentheses, in the text itself; however, if more extensive documentation is needed and footnotes are required, then consult a reliable guide, such as the *MLA Style Sheet,* for proper footnote form.

Strategies for Presenting a Persuasive Argument

Strategy I

Introduction

1. State the problem so that the issue is clear.

2. Define your terms if necessary.
3. State your thesis in one clear sentence.

Body

1. Present first main point and supporting evidence.
2. Present second main point and supporting evidence.
3. Present third main point and supporting evidence.
4. Present fourth main point, and so on, as needed.

Conclusion

Wrap up your discussion and reemphasize your thesis.

Strategy II

When there is strong opposition to your thesis, an effective strategy is to state the evidence first and conclude with your thesis sentence. In this way, you can pile up the evidence to break down the opposition, then state your thesis after you have had ample opportunity to convince your reader. This type of persuasive argument is flexible in structure, and it offers you a better opportunity to combine logical and emotional appeals. Such an argument might follow these three basic steps:

1. Bring the issue to your reader's attention with a striking example.
2. Pile up more and more details, all pointing toward one conclusion.
3. State your thesis. (In this instance, your thesis and conclusion are the same.)

When your thesis clearly follows from the evidence you have presented, you will have earned an acceptance of your conclusion even from an apathetic or hostile audience. Suppose, for example, that you wanted to convince your readers of the horrors that youthful offenders sometimes face inside our jails and prisons. Some careful research could provide you with telling case histories, and your most effective argument might be one which simply presented case after case of well-documented abuses. By carefully presenting the evidence and avoiding any suggestion of argument, you could lead even the most skeptical reader to accept your thesis.

CONCLUSION

Offer a conclusion that pulls together the main supporting points of your discussion and reinforces the controlling idea of your thesis sentence. Avoid overstating your case; your conclusion should be

warranted by the evidence you have presented. An effective concluding paragraph may provide a careful statement of the implications of
the evidence, a striking example or quotation to drive home your
main point, a forecast based solidly on the evidence you have presented, or a call for action to remedy the problem you have brought
to the reader's attention. An effective conclusion is never just some
words tacked on at the end of your essay; it should bring your
discussion to a definite close. Having presented your best evidence,
you rest your case with the reader.

Many methods may be used in developing a persuasive argument. In some instances, it may be necessary to dispose of an opposing argument before you can present your own argument effectively.
When you have two sharply opposing views on a particular issue,
you may need to set forth both the pro and con positions. Then,
when you have examined these clashing views, you can lead your
reader to a more balanced view, a carefully reasoned compromise
between the two extremes. Whatever pattern of development you
employ, however, you must present your reader with a sensible
progression from evidence to reasoned conclusion.

EXERCISE 11C: TESTING CONCLUSIONS

*All the time the arguer is trying to persuade you, as an intelligent reader,
you are testing that person on the worth of his or her argument. What do
you think of the following conclusion? This is the final page from a book
titled* Intellectuals, *by Paul Johnson, an established and respected
writer. All 374 preceding pages are biographical studies of twelve intellectuals who were of vast influence in their respective disciplines. Nevertheless, Johnson questions the value of their contributions. What do you
think?*

It is just about two hundred years since the secular intellectuals began to replace the old clerisy as the guides and mentors of
mankind. We have looked at a number of individual cases of
those who sought to counsel humanity. We have examined
their moral and judgmental qualifications for this task. In particular, we have examined their attitude to truth, the way in
which they seek for and evaluate evidence, their response not
just to humanity in general but to human beings in particular;
the way they treat their friends, colleagues, servants and above
all their own families. We have touched on the social and political consequences of following their advice.

What conclusions should be drawn? Readers will judge for
themselves. But I think I detect today a certain public scepticism when intellectuals stand up to preach to us, a growing

tendency among ordinary people to dispute the right of academics, writers and philosophers, eminent though they may be, to tell us how to behave and conduct our affairs. The belief seems to be spreading that intellectuals are no wiser as mentors, or worthier as exemplars, than the witch doctors or priests of old. I share that scepticism. A dozen people picked at random on the street are at least as likely to offer sensible views on moral and political matters as a cross-section of the intelligentsia. But I would go further. One of the principal lessons of our tragic century, which has seen so many millions of innocent lives sacrificed in schemes to improve the lot of humanity, is—beware intellectuals. Not merely should they be kept well away from the levers of power, they should also be objects of particular suspicion when they seek to offer collective advice. Beware committees, conferences and leagues of intellectuals. Distrust public statements issued from their serried ranks. Discount their verdicts on political leaders and important events. For intellectuals, far from being highly individualistic and non-conformist people, follow certain regular patterns of behaviour. Taken as a group, they are often ultra-conformist within the circles formed by those whose approval they seek and value. That is what makes them, *en masse,* so dangerous, for it enables them to create climates of opinion and prevailing orthodoxies, which themselves often generate irrational and destructive courses of action. Above all, we must at all times remember what intellectuals habitually forget: that people matter more than concepts and must come first. The worst of all despotisms is the heartless tyranny of ideas.

Paul Johnson

QUESTIONS FOR DISCUSSION

Is Johnson's evidence pertinent?
Do you suspect *a priori* thinking?
Are twelve examples of evidence sufficient?
Will you accept twelve people as true and valid evidence?
Were you or were you not convinced of his argument?

FORMAL ARGUMENT

Although the success of your persuasive effort depends on more than just the structure of your argument, some knowledge of the formal structure of arguments can help you to present your case more effectively. The term *formal argument* refers to the structure of an argument. Is the argument logically constructed? Is the logic inductive or deductive? The term *persuasion* refers to the use of an argument for a specific purpose. When you are persuading, you have to be concerned with how your arguments will affect your audience, so you have to consider more than just the logic of your argument: you have to consider its emotional appeal and the appeal of your "image" as a writer. Do you come across as sincere, authoritative, worth listening to? You need not show every single step in your argument; in fact, you can show your reader valid cause-and-effect relationships without stating all the assumptions and the minor premise of your argument. For example, consider the following statement from a persuasive essay that explores the need for remedial classes:

> Many of the high school graduates in ABC County can't read above the fifth-grade level, so ABC County Community College should offer some classes in reading improvement.

This statement shows a clear cause-and-effect relationship even though the minor premise of the argument is not stated. If this statement were presented as a formal argument, it would look like this:

MAJOR PREMISE:
Many of the high school graduates in ABC County can't read above the fifth-grade level.

MINOR PREMISE:
College students who can't read their textbooks are likely to fail their courses.

CONCLUSION:
ABC County Community College should offer some classes in reading improvement.

The statement also makes several assumptions, but they are so obvious that they don't need to be stated. For example:

ASSUMPTION 1:
Many of the students who attend ABC County Community College went to high school in ABC County.

ASSUMPTION 2:
College textbooks are written at a reading level above the fifth grade.

ASSUMPTION 3:
Classes in reading improvement should help students learn to read at a higher grade level.

So don't automatically equate the terms *argument* and *persuasion*. Think of the word *argument* as a process of reasoning. (Certainly don't think of it as a quarrel, as in "She had an argument with her boyfriend.") Argument is a formal structure of reasoning, which has two basic patterns: *induction*, which means "to lead into," and *deduction* which means "to lead away from."

Inductive Reasoning

The process of reasoning from particular facts or observations to a generalization is called *induction.*

In simplified form, the process could be described as

S ———————————→ G
Specific examples   to   Generalization

By carefully observing a great many particular examples—of animal behavior, plant growth, people's spending habits, or whatever—you are able to arrive at a reliable generalization or conclusion. For instance, through a great many observations over an extended period, ornithologists (scientists who study birds) have been able to arrive at reliable conclusions about whooping cranes—their flyways, their nesting grounds, and their breeding habits. In a similar process, a poll taker may interview a thousand shoppers concerning their spending habits; then, if the poll is carefully conducted, the interviewer may arrive at a reliable generalization, such as "the majority of American shoppers are comparing prices carefully before making major purchases."

Even though it may be on a smaller scale, you make use of inductive reasoning on a day-to-day basis; that is, you look at certain evidence and arrive at a conclusion on the basis of that evidence. If you see that, for the third day in a row, your left rear tire is low, you conclude that it must have a slow leak.

You must keep in mind, however, that any conclusion based upon induction is a **probability.** Generally, the more instances or examples and the more careful the observation, the more reliable the conclusion; however, the conclusion does **not** necessarily follow from evidence, no matter how strong that evidence may be. Sloppy reasoning or hasty examination of the evidence can lead you to a false conclusion. If you see that a neighbor drives a new car every year, you might easily conclude that she must be able to afford to trade-in her car every year. However, that conclusion may be unwarranted; she may be leasing the car, not buying it, or her employer may provide her with a new car each year.

A generalization arrived at through induction should never be considered an absolute certainty. However, there are some sensible guidelines that can help to ensure the reliability of your conclusion:

1. Do you have enough examples to support the generalization? If you're not careful, you may be jumping to a conclusion on the basis of too little evidence.
2. Is the generalization carefully limited to what the evidence will support? You need to be especially careful in making generalizations about **all** members of a group. You can seldom justify a generalization that contains such words as *all, always, no one,* or *everyone.*
3. Are the examples typical? You cannot make a fair and accurate generalization based upon bizarre examples or exceptional cases.
4. Is the evidence drawn from up-to-date and reliable sources? If your evidence is out-of-date, or if you rely on biased sources, you're not apt to arrive at a reliable conclusion.
5. Is the evidence relevant to the generalization being drawn from it? Even dozens of examples of poverty-stricken youngsters who became famous athletes earning huge salaries do not support the conclusion that athletics provides a way out for the youth of the ghetto.

Deductive Reasoning

The process of reasoning from a generalization to a special application of that general principle is called *deduction.* In a schematic form invented by Aristotle, the process is described as a *syllogism.* The syllogism argues from general statements, called *premises,* which follow a fixed form. The argument always goes like this: If *A* is true, and if *B* is true, then *C* must be true. Most books of elementary logic give this as an example of syllogistic form:

MAJOR PREMISE:
All men are mortal.

MINOR PREMISE:
Socrates is a man.

CONCLUSION:
Therefore, Socrates is mortal.

The broad statement at the beginning is the *major premise.* The more particular statement in the middle is the *minor premise.* The final statement is the *conclusion,* which follows from the major and minor premises. If you examine these three statements, you see that they are related on the basis of a common element, or *middle term,* which appears in both the major and minor premise.

All syllogisms are built on these three terms, which you can identify by grammatical analysis:

The **major term** (*mortal*) is the predicate of the conclusion.
The **minor term** (*Socrates*) is the subject of the conclusion.
The **middle term** (*men–man*) appears in both premises but does **not** appear in the conclusion.

The *form* of the syllogism does not often appear in real life; you are much more likely to say, "Since Socrates is a man, he must die." However, syllogistic form underlies all argument that moves from the general to the specific. What's more, it serves as an excellent test of the logic of statements you write and read.

For example, if you wanted to convince someone that your local council president should be reelected, you might point out that she has done a lot for the people of the community. Here you are using a generally accepted premise that "Officials who do a lot for the people should be reelected" to support a specific case, the reelection of the council president.

Stated as a syllogism, this would read:

MAJOR PREMISE:
Officials who do a lot for the people should be reelected.

MINOR PREMISE:
Our local council president has done a lot for the people.

CONCLUSION:
Therefore, our local council president should be reelected.

If the persons you are trying to convince agree with your major and minor premises, they must agree with your conclusion.

The Chain of Reasoning

In everyday situations, induction and deduction go hand in hand. Through induction you arrive at a generalization; then you apply that generalization to a particular situation and draw a conclusion, which is deduction.

Although both of these patterns of logical arguments are necessary, there is one important difference between them. Inductive reasoning, no matter how painstaking, can never lead to any conclusion stronger than probable, even though it may be very persuasive. Deductive reasoning has greater force because if the syllogism is both valid and true, the conclusion cannot be denied by any reasonable person. Deductive reasoning leads to certainty.

Special Cautions

Distributed Middle Term

Logicians say that a valid syllogism must have a *distributed middle term*. This middle term puts the major term and the minor term in the same classification; it provides an overlapping of meaning so that the conclusion follows logically from the premises. For instance, in our example about Socrates the middle term in the major premise is *men* and the middle term in the minor premise is *man;* since *men* and *man* are clearly the singular and plural of the same term, the two belong in the same category and are therefore **distributed,** one in each premise. If the middle term is not distributed, that is, if it does not appear in both major and minor premises, the conclusion is not valid. In the following syllogism, you can instantly spot the fallacy of the undistributed middle by noting that the middle term, *B,* is the **predicate** of both premises and thus is not distributed in subject and predicate. The conclusion is therefore not valid.

> All *A* is *B.*
> All *C* is *B.*
> Therefore, all *C* is *A.*

If the syllogism is to yield a valid conclusion, the middle term not only must be distributed but must remain clear and stable; it must have the same meaning each time it appears.

Now look at the following syllogism:

> All nuts are high in nutrients.
> My Uncle Fritz is a real nut.
> My Uncle Fritz is high in nutrients.

Here, the conclusion is obviously ridiculous because the meaning of the middle term has shifted.

Validity and Truth

When you ask if a syllogism is valid, you are interested in its **form.** When you ask if it is true, you are concerned with its **content.** If you question the truth of a syllogism, you are asking if the premises are statements you consider true. For example, is "All men are mortal" a true statement? Common human experience confirms it to be true; there are no exceptions to disprove it. Therefore, the syllogism about Socrates is both valid and true. Some syllogisms, however, are valid but not true. For instance:

All cats speak French.
Some chickens are cats.
Therefore, some chickens speak French.

This is an example of a valid but untrue syllogism.

If you disagree with the conclusion, you must first determine whether you find it invalid or untrue. If you find it invalid, you can immediately offset the argument. If you find it untrue, you may find it harder to disprove the premise—although not in the case of the cats.

EXERCISE 11D: SYLLOGISMS

The syllogism about the French-speaking cats was written by Lewis Carroll, who is best remembered as the author of the Alice *books but who was also an important logician. Here are some sets of premises he wrote for students. Make up conclusions for these, trying to make them valid and/or true (even if many of them are just jokes). If you cannot make valid and/or true conclusions, tell what prevented you from so doing.*

1. Some oysters are silent.
   No silent creatures are amusing.
   Therefore, _____

2. No riddles interest me that can be solved.
   All these riddles are insoluble.
   Therefore, _____

3. All wasps are unfriendly.
   All puppies are friendly.
   Therefore, _____

4. All ducks waddle.
   Nothing that waddles is graceful.
   Therefore, _____

5. Bores are terrible.
   You are a bore.
   Therefore, _____

6. No fossils can be crossed in love.
   An oyster may be crossed in love.
   Therefore, _____

7. A prudent man shuns hyenas.
   No banker is imprudent.
   Therefore, _____

8. Some pillows are soft.
   No pokers are soft.
   Therefore, _____

9. No country that has been explored is infested by dragons.
   Unexplored countries are fascinating.
   Therefore, _____

10. "I saw it in the newspaper."
    "All newspapers tell lies."
    Therefore, _____

11. No emperors are dentists.
    All dentists are dreaded by children.
    Therefore, _____

12. No military personnel write poetry.
    No generals are civilians.
    Therefore, _____

13. All owls are satisfactory.
    Some excuses are unsatisfactory.
    Therefore, _____

14. No unexpected pleasure annoys me.
    Your visit is an unexpected pleasure.
    Therefore, _____

TESTING THE COMPLETE ARGUMENT

Torture: The word itself brings shivers to our spines and sickness to our stomachs. It conjures up pictures of bamboo strips being driven under fingernails, electric shocks being applied to delicate body parts, toes and ears being systematically cut off. We feel immediate sympathy for the one being tortured and revulsion for the torturer.

The author of the following essay presents a different view of torture. After reading the essay, answer the questions that follow.

··

THE CASE FOR TORTURE

··

It is generally assumed that torture is impermissible, a throwback to a more brutal age. Enlightened societies reject it outright, and regimes suspected of using it risk the wrath of the United States.

I believe this attitude is unwise. There are situations in which torture is not merely permissible but morally mandatory. Moreover, these situations are moving from the realm of imagination to fact.

Death: Suppose a terrorist has hidden an atomic bomb on Manhattan Island, which will detonate at noon on July 4 unless . . . (here follow the usual demands for money and release of his friends from jail). Suppose, further, that he is caught at 10 A.M. of the fateful day, but—preferring death to failure—won't disclose where the bomb is. What do we do? If we follow due process—wait for his lawyer, arraign him—millions of people will die. If the only way to save those lives is to subject the terrorist to the most excruciating possible pain, what grounds can there be for not doing so? I suggest there are none. In any case, I ask you to face the question with an open mind.

Torturing the terrorist is unconstitutional? Probably. But millions of lives surely outweigh constitutionality. Torture is barbaric? Mass murder is far more barbaric. Indeed, letting millions of innocents die in deference to one who flaunts his guilt is moral cowardice, an unwillingness to dirty one's hands. If *you* caught the terrorist, could you sleep nights knowing that millions died because you couldn't bring yourself to apply the electrodes?

Once you concede that torture is justified in extreme cases, you have admitted that the decision to use torture is a matter of balancing innocent lives against the means needed to save them. You must now face more realistic cases involving more modest numbers. Someone plants a bomb on a jumbo jet. He alone can disarm it, and his demands cannot be met (or if they can, we refuse to set a precedent by yielding to his threats). Surely we can, we must, do anything to the extortionist to save the passengers. How can we tell 300, or 100, or 10 people who never asked to be put in danger, "I'm sorry, you'll have to die in agony, we just couldn't bring ourselves to . . . ."

Here are the results of an informal poll about a third, hypothetical, case. Suppose a terrorist group kidnapped a newborn baby from a hospital. I asked four mothers if they would approve of torturing kidnappers if that were necessary to get their own newborns back. All said yes, the most "liberal" adding that she would like to administer it herself.

I am not advocating torture as punishment. Punishment is addressed to deeds irrevocably past. Rather, I am advocating torture as an acceptable measure for preventing future evils. So understood, it is far less objectionable than many extant punishments. Opponents of the death penalty, for example, are forever insisting that executing a murderer will not bring back his victim (as if the purpose of capital punishment were supposed to be resurrection, not deterrence or retribution). But torture, in the cases described, is intended not to bring anyone back but to keep innocents from being dispatched. The most powerful argument against using torture as a punishment or to secure confessions is that such practices disregard the rights of the individual. Well, if the individual is all that important—and he is—it is correspondingly important to protect the rights of individuals threatened by terrorists. If life is so valuable that it must never be taken, the lives of the innocents must be saved even at the price of hurting the one who endangers them.

Better precedents for torture are assassination and preemptive attack. No Allied leader would have flinched at assassinating Hitler, had that been possible. (The Allies did assassinate Heydrich.) Americans would be angered to learn that Roosevelt could have had Hitler killed in 1943—thereby shortening the war and saving millions of lives—but refused on moral grounds. Similarly, if nation A learns that nation B is about to launch an unprovoked attack, A has a right to save itself by destroying B's military capability first. In the same way, if the police can by torture save those who would otherwise die at the hands of kidnappers or terrorists, they must.

Idealism: There is an important difference between terrorists and their victims that should mute talk of the terrorist's "rights." The terrorist's victims are at risk unintentionally, not having asked to be endangered. But the terrorist knowingly initiated his actions. Unlike his victims, he volunteered for the risks of his deed. By threatening to kill for profit or idealism, he renounces civilized standards, and he can have no complaint if civilization tries to thwart him by whatever means necessary.

Just as torture is justified only to save lives (not extort confessions or recantations), it is justifiably administered only to those *known* to hold innocent lives in their hands. Ah, but how can the authorities ever be sure they have the right malefactor? Isn't there a danger of error and abuse? Won't We turn into Them?

Questions like these are disingenuous in a world in which terrorists proclaim themselves and perform for television. The name of their game is public recognition. After all, you can't very well intimidate a government into releasing your freedom fighters unless you announce that it is your group that has seized its embassy. "Clear guilt" is difficult to define, but when 40 million people see a group of masked gunmen seize an airplane on the evening news, there is not much question about who the perpetrators are. There will be hard cases where the situation is murkier. Nonetheless, a line demarcating the legitimate use of torture can be drawn. Torture only the obviously guilty, and only for the sake of saving innocents, and the line between Us and Them will remain clear.

There is little danger that the Western democracies will lose their way if they choose to inflict pain as one way of preserving order. Paralysis in the face of evil is the greater danger. Some day soon a terrorist will threaten tens of thousands of lives, and torture will be the only way to save them. We had better start thinking about this.

Michael Levin

QUESTIONS FOR DISCUSSION

1. Point out two examples of the use of the argumentative edge in Michael Levin's essay.
2. Discuss the methods of development used in the essay.
3. In "The Case for Torture," the author begins with the most dramatic reason for employing torture (millions will die) and then goes on to a single death as justifying torture. Is this the most effective chronology to use? Why or why not?
4. How does the author justify ignoring a person's human rights?
5. According to the author, when is torture justified, and when is it wrong?
6. When would it be morally wrong *not* to torture someone?
7. The author makes several assumptions in the essay. Pick out a few and explain why you agree or disagree with them.
8. In this short essay, Michael Levin opposes the views of most "enlightened societies" and the conviction of most of the educated, moral individuals in the world. How passive is he? How does he manage to make such an unpopular view convincing?
9. Can you refute his argument?
10. Can you reduce Levin's argument to a syllogism?

PITFALLS TO AVOID

1. Don't confuse opinion with fact. A fact is subject to verification. The truth or falsity of a statement such as "Hitler was born in 1889" can be verified because there are documents that establish this fact. An opinion, however, is a judgment based upon some sort of evidence—for example, "Hitler was a maniac." Whether this opinion is valid or not is open to question. Someone else might present evidence to show that Hitler was not insane.
2. Don't sound too shrill. No matter how strongly you feel about an issue, a carefully reasoned approach will have a far better chance

of persuading intelligent readers than would overblown, hysterical language.

3. Avoid a long-winded introduction. Get to the point. Get down to the question in one brief introductory paragraph.

4. Avoid making statements that are simply unsupportable, such as, "Americans all want smaller, more fuel-efficient cars." Then why are some people still buying the big luxury cars? Watch out for statements that imply "all" or "every"; a single exception can refute any such assertion.

5. Avoid relying on one source for all of your evidence. Unless you can be sure that the source is reliable and unbiased, you could be badly misled, especially on a subject about which you have little or no knowledge.

6. Don't assume that because something appears in print it must be true. Every publication, even the most reliable, contains inaccuracies from time to time. If the printed facts don't square with common sense, check other sources to verify the information.

SUGGESTED TOPICS

Take a stand on one of the topics below and write a carefully worded persuasive essay directed toward an audience of college students. Consider both logical and emotional appeals.

1. Mandatory retirement
2. Gun control
3. Ceiling on salaries
4. Paddling in elementary schools
5. Drafting of women
6. Saving the rain forests
7. Expelling students for cheating
8. Jail sentences for drug users
9. Rating records
10. Censorship on television
11. Smoking in public places
12. Alimony
13. Freedom of information
14. Four-day work week
15. Test-tube babies
16. Equal rights amendment
17. Abortion
18. Capital punishment
19. Mandatory class attendance
20. Equitable taxation
21. Public housing
22. Pass/fail grading
23. Money for space exploration
24. Plea bargaining
25. Public employee strikes
26. Banning auto imports
27. Credit cards for children
28. Becoming a vegetarian
29. Flag burning and free speech
30. Longer school year
31. Right to die naturally
32. Immigration quotas
33. Punishment for corrupt government officials
34. Generic food products
35. Chemical preservatives in food
36. Education in U.S. high schools
37. Socialized medicine
38. Natural childbirth

39. Pollution control
40. Foreign language requirements
41. Endangered species
42. Employee loyalty
43. Mandatory union membership
44. Women in the priesthood
45. Homeless in the United States
46. Aid to private schools
47. Pay television
48. Free college education in the United States
49. Civil liberty or police power in war on drugs
50. Marriage

TECHNIQUES OF CLEAR WRITING

SENTENCE COMBINING FOR BREVITY AND CLARITY

A sentence is defined as a complete thought. However, in sophisticated writing, you are interested in showing your reader the relationships among your complete thoughts. This is done by *sentence combining.* Sentence combining shows your reader which thoughts are most important, which thoughts are subsidiary, and in which ways they are subsidiary. (Types of sentences are explained fully in Chapter 9.)

EXERCISE 11E: SENTENCE COMBINING, COMPLEX AND COMPOUND–COMPLEX

Following are lists of simple sentences. The sentences in each group can be combined in various ways to make complex or compound–complex sentences. For each group, combine all the sentences in two different ways as shown below.

EXAMPLES

GROUP A:
The bull pawed the ground.
The bull was in the meadow.
The bull snorted.
The bull was angry.

COMBINED:
In the meadow, the angry bull snorted and pawed the ground.
The bull, angry and snorting, pawed the ground in the meadow.

GROUP B:
The farmer was alarmed.

He told the hired man to help him.
He needed to tether the bull.

COMBINED:
The alarmed farmer told the hired man he needed help to tether the bull.
Alarmed, the farmer told the hired man to help him tether the bull.

GROUP C:
The bull was dangerous.
He was untied.
He had a ring in his nose.

COMBINED:
The dangerous bull had a ring in his nose although he was untied.
Although he had a ring in his nose, the dangerous bull was untied.

GROUP D:
A chain could be attached to the ring.
The chain could be attached to a heavy stake.
The bull could be tied.
He wouldn't be a threat anymore.

COMBINED:
To keep him from being a threat, the bull could be tied with a chain attached to the ring and to a heavy stake in the ground.
A chain could be attached to the ring in the bull's nose and to a heavy stake in the ground to keep him from being a threat.

Now try it with the following groups. Remember to combine each group of sentences in two ways.

1. **Group A:**
   The tall girl leaned on the farm gate.
   She was lovely.
   Her nose was snub.
   Her hair was golden.

   Group B:
   The farmer's son strolled down the lane.
   He glanced shyly at her.
   He thought she was attractive.
   He was lonesome.

   Group C:
   The girl noticed him looking at her.
   She was amused and touched.
   She smiled up at him.
   She was lonesome, too.

2. **Group A:**
   They didn't speak that evening.
   They smiled at each other a lot.

The boy looked after her over his shoulder.
They hoped they would meet again.

Group B:
The next night the girl was waiting.
The boy again strolled down the lane.
Their minds were made up.
Tonight they would speak.

Group C:
They worked up their courage.
She vowed to say hello.
He swore to ask her name.
At last they were talking.

3. **Group A:**
They had lots to talk about.
He had plans to be a farmer.
She had unannounced plans to be a farmer's wife.
They were happy all the long summer evenings.

Group B:
By fall they were in love.
They wanted to marry.
Would their parents agree?
They were very young.

Group C:
They finally asked their parents' permission.
Their parents had been waiting for them.
Their parents happily granted permission.
They were married on Christmas.

4. **Group A:**
This simple romance is old-fashioned.
Modern romances move faster than this.
The people who lived it liked it.
My grandmother told me she loved every minute.

Group B:
She and my grandfather lived 40 years together.
They had three children.
They all lived peaceably together on the farm.
She felt their lives were happy and fulfilled.

Group C:
Grandfather died.
Grandmother tried to live on the farm alone.
She was too lonely.
She moved in town with us.
She lived serene with her happy memories.

EXERCISE 11F: SENTENCE COMBINING, LOOSE SENTENCES

From each of the following groups of sentences, choose the idea you wish to make most important. Write a sentence expressing that idea in an independent clause and putting it first in the sentence, subordinating the other ideas to it.

EXAMPLE

a. The candidate has seven years' experience.
b. The candidate has proved herself competent.
c. The candidate should be reelected. (most important)
d. She had proved herself trustworthy.

COMBINATION A: INDEPENDENT CLAUSE AT BEGINNING OF SENTENCE

The candidate should be reelected because in her seven years' experience she has proved herself competent and trustworthy.

Now, using the same four sentences, put one subordinate element before and another after the independent clause.

COMBINATION B: INDEPENDENT CLAUSE IN MIDDLE OF SENTENCE

Having proved herself through seven years' experience, the candidate should be reelected for her competence and trustworthiness.

Combine each of the following groups of sentences in the two ways suggested above.

1. a. Block Island is a fine place for a seaside vacation.
   b. You have to reach Block Island by ferry boat.
   c. It is about 20 miles off the coast of Rhode Island.
   d. Block Island is uncrowded and somewhat old-fashioned.

2. a. Graduation at our community college is especially rewarding.
   b. This year the graduates ages ranged from 17 to 71.
   c. More than half of the graduates were going on to four-year colleges.
   d. Almost all the others had jobs.
   e. Everyone was emotional about leaving, even the discontented ones.

3. a. We had a Winter Festival Weekend at our college.
   b. It was the biggest party of the school year.
   c. We didn't have a ski slope.

    d. We did have sleigh riding, ice skating, snowball battles, and dancing, dancing, dancing.

4. a. We are constantly adding new courses to our liberal arts curriculum.
    b. We add things at the suggestion of the four-year schools.
    c. This way our students have the basic courses the senior schools want.

5. a. Fairy tales are more than stories for children.
    b. Children, however, like them.
    c. Fairy tales express the desires of simple but adult people.
    d. Fairy tales emphasize the values of common sense, courage, and kindness.
    e. These values give fairy tales a kind of "social cement."

EXERCISE 11G: SENTENCE COMBINING, PERIODIC SENTENCES

Using the groups of sentences in Exercise 11F, again decide upon the most important idea and place it at the end of the combined sentence, with all the other sentences subordinated to and preceding it.

EXERCISE 11H: SENTENCE COMBINING, BALANCED SENTENCES

Combine the following groups of sentences by making them, or some parts of them, parallel.

EXAMPLE

Jack Sprat wasn't allowed much cholesterol.
His wife didn't like lean meat.
Jack Sprat could eat no fat; his wife could eat no lean.

1. a. The lion tamer never took his eyes off the big cats.
    b. Their every move he observed closely.
    c. His whip was quiet.
    d. It was always prominently displayed to the cats.

2. a. The night at the ski lodge was perfect.
    b. The full moon was shining on the snow.
    c. The smell of the pines filled the air.
    d. Crisp and cold, the air was exhilarating.
    e. The light from the cabin windows streamed across our path.

3. a. The poetry of Robert Frost is based on natural images.
    b. Frost's themes in his poetry are universal.
    c. The language of Frost's poems is simple.
    d. His style is flexible and fluent.

4. **a.** The boxer argued for six months about his share of the gate.
   b. He threatened several times to break his contract.
   c. He insulted his trainer on television.
   d. He was knocked out in one minute and twenty-three seconds.

5. **a.** Patrice was a woman of strong character.
   b. She never permitted anyone to sway her decisions.
   c. She never changed her decisions.
   d. She felt her principles were right.

EXERCISE 11I: SENTENCE COMBINING ANTITHETICAL IDEAS IN VARIED SENTENCE FORMS

The following groups of sentences contain opposing ideas. Decide what the two ideas are, and, through subordination of some sentences, combine them into one sentence in which the relationship of opposition is clear.

EXAMPLE
a. The crowd was eager to see the rock stars.
b. The wait for the doors to open seemed endless.
c. Most of the crowd had been fans of this group for years.
d. Rain and a chilling wind made the wait uncomfortable.

COMBINED:
The crowd, fans of the rock stars for years, were eager to see them, but the wait in the rain and chilling wind for the doors to open seemed endless. Although it seemed endless waiting in the rain and chilling wind for the doors to open, the crowd, fans for years, were eager to see the rock stars.

1. **a.** Choosing the right word takes care and time.
   b. The vague and trite word comes quickly to mind.
   c. The right word is precise and convincing.
   d. The vague word is easily forgotten.

2. **a.** The detour is long.
   b. The detour takes an extra half hour.
   c. The detour goes through lovely farming country.
   d. The roads of the detour were winding, and they had splendid views at every curve.

3. **a.** The concert was exciting to a few in the audience.
   b. The music was all twentieth-century compositions.
   c. Most of the audience disliked modern music.
   d. They preferred established classics from the eighteenth and nineteenth centuries.

WORD POWER

WORDING YOUR ARGUMENT

Language is your great tool in swaying an audience. As a writer, the vocabulary you use will be determined, to a large extent, by the educational level of your audience. You don't want to talk over the heads of your audience, nor do you want to insult them by oversimplifying ideas. You have to communicate with readers on their own level. If, for example, you were a graduate student in marine biology writing a doctoral dissertation on water pollution, you would probably use some highly scientific terminology. Terms such as *chlorinated hydrocarbons* and *phosphoric acids* would be appropriate. But if you were writing an editorial about water pollution for your local newspaper, you would use terms like *insecticides* and *pollutants*, and you would call small gnats *small gnats*, not *Chaoborus asticopus*. Such specialized terms require caution. Also beware of dependence on abstract terms. A highly educated audience can usually deal with abstract terms, but other audiences frequently respond better to more concrete language.

You also have to take your readers' value system into account when you are deciding how to word your argument. If you were trying to convince the National Athletic Association to support an investigation of drug abuse among professional athletes, you wouldn't refer to the athletes as *jocks*. Your use of the term *jocks* would convey a condescending attitude toward sports. You would be likely to lose your goal from the start. The thoughtless use of even one offensive word in an otherwise intelligent essay can destroy all hopes of establishing any common ground between you and your readers. Calling a legislator a "dupe" of organized labor would thwart any hope of your persuading that person to work with you. Remember, the language you use will shape your readers' response, so **choose your words carefully.**

LABELING

"Sticks and stones will break my bones, but names will never hurt me." Unfortunately, however, names can and do hurt people very much. Phyllis McGinley, a popular poet, rewrote that old saying in a more realistic way:

Sticks and stones are hard on bones
When thrown with hateful art.
And words can sting like anything
But silence breaks the heart

One of the most common ways that words can sting is in **labeling** people. Identifying people through labels happens constantly in our society: "She's a typical dumb blonde," "He's just a paper shuffler," "They're all a bunch of radicals." A person is thus no longer seen as an individual but only as part of a group. This is what makes labels so dangerous.

> . . . what we call an object or person or situation is going to influence the way we see it and evaluate it, and as a result, affect the way we respond to it . . . in our encounters with the world, we are responding more often than we realize not just to something as it exists "out there" . . . but rather to something "out there" **as modified by the label we've applied to it.** . . . To the extent that our behavior is affected by labels . . . we are not entirely sane.
>
> *William Dresser and S. I. Hayakawa*

As the authors point out, stereotyped thinking that often goes with certain labels can lead us into false perceptions of the world around us. Here is an example that you should recognize: some people associate the word *Mexican* with a stereotyped image of someone leaning against a giant cactus, fast asleep under his broad sombrero. However, the label, when it provokes that kind of non-thinking response, does **not** correspond with reality. Among other things, cactuses (or cacti) are not designed for leaning against; besides—and more to the point—Mexicans would have every right to resent that image of themselves. In fact, millions of people in our own country have suffered because of labels that unfairly characterize an entire group as being dirty, lazy, dumb, or unpatriotic.

So don't use labels thoughtlessly. What you need to do is look behind the label. What are the facts? If a person is labeled as a "troublemaker" or a "pathological liar," make sure that you examine the facts. What did that person do? What did that person say? Who has applied this label, and is that person prejudiced?

EXERCISE 11J: LABELS

Examine the list of words below. What do you think of when you hear these labels? Beside each word, write down your understanding of the term. Next ask someone whose views or background differs from yours to define the terms. Then compare his or her definitions with yours. Notice the variety of emotional responses associated with each label.

1. Go-fer _____
2. Wimp _____
3. Jock _____
4. Good 'ole boy _____
5. Paper shuffler _____
6. Loser _____
7. Do-gooder _____
8. Teddy bear _____
9. Redneck _____
10. Daddy's girl _____
11. Stuffed shirt _____
12. Hillbilly _____
13. Hunk _____
14. Bookworm _____
15. Mama's boy _____
16. Party animal _____
17. Egg head _____
18. Bad _____
19. Nerd _____
20. Playboy _____

EXERCISE 11K: PERSUASIVE STRATEGIES

Out of the five proposals listed below, choose one and briefly explain the persuasive strategies you would use in situation A and in situation B to convince the respective audience to accept your position.

1. Terminally ill patients deserve the right to die naturally instead of being kept alive through artificial means.
   - **A.** Their attending doctors
   - **B.** Their loving families
2. AIDS carriers should be placed in isolated hospitals.
   - **A.** A gay activist group
   - **B.** A group of parents
3. There should be mandatory jail sentences for drunk drivers.
   - **A.** Defense attorneys
   - **B.** AA members
4. There should be more shelters for battered women.
   - **A.** U.S. budget makers
   - **B.** Social service workers
5. There should be a war against pollution to protect our planet.
   - **A.** National Association of Manufacturers
   - **B.** Environmentalists

Writing About Literature

It's a great pleasure to read a good book, but sometimes it's almost as much fun to talk about it with someone else who has read it. Have you ever said to anyone, "Here, read this book; it's terrific!"? Then, every day you ask, "How far have you gotten in the book?" because you want to discuss the parts you really liked or disliked or wondered about. Literature of any type—books, plays, poems, short stories, essays, even movies and TV programs—often present new ideas or new ways of looking at life. After you have thought about these "new" things, you often want to talk about them, to test them, perhaps to adjust your own life to them; therefore you want to hear how others reacted. Did the other person get the same ideas you did? Did he or she agree or disagree with what the author wrote? As you discuss the work, your understanding of it increases, and what you learned from it becomes a part of you. Thus, communicating your ideas about literature is both important and enjoyable.

READING LITERATURE AND PREWRITING

In most of the writing you have been doing throughout this book, you have been responding to direct experience, something you have either lived through or observed around you. In writing about literature, you are responding to another writer's interpretation of people's experience or observation.

Why should you be concerned with someone else's interpretation when you could be making your own? There are a number of answers to this question, but perhaps the most obvious is this: any individual's life is limited. Literature, of course, is not life, but it is vicarious living, living through imagination. No matter how fortunate an individual may be, his or her experiences in comparison with all the possibilities of human life are extremely limited. Obviously, you can't experience life as a man and a woman, as an American and a Japanese, as a twentieth-century citizen and a thirteenth-century feudal baron. Good writers can make all experiences come alive for you through imagination. Good writers can vastly extend your experiences.

There is also another answer. Good writers can create experiences similar to, perhaps identical with, your experiences, and as you watch the characters in literature coping with such experiences, you often are better able to interpret what you yourself have lived through. Literature thus can expand your life and make it more understandable.

In trying to reach the understanding that comes through imaginative literature, you might apply what are called "the four critical questions."

1. What is the author attempting to communicate?
2. How does he or she go about communicating it?
3. Is it worth communicating?
4. What does it mean to you, the reader?

Although these four questions seem simple, good answers to them depend on your ability to read sensitively and intelligently. Such reading depends, in turn, upon a careful consideration of the "elements" of literature, which vary from one genre to another; that is, the elements of poetry differ from those of drama and those of drama from those of fiction.

ELEMENTS OF FICTION

Since fiction—short stories and novels—is the most widely read genre (type) of literature, you'll find its elements make a good starting point for improving your critical reading.

Plot

Plot involves action, the sequence of events which takes place in a story. Plot also involves motivation, the reason for each action in the sequence. As the plot unfolds, one action impels another until the conclusion. (When you say "That was an exciting story," you are generally referring to the plot.)

The *opening action,* sometimes called exposition, shows the reader the situation (gives the setting, introduces the characters, and starts the action). The *rising action,* sometimes called complication, shows the main character (protagonist) in conflict with some antagonist (nature, other people, or some conflict within himself or herself). The *climax,* sometimes called crisis, is the point at which some decision is made or some action is taken that determines the outcome of the story. You have probably heard the term used medically. If the patient is said to "have passed the crisis," that means the patient will survive. In a fictional crisis the coward may run into the burning building to save the child, in which case the story ends one way. Or, the coward may run away, in which case the story must end another way. In the fairy tale, the only clue the prince has to find Cinderella is her golden slipper. He tries the slipper on many girls, including the ugly stepsisters, but only at the last, the crucial moment, does he try it on Cinderella. The crucial moment is the crisis or climax. Once the climactic decision or action has been made, the action which follows, sometimes called the denouement, leads to the logical ending of the story.

Notice in the diagram that the falling action is much shorter than the rising action because, once the climax is reached, that particular story is practically over. Plots, like your essays, must have unity. Even though human experience tells you that a falling action as simple as "And so they were married and lived happily ever afterward" is unlikely, what happens after they are married is another story.

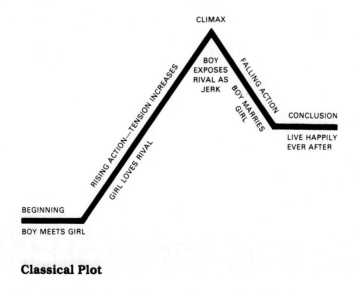

Classical Plot

These actions are all based on conflict. If there is no conflict or struggle, there is no story. If you have a story about a pilot whose tiny plane crashes in a vast wilderness, the essential conflict is going to be that of man against nature. If you have a man who defies the rules of the society to which he belongs—for good reasons or bad— then a central element will be the conflict between man and society. If you have a story about a man who has gained wealth and power but comes to hate himself for the way he has succeeded, then you have man against himself.

These types of conflict are not imposed upon fiction by critics but are the structures by which the authors build their plots and which careful readers can easily observe. For example, conflict between man and nature is seen in Jack London's "To Build a Fire," in which man is pitted against the killing cold of an Alaskan winter; such a conflict appears again in Stephen Crane's "The Open Boat," which is man against the ocean.

The conflict of man or woman against society takes place in two forms. In one, the conflict is between two individuals. An example of this is *Les Misérables*, a great novel of Victor Hugo's in which a detective makes it his life work to hunt down the protagonist, who once committed the "crime" of stealing bread. The second form of the conflict of a person against society is the individual against a group or social institution—for example, the kind of detective fiction in which an entire police department seeks to capture the villain.

Perhaps the most subtle of conflicts is that within an individual, where a person is torn between love and friendship, or love and duty. Such a conflict is that of the hero in James Joyce's *Portrait of the Artist;* he wrestles with his conflicting desires to follow the wishes of his dying mother but also to follow his own opposing wishes.

Very often, however, the conflict is not so simple as these examples seem to indicate. There are frequent overlapping conflicts. Even in a story as relatively simple as "To Build a Fire," the protagonist not only is involved in the man–nature conflict, but has secondary conflicts with the group he lives with and with his own personality. Yet, whether they are one or many, conflict is the essence of plot.

After you have read a work and wish to evaluate the element of plot, ask yourself:

1. Did the action carry me along? Was I interested in what happened? (If the answer to this is no, you probably won't go any further for you probably have not finished the work.)
2. In the circumstances that the author created, were the actions believable? Do people behave like this?

3. Given the characters and circumstances that the author created, was the conclusion logical or was common sense defied to force a happy ending?

Character

Characters are the people who act out the plot. The protagonist is the leading actor who struggles against his antagonist, whether that antagonist is another person or nature or a social force. If you love the protagonist and hate the antagonist, the writer has won your interest so that you will follow the plot avidly in the hope that all will go well for the protagonist.

Basic classifications of characters are **round characters,** whom you can see from all sides, just as you can walk around a statue to see it from all angles, and flat characters. With well-rounded characters, you learn much more than the physical description. You learn about their natures through what they say about themselves and what others say about them. You discover so much about them that you understand what they do (or don't do). Even if you are surprised at first at their actions, you know them well enough to understand why they took that action. Not all characters in a work must be round, but the protagonist must be, and if the antagonist is a person, he or she usually should be round. **Flat characters** are those of secondary interest, whose function in the story is to present just one or two traits—for example, a lovable but interfering neighbor. **Stereotyped characters** are also flat, but in addition they lack originality and individuality. They just fit an overly used role—for example, a mean stepmother.

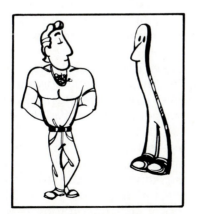

Round Character—Flat Character.

Another way of considering characters is on the basis of universality and individuality. Good character creations have both these qualities: They are universal in that you recognize in them the common humanity they share with everyone; they are individual in that you find in them distinctive and unusual touches that make them interestingly unlike everybody else. Some characters fall between these two extremes; they represent a segment or class of society that is typical, like a conservative businessman.

Still a third way to analyze characters is to determine if they are dynamic or static. Those who are dynamic grow, develop, change, learn to know themselves in the course of the plot. By the end of the story they are not what they were in the beginning. Static characters are at the end just as they were in the beginning. The protagonist, and sometimes other important characters, are usually dynamic; minor characters usually are static.

Sometimes, however, a minor character does change. When the story is narrated by a character who takes no important part in the action but simply observes and reports, he or she is often the one who is changed by the experience. He compassionately watches the main characters hurrying on to their happy or tragic ends. The characters themselves are unaware of the meaning of their experience, but the narrator perceives the significance, so his understanding deepens, as does the reader's.

Theme

Theme is the most important element in serious fiction. It is the author's controlling idea, the truth about life that he or she wishes to convey to the reader. Theme is often implied rather than directly stated. Some stories (frequently called "escape fiction") do not even have a theme; they are written just to scare you or make you laugh or test your wits against those of the detective. Serious writers, though, reveal some aspect of life as they see it; what they reveal is the theme.

Theme is not to be confused with a moral, which is a characteristic of the fable, a piece of literature designed primarily to teach. In fact, the writer of the fable is so eager to get the moral across that he or she often repeats the moral point at the end of the story and labels it Moral.

Theme is often revealed to the reader through the increased awareness of a character, usually either the protagonist or the narrator, the person from whose point of view the story is seen. Because of what happens to the characters in the story, one character learns something which deepens his or her understanding. Since the character has learned this, the author hopes that the reader has also learned it.

Setting

Setting is the time and place of the action. Sometimes it simply provides a background for the characters and their action. After all, they can't exist in a vacuum. Setting can also add flavor of its own to a work. It makes a difference in the reader's appreciation if the setting is Algiers before World War II or New York City today. But setting is most important when it functions as environment that determines the types of characters and influences the events of the plot.

Sometimes the setting almost becomes an actor. For example, in Stephen Crane's "The Blue Hotel," setting is as important as characters. A man, identified only as "the Swede," is murdered because the setting, from the large background of the desolate plains to the interior of the hotel saloon where even the stove "was humming with god-like violence," leads to brutality and viciousness.

Tone

Tone is the author's attitude toward the material. Authors may be sympathetic or hostile toward characters. They may pity or make fun of them. They may be straightforward or ironic. But whatever the authors' attitude, they must be consistent in it.

Here is a bit of verse and a short poem, both on the subject of the immediate sense of liking or disliking someone.

> *I do not like you, Dr. Fell,*
> *The reason why I cannot tell.*
> *But this I know, and know full well,*
> *I do not like you, Dr. Fell.*
>
> **Thomas Brown**

> *The soul selects her own society,*
> *Then shuts the door:*
> *On her divine majority*
> *Obtrude no more.*
>
> *Unmoved, she notes the chariot's pausing*
> *At her low gate;*
> *Unmoved, an emperor is kneeling*
> *Upon her mat.*
>
> *I've known her from an ample nation*
> *Choose one;*
> *Then close the valve of her attention*
> *Like stone.*
>
> **Emily Dickinson**

Although the subjects of these are similar, the tone is widely different. Which one do you think is flip? Which one is serious? What words or phrases make you think this?

Point of View

Point of view is the vantage point from which the author looks at the story. Imagine yourself caught up in a mob of excited fans who are trying to get close to their idol. What would you see and hear and feel? How would you see the same situation if you were looking out of a fifth-story window across the street from the mob scene? How would you describe the scene ten years later? Do you see that the descriptions of the same event would be vastly different? What you see depends upon your perspective: your point of view. An author chooses to see the characters and their actions through one of several visions. The point of view chosen determines the reader's understanding of the story. Think what a difference it would make if the story of Little Red Ridinghood were told from the point of view of the wolf, or if Cinderella were told by the stepsister.

In a novel called *What Maisie Knew*, Henry James tells the story from the point of view of a twelve-year-old girl whose parents are divorcing. What Maisie knows is limited by her twelve-year-old mentality and experiences. It would be an entirely different story were the same events related by Maisie's mother and still another if those events were told by her father.

Although there are many ways to analyze the point of view, you need be concerned only with the basic types.

1. In the omniscient point of view, the author knows all. He or she goes into the minds of all the characters and tells what each is thinking or feeling. When an author uses this point of view, the reader has no doubt as to what the character is: good or evil, bright or slow, confident or unsure.

2. In the limited point of view, the author goes into the mind of only one character. This character may be central to the story or may be on the outskirts. The author may use first or third person. The important thing is that the story is told as it is seen and understood by this character. This point of view appeals to readers for it parallels the way they see the world every day: through one pair of eyes—their own. It also appeals to authors, for it allows them to reveal the truth as it might be seen by someone other than themselves.

3. The objective point of view is the most demanding on both author and reader. Here, the author goes into no one's mind, makes no speculations or explanations. He records what happens, what

is said and done, and the reader must determine the meaning and significance of the actions. The writer must get the point across by showing, not telling.

Here is a short story by the contemporary writer Ray Bradbury. Read it carefully and then see if you agree with the discussion following it.

I SEE YOU NEVER

The soft knock came at the kitchen door, and when Mrs. O'Brian opened it, there on the back porch were her best tenant, Mr. Ramirez, and two police officers, one on each side of him. Mr. Ramirez just stood there, walled in and small.

"Why, Mr. Ramirez!" said Mrs. O'Brian.

Mr. Ramirez was overcome. He did not seem to have words to explain.

He had arrived at Mrs. O'Brian's rooming house more than two years earlier and had lived there ever since. He had come by bus from Mexico City to San Diego and had then gone up to Los Angeles. There he had found the clean little room, with glossy blue linoleum, and the pictures and calendars on the flowered walls, and Mrs. O'Brian as the strict but kindly landlady. During the war he had worked at the airplane factory and made parts for planes that flew off somewhere, and even now, after the war, he still held his job. From the first he had made big money. He saved some of it, and he got drunk only once a week—a privilege that, to Mrs. O'Brian's way of thinking, every good workingman deserved, unquestioned and unreprimanded.

Inside Mrs. O'Brian's kitchen, pies were baking in the oven. Soon the pies would come out with complexions like Mr. Ramirez'—brown and shiny and crisp, with slits in them for the air almost like the slits of Mr. Ramirez' dark eyes. The kitchen smelled good. The policemen leaned forward, lured by the odor. Mr. Ramirez gazed at his feet, as if they had carried him into all this trouble.

"What happened, Mr. Ramirez?" asked Mrs. O'Brian.

Behind Mrs. O'Brian, as he lifted his eyes, Mr. Ramirez saw the long table laid with clean white linen and set with a platter, cool, shining glasses, a water pitcher with ice cubes floating inside it, a bowl of fresh potato salad and one of bananas and oranges, cubed and sugared. At this table sat Mrs. O'Brian's children—her three grown sons, eating and conversing, and her two younger daughters, who were staring at the policemen as they ate.

"I have been here thirty months," said Mr. Ramirez quietly, looking at Mrs. O'Brian's plump hands.

"That's six months too long," said one policeman. "He only had a temporary visa. We've just got around to looking for him."

Soon after Mr. Ramirez had arrived he bought a radio for his little room; evenings, he turned it up very loud and enjoyed it. And he bought a wrist watch and enjoyed that too. And on many nights he had walked silent streets and seen the bright clothes in the windows and bought some of them, and he had seen the jewels and bought some of them for his few lady friends. And he had gone to picture shows five nights a week for a while. Then, also, he had ridden the streetcars—all night some nights—smelling the electricity, his dark eyes moving over the advertisements, feeling the wheels rumble under him, watching the little sleeping houses and big hotels slip by. Besides that, he had gone to large restaurants, where he had eaten many-course dinners, and to the opera and the theater. And he had bought a car, which later, when he forgot to pay for it, the dealer had driven off angrily from in front of the rooming house.

"So here I am," said Mr. Ramirez now, "to tell you I must give up my room, Mrs. O'Brian. I come to get my baggage and clothes and go with these men."

"Back to Mexico?"

"Yes. To Lagos. That is a little town north of Mexico City."

"I'm sorry, Mr. Ramirez."

"I'm packed," said Mr. Ramirez hoarsely, blinking his dark eyes rapidly and moving his hands helplessly before him. The policemen did not touch him. There was no necessity for that.

"Here is the key, Mrs. O'Brian," Mr. Ramirez said, "I have my bag already."

Mrs. O'Brian, for the first time, noticed a suitcase standing behind him on the porch.

Mr. Ramirez looked in again at the huge kitchen, at the bright silver cutlery and the young people eating and the shining waxed floor. He turned and looked for a long moment at the apartment house next door, rising up three stories, high and beautiful. He looked at the balconies and fire escapes and back-porch stairs, at the lines of laundry snapping in the wind.

"You've been a good tenant," said Mrs. O'Brian.

"Thank you, thank you, Mrs. O'Brian," he said softly. He closed his eyes.

Mrs. O'Brian stood holding the door half open. One of her sons, behind her, said that her dinner was getting cold, but she shook her head at him and turned back to Mr. Ramirez. She remembered a visit she had once made to some Mexican border towns—the hot days, the endless crickets leaping and falling or lying dead and brittle like the small cigars in the shopwindows, and the canals taking river water out to the farms, the dirt roads, the scorched landscape. She remembered the silent towns, the warm beer, the hot, thick foods each day. She remembered the slow, dragging horses and the parched jack rabbits on the road. She remembered the iron mountains and the dusty valleys and the ocean beaches that spread hundreds of miles with no sound but the waves—no cars, no buildings, nothing.

"I'm sure sorry, Mr. Ramirez," she said.

"I don't want to go back, Mrs. O'Brian," he said weakly. "I like it here. I want to stay here. I've worked, I've got money. I look all right, don't I? And I don't want to go back!"

"I'm sorry, Mr. Ramirez," she said. "I wish there was something I could do."

"Mrs. O'Brian!" he cried suddenly, tears rolling out from under his eyelids. He reached out his hands and took her hand fervently, shaking it, wringing it, holding to it. "Mrs. O'Brian, I see you never, I see you never!"

The policemen smiled at this, but Mr. Ramirez did not notice it, and they stopped smiling very soon.

"Good-by, Mrs. O'Brian. You have been good to me. Oh, good-by, Mrs. O'Brian. I see you never!"

The policemen waited for Mr. Ramirez to turn, pick up his suitcase, and walk away. Then they followed him, tipping their caps to Mrs. O'Brian. She watched them go down the porch steps. Then she shut the door quietly and went slowly back to her chair at the table. She pulled the chair out and sat down. She picked up the shining knife and fork and started once more upon her steak.

"Hurry up, Mom," said one of the sons. "It'll be cold."

Mrs. O'Brian took one bite and chewed it for a long, slow time; then she stared at the closed door. She laid down her knife and fork.

"What's wrong, Ma?" asked her son.

"I just realized," said Mrs. O'Brian—she put her hand to her face—"I'll never see Mr. Ramirez again."

ANALYSIS OF "I SEE YOU NEVER"

If, in preparing to write a critical analysis of "I See You Never," you apply the first critical question to this story (What is the author attempting to communicate?), you are dealing with the element of theme. Your interpretation of theme is subjective; that is, it is your interpretation so long as it does not violate what the story obviously says. To support your interpretation, you look constantly at the story. Here is one possible statement of the theme:

> In "I See You Never," Ray Bradbury is conveying his concept that social forces frequently wound—or even destroy—the "little man" because he does not understand them or understand how to cope with them. The law of the country, attempting to protect the majority of the citizens, regulates aliens. Mr. Ramirez has, unknowingly, violated the law which determines the length of time he can work in the United States. The law is not wrong; moreover, its representatives, the two policemen, are kind, courteous, and human. (Bradbury comments on their humanity when he has them lean toward Mrs. O'Brian's door to smell her pies.) The conflict between the law and Mr. Ramirez would be solved if he knew enough to go through the proper channels to have his visa extended and to apply for naturalization. But he doesn't know that; nor does he even know enough to get a lawyer. Mrs. O'Brian, despite her kindness and compassion, doesn't know either. Ignorance is the villain. And social forces destroy Mr. Ramirez.

The second critical question (How does the author go about communicating it?) deals, first, with identifying the genre. This would be quickly done, perhaps in a subordinate clause or a modifying phrase: "In Ray Bradbury's short-short-story 'I See You Never,' . . ."

The second critical question, however, usually is the largest part of your critical essay because, in answering it, you discuss elements of fiction other than theme. You need not discuss them all, of course, but you would indicate in your thesis statement just what you were going to discuss. For instance, if you were going to discuss plot, you might say this:

> Plot, in Ray Bradbury's "I See You Never," is of slight importance. It really is only an incident—a Mexican boarder says goodbye to his American landlady. He explains why he must say goodbye: his visa has expired. And, in flashback, his experiences in the United States are sketched, but they are ordinary. Indeed, the very lack of plot, of action, contributes to the significance of the theme.

To satisfy the second critical question, you probably would need to discuss setting:

Setting in this story is important, perhaps more important than any other element except theme. There are really two settings contrasted with each other to show why Mr. Ramirez wants to stay in the United States. The Mexican setting is lonely, uncomfortable, almost lifeless; the American setting is peopled, comfortable, intensely alive.

The lower-middle class environment is of vital importance. Bradbury establishes that with a few understated touches—linoleum instead of carpeting, calendars instead of pictures. But the story depends on this environment. Neither Mrs. O'Brian nor Mr. Ramirez has the practical knowledge that would be natural in more sophisticated settings. Although their setting is sound and sweet (the house is clean, the food is wholesome and appetizing), it is limited by ignorance. Mr. Ramirez forgot that he had to keep up his car payments; he made parts, during the war, "for airplanes that flew off somewhere."

Setting would then lead into a discussion of character. In such a setting people like Mrs. O'Brian and Mr. Ramirez would be fated to lose. You then might want to identify what kinds of persons these two characters are. They are typical characters, a fact Bradbury underscores by giving them only last names. They have, however, endearing traits that individualize them. Such traits are Mrs. O'Brian's conviction that a good workman ought to be allowed to get drunk once a week and Mr. Ramirez's joy in living, even riding streetcars all night.

Tone also would be considered in the second critical question. Bradbury's tone is compassionate, which he reveals both directly as the omniscient author and by showing compassion developing in Mrs. O'Brian. As the omniscient author, he takes us into the minds of both his characters, and almost always, when we see people through their own eyes, we learn the author's compassion. He does not idealize his characters—indeed, his tone has some overtones of humor—but he consistently shows the pathos of the little man who cannot control his destiny.

Even with so short a story, there are many more points that could be made. These observations are just to give you an idea of approaching a work critically.

For the third question (Is it worth communicating?), the answer is usually yes if the author is artistically serious. Even if the work fails, an honest failure can be enlightening.

The fourth question (What does it mean to me?) will probably be your conclusion, the summing up of your response to the work. Here you must be sure to keep your emphasis on the work, not on the response. You want to avoid conclusions like "I was interested in this book. I couldn't put it down." Focus on the work: "This is a simple, poignant story of good little people who are crushed by social forces which are not evil in themselves."

Writing about literature serves the same purpose as talking about it, but the process is different. It is solitary: you are communicating your thoughts to someone not present, someone who cannot question or react or discuss or present his or her ideas immediately. Therefore, writing about literature is more concentrated and more specific, and the ideas are more carefully supported than they are in talking about it.

ORGANIZATION

CHOOSING YOUR TOPIC

After reading the piece of literature and rereading it if necessary to make sure that you understand it, you must choose some aspect of the work to write about. Here, as with all other essays, you must narrow your topic; you cannot discuss everything.

When you are asked to write about fiction, whether a novel or short story, one of the first things you need to do is to decide upon a manageable topic. A complex novel, for example, may present almost limitless possibilities, yet you must narrow your focus to some specific topic before you can begin to put together a unified essay. Following are six practical approaches to finding a manageable topic.

Historical Approach

Does the work have some historical significance? What does it tell us, for example, about life in Czarist Russia or in Paris in the 1920's? What does the work show us about a specific time and place?

Biographical Approach

What is the relationship between the author's life experience and the work of fiction he or she has created? Is the work based upon the author's direct experience? What light is shed upon the work by the author's life, letters, and public statements? (Here you need to be wary of oversimplification. Even though a character in a novel, for instance, may seem to represent the author in thought and experience, this person is not the author, but a fictional character within the work.)

Comparison-Contrast

Does comparing the work of one author with that of a different author who is writing about the same subject reveal something worthwhile? What specific points of comparison do you see between two characters in different works by the same author? Or between two characters in works by different authors? Or between two characters in the same work?

Analysis of a Single Character

How does the author reveal a particular character? What does the author say about the character? What do other characters say about him or her. How do they react to this character? What does the character think and say? What do the character's actions reveal?

Analysis of Theme

What main idea or set of ideas does the author bring home to the reader? Does the author state the theme? If not, what do you see as the main idea that emerges from the work? What does the story tell us about love, death, honor, duty, ambition, depravity, or human dignity?

Detailed Analysis of a Single Feature

Is irony, satire, or symbolism important in the work? Does the effectiveness of the story or novel depend upon a certain point of view? Does conflict provide a focal point of interest? Is the author's style—whether simple and straightforward or complex and tortuous—an important element in the story?

There are many possible topics to discuss in any worthwhile piece of literature. The possibilities are by no means limited to these six approaches, but each does provide a sensible starting point. The more carefully you read, the more you will find topics suggesting themselves to you.

INTRODUCTION

Once you have decided on your topic, you should decide exactly what you want to say about it. Make sure that early in your introduction you give the full title of the work to be discussed and the author's full name. Then write a carefully worded thesis sentence that tells the reader exactly what you are going to write about.

INCORRECT:
Satan, in Mark Twain's "The Mysterious Stranger," is unbelievable. [not specific]

CORRECT:
Seldom in fiction has Satan been so fully characterized as in Mark Twain's "The Mysterious Stranger," where the monarch is shown as beautiful, compelling, accommodating, and completely without conscience or empathy.

Once you have clearly established your subject and attitude, you should write an introduction that captures the reader's interest and leads into the thesis statement. A quotation from the work itself, a striking comment or anecdote about the work or the author, or a brief definition are among the good introductory gambits.

If, for example, you were writing about *One Day in the Life of Ivan Denisovich*, you might quote Ivan's highly significant line that "A man who is warm cannot understand a man who is cold." This quotation is striking in itself, is applicable to many situations, and is pertinent to the theme of the novel.

If you were writing about *Uncle Tom's Cabin*, you might want to repeat the anecdote about Abraham Lincoln's remark to the author, Harriet Beecher Stowe, when he first met her. Lincoln said, "So you are the little woman who started this great war." This would be a good opening for a discussion of books that changed our lives.

If you were going to write about the comedy in Woody Allen's movies, it might be well to start with a definition of comedy in general. Perhaps something like:

> Comedy is literature that aims to amuse, to provoke laughter, to arouse thought. It ends happily. But until it reaches that happy ending, it skirts disaster and sorrow. Its aim is essentially serious. Someone, years ago, trying to define comedy, said "Comedy is no laughing matter." A Woody Allen movie certainly gets plenty of laughs, but its theme is no laughing matter.

Interpretation in the Thesis Sentence

No matter how you introduce your essay, it is imperative that your thesis statement be an interpretation rather than a mere statement of fact. Although it is **your** interpretation, remember that it must come from ideas you have gathered from the work read, not just any that popped into your head. That is, it must be relevant and supportable.

Your job is to provide interpretation and explanation of the work; just retelling what happened in the story or just repeating what the author says is totally inadequate.

Since your essay should be the result of your own thinking, the thesis statement and the topic sentences of the body paragraphs should be in your own words, not words borrowed from some other writer. Although sometimes you may want to use professional criticism to support your points, you are using it **only as support** for your own thoughts expressed in your thesis statement and your topic sentences. **To interpret is the purpose of critical writing.**

A review, on the other hand, has a different purpose. In a review, the writer assumes that the readers want to know what happens, what a work is about, so that they can decide if they want to read the book or go to the movie or buy the record. In critical writing, the writer assumes that the readers already know what the work is about but want to know more and know more deeply.

BODY

In the body of your essay you must support your thesis sentence, just as in the other essays. When writing about literature, however, you have your support right at your fingertips—the work itself. You will use quotations and paraphrases from the literature to prove the statements in the body.

There are two possible directions that you might take once you have your thesis statement: (1) outlining first and then looking for support for your subtopics, and (2) searching for items that support your thesis first and then dividing these bits of evidence into classifications that become your subtopic sentences. Both methods work; it is a matter of personal preference.

Getting the Subtopics First

In support of the thesis statement on Mark Twain's "The Mysterious Stranger," you might use the following topic sentences:

TOPIC SENTENCE 1

Satan is beautiful; he is "handsome and had a winning face and a pleasant voice, and was easy and graceful and unembarrassed."

TOPIC SENTENCE 2

Satan is compelling; whether they want it or not, the boys are drawn to him, held by him, bound to obey his wishes.

TOPIC SENTENCE 3

Satan is accommodating; he does what the boys wish, though the result of his actions often turn out to be not exactly what the boys want.

TOPIC SENTENCE 4

Satan seemed to have neither conscience nor empathy; when two of the little workmen quarreled, "Satan reached out his hand and crushed the life out of them with his fingers" and ignored the grief of the wives who mourn them.

Once you have decided on a thesis sentence, you become a kind of detective. Much as the detective looks for clues, you look for evidence to support your thesis.

For example, in supporting topic sentence 3, you would read through the story, finding and jotting down on notecards all material to prove that Satan is accommodating but that the results are not always what the boys wish:

CARD 1

Feeling sorry for the grief-stricken mother of a friend of theirs, the boys ask Satan to examine her possible futures. He reports that "the longest . . . gave her forty-two years and her shortest twenty-nine, and that both were charged with grief and hunger and cold and pain." The boys beg Satan to change her future. Satan does. "In three days time, she will go to the stake," he promises.

CARD 2

By this same act, Satan changes the future of Fischer, who will now betray the mother. Instead of dying the following year as was originally his fate, Fischer would "live to be ninety and have a pretty prosperous and comfortable life of it. . . . " The boys are delighted to have done Fischer such a service until Satan adds that his fate after death has also been altered. Had he died in the following year as originally scheduled, he would have gone to heaven. With his new future he is doomed to hell.

CARD 3

Another example of Satan's "accommodation" is his agreeing, at the boys' request, to release Father Peter from prison and ensure him a happy life. Satan does as he is asked, but only later do the boys discover that Father Peter will also be insane.

Then go on searching through the story for more clues, more evidence to prove each of your points.

Getting the Evidence First

If you use the second method, you would start the same way—reading the story, thinking about it, and coming up with some general impression you would turn into a tentative thesis statement.

Suppose the assignment is a critical paper on Nathaniel Hawthorne's "Young Goodman Brown." After reading the story, perhaps you are a little baffled. The story seems simple enough, but what does it mean? A young man leaves his bride, goes into the forest for a night, meets someone who may or may not be the devil, learns from him that his father and grandfather may not have been the good men he thought they were. He sees and hears—or thinks he does—all the fine, respected people he knows bound on an evil journey, just as he is. They all arrive—or he imagines that they do—at a great witch meeting dedicated to evil. He even thinks he hears his parents and his wife. Hearing them, he faints. When he comes to, the forest is only the forest, silent and solitary. He never knows whether he only dreamed this vivid and awesome scene, but all the rest of his life is sad and "distrustful."

From this plot summary you can see that at every step of the way through his journey and through his story, Goodman Brown either does or does not experience something evil. In the Word Power section at the end of this chapter you will see that this either—or situation is called *ambiguity*. So you are ready to try a tentative thesis statement.

> Through his repeated use of ambiguity, Hawthorne arrives at his theme that a sense of evil, regardless of whether it is real or imagined, spoils life because it destroys faith in the goodness of man.

Now you collect evidence that can later be classified into subtopics to support your thesis statement. The first thing you notice is the title, "Young Goodman Brown." *Goodman* isn't a name, you find, but a form of address to the ordinary men of early New England colonies. And *Brown* is a common name among the English and their American descendents. Thus, from the title alone, you have learned that the chief character is an ordinary young man, not individualized even by a full name. Thus, you can infer that young Goodman Brown is meant to represent man in general.

The title, also, as mentioned, indicates the setting of early New England. In the early paragraphs, calling Salem a village also indicates time past as well as a specific place. And the terms *tarry*, *prithee*, and *afeard* all help to set the scene in early days.

You notice that the wife's name is Faith, which of course is a feminine name but is also the name of a quality. This, you recognize, is the first of the ambiguities in the story (unless, of course, there is some doubt about the *good* in Goodman). You see it played upon when Brown tardily meets the man in the forest and says, "Faith kept me back a while."

Within a few lines you have three possible subtopics: first, the universality of the characters; second, the setting; third, the ambiguity of the characters. Careful reading will reveal to you many items under these headings and many other possible headings. Once you classify these bits of information, you will probably have more subtopic ideas than you need, so you will choose the best to form your subtopics and use the others to support them. Some, of course, you will discard. Those selected for subtopics will provide the organizational framework for the body of your essay.

CONCLUSION

The conclusion of your essay about literature follows the same pattern as the conclusion to any other essay. You may summarize your main points and restate your thesis. Here, also, an apt quotation or a pertinent anecdote often works well.

In writing a possible conclusion for the suggested interpretation of "I See You Never," you might say:

> Almost plotless and with characters so little familiar that we don't even know their first names, this simple story nevertheless conveys a great theme: man's enemy is ignorance. The social forces that exile Mr. Ramirez are destructive only to those who don't know enough to work within those forces. His cry of human loneliness, "I see you never," pertains to more than just Mrs. O'Brian. He cannot "see" his world at all. Mr. Ramirez is one of the good little people who, through ignorance, are crushed by social forces that are not evil in themselves.

PITFALLS TO AVOID

1. Don't forget to mention the full title and full name of the author early in your essay. Do not start out with "This story . . . " or "I really love this book."
2. Do not retell the story; you are writing a critical paper, not a book report. In writing a critical essay, you need to show not just what happens, but the significance of what happens.
3. Narrow your topic carefully. Do not try to write on too broad a subject or on too many aspects of a work.
4. Do not use the works of critics without giving credit. This is plagiarism, which is a crime.

5. Do not pretend to more knowledge than you have. Write simply and honestly.

6. Do not state the obvious. "Mark Twain was a great American humorist."

7. Don't just patch together long quotations from various critical works. You need to do your own thinking and provide your own interpretation of the work. But make sure you understand the story before you trust your own interpretation.

8. Don't fail to cite specific evidence from the story that will make your interpretations clear and convincing.

The following passage from Lionel Trilling's "Of This Time, Of That Place" illustrates a situation in which the student clearly does not understand the work he has written about:

....

There was a silence between them. Both dropped their eyes to the blue-book on the desk. On its cover Howe had pencilled: "F. This is very poor work."

Howe picked up the blue-book. There was always the possibility of injustice. The teacher may be bored by the mass of papers and not wholly attentive. A phrase, even the student's handwriting, may irritate him unreasonably. "Well," said Howe, "let's go through it."

He opened the first page. "Now here: you write, 'In "The Ancient Mariner," Coleridge lives in and transports us to a honey-sweet world where all is rich and strange, a world of charm to which we can escape from the humdrum existence of our daily lives, the world of romance. Here, in this warm and honey-sweet land of charming dreams we can relax and enjoy ourselves.' "

Howe lowered the paper and waited with a neutral look for Blackburn to speak. Blackburn returned the look boldly, did not speak, sat stolid and lofty. At last Howe said, speaking gently, "Did you mean that, or were you just at a loss for something to say?"

"You imply that I was just 'bluffing'?" The quotation marks hung palpable in the air about the word.

"I'd like to know. I'd prefer believing that you were bluffing to believing that you really thought this."

Blackburn's eyebrows went up. From the height of a great and firm-based idea he looked at his teacher. He clasped the crags for a moment and then pounced, craftily, suavely. "Do you mean, Dr. Howe, that there aren't two opinions possible?"

It was superbly done in its air of putting all of Howe's intellectual life into the balance. Howe remained patient and simple. "Yes, many opinions are possible, but not this one. Whatever anyone believes of 'The Ancient Mariner,' no one can in reason believe that it represents a—a honey-sweet world in which we can relax."

"But that is what I **feel**, sir."

This was well done too. Howe said, "Look, Mr. Blackburn. Do you really relax with hunger and thirst, the heat and the sea-serpents, the dead men with staring eyes, Life in Death and the skeletons? Come now, Mr. Blackburn."

There is a moral to this story. Trilling's theme is that to criticize intelligently, you must read the story closely, then react to it. Don't try to bluff; instructors have read the story and understood it; so must you. To be criticism, opinions must be supported by the work being criticized.

TECHNIQUES OF CLEAR WRITING

THE HISTORICAL PRESENT TENSE

Writing about literature will involve you in using the historical present tense. You use the historical present now whenever you narrate events that happened in the past as though they were happening in the present. For instance, you might write:

> Mr. Pumpernickel **jerks** open the door and **shouts,** "Down with Democrats!"

Correct use of the historical present lends a sense of immediacy and action to such writing. Using the historical present for narratives is a stylistic choice available to you, but be sure to stay in the tense if you do choose it. Don't shift inconsistently from the historical present to the past. Avoid mistakes like this:

> Mr. Pumpernickel **jerks** open the door and **shouted,** "Down with Democrats!"

Two special circumstances require the historical present. First, it is the right form for expressing universal truths:

Aging is a reality that no one escapes.

Second, when you write about literature, using the historical present permits you to convey the idea that although the work you are discussing was written in the past, the effect and meaning of the words—what they say—exist in the present.

In writing about literature, using both past and historical present tenses lets you make a distinction between what authors have done and what their words convey. In other words, the events of the writer's life are in the past, but the words they produced still exist and speak. For instance, you might say:

> Shakespeare **wrote** many of his sonnets before 1598 and **published** at least part of them by 1609. They **are** among the world's greatest love poems. In them, he **expresses** his belief that literature **exists** far beyond the lifetime of the writer. One sonnet **ends** with the lines:
> So long as man can breathe or eyes can see,
> So long live this [poem] . . .

FIGURATIVE LANGUAGE

As you have gone through this book, you have learned that writing that communicates clearly is frequently the result of choices. You choose a topic; then you choose an attitude toward it; then you choose what method will best develop it. When you are writing sentences, you choose among different structures to make sure that the relationships among your ideas are clear. But when you come to selecting individual words and phrases, you have a vast range of choices.

Ford Madox Ford tells how he and Joseph Conrad practiced choosing the right word. Both were novelists who are considered among the great craftsmen of literature. Because they were friends, they spent much time together testing their skills in choosing words. Driving along a country road, for instance, they would challenge each other to choose words to best describe a meadow they were passing. Or, stopping in a country inn, they would test themselves on words that would best convey the atmosphere of the place or the appearance and personality of the landlord. So, you see, even for professional writers, the choice of words takes discrimination— you must choose those words that express exactly what you mean.

The sum total of your choices becomes your style, and your style reveals you. Goethe, the great German writer, said, "We should try to use words that correspond as closely as possible with what we feel, see, think, imagine, experience, and reason,"

You have already studied word choice under several headings: the specific word and the general word; the concrete word and the abstract word; the denotative word and the connotative word. Still another consideration in effective choice of words is that between literal language and figurative language.

Literal language points to very definite objects or actions or ideas, like a football, or kicking a football, or football strategy. It is concerned chiefly with facts which are stated as plainly and precisely as possible. At its most precise, literal language becomes a scientific language. For example, the literal statement that "Man is an animal who reasons" could be expanded to a biological definition such as: "Man is a biped mammal characterized by his erect posture, his plantigrade foot which permits such posture, a perfectly opposable thumb, scarcity of hair, and, above all, a large cranial cavity which permits the development of a large brain, and, so, of large intellectual capacity."

Figurative language is the opposite of literal; it is imaginative. It is closely allied to connotative language because, like connotation, it has emotional overtones. Figurative language usually depends on the extended rather than the primary meaning. All words have a primary meaning; many words go beyond that first meaning to meanings suggested by it. For example, the primary meaning of green denotes a specific range of color, but its extended meanings refer to things that are green, like a golf course, or money, which, in slang, is sometimes called the "long green." But extended meanings go even beyond that. At a horse show you might hear about a "green horse." Or your grandfather might say about your brother (never about you), "That boy certainly is green." Obviously, neither the horse nor your brother is literally green. What is meant is that both the horse and the boy are inexperienced. How did a color come to express a condition like "inexperienced"?

Language expands through associations. Green is the color associated with spring. After the drab browns and blacks of winter, or the white of its snows, the first sign of spring is the world turning green again. Spring is associated with youth because spring is a new beginning. Youth, of course, does not have the experience of age. Language skips over some of the steps of the associative process and dubs the inexperienced horse and boy "green." (Even that last sentence, though attempting literal definition, uses figurative speech in saying that language "skips" and "dubs.")

You can see language working figuratively throughout literature. In Shakespeare's *Antony and Cleopatra*, the lovers tease each other, sometimes so much that one or the other grows bad-tempered. Antony, cross with Cleopatra, twits her about Julius

Caesar, who had earlier been her lover. Cleopatra, to reassure Antony, replies, "Those were my salad days, when I was green in judgment." Had she been speaking literally, she would have said something like "Those days with Caesar happened when I was too inexperienced to have the good judgment to wait for you." The term *salad days* has come to mean the times of early maturity, springtime, when the lettuce and other salad greens come up. Later the term picked up another implication. Since youth, when it is looked back to, suggests a carefree happiness, *salad days* implies the good old days.

Language can be almost endlessly extended by association. A poem of Robert Frost's begins "Nature's first green is gold." Again, we associate green with spring and more precisely with the first greening of the trees. But in no literal sense is green gold. The literal statement would be something like this: "The first color that shows on the trees in spring is a yellowish green." That literal statement is not only longer, but it leaves out the suggestion that the turning of the color is both universal and good.

Figures of Speech

In addition to having emotional overtones, extended meanings, and suggested associations, figurative language is characterized by its dependence on *figures of speech*. Figures of speech are expressions made up of words used not in their literal sense but to make a forceful and dramatic image. Scholars say that in classical and medieval times students had to learn as many as 250 figures of speech. Modern students need to be familiar with only a handful of the most common.

Antithesis

Antithesis is a figure of speech in which two ideas are contrasted through parallelism. To emphasize the contrast, one idea is balanced against its opposite, with each term in similar grammatical form. For example, "You're wrong, I'm right," or "Man proposes, God disposes." A thesis (the same concept as a thesis statement) is stated and an anti- (or opposing) thesis is made against it.

Hyperbole

Hyperbole is a figure of speech based on exaggeration. You use it frequently in ordinary conversation: "I'm starved" or "He's a real nut" or "I'll die if she doesn't give me an A on this paper." Such statements are not made to deceive but to emphasize. This is also true of literary hyperbole. In order to emphasize his faithfulness to the girl like the red, red rose, Robert Burns exaggerated:

> *And I will luve thee still, my dear,*
> *Till a' the seas gang dry.*
> *Till a' the seas gang dry, my dear,*
> *And the rocks melt wi' the sun.*

Samuel Hoffenstein, a comic poet, uses both hyperbole and antithesis in this little verse:

> *When I took you for my own,*
> *You stood 'mong women all alone.*
> *When I let the magic go,*
> *You stood with women in a row.*

In literal language, he is saying that when he loved her, she was to him the most important of women; when he no longer loved her, she was just like all other women. Both are exaggerations. In addition, the last two lines are an antithesis to the first two.

Personification

Personification is a figure of speech which gives human characteristics to nonhuman things. This, too, you use in everyday speech. You might say of your car on a winter morning: "She's cranky today. She's always hard to get along with on cold days." On a more literary level, John Donne personified death when he wrote, "Death, be not proud." (This line also includes the figure of speech known as *apostrophe*, in which the nonhuman entity or an absent person is spoken to directly.)

Here is a verse by John Hay in which good and bad luck are personified as women. After identifying good and bad luck as women, Hay discusses them totally as if they **were** women.

Identification of good luck as a "gay girl"

> *Good luck is the gayest of all gay girls.*

Characteristics of the gay girl

> *Long in one place she will not stay.*
> *Back from your brow she strokes the curls.*
> *Kisses you quick and flies away.*

Identification of bad luck as a sober-sided matron
Her characteristics

> *But Madame Bad Luck soberly comes*
> *And stays—no fancy has she for flitting—*
> *Snatches of true-love songs she hums.*
> *And sits by your bed, and brings her knitting.*

Metonymy

Metonymy is a figure of speech in which a part of the thing meant or something closely related to it stands for the thing itself. Metonymy is frequently used in everyday speech. You might refer to a king as "the crown" and to the king's power as the "scepter." King Richard I often called himself "England" because he so closely associated himself with his country. But he is called by history "the Lionhearted" in a metonymy for the courage of a lion, for normal courage is sometimes called "heart" ("He has no heart for a fight") and extraordinary courage is "lionhearted."

The part chosen to represent the whole must be an important part. You might refer to your car as your wheels, but if you wished to be understood, you would scarcely refer to it as your gas cap. Likewise, because of all the marching they must do, infantry are referred to as "foot" soldiers. It is a metonymy of an important part when the captain of a ship commands, "All hands on deck." He expects the entire sailor to show up, but he calls him a hand because of the amount of manual labor the sailor must do. The same principle is applied in "field hands." By focusing attention on an important part or function, the writer gains emphasis and vividness.

Metaphor

Metaphor is the most important of the figures of speech. Indeed, most of the others are really just subdivisions of metaphor. Metaphor is based on comparison, not literal but imaginative. The word itself means "transfer," the transfer of one kind of meaning to another through comparison. To say that language is metaphoric is almost identical with saying that it is imaginative. The comparisons made by metaphor are essential to any satisfactory handling of language. (Notice that the phrase *handling of language* is a metaphor.) Without metaphor, the users of language could denote only those things that were present with them in time and space. All abstraction rests on metaphor. In fact, every word has a metaphorical root. (Notice that *root* in that sentence is a metaphor.)

Metaphor uses nonliteral comparison to describe and identify one thing in the terms of another. Such describing and identifying is basic to the growth of language, but, even more important, it is basic to understanding. You use metaphor because you can't escape it, but also because, when you use it successfully, it is a swift and vivid way to convey understanding.

Sometimes metaphor is broken down into *simile* and *metaphor* for the sake of analysis. Simile uses *like, as,* and *than* to make explicit comparisons. Simile says that *A* is like *B*, as in the following quotations:

> He roared *like* a lion.

> Let us go then, you and I,
> When the evening is spread out against the sky
> *Like* a patient etherized upon a table.

See a full discussion of metaphor in Chapter 5.

USE OF OTHERS' WRITINGS

Before you make use of the writings of other people, you must learn the accepted ways of summarizing, paraphrasing, and quoting. These techniques allow you to include the writings of others in your essays without committing the crime of plagiarism. In all of these, you give credit to the original writer by footnote, parentheses, or reference.

Before beginning to write any of these, however, you must first make sure that you understand exactly what the author means. Read the passage as many times as is necessary to feel confident that you know the author's purpose and tone as well as his or her meaning. Once you have a clear idea of the meaning, you must decide which of the devices you wish to use: the summary, the paraphrase, or the quotation.

The Summary

The use of the summary is not new to you. You used it in high school when you wrote a book review; you used it when you told your friend the plot of a book you read or a movie or a TV program you watched. You probably have used the summary to answer essay questions. The summary is a brief recounting given in your own words. It is usually less than one half as long as the original work, and it follows the same order as the original and includes its major points, major supporting detail, any key facts, and examples.

The Paraphrase

A paraphrase is a restatement, in your own words, of what someone else has written. The paraphrase may be shorter than the original, or it may be as long as or longer than the original, for the purpose here is not so much to condense, as is the case with the summary, but to retell the work in your own words and your own style. Paraphrase allows the writer to concentrate on only one part of the original work or to shift the point of emphasis in the original. However, paraphrase only what the author says, not what you think is implied.

You may, if you wish, quote key words or phrases if they seem better than anything you can come up with. However, the quotations should be clearly marked as such and should be blended into your writings so that the sentences are not choppy. Again, you must have a clear understanding of what the original author is saying, and you must completely reword it. Changing the order of the words, changing direct quotation to indirect quotation, or moving a few phraes around is not paraphrasing—it's plagiarizing.

DISCUSSION ACTIVITY: PARAPHRASING

Suppose two students are paraphrasing on notecards the following passage. Discuss the errors in and merits of each paraphrase.

PASSAGE TO BE PARAPHRASED

A literary symbol means itself plus more. It stands for what it is and other things that it brings to mind. The flag is a symbol; it stands for a flag plus all the feelings of patriotism, honor, bravery, freedom, and love of country that the flag may bring to mind. Other symbols such as the cross, the swastika, the Statue of Liberty, and the skull and crossbones evoke their own connotations. In any given story, however, the symbol could take on a different meaning. Certain literary symbols have been used so often that they are almost standardized:

journey = life
spring, summer, fall = youth, adulthood, old age
morning, afternoon, night = youth, adulthood, old age
crossing a bridge = changing your life
water = purification, life-giving force
light = good, hope, civilization
dark = evil, despair, primitiveness
star = hope

Other symbols have unique meanings; they have a special meaning only in the story in which they appear. The raft, for example, in *Adventures of Huckleberry Finn* represents a kind of Eden, a Paradise, but the raft is not a universal symbol. In other stories, it might represent danger or impermanence, or something else, or nothing else.

PARAPHRASE A

If something means itself plus something else, it is a literary symbol. It stands for what it is and other things that it brings to mind. A military uniform, for example, means a uniform plus all the feelings a uniform brings forth—feelings of patriotism, and bravery, and honor. The same is true of many things, like a skull and crossbones, which makes you think of poison or pirates. Light usually means good things, and dark means bad things, but symbols don't always mean the same things. Sometimes a raft might mean good, but sometimes it might mean evil.

PARAPHRASE B

"A literary symbol means itself plus more."[1] There are two types of literary symbols; one type of symbol has a traditional meaning because it has been used so often: light, for example, has come to symbolize hope or civilization or goodness, while dark represents the opposite. Seasons and times of day have come to be recognized as also representing ages of man. Feeling of patriotism are often evoked by the flag, and other symbols evoke other emotions. Sometimes "symbols are unique; they have a meaning only in the story in which they appear;"[2] in the *Adventures of Huckleberry Finn*, for example, Twain uses a raft as a symbol of Paradise, or it may mean the opposite. Or it may mean just a raft, having no symbolic meaning at all.

EXERCISE 12A: PARAPHRASING

Paraphrase the following paragraphs.

STORY AND STRUCTURE

There are no easy rules for literary judgment. Such judgment depends ultimately on our perceptivity, intelligence, and experience; it is a product of how much and how alertly we have lived and how much and how well we have read. Yet at least two basic principles may be set up. First, every story is to be initially judged by how fully it achieves its central purpose. Each element in the story is to be judged by the effectiveness of its contribution to the central purpose. In a good story every element works with every other element for the accomplishment of this central purpose. It follows that no element in the story may be judged in isolation.

Once a story has been judged successful in achieving its central purpose, we may apply a second principle of judgment. A story, if successful, may be judged by the significance of its purpose. . . . If a story's only aim is to entertain, whether by mystifying, surprising, thrilling, provoking to laughter or tears, or furnishing a substitute dream life, we may judge it of less value than a story whose aim is to **reveal.** When a story does provide some revelation—does make some serious statement about life—we may measure it by the breadth and depth of the revelation.

Some stories, then, provide good fun and innocent merriment. Others afford the good reader a deeper enjoyment through the insights they give into life. A third type, like many of the soap operas of television and radio, offer a cheaper and less innocent pleasure by providing escape under the guise of interpretation. Such stories, while professing to present real-life situations and everyday people and happenings, actually, by their shallowness of characterization, their falsifications of plot, their use of stock themes and stock emotions, present us with dangerous oversimplifications and distortions. They seriously misrepresent life and are harmful to the extent that they keep us from a more sensitive, more discriminating response to experience.

Laurence Perrine

The Quotation

A direct quotation is the use of another's writing exactly as it was written, word for word. You may use a phrase, a clause, a sentence, or even a group of sentences and put it in your paper verbatim. The quotation should be used primarily if the material is written brilliantly, or if the material is controversial or unknown. Otherwise, the paraphrase is usually better, as it is in your style and the writing remains smoother. However, the careful use of quotations can enhance your writing and provide excellent support for your thesis. Generally, phrases, sentences, and short passages are preferable to long passages. **All quotations must be introduced.** Long quotations from various authors strung together with little of your own introductions and comments make for choppy and generally unclear writing. Quotation is not a substitute for your thought and your words. Some instructors restrict the use of quotations to no more than 20 percent of your paper.

Techniques of Quoting

The quotations that you use (a few words or part of a sentence) must fit with the rest of the sentence; that is, the sentence must make sense. A sentence such as

> Knowledge, at that time, was not considered essential "could make them discontented with the lot which God had appointed for them."

is unclear and will confuse the reader. To make the meaning clear, the sentence should be changed to

> During the Middle Ages, the lower classes were not encouraged to learn because it "could make them discontented with the lot which God had appointed for them."

The Long Quotation

Any quotation of three lines or more is indented five spaces and single-spaced. No quotation marks are necessary; the indentation and single-spacing show that it is a direct quotation.

   With all quotations, and especially long ones, you must make clear to the reader the relationship between the quotation and the point you are making. This is usually done in your introduction to the quotation. If, for example, you are attempting to prove that the work you were discussing was, contrary to popular opinion, a tragedy, you might write:

> This work is a tragedy because it has the classical properties of a tragedy. John Dryden defined the qualities of tragedy in a 1679 essay:
>> It ought to be great, and to consist of great persons, to distinguish it from comedy, where the action is trivial and the persons of inferior rank . . . it ought to be probable, as well as admirable and great . . .   the end or scope of tragedy . . . is, to rectify or purge our passions, fear and pity.

Then you would show that the work has all of these qualities.

   Notice that in the text of the paper the writer has given credit to the author. Mentioning the author immediately before using his or her ideas or words is useful in showing where your idea (or someone else's ideas) ends and this author's begins.

Documentation

To document is to give credit to the sources of your information either formally or informally. If you are writing an important and serious paper, like a research paper, a thesis, a dissertation, you should use *formal documentation.* In an essay based on a single work, you may generally use *informal documentation.* Your instructor will usually tell you which type is required.

The documentation suggested in this textbook is taken from a highly regarded publication of the Modern Language Association known as the *MLA Handook.* The textbook you are reading contains only general instructions and a few samples of the most frequently used specifics relating to documentation. For complete and detailed documentation you will need to consult the *MLA Handbook* (or some other recommended handbook).

Works Cited, or Bibliography

Although *Works Cited* comes at the conclusion of your paper, it is well to write it first, for that will simplify your footnoting. The *Works Cited* is simply a list of all the sources *you have quoted,* directly or indirectly, in your own paper. The sources include books, of course, and any articles, journals, pamphlets, charts, illustrations, films, etc., you plan to use.

An *Annotated List of Works Cited* is the same list with descriptive or evaluative comments after each citation.

The information listed in *Works Cited* is normally arranged in this order:

1. Author's (or authors') name
2. Title of work
3. Name of editor, translator, or compiler (if applicable)
4. Edition used (except first)
5. Number of volumes (if applicable)
6. Name of series (if applicable)
7. Facts of publication (place of publication, name of publisher, date of publication)
8. Page numbers (if applicable)

(See sample entries for *Works Cited* list below.)

Works Cited

Arnold, Matthew. "Dover Beach." *Norton Anthology of English Literature,* 4th ed. 2 vols. Ed. M.H. Abrams et al. New York: W.W. Norton, 1979, 2: 1378–79.

Donald, Robert B. et al. *Writing Clear Essays,* 2nd ed. Englewood Cliffs, N.J.: Prentice Hall, 1992.

————. *Models for Clear Writing*, 2nd ed. Englewood Cliffs, N.J.: Prentice Hall, 1992. (NOTE: Do not repeat author's name in subsequent entries.)

These few samples give you the basic form as well as the required punctuation for entries in the list of *Works Cited.*

Formal Documentation

Footnotes and entries in the *Works Cited* list offer the same information but differ in form. A *bibliographic entry* has three main divisions, each separated by a period: (1) the author's name reversed for alphabetizing; (2) the title of the work; and (3) the facts of publication. A footnote has four main divisions with only one period at the end: (1) the author's name in the usual order, (2) the title of the work, (3) the facts of publication in parentheses, and (4) the page or pages cited. See sample footnotes for correct style.

1. Ford Madox Ford, *The Rash Act* (Manchester, England: Carcanet New Press, 1933), 187.

2. Robert B. Donald et al, *Writing Clear Essays*, 2nd ed. (Englewood Cliffs, N.J.: Prentice Hall, 1992), 311.

Subsequent Footnote Forms

It is imperative that you document *everything* you borrow, not only quotations but also information and ideas. Needless to say, you don't have to document proverbs, well-known quotations, or commonly known facts, but you must acknowledge and thereby give credit for any borrowed material that could be mistaken for your own. (If you're not positive about what to document, give credit.)

The footnoting references in the text must clearly point to specific sources in the *Works Cited* list at the end of your paper. The *Works Cited* list is an important part of giving credit to your sources, but it is not specific enough in its details to give precise documentation. The *MLA Handbook* states:

> You must indicate exactly what you have derived from each source and exactly where in that book you found that material. The most practical way to supply this information is to insert brief parenthetical acknowledgments in your paper wherever you incorporate another's words, facts, or ideas. Usually, the author's last name and a page reference are enough to identify the source and the specific location from which you have borrowed the material. *(MLA Handbook,* 136)

For example:

Ford's compassion for his characters is quiet but unfaltering (Sisson, 147).

However, if Sisson's name (or the name of any other author you have quoted) appears in the quotation, the parenthetical note would simply be (147). Anything that appears in the text should not be repeated in the parenthetical footnote.

You must remember two things about documentation: First, there are a number of styles of documentation that are equally as satisfactory as the *MLA Handbook;* second, each of the systems has a vast number of details of documenting far beyond the scope of this textbook. But no matter what system you and your instructor decide on, you must always make sure to give credit, and you must be consistent in following that system.

Informal Documentation

Informal documentation is used when you are writing about only one literary work and using only one source. You identify your source in a single footnote, and thereafter you include the necessary information (usually just the page number) in parentheses in the text of your essay.

For example:

The change in Goodman Brown's attitude toward the townspeople was evident. "He shrank from the venerable saint, as if to avoid an anathema. . . ." (507) He "looked sternly and sadly into [his wife's] face, and passed on without a greeting." (508)

WORD POWER

USEFUL TERMS FOR LITERARY CRITICISM

There are various terms you need to know when discussing literature.

Allegory

Allegory is a form of fiction in which the characters and actions represent abstractions, like Knowledge, Good Deeds, Beauty, Power. The characters and their actions are less important than the political, religious, and moral ideas they stand for. The surface story is just a way to discuss the ideas underlying it.

In an allegory, the characters and incidents are clearly related to the underlying but more important story in a clear-cut and definite relationship. Often the character of Everyman stands for all people. In the most famous of allegories, John Bunyan's *Pilgrim's Progress*, characters such as Christian, Faithful, the Giant Despair, and Mr. Worldly Wiseman represent religious ideas.

Allusion

An allusion is a reference to some person or event in history or literature with which the reader is presumed to be familiar. When employed by a skillful writer, an allusion—whether to Hiroshima or Adolf Hitler—can bring into play a whole set of ideas and emotional responses without the author's having made a direct statement about people or events of the past. Much of the work of such modern authors as James Joyce and T.S. Eliot is impossible to understand without some knowledge of the classical allusions.

The title of William Faulkner's novel *The Sound and the Fury,* in which the first section is told by an idiot, is an allusion of these lines from Macbeth:

It is a tale told by an idiot, full of sound and fury, signifying nothing.

Ambiguity

Ambiguity refers to the possibility that an object, action, or situation may be subject to more than one interpretation. It is an artistic device used deliberately to enrich the work by suggesting that multiple meanings can be drawn from a single detail. For example, a character may be impelled by contrary impulses, such as ruthless pursuit of power and genuine love for his friends; thus his every move up the ladder is open to contrary interpretations.

In expository writing, where your aim is clear communication, ambiguity is a fault; it simply means vagueness. In literature, however, ambiguity, because it permits more than one interpretation, reflects the richness of human experience. It also reflects the difficulty of perceiving the significance of experience.

Atmosphere

Atmosphere is a general term used to describe the combined effects of setting, tone, and mood. It is the feeling created by the work as a whole. In Edgar Allan Poe's " The Fall of the House of Usher," for instance, the atmosphere is established in the very first sentence:

> During the whole of a dull, dark, and soundless day in the autumn of the year, when the clouds hung oppressively low in the heavens, I had been passing alone, on horseback, through a singularly dreary country, and at length found myself, as the shades of the evening drew on, within view of the melancholy House of Usher.

The authors' tone, their attitudes toward their subjects, also contribute to the atmosphere. Whether they are distant and contemptuous or close and sympathetic, their attitudes affect our feeling about their work. Then, too, a skillful writer may establish a mood of wild frenzy, quiet resignation, or romantic moonglow; the sound of the words themselves can powerfully influence the atmosphere.

Catharsis

Catharsis is a term associated with tragedy and its effect upon the audience. Through emotional participation in the pity and fear of tragedy, the reader or viewer experiences a purifying or cleansing of the emotions—if not a spiritual renewal, at least relief from anxiety and tension.

Comedy

One curious feature of comedy is that every attempt to define it turns out to be singularly unfunny. Socrates is said to have put the comic poet Aristophanes to sleep with a lecture on the comic spirit, and modern scholars have written volumes in an attempt to explain what comedy is, so any brief definition is almost certain to prove inadequate. In the traditional sense, comedy implies a situation in which people's fortunes turn from bad to good; they get either what they deserve or better than they deserve. However, in a broader sense, there is no universally accepted set of characteristics which mark the boundaries of comedy, except that it ends well for the protagonist. Much of modern comedy, however, deals with the futility and absurdity of life; thus it could be said that it springs from tragic roots. The distinction between comedy and tragedy that will serve well in most instances is that comedy deals with the light rather than the dark, that it offers an optimistic outloook in the face of folly, absurdity, and death.

Deus Ex Machina

As originally applied to Greek drama, *deus ex machina* meant the timely intervention of a god who was suddenly lowered onto the stage to resolve the insolvable problems of the human characters.

Today, the term is applied to any trick or improbable coincidence used by an author to untangle the difficulties of the novel or story and provide a neat conclusion. In a second-rate romantic novel, for example, you might have the pirate hero snatched from the gallows by the king's pardon or a sudden declaration of war.

Fable

A fable is a brief tale which carries some sort of moral or cautionary point. The most common form is the beast fable, in which animals talk and act like people, as in Aesop's *Fables* or the Uncle Remus stories of Joel Chandler Harris. James Thurber uses animal fables for his satires on religion, politics, and human relationships in *Fables for Our Time.*

Farce

Farce is a type of low comedy marked by improbable characters and actions. The typical farce is a short, loosely structured play designed to amuse with nonsensical antics of one-dimensional characters.

Genre

In its most commonly accepted meaning, genre refers to the particular form or category to which a literary composition belongs, such as novel, short story, epic, elegy, sonnet, ode, and so on.

Imagery

Imagery is the creation in words of some sensory experience. It is usually visual, but it can be an experience of any of the other senses; sometimes it is more than one. For example, the line "the little dog laughed" creates a picture and also a sound.

The purpose of imagery is to describe and illustrate, but usually the description implies some meaning, suggests some emotion. When you wrote your descriptive essay, you aimed at creating images—helping your readers see what you saw—but you also wanted them to feel what you felt, your implied meaning.

In the following poem Samuel Allen describes the great baseball pitcher, "Satch" Paige. Paige played for over twenty years on black teams before he went into the big leagues, and there he played until he was almost fifty years old. It seemed as if he would go on forever.

To Satch

Sometimes I feel like I will never stop
Just go on forever
Til one fine mornin'
I'm gonna reach up and grab me a handfulla stars
Throw out my long lean leg
And whip three hot strikes burnin' down the heavens
And look over at God and say
How about that!

This little verse creates, first, an image of a pitcher winding up and then a second image of Satch's almost gloating satisfaction as he delivers three strikes in heaven.

Read the following poem to note how the poet moves back and forth from straightforward language to imagery in order to emphasize his theme that, even in small things, there are great meanings.

The Death of a Toad

A toad the power mower caught,
Chewed and clipped of a leg, with a hobbling hop has got
To the garden verge, and sanctuaried him
Under the cineraria leaves, in the shade
Of the ashen heartshaped leaves, in a dim,
Low, and a final glade.

The rare original heartsblood goes,
Spends on the earthen hide, in the folds and wizenings, flows
In the gutters of the banked and staring eyes. He lies
As still as if he would return to stone,
And soundlessly attending, dies
Toward some deep monotone,

Toward misted and ebullient seas
And cooling shores, toward lost Amphibia's emperies.
Day dwindles, drowning, and at length is gone
In the wide and antique eyes, which still appear
To watch, across the castrate lawn,
The haggard daylight steer.

Richard Wilbur

Read the following essay to see how the student writer narrows her discussion to the poet's use of imagery in support of his theme.

....
IMAGERY IN "THE DEATH OF A TOAD"
....

Complete title and full name of author given.

  "The Death of a Toad" by Richard Wilbur relies heavily for its effectiveness upon its imagery. The poem begins with blunt, specific, unconnotative language; the power mower "chewed and clipped" the toad's leg. The despair and helplessness of the

Evidence cited from poem to contrast denotative language about the machine with connotative images about the toad's death.

toad is heightened by his retreat in a "hobbling hop" to the only place he knows protection—his "sanctuary" of "ashen, heart-shaped" leaves, where actually he is afforded no protection at all, not even from death. The choice of "ashen" and "heart-shaped" are again specific terms of description, but these have connotative overtones of death and compassion. The image of a "dim and final glade" begins a continuing image of the failing of light and sight as a metaphor for the failing life. Blood flows into his eyes, the seas are "misted," "day dwindles and is gone," the daylight grows "haggard."

Further citing of source to support student's interpretation.

Wilbur refers to the "earthen hide" on which the "rare, original heartsblood goes" to show the baseness and importance of this creature. The toad is one of the few creatures existing in its unaltered genetic form today, and it still performs its rudimentary functions of a toad of a million years ago. Wilbur reinforces this view of the primitiveness of the toad by stating that "he lies as still as if he would return to stone," suggesting that the toad cannot regress further into evolution without becoming nonexistent.

Student's analysis of poet's tone by quoting pertinent images.

Wilbur's lament for the loss of the toad is obvious in the last stanza. He refers to the toad's domain as "Amphibia's emperies," suggesting the greatness and power this primitive animal has over his territory, the now "castrate" lawn—"castrate" because it has lost one of the basic elements for its survival, the toad.

Erin Duffy
(Student)

Irony

In essence, irony is saying one thing and meaning something else. Suppose that you stay out late and have to get up early, but in the morning, feeling half dead, you say, "Oh, I feel great." Then you are using simple irony. Irony can also be shown through a discrepancy or gap between what one says and what one does, between what a character is and what he or she professes to be, or between what a character expects and the true outcome of events. In Shakespeare's Macbeth the central irony is that Macbeth thinks that by killing Duncan, the king, he will gain power, prestige, and a life of ease; but he gains only sleepless nights of torment until he finally goes to meet his death. In a soap opera, on the other hand, you might have a slick con artist who snares a wealthy widow, only to find out afterward that the widow is bankrupt but believes that he is rich.

Melodrama

The term *melodrama* is applied to a dramatic presentation heavily marked by the use of sentiment and sensationalism. Its heroes and villains lack complexity and the conflict between good and evil is oversimplified; you have only the "good guys" and the "bad guys." The evil characters always get their comeuppance, and a happy ending is predictable. You have a melodramatic situation when, for instance, the mean cattle baron drives the noble Indians from the land of their forefathers. If he ends up with an arrow through his middle, so much the better—especially if it is the chief's rebellious but beautiful daughter who lets fly.

Whenever you have the sun suddenly breaking through the dark clouds as the lovers kiss, see the hero being snatched from certain death at the final moment, or find the heroine miraculously escaping the clutches of some fiend, you can be sure that you are in the midst of melodrama.

Motif

In literature, *motif* is the term applied to a recurring idea or situation. Just as a few bars may recur from time to time throughout a musical composition, a certain idea or situation may keep recurring in different ways throughout a literary work. The motif may take such forms as a recurring lament for the past, repeated expressions of the joy of life, a wistful longing for a different world, or a merry-go-round of futile activity, but it usually bears some relationship to the dominant theme of the work.

Myth

A myth is a traditional story of unknown authorship, originally passed on by word of mouth. Typically, myths deal with the heroes, gods, and rituals of a preliterate society. Although once accepted as fact, such stories are now regarded as the fictions of earlier societies. The Greeks and the Norse have provided us with an especially rich collection of myths peopled with monsters, giants, supernatural beings, and ancestral heroes. In a more general sense, but not in the literary sense, the word *myth* is applied to any of the fictions or half-truths that make up the common beliefs of a society: the myth of Hitler's invincibility perished in the Battle of Stalingrad.

Realism

Realism concerns both the subject of a piece of writing, usually fiction, and the author's attitude toward the subject. The subject of *realism* is **real,** or actual, life as it is lived by ordinary people in an observable world. The realist, being a believer in the value of the common person, focuses on average and everyday events in the lives of ordinary people. These people are not idealized or sentimentalized but are credible human beings attempting to cope with workaday conflicts and emotions.

Romanticism

On the other hand, romanticism tends to place its stories in the faraway and long ago. The romantic writers tend to look at the world through glasses tinted rose by sentimental feelings. Their characters yearn upward toward ideal. In the novel, the romantic writer is usually more interested in the hero's adventures than in the hero's character. For the reader romanticism frequently means an escape from life rather than an interpretation of it.

Sarcasm

The word sarcasm derives from the Greek *sarkazein,* meaning "to tear flesh." As its origin suggests, sarcasm consists of biting language or cutting remarks. Its subsequent meanings indicate harsh criticism either verbal or visual and usually against an individual. For example, a widely syndicated cartoonist frequently portrays the Vice President as a figure without a head but with two feathers where his head should be.

Satire

Although satire frequently makes use of irony, sarcasm, and caricature, it has a serious underlying purpose: reform. By holding up to ridicule or poking fun at the folly and vice of people and their institutions, satire makes its attack indirectly. For example, instead of telling us that some members of congress are less than honest, a satirist might show us a Bible-quoting congressman swilling liquor on a luxurious yacht provided through the generosity of defense contractors. Satire comes in many shades, from gentle humor to scathing ridicule and contempt.

Stream of Consciousness

The term *stream of consciousness* refers to a technique of fiction in which the writer attempts to capture thoughts as they flow through the mind of a character. In attempting to set forth the thoughts of the character, the writer tries to get closer to the inner reality of ideas and sensations which pass through the mind in a stream of bits and pieces. Conventional sentence structure and punctuation are abandoned in an effort to convey immediate sensations and impressions. The best-known example of the technique is found in James Joyce's *Ulysses.*

Tragedy

According to the definition laid down by Aristotle in his *Poetics* (c. 350 B.C.), tragedy involves much more than mere coincidence or a change of fortune from good to bad. Tragedy, Aristotle insists, must inspire pity and fear: "pity . . . aroused by unmerited misfortune, fear by the misfortune of a man like ourselves." The misfortune must be "that of a man who is not eminently good and just, yet whose misfortune is brought about not by vice or depravity, but by some error or frailty." Classical tragedy typically involves a representative person who acts out of ignorance, only to recognize afterward the tragic error he or she has committed. Neither indifferent nor vicious, the person commits a tragic error out of some weakness or frailty of character, known as "the tragic flaw." Thus, Oedipus, spared by fate from death in infancy, grows to manhood ignorant of his true parentage. He kills his father in a rash quarrel and then marries his own mother. Not until years later does he discover the horror of what he has done.

Aristotle's definition of tragedy has been altered quite drastically over the centuries so that today tragedy is often more loosely defined as a human struggle that ends disastrously. However, there can be no tragedy without some exercise of free will and some sort of recognition or tragic knowledge. In Arthur Miller's play *Death of a Salesman,* Willie Loman, the salesman, kills himself after he finally comes to recognize the lies and contradictions of his life.

NOTE: The term *tragicomedy* is used to describe dramas in which the action seems to be moving toward a tragic end but which manages to switch direction and does end happily.

The Essay Test

When you are answering an essay question, you are simply repeating a process that you are already familiar with. There is no major difference between an essay and an essay test. The principles you learn in one apply to the other—with one added advantage: in an essay test, you don't have to think of a topic; your instructor has already done that for you. Actually, many students who once dreaded essay tests find that their attitudes change completely after they have taken one. They begin to like essay tests because they find it much easier to answer questions in their own words than to adapt their thinking to someone else's vocabulary. When you are studying lecture notes, for example, you will sometimes find that concepts are easier to understand once you put them in your own words. So remember, if you can write a paragraph, you can take an essay test—assuming, of course, that you studied.

You don't scare me any more.

HOW TO PREPARE FOR AN ESSAY TEST

Take Good Notes

Learn to distinguish between hearing and listening in class. Hearing is an automatic process, but listening requires a concentrated mental effort on your part. You can't evaluate what your instructor is saying if you are just hearing words. You have to **listen** carefully in order to pick out important points and major supporting details.

You must use judgment in deciding what your instructors are emphasizing. They may emphasize by repetition, repeating a point in several different ways; they may give several examples to illustrate a key point; they may explain its causes and effects, point out parallels between two ideas or events; may underscore a point by tone of voice or gesture.

Those points which are not emphasized are not to be ignored, of course, but must be subordinated to major points. Get the important things on paper first, and then, as you have time, expand them with the instructor's relevant lesser supports.

NOTE: Don't take notes only when you see your instructor write something on the board. Few instructors will put **all** of their important notes on the board.

Read All Assigned Material More Than Once

Some students believe that they can breeze through their reading assignments a night or two before a test and still get a decent grade on their exam. No one, including your instructors, can remember every important point in a chapter, detail by detail, after reading it only one time. The human memory doesn't usually work that way. In fact, psychological studies have shown that when you learn something new, you are likely to forget over 60 percent of it. That's why cramming is so dangerous. You will retain more information from ten separate half-hour study periods than you will from one all-night cramming session.

Learn to Use Your Textbooks

Don't be afraid to write in your textbooks. They're your books, so use them. Highlight important points, underline definitions, insert additional examples, rewrite difficult concepts in your own words, and jot down any questions that occur to you as you are reading. Make up your own essay questions and see how well you can answer them from memory. Then compare your answers with the information contained in your notes and in your text. If you find that you are particularly weak in a certain area, you will still have time to correct the problem before the test.

Study

Study! Study! Study!

HOW TO TAKE AN ESSAY TEST

Budget Your Time Carefully

Before you begin to answer an essay test, find out approximately how much time you can devote to each question. If you have two questions to answer in a fifty-minute period, then don't spend forty-five minutes on one question. If you don't have a watch, then ask your instructor to post the time on the board periodically. Remember, although quality is more important than quantity, your instructor will expect the length of your essay to correspond with the

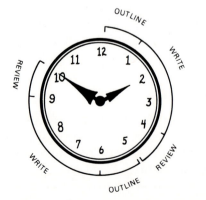

Budget your time.

amount of time you have to write it. The more time you have, the more details you should include.

You can reduce your anxiety and make the best use of your time by answering the easiest questions first.

Look Closely at the Verb in Each Question

Students often misinterpret essay questions by overlooking verbs. Make sure that you understand exactly what the question is asking you to do. Does it ask you to . . .

explain	to give reasons for something
evaluate	to decide on the value or significance of something
analyze	to explain something by breaking it down into parts and showing how each part relates to the whole and furthers an understanding of the whole
illustrate	to give examples of something
define	to explain the meaning of something
discuss	to tell all you know about a subject
compare	to point out similarities
contrast	to point out differences
compare and contrast	to point out **both** similarities and differences

When you read an essay question, learn to look for verbal signals—wording that indicates what particular method of development the question is calling for. For example:

EXPLAIN:

If you see words such as *reasons, how, why, expound,* or *clarify,* then you'll know that your instructor wants you to explain.

EVALUATE:

If you see *judge, weigh, appraise, give the significance of, write a critical analysis* or *a critical commentary,* then you'll know that your instructor wants you to evaluate.

ANALYZE:

If you see *kinds, types, classes,* or categories, then you'll know that your instructor wants you to show interrelationships among these elements—to analyze.

ILLUSTRATE:

If you see *examples, instances, cases, samples, specimens,* or *incidents,* then you'll know that your instructor wants you to illustrate.

DEFINE:

If you see the *meaning of,* your *understanding of,* the *distinctive properties of,* or the *nature of,* then you'll know that your instructor wants you to define.

DISCUSS:

If you see *examine, consider,* or *comment on,* then you'll know that your instructor wants you to discuss.

COMPARE:

If you see *likeness, similarities, parallels,* traits shared *in common with,* or how *A is like B,* then you'll know that your instructor wants you to compare.

CONTRAST:

If you see *differences, dissimilarities, in opposition to,* or how *A is unlike B,* then you'll know that your instructor wants you to contrast.

Make a Rough Outline Before You Begin to Write

Read the directions and see how many questions you are supposed to answer, but before you begin to write, jot down any points that you can think of that will help you answer the question. If you don't write them down right away, you might forget them. You'll just end up wasting time and making yourself nervous trying to think of them later. Putting these points into some sort of rough outline can help you a great deal. It's much easier to write a good answer within a limited time if you are following an outline.

Get to the Point

Avoid long-winded introductions. Normally, ten or fifteen minutes is not enough time to spend on an introduction to an essay, but spending that much time on an introduction during an essay test can be fatal, especially if you have less than a half hour to answer the question. The evidence that you present in the body of your essay is more important to your instructor than how you introduce that information. So don't waste time. Get to the point.

A simple but effective way to get to the point quickly is to turn the question into a declarative sentence and treat that sentence both as your thesis statement and as a one-sentence introduction. When you do this, you don't have to spend much time on wording; your instructor has already carefully worded it. More important, since your thesis statement controls what you write, by using a rephrasing of the question, you guarantee that your answer is to the point. Suppose in an English Composition exam your instructor directs, "Discuss the techniques of achieving coherence in an essay." You can turn it around to "Achieving coherence in an essay depends upon two techniques: the first is to establish a sound overall organization; the second is to link the smaller elements within the large plan." Then you would go on to talk about Intro-duction–Thesis Statement–Development–Conclusion, and the or-dering of details within that structure. You would then go on to deal with the subtopics—the smaller elements; there you would discuss enumeration, pronoun reference, transitional phrases, repetition of key terms, and parallelism.

Or suppose your history instructor asks, "Explain by the use of examples the philosophy known as Nineteenth-Century Liberalism as the term refers to government, economics, and the movement called "romantic nationalism." You might turn it around to answer, "Nineteenth-Century Liberalism can be well explained through ex-amples taken from government, from economics, and from 'roman-tic nationalism.'"

Proofread Your Answers

Too often, when students are taking an essay test, they are so happy to finish that they dash out of the classroom without ever looking at what they have written. This is foolish. When you are writing under the pressure of time, you might make mistakes that you don't nor-mally make— not just in grammar, but in content. You might have left out an important point, or you might have said the exact oppo-site of what you intended to say. So take a few minutes to reread your answer. It could make a big difference in your grade.

FIVE WRONG WAYS TO ANSWER AN ESSAY QUESTION

1. List a series of facts without relating them to the question.
2. Use a lot of general statements with no specific examples.
3. Pad your answers with irrelevant details.
4. Present your information haphazardly.
5. Express your points in incomplete sentences.

Listing a Series of Facts Without Relating Them to the Question

When you are answering an essay question, you cannot simply list details. You have to use those details to prove a point. A list of facts will not prove to your instructor that you understand the material you're being tested on; it might only prove that you memorized those facts. After all, an essay is the development of an idea, and you can't develop an idea by listing facts. Look at the following answer to an essay question on the art of American film-making:

QUESTION: Discuss the impact of *Citizen Kane* on the art of film-making.

ANSWER: *Citizen Kane* was directed by Orson Welles when he was 25 years old. He signed a contract which gave him 25 percent of the profits in addition to the authority to write and direct the film. He was also the chief actor in the movie. Most of the actors had a background in theater, but Welles's background was in radio.

Citizen Kane was filmed with a wide-angle lens and high-speed film. Welles used sets with ceilings on them. Welles's basic editing technique consisted of lap dissolves, and he used broad arc lamps for lighting. The sound track blended background music with natural sounds.

The story of Charles Foster Kane, a big newspaper tycoon, was told mostly in flashbacks—through interviews of people who knew Kane. Many people believed that the film was really the life story of William Randolph Hearst, the controversial newspaper publisher of the late nineteenth century. Basically, the story of Charles Foster Kane was the story of a man who could buy everything—except love.

After reading this answer, you still would not know **why** *Citizen Kane* was an important film because the factual details listed are not connected to ideas. In the first paragraph, for example, the student should not have just listed the details of Welles's contract; he should have explained that the contract was the first of its kind. Before *Citizen Kane*, an actor was expected to confine himself to acting, but Welles managed to get a contract that gave him the authority to supervise the production of a film that he was going to star in. The details about the backgrounds of the actors also mean nothing until one understands that the actors used in *Citizen Kane* represented a different approach to film-making. They proved that the transition from stage to screen could work. In fact, many critics believe that the excellent performances of Joseph Cotton and Agnes Moorehead stemmed partly from the fact that they had never acted in front of a camera before. Presumably, they took direction well because neither had yet developed a specific screen style.

The second paragraph also contains many facts, but they don't mean anything unless the student explains that most of the details refer to specific technological innovations in film-making. The creation of the wide-angle lens shot, for example, was a relatively new concept in cinematography. Welles wanted his audience to see things on the screen just as they saw them in real life. When you look at a room, for instance, you can clearly see the furniture in the foreground, the middleground, and the background, which is exactly what the wide-angle lens made possible on the screen. Before *Citizen Kane*, movie audiences had to see things through the eye of the camera, whose focus was limited to one area at a time. The use of ceilinged sets was also a novel idea that achieved a new realism in the art of film-making. It led to more natural lighting effects and more interesting camera angles. For example, filming Charlie Kane from floor level magnified his importance. The audience was looking up at a figure who seemed to be towering over them. Before *Citizen Kane*, actors couldn't be filmed from low angles without showing that "rooms" in films had no ceilings.

In the last paragraph the student should have explained that the complex narrative structure of the film represented a refreshing change from the traditional method of using simple chronological order to tell a story, and the final details about the similarities between Kane and Hearst should have been discussed in terms of the social impact of the film. The controversy became so heated at one point that the Hearst factions actually tried to have the film burned.

Using a Lot of General Statements With No Specific Examples

You will never convince your instructor that you understand the material you're being tested on if you can only discuss it in general terms. Vague definitions and general explanations are a clear indication that you don't really understand what you're talking about. Even if all of your general statements are correct, your answer will still be incomplete. Accurate generalizations are simply not enough. An instructor doesn't prepare six lectures on a subject and assign a hundred pages of reading just so her students can get a **general** idea of what she has been explaining in painstaking detail for several weeks. The following answer, for example, would get a very poor grade. It is filled with unsupported generalizations, a clear indication that the student was unprepared to take the test.

QUESTION: Discuss the causes and effects of the Homestead Steel Strike in 1892.

ANSWER: Working conditions in the late nineteenth century were terrible. The economy was bad too, but the head of the Homestead plant didn't like the union. He wanted the workers to take a cut in pay. Henry Clay Frick was running the plant because his boss, Andrew Carnegie, was off in Scotland, so Frick could run the place the way he wanted—and that's exactly what he did. The workers eventually went on strike.

They battled it out with the Pinkerton detectives that Frick hired, but, in the end, Frick won and the workers lost. In general, the Homestead Steel Strike had some very damaging effects on the labor movement in this country.

If the student had twenty or thirty minutes to answer this question, the instructor would certainly expect an answer more than a paragraph long. She would expect specific details: what kind of "terrible" working conditions existed in the late nineteenth century? How bad was the economy? How much of a pay cut did Frick impose on the workers? What union did they belong to? What happened when they went on strike? How did the Homestead strike affect American steelworkers? How did it affect the labor movement in general?

Padding Your Answers With Irrelevant Details

Students often jokingly refer to padding as "the snow job," but they usually stop laughing when they get their tests back: D's and F's are not very funny. Sometimes, in an attempt to tell the instructor everything they know, students make the honest mistake of getting sidetracked on an unimportant detail, but careful outlining can help to eliminate this error. Remember, every irrelevant detail wastes precious time, so make sure that all of your details pertain to the question being asked. Notice the irrelevant details in the following answer from an essay test in Black History:

QUESTION: Contrast the progress of the anti-slavery movement during the Revolutionary period with the strength of the anti-slavery movement during the Constitutional period.

ANSWER: During the Revolutionary era, anti-slavery sentiment in this country was rather strong. The signing of the Declaration of Independence bolstered the spirit of freedom and independence in general, so many people thought that the abolition of slavery was only a matter of time. Slaves began to petition for their freedom, and Northern states began to pass their own laws ending slavery in their states. Perhaps if more people today would think about what the Declaration of Independence really says, there would be fewer racial problems in our schools and in our cities. Over 200 years after the signing of this great document, there are still people in this country who don't believe that "all men are created equal." I guess they think that the Declaration of Independence was written just for white people. Some even act like it was just written for men—not women. Other examples of the strong anti-slavery sentiment during the Revolutionary era were the formation of the first anti-slavery society in America and the public recognition of the accomplishments of free

Turning in the Snow Job.

blacks. The fact that blacks fought in the Revolutionary War also emphasized the hypocrisy of fighting for independence and, at the same time, owning slaves.

Within a decade, however, the fate of blacks in America took a turn for the worse. The Constitution was written in 1787, and it wiped out much of the progress made by anti-slavery forces during the Revolutionary period. Our founding fathers evidently considered the right to own property (slaves) more important than the right to be free. The power of the slave states at the Constitutional Convention ended any hopes of victory for the anti-slavery forces. Three clauses in the Constitution clearly recognized the existence of slavery. One was particularly dehumanizing—the three-fifths compromise. It provided that every slave would count as three-fifths of a person for purposes of both taxation and representation (5 slaves = 3 whites). The other two clauses were directed toward the slave trade and runaway slaves. Many runaway slaves were aided by the Underground Railroad. It helped thousands of slaves escape to the North and to Canada. The most famous leader of the Underground Railroad was Harriet Tubman. She was a very brave and clever woman. So the Constitution actually legitimized slavery. It would be another forty or fifty years before anti-slavery sentiment would be as strong as it was during the Revolutionary War.

Although this answer contains a lot of specific information, much of it is irrelevant. In the first paragraph, for example, the student got carried away with the discussion of the Declaration of Independence. His comments on twentieth-century political hypocrites and male chauvinists are completely unrelated to the question. In the time it took to formulate those thoughts and write them down, the student could have been presenting details on the significance of the first anti-slavery society—an important point which he glossed over—or discussing the anti-slavery pronouncements of prominent Revolutionary figures. In the last paragraph the student made a similar mistake. Instead of explaining the provisions of the clauses in the Constitution dealing with the slave trade and runaway slaves, he got off on a tangent about the Underground Railroad.

Presenting Your Information Haphazardly

Sometimes students don't understand the importance of presenting their information in some sort of logical order. They think that as long as they cover the most important points, it doesn't matter **how** they present their material. The instructor who is faced with this jumble of disorganized thoughts often has to plod through the answer several times to make sense out of it. If you can't put your thoughts down in any kind of organized format, then you're really telling your instructor that you don't fully understand the material. If you did, you would see the relationship between one point and another. For example, if *A* caused *B*, then you would logically discuss *A* before *B*. If you are analyzing reasons for citing examples, you should begin with the least important and end with the most important. The following answer to a test in Child Psychology is very confusing because the details are not placed in any kind of logical order:

QUESTION: Analyze the general trends in a child's physical development.
ANSWER: By the age of 6, a child's growth process starts to slow down. An average American child at this age usually weighs around 50 pounds and is close to 4 feet tall. During the first year of life a child experiences extensive growth. His body length increases over one-third, and his weight almost triples. By the age of 3, bone begins to replace cartilage in the child's skeletal system. By the age of 2, the average child is about 2 and a half feet tall and weighs around 30 pounds. Myelinization also occurs during this period. During the first few years of life a child's brain increases in weight, becoming three-fourths of its total weight by the age of 2. Immature nerve fibers also develop protective tissues around them. This is a process known as myelinization. During the early adolescent years, from 11 to 15, the child's heart grows faster, but there is no significant increase in brain size. There is also a marked increase in height and weight. Between the ages of 6 and 12, a child's bones become harder, his blood pressure increases, and his pulse rate decreases.

As you can see, the details in this answer are arranged so haphazardly that they make little sense. The confusion could have been eliminated through the use of simple chronological order: first year, second year, preschool years, middle childhood, and adolescence. Also, a term such as *myelinization* should have been defined before it was discussed.

Expressing Your Points in Incomplete Sentences

When you are answering an essay test, you have to remember that your instructor expects coherent paragraphs containing complete sentences. When you are taking notes in class, you have to use fragments because you are copying information as fast as you can, but on an essay test you can't just jot down bits and pieces of information. If your instructor had wanted two- or three-word answers, she would not have given you an essay test. So don't write any answers like the following from a class in Sociology through Literature:

QUESTION: Describe the various stages in the evolution of Malcolm X from a Nebraska preacher's son to the creator of a new political religious movement.

ANSWER: Malcolm X—born a preacher's son
—father killed and mother went insane
—sent to reform school
—lived with white family
—moved to big city and lived with half-sister
—got a white girlfriend in the city
—wanted to look white and act white
—got his hair straightened
—got a job as a shoe-shine boy, then peddled dope—got caught and went to jail
—became a Black Muslim (influence of family)
Muslim religion—all white men devils, black race superior
—became a preacher for Black Muslims
—heaven and hell equals your life on earth
went to Africa—changed—saw both black and white Muslims
—white men no longer devils
—good and bad in both blacks and whites

The following is an example of a well-written, well-organized, well-documented answer to an essay question in Black History. It is coherent, accurate, and specific. It was also the student's very first essay test:

Trace the development of the Atlantic slave trade from the 1400s to the 1800s.

ANSWER: The Atlantic slave trade took place over a period of 450 years. It occurred along the African coast from Senegal to Angola, a total of 3,000 miles.

The first contact was made in 1441. Portugal was under

the rule of King Phillip, and a Portuguese vessel captained by a man named Gonzales brought home a few slaves along with his material commodities. One of these slaves was the descendent of a chief. He begged for his return to Africa and promised more slaves in exchange for his freedom. In 1452 he was taken back, and his family gave ten other slaves in return for his safety.

Throughout the 1500s, Portugal and Spain dominated the slave trade. Although a trading system had already developed in gold, iron, and copper, the trade in human cargo developed more gradually. During this early period, slaves were taken mainly from the Upper Guinea Coast. From Senegal and Guinea, Mandingoes and Susus were traded. The trade was relatively small at that time—for example, in 1506, 3,500 slaves were taken from the Upper Guinea Coast. By the 1680s however, 20,000 a year were taken from the slave coast.

In the 1600s, the Dutch took control of the slave trade, conquering Spanish and Portuguese posts along the coast. By 1640, the demand for slaves had increased so tremendously that the Lower Guinea Coast was tapped for slave supply. From Benin, Nigeria, and Whydah came Ashanti and Fanti tribes, among others. A major reason for the drastic increase in the slave trade at this time was the discovery of the New World and the subsequent need for cheap labor. Africa's needs also played an important part. She needed horses, textiles, and most importantly, guns and gunpowder.

Although France condemned slavery in 1571, the 1700s found France and England dominating the slave trade. Throughout the slave period, the African chiefs cooperated with the traders. Although the first captures were done by piracy, the chiefs soon became the major suppliers of slaves. They captured prisoners of war, and kidnapped and deported criminals and rebels. The slaves did not all go readily into bondage. In 1753, for example, slaves revolted in mid-ocean on the Narborough and killed all of the crew except those necessary to take them home.

The slave trade was declared illegal in 1808. However, illicit slave trade continued until 1862, with most of these slaves being sent to Brazil for work on sugar plantations. An estimated 8 million to 50 million human beings were victims of the slave trade. The second figure includes those who never even made it to slavery, unable to survive one of the many terrible steps to its completion. Basically, slavery flourished because people held their own self-interests above those of humanity.

Pat Tonkovich
(student)

The test question called for a chronological understanding of events over a long period of time ("**Trace** the **development** of . . . "). The student, therefore, organized her information century by century and supported her major points with specific data, mostly facts and statistics.

Many essay questions, like the previous one, will call for a specific method of development (comparing, defining, analyzing, and so on) but others will be worded in more general terms. Then it's up to you to decide how to develop your answer. If, for example, an essay question tells you to "discuss" something, you might need to use a combination of methods to develop a good answer.

The essay below was done in a Sociology class after a lecture and discussion on the five major perspectives of sociology. In neither the lecture nor the discussion were education and law discussed. Therefore, the student had to *analyze* the perspective of the structural functionalist and the conflict theorist and apply his knowledge to different subjects. Testing students' ability to apply their knowledge and show their competence in using information is one of the major advantages of the essay test. After all, the problems you face in the world will not always be the ones you discussed in class.

....

The viewpoints of a structural functionalist versus a conflict theorist in regard to the American educational system are diametrically opposed. Let us first consider the structural functionalist point of view. A structural functionalist views society as a living, changing organism having certain needs. These needs are met by the development of systems or structures which help provide social equilibrium, stability, and integration for society as a whole.

A structural functionalist is concerned with the question of how these systems benefit society. Functional systems are considered good for society, dysfunctional systems bad for society. The structural functionalist would most likely view the educational system in America as being functional, or good for society. Upon examination he or she would note that education's manifest function or intended purpose is to disseminate information as a whole. This action would be viewed as functional since it benefits society.

Furthermore there are latent functions or residual effects of the educational system. The educational system provides jobs for administrators, teachers, secretarial and custodial personnel, all of whom earn incomes, pay taxes, and buy goods, which in turn benefit and support society. Students, besides being educated in formal subject matter, gain experience in social skills, personal interaction, and dealing with authority figures. The structural functionalist might argue that many children's nutritional needs might not be met if it were not for the balanced meals they receive while in school. Further argument could be made on behalf of these children that the only exposure to a functional environment they experience is during school hours since many are products of dysfunctional family and community systems. Another practical latent function of the educational system is that it regulates the flow of new personnel into the work force, helping to control unemployment and stabilize the economy.

The conflict theorist takes an opposing view. To him society represents a power struggle with some having a huge advantage over the rest. To the conflict theorist, systems and structures represent a means of control, manipulation, maintaining the status quo, and adopting a "don't rock the boat" type of attitude. Rather than saying all things are equal and shared, he says power, privilege, and opportunity are unequally distributed.

A conflict theorist points out the constant competition for more benefits by some even if it means depriving others. The conflict theorist continually addresses this very question. Who benefits and who is deprived through the structures and systems society creates? In regard to education the conflict theorist might question who really benefits from the system, the student or the faculty? Who determines what information is suitable to disseminate? How much information to be released? To whom? Who controls decision-making policies in regard to these questions? What are their motives when making these decisions? His argument might follow a line that structured educational practices tend to stifle creativity and promote conformity.

Economic inequality would be high on his list of objections. The conflict theorist would be quick to point out that students from economically depressed areas generally do not enjoy the same educational quality as students from affluent areas. Does this influence future consideration for job placement or higher education? Could this be an attempt by those with power to retard the progress of those without?

The conflict theorist's attitude toward society is one of challenge. He does not believe that all is harmonious and stable. To the contrary, he feels there is much discord and conflict.

He sees functionalism as an attempt to make legitimate the constant struggle for dominance. The conflict theorist would view education, the obtaining of information and knowledge, as one more struggle for dominance, power, and position.

Though totally opposed in theory, I personally believe both the structural functionalist and the conflict theorist serve vital roles in today's society, offering checks and balances and differing thought-provoking opinions on the same subjects.

Jim Krauza
(Student)

The final essay question, given in an American Literature class, called for a *discussion*, the broadest category of answer. Respondents were allowed to talk about any *pertinent* point they wished to comment on.

QUESTION: Discuss Mark Twain's major theme in *Huckleberry Finn.*

ANSWER: A noted psychiatrist, Dr. Karl Menninger, made a touchingly perceptive statement which describes at least one of Mark Twain's themes in *Huckleberry Finn.* "Anything that can be made funny must have at its heart some tragic implications."

Like Twain, humorists generally view their world with their priorities slightly askew. The more radical their view, the more entertaining their work. What causes their comic genius, their bite? Unquestionably, Twain bites with a vengeance.

On the Thames Embankment in London an inscription dedicated to W.S. Gilbert could easily describe Mark Twain. "His foe was folly and his weapon wit." Yet Twain's bite went deeper and was more despairing than Gilbert's. More often than not, Twain's works parody the injustices he observed in the "damned human race."

The gross injustice of slavery is a major target for Twain in *Huck.* Huck doesn't understand the complexities of slavery, but he knows that something is wrong. And his struggles to find out what is wrong are bitterly comic. Twain used the intensely close relationship between Huck and Jim to reflect on the contradiction that was southern racism. Huck's dilemma comes to light when he says, "I was trying to make my mouth *say* I would do the right thing . . . and tell Jim's owner . . . where he was; but I knowed it was a lie." Huck could no more tell the owner where Jim was than he could think of owning Jim himself. Huck *thinks* he believes in the rights of the slaveowner; he of course believes in the rights of man.

Perhaps the most moving scene in the whole book is when Jim chastises Huck because Huck had so horribly teased him by pretending to have been swept overboard. We see here a man of quiet dignity greatly affronted and a boy transcending his childishness to "humble himself." But of course Huck is doing the opposite of "humbling himself"; he is showing that he has genuinely grown.

Misanthropic and comic Twain paints an ugly picture of humankind. Comedy and despair for Twain go hand in hand. Still, he does suggest one antidote. In every episode, his best answer is common human decency.

David McNutt
(Student)

TEXT CREDITS

I N D E X